GLENALLACHIE

12

Single Highland Malt
Scotch Whisky

TOMINTOUL

12

GLENLIVET

SCOTCH WHISKY

CLY

COAST

Scotch
Whisky

Years 14 Old

46% vol.   70cl e

THE
E·DRADOUR

Single Highland Malt
Scotch Whisky

SCAPA

SINGLE HIGHLAND MALT
SCOTCH WHISKY

1989

CONNOISSEURS
CHOICE

HIGHLAND

Single Malt Scotch Whisky

GLENCADAM

1987

Gordon & MacPhail

MALT

GLEN
ORD

SINGLE MALT

Vintage 1975
Single Highland Malt Scotch Whisky

Distilled at Glentauchers Distillery

Schenley
OFC

ORIGINAL FINE CANADIAN

CANADIAN WHISKY CANADIEN

SINGLE MALT SCOTCH WHISKY

ROYAL BRACKLA

BAKERY
HILL

PEATED   MALT

SINGLE MALT
WHISKY

THE

TYRCONNELL

Estd 1762 Since

Single Malt

IRISH WHISKEY

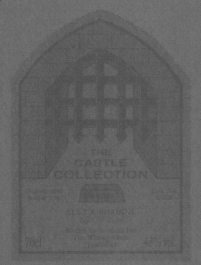

THE
CASTLE
COLLECTION

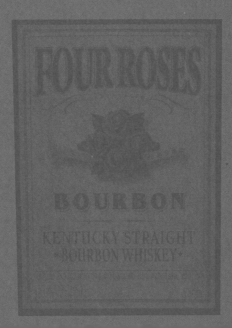

FOUR ROSES

BOURBON

KENTUCKY STRAIGHT
BOURBON WHISKEY

Inverleven

WHISKY

WHISKY

A FASCINATING JOURNEY THROUGH
THE MOST FAMOUS WHISKIES AND
DISTILLERIES WORLDWIDE

MARC A. HOFFMANN

Bath · New York · Singapore · Hong Kong · Cologne · Delhi · Melbourne

IMPRINT

Copyright © Parragon Books Ltd
Queen Street House
4 Queen Street
Bath BA 1 1HE, UK

Original edition production:
  bookwise Medienproduktion GmbH
Project coordination: Daniel Hoch
Design and layout:
  Cordula Schaaf, Jürgen Braun
Picture research:
  Sandra Schaeff, Andrea Schick
Cartography: Michael Slomski

English edition produced by:
  APE Int'l, Richmond, VA
Translation from German: Markus Flatscher,
  Dr. Maureen Basedow, Russell Cennydd
Editing of English edition: Tammi Reichel
  for APE Int'l

ISBN: 978-1-4075-1632-5

Printed in Malaysia

ACKNOWLEDGEMENTS

To write a book would be an impossible endeavor if it were not for the help of a wide range of people. I am indebted to the passionate whiskey lovers I know, to members of the industry and to those who were directly involved with this book. I also owe a great debt of gratitude to my family and friends, who had to do almost entirely without me, in particular during the final months. Their patience and understanding has been an invaluable aid in writing the book.

I obtained a wealth of valuable information on guided tours of distilleries and through personal communication. The following list is not exhaustive, but names some of the people who have been particularly helpful: Claudio Bernasconi (Waldhaus am See, St. Moritz), John Black and Gavin Cunningham (Tullibardine), Angela Bray (Pernod Ricard Swiss), Daniele Bruggmann (Best Taste), Peter Currie (Springbank), Jim McEwan (Bruichladdich), Daniel Graf and Yvonne Meyer (Scot & Scotch), Frank McHardy (J.&A. Mitchell), Iain Henderson (formerly with Edradour), Alois Immoos (Chocimo), Christian Lauper (World of Whisky), Patrik Marty (Dettling & Marmot), Rob MacPherson (Balvenie), Berthold Pluznik (Lateltin), Brian Robinson (Glenfiddich), Trisha Savage, Alistair Walker and Billy Walker (Benriach), Andrew Symington (Signatory, Edradour), Yvonne Thackeray (Chivas Brothers, Pernod Ricard), Ian A. McWilliam (Glenfarclas).

MADE IN TENNESSEE

CONTENTS

Foreword

THE COMMUNITY OF WHISK(E)Y LOVERS has always been a large one, but in recent years the popularity of the "water of life" has boomed. The general trend of increasing consumer appreciation for high-quality, thoughtfully produced food and drink—from artisan wines to ham and cheese specialties that are aged for years—has had a positive impact on whiskey, as well.

Because the whiskey market has to adapt to customers' ever-changing demands, whiskey itself is constantly evolving. Among many notable recent innovations, the trend toward single-cask bottling stands out: most single-cask whiskies are sold out before they even appear on the market. In terms of business, too, the market is in constant flux: distilleries are taken over, brands are sold, important industry figures change affiliations and sales markets shift.

A single book can do no more than provide a snapshot of the current situation. Even during the period in which this book was written, some things were changing, and the text had to be adapted to reflect those changes. Even so, with this book you have surely acquired one of the most interesting illustrated books on whiskey currently available.

For all the recent developments and changes mentioned above, the whiskey industry is characterized by one factor above all: tradition. In some countries, whiskey is an integral part of history and culture. Customs and traditions maintained for decades, even centuries, remind us that some of the seemingly revolutionary things happening on the whiskey market today will prove to be no more than a series of building blocks in the history of whiskey production.

The "Brands of the World" section presents whiskey brands according to countries and regions; within those groups, the order is alphabetical. An exception has been made for distilleries no longer in operation, which are included if their whiskies are still commercially available; these were added to the end of the respective country or region sections.

We hope you will enjoy reading this book. Settle back, relax and browse, maybe even while enjoying a wee dram of whiskey.

The Strathisla Distillery, Scotland, in winter.

WHAT IS
WHISKEY?

Definition

EXACTLY WHAT CAN BE CALLED A WHISKEY (or a whisky) varies from country to country and sometimes depends on legal regulations. One thing is universally true: it has to be a distillate made from grain, yeast and water that matures in wooden casks for a certain period of time, resulting in a strong spirit that is called whiskey (with an "e") in the case of Irish and American whiskies, or whisky (without the "e") in Scotland, Canada, Japan and elsewhere. The spelling "whiskey" is generally used in this book, except in reference to specific spirits that are spelled "whisky" and discussions of whiskey in countries that use that spelling. A difference exists even in the Gaelic words from which the name is derived: *uisge beatha* in Scotland, as opposed to the Irish Gaelic *uisce beatha*. Both expressions mean "water of life" (as do the Latin term *aqua vitae* and the German *Aquavit*). The present name originated from *usquebaugh*, which became *uisge*, then *usky* and eventually whiskey. Whiskey is not a protected term, and can therefore be used all over the world. The same is not true, however, of the labels "Scotch," "Irish" or "Bourbon": those expressions are protected by various legal provisions, in particular as trademarks.

Whiskey is a strong spirit. Consumed to excess, it may—and it is important to be aware of this fact—lead to alcoholism and damage one's health. Alcohol is an addictive drug, and that's a fact. Strictly speaking, any consumption of alcohol is unhealthy, although there seems to be scientific evidence that drinking whiskey in quantities of up to 100 ml (3.4 oz) per week may actually reduce one's risk of a heart attack. Even so, this should not be taken as an incentive to drink without moderation. High-quality whiskey is a refined and usually quite expensive drink; it is certainly not intended for chugging. Moderation is an essential quality for any true connoisseur of whiskey.

The following pages will introduce many, but by no means all, of the wonderful whiskies available around the world. This overview will be limited to the most important countries of origin and kinds of whiskies.

IRISH WHISKEY
According to law, Irish whiskey must be produced in Ireland and matured for at least three years.

SCOTCH WHISKY
This term has been legally defined since 1909, and the definition was amended in 1988. In order to be called Scotch, the whisky has to be produced in a Scottish distillery and must be made from malted barley or another type of grain that has been mashed with water. The mash is fermented by the addition of yeast and then distilled to an alcoholic strength of no more than 94.8 percent alcohol by volume (ABV). Finally, Scotch whisky has to mature in a wooden cask (usually made of oak) in Scotland and must contain at least 40 percent alcohol at the time of bottling.

AMERICAN WHISKEY
While many people consider Bourbon to be the quintessential American whiskey, there is no strict definition of what constitutes American whiskey. Bourbon is by no means the only kind of American whiskey: there is also Tennessee whiskey, for instance, as well as variants made from rye, wheat, corn or a blend of more than one grain.

MALT WHISKEY
Malt whiskey is made entirely from malted barley, and cannot contain any other types of grain.

The lowest common denominators for all the myriad kinds of whiskies from all over the world: grain, water, yeast and maturation in wooden casks.

Whiskey is an exceptionally popular drink all over the world, whether it's a smoky single malt, a sweet Kentucky Bourbon, a sophisticated blend of as many as fifty different whiskies, or simply one ingredient in a delicious cocktail.

SINGLE MALT

Most whiskey distilleries in Scotland produce single malts. The Scotch Whisky Association defines a single malt as follows: it must consist exclusively of malt whiskey, and it has to be distilled at a single distillery. If the whiskey in question is not a single cask (i.e., bottled from *one* single cask), it is usually a blend created from the contents of several casks of varying alcoholic strength, and sometimes even maturation periods. This practice, which is called vatting, ensures that a brand can maintain a constant and characteristic taste, since the contents of the individual casks may differ quite widely in terms of flavors. If whiskies of different ages are blended, only the maturation of the youngest whiskey may be stated on the label. Single malts are usually distilled in pot stills.

Single malt is by no means an exclusively Scottish product, however. Until World War II, large quantities of single malt were produced in Ireland, as well. Today, a sense of this tradition is slowly reawakening on the Emerald Isle, and single malts modeled on Scotch single malts are produced by distilleries in almost all of the regions of the world that produce whiskey.

(SINGLE) GRAIN WHISKEY

According to the Scottish definition, grain whiskey has to be produced by a grain distillery. It is usually made from corn, wheat, rye and/or malted and unmalted barley. While barley is the most expensive of these types of grain, a certain amount of it—up to 20 percent—is required, since barley is the only grain that can supply the enzymes necessary to convert the starches contained in the grain to sugar. Grain whiskies are almost always blended. In general, Irish grain whiskey variants are lighter; their low wines frequently contain 94.8 percent alcohol by volume. Single grain whiskies are rarely bottled, since most of the grain whiskey production is used for blends.

PURE POT STILL

This type of Irish whiskey has been in existence since the early eighteenth century, when unmalted and malted barley were regularly mixed and distilled in pot stills in an attempt to bypass the high malt taxes. It wasn't long before the distillers realized that this unusual practice led to exceptionally fine whiskies, which eventually made pure pot still whiskey world-famous. While it may not play such an important role today, it still has a

Definition

loyal following. Although many people in other parts of the world think the USA produces nothing but Bourbon, in fact, a wide range of pure pot variants are made in America. These are usually referred to as straight whiskies.

STRAIGHT WHISKEY

Straight whiskey, also called pure whiskey, has to be made from at least 51 percent of a single kind of grain, and the alcohol content may not exceed 80 percent by volume. Straight whiskies have to

BLENDS

Apart from the whiskey varieties mentioned above, there are a wide range of blends. A blend is a mixture of several different whiskies. If information on the blend's vintage is given, it is the year of the youngest whiskey. Blended whiskies launched the international triumph of Scotch whiskies. They also play an important role in Ireland, Canada and other countries all over the world. In the USA, however, they are only produced in small quantities. For information regarding the production of blends, see pages 42ff.

Scotch blends

Scotch blends usually consist of a great number of different whiskies, sometimes fifty varieties or more. The quality of the blend increases with the proportion of malt whiskies included in it. A Scotch blend with more than 40 percent malt whiskies is called a deluxe blended Scotch. Manufacturers trade casks of different brands of whiskey in order to achieve the necessary diversity and quantity. In Scotland, some manufacturers now concentrate exclusively on the production of blended Scotch whiskies.

Irish blends

The comparatively low number of distilleries in Ireland made it impossible to achieve the same level of diversity as in Scotland. Nonetheless, the special quality of pure pot still whiskies still allows a range of possibilities for different blends. The Cooley Distillery, for example, has caused a stir on the blends market. Some of the traditional Scottish production methods have been adapted, allowing Cooley to produce blends more flexibly and in greater variety.

Canadian blends

Most of the whiskey produced in Canada is blended and sold on the US market. Many Canadian distilleries produce neutral spirits to serve as a basis for the blends. The resulting whiskey has a light, soft taste that has become especially popular in the USA.

American blends

American blends make up only a small share of the blends market. US blends are created from straight whiskey mixed with up to four-fifths neutral grain whiskey, usually of lesser quality—which is also why American blends are not especially widespread.

Molasses-based whiskey

In India and Thailand, inexpensive whiskey is distilled from molasses, a sugar substitute that can be produced at very little cost. By Western standards, however, molasses-based whiskey is closer to the family of rums than to whiskies.

mature for at least two years in new oak casks that have been charred, and cannot contain any added coloring. At the time of bottling, they must have between 40 and 62.5 percent alcohol by volume. In order to ward off certain bacteria, a portion of the backset (discarded mash from the previous batch) is mixed in during the mashing process. This practice is known as sour mashing. If it is not used (which is rarely the case), the mixture is called sweet mash. In general, most straight whiskies contain a certain amount of malted barley, not least because of barley's richness in enzymes.

STRAIGHT BOURBON
Straight Bourbon must be made from no less than 51 percent and no more than 80 percent corn. The rest of the blend consists of unmalted and malted barley, as well as wheat or rye. If the spirit's maturation peiod is less than four years, this has to be explicitly mentioned on the bottle's label. On a side note, corn has the highest sugar content of all grains.

STRAIGHT TENNESSEE
This whiskey only received its official legal designation in 1941. Today, it is most often made from 51 percent corn, similar to straight Bourbon, although the use of corn is not legally binding.

What sets straight Tennessee whiskey apart is the additional step of charcoal mellowing, also known as the "Lincoln County Process," which involves filtering the whiskey through a layer of charcoal 10 feet (3 m) thick before it is filled into casks for maturation.

STRAIGHT RYE
Straight rye whiskey consists of at least 51 percent rye. Before Bourbon became the most popular type of whiskey in the USA, straight rye was long the most widespread of American whiskies. In recent years it has experienced a kind of revival.

STRAIGHT CORN
Isn't straight corn the same thing as straight Bourbon? The answer is no. Straight corn whiskey has to consist of at least 80 percent corn, but it does not necessarily have to be aged in oak casks. There is also a special corn spirit that is used for creating blends; its quality, however, does not even come close to the quality of grain whiskies.

The well known Famous Grouse blended whisky in the bottling line of the Scottish Glenturret Distillery.

Ingredients

In the few Scottish distilleries where barley is still malted on-site, such as at the Springbank Distillery shown here, no effort is spared: rakes are drawn through the barley by hand, forming furrows in the grain that provide extra ventilation during germination.

Whiskey Distillation

AT ITS MOST BASIC LEVEL, whiskey production always involves the same fundamental ingredients: grain, water and yeast. Of course, there are other factors that play an important role in shaping the outcome, too, such as the peat used to fire the kiln, the water used to cut the spirit, or the wood from which the casks are made. To begin with, we will take a look at the three essential ingredients.

Grain

EACH WHISKEY CONSISTS of at least one (in the case of malt whiskey) or several types of grain. Each distillery that uses multiple varieties of grain has its own unique and top-secret recipe for blending them just so.

BARLEY
Barley is a grain of the genus *Hordeum* and belongs to the family of *poaceae*, or grasses. It has been cultivated since ancient times in the Middle East and in the eastern Balkans; the earliest historical evidence dates back to the year 10,500 BCE. Western Europe has a long tradition of growing barley as well, including Scotland and Ireland. Scottish and Irish settlers eventually brought the crop to America, where it became popular primarily in North Dakota, Wisconsin, Minnesota, Idaho and Washington, the most important growing areas for the US whiskey industry. Canada is another important supplier of barley.

They are the second-most important producer on the world market, second only to the CIS member states. The USA ranks only ninth on that list.

There are two main types of barley: wild barley and domesticated barley. The latter is in turn divided into two-row and multi-row barley. Two-row barley is cultivated mainly in Europe, six-row barley in the USA. These are again subclassified into the groups of narrow-eared and wide-eared barley, as well as summer and winter barley. For malt production, the two-row summer barley varieties are the most suitable. Of the approximately 300 types of summer barley, some sixty of them can be used for the production of brewing malt, the elementary ingredient for many whiskies.

In Ireland, barley is cultivated in the regions around Cork and Athy. Connoisseurs claim that Irish barley is the best in the world.

Most of the barley used in Scotland is grown domestically, though small quantities of barley are also imported from the English regions of Norfolk and Northumberland. The main growing areas in Scotland are Black Isle, Morayshire, Aberdeenshire, Fife, Angus and Lothian. Beer brewers, incidentally, prefer barley crops rich in nitrate, which are not suitable for whiskey production. That is also the case for varieties that contain a high proportion of protein, because that richness in protein comes at the expense of starch. Grain that contains less starch yields less spirit. Barley suitable for the production of whiskey should also have a low nitrogen content; nitrogen values higher than 1.7 percent are an indicator of both high protein content and high levels of fertilizer, both of which are undesirable for whiskey production. Moreover, the barley used for whiskey should have a low water content, definitely no more than 17 percent.

The reason barley is so attractive for the production of whiskey is its characteristic ability to convert starch into fermentable sugars. The barley varieties that were being used around 1900 had the capacity to yield approximately 80 gallons (300 l) of spirit per ton of barley. Today's high-efficiency crops yield up to 130 gallons (500 l) per ton. When cultivating new varieties of grains,

VARIETIES OF BARLEY

Bere
The traditional type of barley in northern Scotland and the archetypal form of domesticated barley.

Camarque
A variety that was popular during the early 1990s.

Chalice
An organic barley used by Benromach, Bruichladdich, Kilchoman and others.
Yields ca. 105 gallons (400 l) of spirit per ton of malt.

Chariot
Chariot has been grown since 1995.
Yields ca. 120 gallons (450 l) of spirit per ton of malt.

Chevalier
Chevalier has been grown since 1900.
Yields ca. 80 gallons (300 l) of spirit per ton of malt.

Golden Promise
Has been cultivated since the 1960s and was the leading variety until the mid-1980s.
Yields ca. 105 gallons (390 l) of spirit per ton of malt.
Used by Macallan and Glengoyne (together with other kinds of grain)

Marris Otter
Grown between 1950 and 1965.
Yields ca. 93 gallons (350 l) of spirit per ton of malt.

Optic
This is currently the leading variety of barley (50–60 percent).
Yields ca. 105 gallons (400 l) of spirit per ton of malt.
Optic barley is used by Port Ellen Maltings, making it the grain of choice for a number of Islay distilleries, including Bruichladdich and Bowmore, among others.

the most important concern—in addition to crop yield—is resistance not only to diseases, but also to strong wind and unfavorable weather. Today's crops of choice usually have shorter but stronger stems.

The most popular barley crops are summer barley varieties that are sown in March or early April. After flowering toward the end of June, seeds are produced. The maturation period depends on the climate. There are varieties, such as Golden Promise, that mature early and can be harvested already in late July. Since this variety is exposed to weather for a shorter period of time, chances are higher that the grain will withstand any bad weather; this is why varieties with short maturation periods are a safe bet. However, each variety has its own characteristic shortcomings, as well. One of the main problem areas is fungal infestation. The known diseases continue to evolve as well, which is why crops that are regarded as highly resistant may still become infested at a later point.

There is a notable trend in recent times toward organic barley, as is used by Bruichladdich or Benromach. This form of agriculture does increase production costs, which is naturally reflected in the selling price.

CORN

The use of corn is a legal requirement for the production of Bourbon. *Zea mays* (as it is called scientifically) is also a member of the *poaceae* family, and was grown by Native American peoples. It originally came from Mexico, but was introduced into present-day Arizona as early as 1100 BCE. While rye was originally the crop most favored by American distillers, with the settlement of Kentucky corn became increasingly popular. Today, corn is the key ingredient for the flavor of Bourbon, lending it its earthy and slightly sweet taste. Corn is also the source of Bourbon's light spicy note, and it yields the greatest quantity of alcohol of any of the grains. Along with rye and malted barley, corn is the most important grain in Canada, as well.

WHEAT

Wheat plays an important role in the production of grain whiskey in Scotland, replacing corn,

Opposite: After steeping in water, the barley is spread out on the malting floor. During germination, it is turned regularly in order to prevent the seeds from sticking together.

which was more frequently used in the past. The scientific name for wheat, which is another member of the family of *poaceae*, is *Triticum aestivum*. Distilleries prefer winter wheat because it has a higher starch content. While its growing period is longer—it is sown in fall and cannot be harvested before the following summer—its harvest season is now starting a little earlier due to climate warming. Summer wheat is significantly less important for whiskey production than winter wheat, because it produces less yield. Its main contribution is a hint of sweetness something like honey, and it also gives whiskey a mellower and more rounded flavor.

RYE

Rye was particularly important during the early period of European settlement in North America. In the eighteenth century, rye whiskey was primarily produced in Pennsylvania and Maryland. Today, this type of whiskey is not terribly significant, though rye is still used to a larger extent in Canadian whiskies. It adds a certain spicy flavor as well as a soft, dry note. Of course, it is also an ingredient in many Bourbons. Rye (*Secale cereale*) is a hardy crop that grows well even on poor soil.

Two-row or multi-row, summer or winter barley: choosing the right variety is important.

Ingredients

Water

SECOND ONLY TO GRAIN, water is the most important ingredient in the production of whiskey: no water, no whiskey. It plays an important role already at the mashing stage, and later on, during distillation, water is used to cool and recondense the evaporated alcohol. When the whiskey is ready to be filled into casks, water is needed once again. Finally, at the bottling stage, the whiskey is cut down to drinking strength with purified water.

This explains why the quality and availability of this natural resource is of major concern for whiskey producers. Even when deciding on the location of a new distillery, the water source is a decisive criterion, arguably even the most important of all. A spring must reliably deliver water even during the warm summer months; it is not uncommon for distilleries to be forced to cease production because a spring runs dry during a drought. If there is no water, whiskey production becomes impossible.

Thus, distilleries pay close attention to water. Glenfiddich is a good example in point. The Robbie Dhu Spring, which provides water for the distillery, has been protected for a long time. In order to ensure this protection, Glenfiddich bought the entire land through which it runs, from

the source of the spring to the distillery, no more and no less than 1,500 acres (600 hectares) of the Conval Hills. In order to safeguard the purity of the water, sheep or cattle are not allowed to graze anywhere near the brook.

WATER IN SCOTLAND

All over the world, there are as many varieties of spring water as there are of whiskey. The water in the Speyside region, for instance, is relatively soft. Because it flows over granite, it only picks up trace amounts of minerals. There are a wide range of special cases: in Cardhu, for instance, the water flows over quartzite, while in Inchgower it flows over red sandstone. On the Mull and Skye Islands, which are partly of volcanic origin, the water flows over basalt, giving the Skye Talisker its unique, fine aroma. Of course, there are also regions with very hard water. The Glenmorangie Distillery in the Northern Highlands, for instance, uses very hard water that flows over limestone and is rich in zinc, calcium and magnesium. It is hard to make a general statement as to whether soft water or hard is more suitable for whiskey production. Both kinds of water contribute to each whiskey's distinctive taste.

Peatbogs and moorlands are not only a characteristic feature of the Scottish scenery, they also contribute to the unique taste of each whiskey.

Choosing the right water for a whiskey is crucial. Here, a water sample is collected from a brook on the Scottish island of Skye, used for the whiskies produced by the Talisker Distillery.

Many distilleries maintain large water reservoirs onsite. The Bushmills Distillery, above, stores water for use in whiskies and for cooling purposes.

WATER IN IRELAND

The water used by the Bushmills Distillery flows over basalt and through layers of peat, which is why it is considered to be quite hard. Middleton, on the other hand, uses soft water originating from a spring in a red sandstone area, which then flows over limestone that is rich in carbon. Still, the mineral content of the water in this region is relatively low.

WATER IN THE USA

Much of the water in the whiskey-producing states of Kentucky and Tennessee flows over limestone, making the water rich in magnesium and calcium. Calcium accelerates yeast growth during fermentation. However, the kind of yeast culture used in the USA is different from the ones used in Scotland or Ireland, because the European cultures work better with less calcium. Although Kentucky has significantly less rainfall than Ireland or Scotland, the region has a relatively stable water supply. Over the course of millions of years, caves and cracks have formed in the limestone, creating large water reservoirs that secure Kentucky's water supply to this day. Moreover, the porous stone functions as a kind of filter and ensures exceptional water quality.

WATER IN JAPAN

Since Japan's landscape is incredibly diverse, not unlike Scotland's in that respect, the hardness and quality of the water also differ between regions. Japan's various whiskey producers use both hard and soft water.

HEATHER

Characteristic of Scottish whiskies, especially those from the Speyside region and the Orkney Islands, is a prominent aroma of heather, as well as flowery notes of eucalyptus, roses and ferns. The three kinds of heather native to Scotland—*Erica tetralix*, *Erica cinera* and *Calluna vulgaris*—all of which flower mainly during late spring and in autumn. Since the spring water frequently flows through moorlands, it picks up flowery flavors that it releases again during the steeping of the barley or during mashing.

Since heather is also a component of peat, it is entirely possible that green malt may pick up heather flavors from the smoke generated by bales of peat burnt while it is drying (malting). Flowery notes may also be intensified during distillation through a greater degree of reflux in the long neck of the still. Finally, Bourbon casks have the characteristic of enhancing these aromas.

Ingredients

On the Scottish island of Islay, water flows through a series of peat bogs before it reaches the distilleries. The strong note of peat in these whiskies, however, is usually achieved by introducing peat smoke in the kiln.

Similarly, whiskies that are matured in casks in distilleries located in coastal areas may well pick up elements of the sea air, that is, notes of salt, algae and iodine. Some distilleries on Islay and Skye or in other coastal regions have storehouses located right by the seaside. The influence this may have on a whiskey is most strikingly noticeable in the case of Laphroaig, a brand with a particularly strong aroma of sea flavors with phenolic and tarry nuances. Apart from the storage location, the peat used is a major source of Laphroaig's unique flavors. Approximately 10 percent of the barley used at the Laphroaig Distillery is still malted in-house, and the peat used in the process contains a great amount of algae, thus lending the end product hints of iodine, sea water and salt. It is worth mentioning, though, that the causal relation of this apparently plausible phenomenon has not been proven scientifically. Even experts quarrel about the exact influence of the various kinds of algae (red, green and brown algae) on the taste of a whiskey.

From a strictly scientific perspective, it is not clear to this day which additives in water determine the flavor of a whiskey, how strongly they do so, or at what stage in the production process they exert most of their influence. Many whiskey producers, for example, believe that peaty water will strongly influence a whiskey's flavor. The spring water used by the Lagavulin Distillery, for instance, is quite brown, an indication of the peat it has picked up along its way from the spring to the distillery. This is not, in fact, what is responsible for the peaty, smoky flavor of Lagavulin, however. In this case, the taste is due to phenols absorbed by the barley from the peat fire during kilning.

The whiskies best known for their strong notes of heather come from the Scottish Highlands and the Speyside region. This flavor results from water flowing through moorlands.

Yeast

YEAST IS THE THIRD essential ingredient for the production of whiskey. Just like water and grain, yeast is a raw material. It is used to convert the sugars—obtained from the starch contained in the grain—into alcohol. After fermentation, the alcohol content of the brew, called the wash, is between 7.5 and 10 percent. Various kinds of yeast are used. Some distilleries swear by brewer's yeast, the same kind that is used for brewing beer, while others have their own yeast culture or have it cultivated by a third party according to a special recipe. Many US distilleries, in particular, take pride in their in-house yeast cultures, some of which have been cultivated continuously for generations.

The yeast cultures themselves are single-celled fungi that belong to the phylum of sac fungi (Ascomycota). They are eukaryotic organisms that reproduce by splitting or budding.

In the Middle East, yeast was already used thousands of years ago to bring about fermentation in the production of wine, beer, and of course bread. In the early days, however, it was not understood that yeast is actually a life form. It was not until the nineteenth century that Louis Pasteur (1822–1895) discovered that yeast consists of microorganisms. Pasteur was also able to demonstrate that the production of alcohol requires fermentation. Yeast was produced synthetically for the first time in history in 1883 at the Danish Carlsberg Brewery. The brewers found that

certain kinds of yeast could be cultured. As early as 1875, Jacob Christian Jacobsen, son of Carlsberg's founder, had established a laboratory in his father's brewery. Louis Pasteur was among his friends at the time; they both contributed to the successful development of a type of yeast that came to be named *Saccharomyces carlsbergensis* in honor of the brewery.

Barley malt does contain some wild yeast, but more potent, cultivated types of yeast are required in order to start the process of fermentation. Distilleries use different varieties of yeast for different whiskies, and the choices made can influence both the alcoholic content and the taste of the final product. This is why distilleries put a lot of care and effort into culturing yeast.

In the large washbacks of Glenfiddich, barley malt is fermented by the addition of yeast. This results in a wash with an alcoholic content of 7.5–10 percent.

LOW WINES STILL
CAPACITY 15,000 LITRES

WASH S
CAPACITY 18,0

PRODUCTION

Whiskey Production

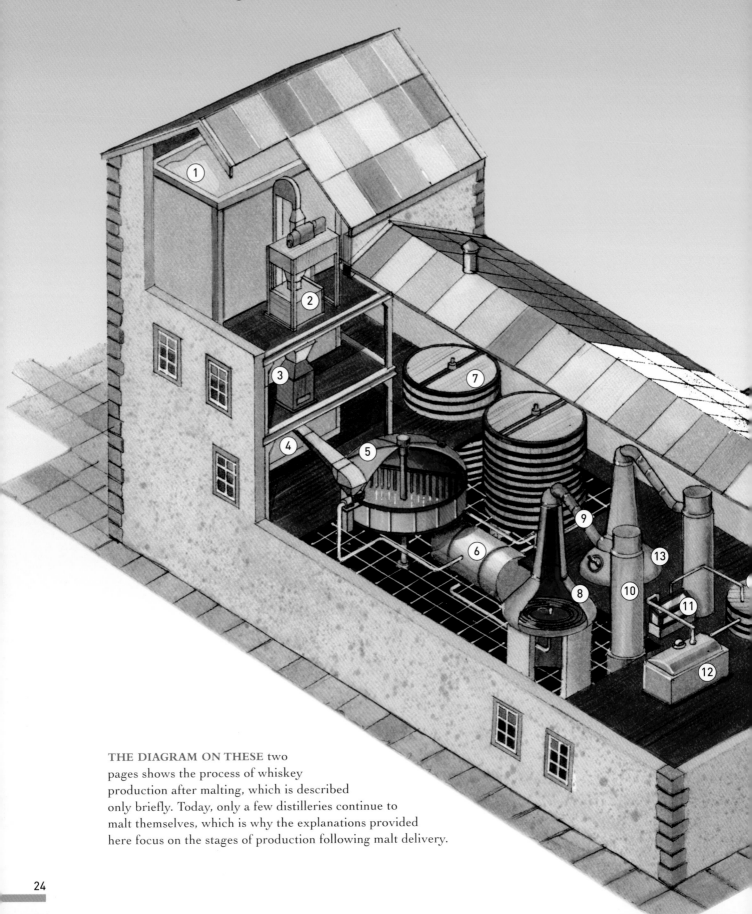

THE DIAGRAM ON THESE two
pages shows the process of whiskey
production after malting, which is described
only briefly. Today, only a few distilleries continue to
malt themselves, which is why the explanations provided
here focus on the stages of production following malt delivery.

When large quantities of barley are delivered, the grain is stored in a barley silo.

In the charge bin, the barley is cleaned and any impurities are removed. Then it is transferred to large steeping tanks and soaked in several changes of warm water for two to three days.

In traditional floor malting, the wet barley is then spread out over a large surface area and turned regularly (aired) to ensure that the temperature of the barley doesn't rise above a certain level during germination. In automated maltings, this process of turning the barley is usually done by a Saladin box or a malting drum.

After germination, the resulting product, which is called green malt, is dried in a kiln. During this step the malt is spread out on a perforated surface in the kiln, which is heated from below by burning charcoal, or if the intention is to give the whiskey a smoky, peaty flavor, peat is burnt instead.

After it is dried, the malt is moved to temporary malt storage. This may be in casks or a silo.

Prior to grinding, the malt is run through the charge bin once again in order to remove any remaining root fibers. The malt is then ground in the malt mill; the resulting product is called grist. ②

If necessary, the grist ③ may again be temporarily stored in a grist hopper.

In the premasher ④, the grist is mixed with hot water from a water tank.

From there, the mixture is fed into the mash tub or mash tun ⑤, which is usually made of stainless steel or cast iron. Most mash tubs are covered in order to retain the heat. The mixture is stirred thoroughly as it releases the wort, which flows to the underback ⑥ through the perforated floor of the mash tub. The spent grain that remains in the tank, called duff, is discarded.

The wort is conveyed first to the wort cooler and then to the washback ⑦, where the fermentation process is initiated by adding yeast to it. This produces alcohol and carbon dioxide. Fermentation continues for two to three days, and the resulting mixture is called the wash.

The wash then flows into the wash charger and the actual process of distillation begins. First, the fermented wash is conveyed to the still ⑧, where it is brought to a boil. Because alcohol boils at a lower temperature than water, alcoholic vapors are the first to rise into the neck of the still ⑨ before being cooled down in a condenser or a worm tub. The condenser ⑩ is kept cool by water from a water tank.

The resulting distillate is called low wine. At this stage it runs through the spirit safe ⑪ for the first time and is collected in a receiving vessel. ⑫

At this point the second stage of distillation begins, in which the low wine is fed into the low wine or spirit still ⑬.

Once again, alcoholic vapors rise into the condenser and are conveyed into a spirit safe. The stillman has to take special care during this stage: only the middle cut of spirits has the proper alcohol content and level of purity to be used for further processing, while the heads and tails (the distillate won before and after the middle cut) are returned to the low wine receptacle to be distilled again with the next round. The heart, as the middle cut is also called, is then received in another storage vessel. ⑭

Finally, this "new make" is transferred to another tank, where it is cut with water to the proper concentration and filled into casks for maturation. ⑮

Malting

THE MALTING PROCESS is the stage during which barley is brought to germination, thus converting stored starch into sugars, which will fuel fermentation. This is a carefully controlled process that has to be closely observed by the maltman, who must be very careful to stop germination at just the right moment.

From a scientific perspective, malting involves the production of enzymes through germination of the barley grain. An enzyme called *amylase* contributes to germination and breaks down the cell walls of the barley, which results in dextrin (i.e., starch in soluble form), which in turn is converted to maltose, a soluble malt sugar.

The maltman lets the barley germinate just long enough for the cell walls to break down. He has to take special care at this stage that the germ bud is not losing any starch; the starch will be needed at a later stage. The maltman needs to arrest the germination process at exactly the right moment.

This is accomplished by extracting moisture from the barley. Missing this moment would be an expensive mistake: malting accounts for two-thirds of the overall cost of making whiskey, naturally including the high cost of the barley itself. This explains why only a few distilleries continue to make their own malt. Most distilleries have their malt produced in large industrial maltings. In the industrial malting process, Saladin boxes, rotating drums or SGKVs (Steep, Germinate and Kilning Vessels) are used to produce malt in a fully automated way, which lowers costs significantly. The flavor of the final whiskey can be strongly influenced during malting, as well. The material used for firing in the kiln, for instance, partly determines how much smoky flavor the whiskey will absorb.

How does this relatively theoretical explanation translate into practice? This will be illustrated by looking at a traditional malting in a distillery.

Some Scottish distilleries still make their own malt. The barley is evenly spread out for germination on malting floors such as the one at Balvenie shown in this picture.

PREPARATION AND STEEPING

When barley is delivered to a distillery, it is usually stored in large silos until it is needed for processing. At this stage, the grain contains less than 12 percent water. After a thorough cleaning, the barley is soaked, or steeped, in warm water in large tubs or tanks called steeps. The steeping period ranges from two to three days, depending on the size of the barley grains, the grains' capacity to absorb water, and the temperature of the water. The moisture content of the barley grains has to be raised to at least 46 percent in order for the process of germination to begin. During steeping, the water is changed two or three times and enriched with oxygen. This accelerates the grains' absorption of water.

GERMINATION

The traditional germination method involves spreading out the moist barley in layers as much as 12 inches (30 cm) deep on stone or concrete floors in long buildings called malting floors. After a short time, the barley starts to sprout. During the germination process, a large amount of heat is released. In order to cool the barley and provide the necessary ventilation, the barley has to be turned over repeatedly. Traditionally, this was done by hand, using wooden shovels and rakes. Today, this process is sometimes automated and performed by a device that looks something like a lawn mower. The entire process of germination takes approximately one week, and the barley loses about half a percent of moisture per day. The sprouts slowly wither as they dry, giving the barley a mealy texture. The maltman has to keep a close eye on the process and assess how far it has progressed. He does so by rubbing the grain in his hands to see if there are still lumps in the barley. If so, it is not yet done; when the grain feels soft and chalky, it is ready. The maltman also checks the taste and the sweetness of the green malt, as it is called at this stage.

Top: Large quantities of barley are stored in big tanks or silos prior to starting the malting process, as in this malting house in the USA.
Bottom: Maltmen, such as this one at Balvenie, keep a close eye on the barley. The germination process releases large amounts of heat. By turning over the grain, the maltman keeps it cool and aerated.

KILNING

The green malt is transferred to the malting kiln, where it is spread out on a perforated floor. Kilns are buildings with distinctive pagoda-shaped roofs that are designed both to allow smoke and water vapor to escape and to ensure a sufficient air supply. Especially in Scotland, these characteristic pagoda roofs are still found in almost all distilleries; the buildings themselves, however, are rarely still being used for their original purpose.

The drying process takes place in several stages. During the first phase, the free drying phase, a great flow of hot air (140–150°F/60–65°C) is blasted through the barley. During the second phase of drying, the temperature is increased by another 18°F/10°C and the air stream is reduced somewhat. This is when the actual drying takes place, reducing the moisture content of the barley to approximately 5 percent. During the third phase, the cooling phase, which can last anywhere between twenty hours and two days, the malt is gradually cooled down.

There are a wide range of factors that have an influence on the individual drying phases: the drying and cooling techniques employed, the amount of green malt to be dried, the size of the kiln floor, the weather (temperature and humidity) and, of course, the firing materials used to dry the malt. In the past, peat was used almost exclusively for this purpose in Scotland and Ireland, if only because it was the only suitable firing material that was available in abundant supply. This practice often resulted in whiskies with distinct smoky flavors.

Since the invention of the railway, progress has visited the many distilleries working with traditional production methods, and in regions with good railway connections, such as the Scottish Highlands, a steady supply of coal became readily available. As a consequence, the smoky flavor started to disappear from the Speyside whiskies. This change in flavor was at first noted with satisfaction by the whiskey market during the early twentieth century; today, however, there is a significant community of whiskey connoisseurs who favor smoky single malts, in particular the smoky whiskies from the island of Islay.

The kiln—here one at the Balvenie Distillery—is fired either with coal or, more traditionally, with peat. Peat gives a whiskey a smoky flavor.

A fire burning in the kiln at Balvenie. Barley absorbs the smoke rising through the kiln. In order to kiln-dry the barley evenly, the temperature has to be controlled with great care and skill.

PEAT

Peat develops mainly in bog regions with a relatively cool climate and ample rainfall. In order for peat to form, the top layer of earth must be impermeable to air. Given the right conditions, such a layer can soak up water like a sponge and turn into peat. It consists mostly of peat moss, heather, various sedges and sweet gale; inland pines and bearberry are part of the mix. In coastal regions, the peat contains more sand and carries salty aromas. Peat bogs may be up to 10,000 years old, though some are much younger, such as those on the Orkney Islands, which are about 1,800 years old. The peat layer there is only about 13 feet (4 m) thick, as opposed to 10,000 year-old bogs, which have a peat layer of approximately 30 feet (9 m). On the Orkney Islands, the top layer consists primarily of heather; the layer beneath it is more compact and generates more heat when burnt, but less smoke. Layers below that often contain lots of wood, and due to the high pressure, this material is not unlike coal. This should come as no surprise: given another 2.5 million years, this substance would actually turn into coal.

Peat has a major influence on the peatiness of the malt, and thus on the flavor of the whiskey. The peaty flavor is determined by the phenolic content, which is measured. Modern production methods make it possible to control phenol levels very accurately. Peatiness is divided into three categories: mildly peaty at 1–5 ppm (parts per million), medium peaty at 10–20 ppm, and peaty at 30–60 ppm; the latter variant is the most common.

Peat is cut either by machines or through back-breaking manual labor, with a spade. The bales of peat, which are ca. 25 x 6 in (60 x 15 cm), have to dry several weeks before they can be used.

Of course, there are exceptions to this rule, as well. Bruichladdich has started producing Octomore, which, as the name implies, contains 80 ppm; however, it is not yet available on the market as a single malt. There is an even stronger version, as well, Octomore II, with 167 ppm.

Peat bogs cover about 12 percent of the surface area of Scotland. Many Scottish distilleries have gone back to this traditional firing material.

Mashing

IN THE NUMEROUS DISTILLERIES that do not have their own maltings, but buy their malt from commercial malt houses instead, the production of whiskey begins with mashing. First, samples of the malt are taken to ensure that it is free of any

Stirring rakes combine grist with water. When mashing is complete, the resulting wort is filtered and drained through small holes in the bottom; the spent grain remains in the mash tun.

Most modern mash tuns, such as this one in Glendronach, are made of copper. A hatch makes it possible to check the progress of the wort inside.

insects, that it is not too moist (less than 12 percent water), and that a germination capacity of at least 99 percent has been reached.

Before the mashing process can begin, the malt has to be ground to grist. This involves grinding the malt in a mill, breaking the grains open in order to release the sugar they contain.

If barley is to be used exclusively, mashing can begin at this point. With some other grains, however, this is not possible, in particular with corn, which is used most often in North American whiskies. With corn, the process of converting the enzymes into fermentable sugar is more involved and requires the corn to be heated in a kind of pressure cooker in order to speed up the breakdown of starch.

Once the starch has been extracted, true mashing can begin. The grist is mixed with hot water and transferred to vats called mash tubs or mash tuns. These tubs are usually made of copper or sometimes stainless steel. The cover, which serves to retain the heat, is often copper.

Just like kilning, the mashing process also has three stages. During the first stage, the grist is mixed with water at a temperature of 147°F/64°C. After twenty minutes, the stirring rakes inside the mash tun start working the mixture. After half an hour, the resulting liquid, which is called wort, is drained through the small holes in the bottom of the mash tun. The next step involves mixing with water again, but this time no additional grist is added. The concoction is brought to a temperature of 158–167°F/70–75°C. This phase continues to extract sugar. The resulting liquid, called the wort, is transferred to a collecting tank known as the underback. During the third phase, the remaining sugar is brought almost to a boil. At this stage, however, not enough starch remains to use the resulting product together with the first two runs of wort in the underback. Instead, it is cooled down and mixed in with another batch of grist at a later time. The spent grain, called draff, is frequently sold to farmers as animal feed.

Large bags of yeast are poured into the washback and mixed with the wort.

Fermentation

THE NEXT PRODUCTION STEP is very similar to beer brewing. However, while it is important to ensure that the entire fermentation process is strictly sterile when making beer, in the case of whiskey, this is not necessary. This is why many of the fermenting tanks, called washbacks, are made of wood and remain open during fermentation. Washbacks are made of larch or pine wood because it has few knot holes, fine pores, and can be cut into long pieces. This is important because large washbacks may hold up to 17,000 gallons (65,000 l). The smallest ones, as used by Edradour, for instance, only hold 265 gallons (1,000 l). Stainless steel washbacks are becoming increasingly popular, some of which hold up to 26,500 gallons (100,000 l), or in the case of grain whiskey, even as much as 66,000 gallons (250,000 l).

What follows is a look at the actual production process, which can be explained quite simply: the wort turns into wash. This is achieved by adding yeast to the wort. The yeast needs oxygen, which it draws from the sugars in the wort, in order to

produce alcohol and carbon dioxide. There are—once again—three stages in fermentation. During the first phase, the yeast "adjusts" to its new environment. The actual process of conversion begins in the next phase, during which the yeast converts sugar to alcohol. The mixture bubbles vigorously at this stage, and the temperature rises to approximately 95°F/35°C. In the final phase, which lasts about twelve hours, the process slows down, since the alcohol increasingly counteracts the yeast's activity. Bacteria, mostly lactic acid bacteria, proliferate at this stage, lowering the pH-value and adding further notes of flavor to the final product. These flavors are caused by esters, which create flowery notes. Acids and long-chain alcohols add complexity to the overall flavor.

The resulting product is a wash with an alcohol content of 5–8 percent, ready for distillation. It is worth mentioning that the tubs have to be cleaned thoroughly after fermentation in order to arrest the growth of bacteria. If this is not done properly, excessive bacteria could prevent the yeast from being effective.

Distillation

DURING DISTILLATION, the alcohol contained in the fermented wort is separated, or distilled, from the water. Since the boiling point of alcohol (at 172°F/78°C) is lower than that of water (212°F/100°C), the alcohol evaporates first, leaving the water behind. The alcoholic vapors are collected and liquefied again in a controlled cooling process.

For malt whiskey production, pot stills made of copper are used almost exclusively. These stills are often set up in pairs, since most distilleries practice double distillation. There are only very few distilleries in Scotland that still practice triple distillation; one of them is Auchentoshan. In Ireland, on the other hand, triple distillation has a long tradition. Distilleries with only one still run the distillate through that same still two or three times, which is, of course, less efficient than using more.

There are three types of pot stills, distinguished by the transition between the head and the condenser. The first type is the traditional onion shape with a wide neck that slows down the rising vapors and cools down the wash, preventing it from foaming over. The second type has a constriction just below the neck, which slows down the vapors and only lets the lightest part rise. The third type has a boil ball in the middle, which basically serves the same purpose as the constriction in the second type of still. The wort cannot overflow, and only the lightest vapors rise into the neck. The ball is sometimes referred to as a Milton ball.

The copper of which the still is made has significant influence on the quality of the distillate. In combination with copper, the alcohol triggers a chemical reaction that, first and foremost, helps prevent an undesirable sulfur taste. Over the years, this reaction causes the copper to wear off; eventually, the walls of the pot still become too thin and have to be exchanged. Special care is taken to ensure that the successor still has the exact same shape and size.

Viewing windows, such as the ones in a still at Talisker shown here, allow the stillman to monitor the formation of foam during distillation.

The Glen Elgin Distillery uses three wash stills and three spirit stills, each of which has a capacity of 2,900 gallons (11,000 l).

Most modern stills are heated via indirect steam, which allows for more precise temperature control. Only a few distilleries are still heating with gas or even coal. Such stills make use of rummagers, rotating copper brushes or a copper chain that is dragged over the bottom of the still head in order to prevent the mixture from burning and sticking to it. There are some illustrious names among the distilleries that still use direct firing to this day, including Glenfiddich, Macallan, Springbank, Glen Grant, Longmorn and Ardmore.

FIRST DISTILLATION

When the wash with its alcohol content of 5–8 percent is ready, the wash still is filled half or two-thirds full. The wash is then brought almost to a boil; as it is heated, the mixture starts to expand and foam. The upper section of the still's neck has a viewing window that allows foam formation to be monitored. By accurately controlling the heat, the foaming can be checked. The alcohol then rises along the swan's neck from the lyne arm to the condenser, where the vapors are converted back into liquid form and then collected in the low wines receiver. The resulting liquid, with a strength of approximately 21 percent alcohol, is mixed with the unused portions of the second distillation and brought up to 28 percent.

SECOND DISTILLATION

The second phase in the distilling process takes place in the spirit still (sometimes also referred to as the low wines still) and involves purifying the low wines, separating it from the impure alcohol that contains esters, aldehydes and other compounds. Many of these impurities determine a whiskey's flavor; some chemists even claim that there are several hundred organic compounds present in whiskey that significantly influence its taste. This is why the stillman needs a spirit safe in order to test the alcohol for purity before measuring its alcoholic content with a hygrometer. As long as the spirit turns cloudy when water is added, more of the foreshots, also called the heads, have to be released.

It is the stillman's task to redirect the clear middle cut and collect it in the proper receptacle. It is only this fine spirit that will later be filled into casks. After a while, the spirit is cut off, and what follows are the tails, heavier spirits that would cause undesirable flavors (organo-sulfur compounds) in the whiskey. The exact timing for switching the middle cut on and off is a well-kept

Using the spirit safe, the stillman is able to control if and how much of the tails are to be added to the fine spirit. A whiskey's character can be significantly influenced at this stage.

TRIPLE DISTILLATION

In Ireland and in the Scottish Lowlands, the triple distillation method is very common, while elsewhere there are few distilleries that still employ triple distillation. The process increases the alcoholic content by another 10 percent, bringing the spirit's strength to approximately 80 percent.

---

trade secret of any stillman. The longer one waits, the more pungent the spirit will be. If the cut is made too early, though, the resulting spirit will be too mild and will lose its character, which is why timing is crucial. The alcoholic strength of the spirit at the end of the second distillation phase is approximately 70 percent.

COOLING AND CONDENSING

The cooling system used influences a whiskey's taste, as well. Worm tubs, which are usually located outside the still house proper, are thought to yield heavier spirit than the more frequently used shell-and-tube condensers. Both of these systems of pipes are made of copper; the latter

Distillation

has a larger cooling surface area, giving the whiskey a slightly lighter aroma.

LOMOND STILL

The Lomond still was developed in the 1950s with the aim of increasing flexibility in producing different whiskies. It looks a little like the traditional column stills. The cylindrical neck has a cooling jacket mounted vertically at the top. Adjustable plates inside the cylinder make it possible to control the degree of reflux; even the angle of the lyne arm can be adjusted in order to control the distillation process more precisely. After twenty years, however, almost all the Lomond stills disappeared because built-up residues tended to block the controlling plates, and maintenance turned out to be too time consuming. Nowadays, Lomond stills are in use only at the Loch Lomond Distillery and at Scapa.

COLUMN STILLS

There is another distillation technique that revolutionized whiskey production. In 1826, Scotsman Robert Stein developed and tested the technique at his own distillery. Shortly thereafter, Aeneas Coffey, an Irish tax collector, perfected the system and made continuous distillation possible, thus greatly increasing production capacity. The new technique also made it possible to use grains other than barley, such as corn, wheat or rye. Finally, column stills can yield spirits with higher alcoholic content (rectification).

Worm tubs are spiralled copper pipes that run through basins filled with cold water, cooling the vapor inside them.

The Jack Daniel's Distillery in Tennessee employs a column still. When this technique was introduced, it became much simpler to distill crops such as corn.

These features provided the basis for producing grain whiskey, and thus the blends that made the Scottish whisky industry world famous. Scotland is not the only place where column stills — also called continuous stills, Coffey stills or patent stills — are in use. They can also be found in Ireland and Canada, most often used in pairs.

THUMPERS AND DOUBLERS

In the USA, the most common technique is to use just one of the column stills, which is then linked to a thumper or doubler. This approach involves conveying the vapors coming from the wash still through the spirit, which leads to further rectification. Thumpers, which are rare nowadays, are still used by Bernheim and at the Brown-Forman Distillery. Doublers, however, are more common. They work like a pot still, and their outward appearance is similar to that of the classic stills, even though their shape is usually cylindrical. Doublers are used for a second distillation stage that brings the spirit's alcoholic content up to just under 70 percent. The resulting product is referred to as high wine or doublings in the USA.

Opposite: The beginning of the distillation phase in one of the big pot stills of the Talisker Distillery on the Isle of Skye.

Cask Production

THE CONTAINERS IN WHICH whiskey is most often aged are oak casks. Worldwide there are about a dozen kinds of oak that are suitable for storing alcoholic beverages, and in the case of whiskey, this can be narrowed down to just two — American White Oak (*Quercus alba*) and English Oak (*Quercus robur*) — which ideally should be around 100 years old. Because new casks have a tendency to impart an overly dominant wood taste, casks that were previously filled with Bourbon or sherry are used almost exclusively for whiskey maturation. In the past, Bourbon and sherry casks were readily available in Scotland and Ireland at moderate prices. For a long time, the prevailing opinion was that the Bourbon or sherry had a decisive influence on a whiskey's taste. In recent years, however, it has become clear that the wood itself has a stronger effect on the flavor than was previously thought. The reasons for using sherry and Bourbon casks have always been pragmatic, actually. Casks that arrived in England and Scotland full of sherry were simply reused for whiskey

COOPERS

Coopers are in charge of making casks. This is hard work, but it pays well if the casks can be made efficiently, since coopers are usually paid per cask. The craft and its tradition are held in particularly high esteem in Scotland. The period of apprenticeship is four years, and secrets of the trade as well as tools are often handed down from generation to generation. All coopers have their own, personal set of tools, and it very bad form for one cooper to use the tools belonging to someone else working next to him or her. Nowadays only a few distilleries, such as Glenfiddich, operate their own cooperage. Instead, the production and repair of casks is outsourced to independent contractors.

This Speyside cooperage still produces whiskey casks from oak in the traditional way.

Glenfiddich casks being thoroughly labeled. The casks are usually not painted because paint does not allow the wood to breathe, and the contents of the cask need to react with oxygen.

The Balvenie cooperage still uses the old, traditional techniques and tools for making casks. The staves are cut to fit exactly and are held in place by rims.

after they had been emptied. Back then, this was a highly practical solution. When sherry consumption declined, casks became less readily available, and their price increased accordingly. For a while, the prevailing practice was to have casks produced directly in Spain and lend them to sherry producers; after the sherry had matured, the casks were brought to Scotland. This solution only worked until sherry producers started importing casks themselves.

Nowadays, a used sherry cask is very expensive: prices can be as high as 400 to 450 Euros ($560 to 625). Bourbon casks, on the other hand, have always been available inexpensively, because there is a legal requirement in the USA stipulating that whiskey can only be matured in new oak casks. Back in the days, the US timber industry was able to get this regulation passed, and ever since then it has not been possible to use Bourbon casks a second time for whiskey maturation within the USA.

The European oak differs from the American White Oak in certain respects. The casks are often made of Spanish common oak, resulting in slightly more porous and more full-bellied casks. Whiskey stored in European oak casks matures more quickly, and its higher tannin content adds notes of apples, apricots and nuts to whiskies matured in it. Whiskey that has matured in American oak

barrels absorbs flavors of vanilla, coconut, banana and has a certain creamy quality. If European oak casks are charred in order to make the staves more pliable, the Bourbon casks are literally roasted. This practice helps eliminate undesirable aromas and to release vanillin. There are three levels of charring: slight, medium, and "alligator char," the strongest version, named after the characteristic char pattern, which is reminiscent of alligator skin.

Before the wood can be processed, though, it has to be dried. The drying process is usually not left to nature alone, because that way the drying period can be shortened from approximately eighteen months to just about twenty-three days. It has been found that it does not matter to the production of Bourbon whether the cask wood has been dried artificially or naturally. For casks that are reused in Scotland, Ireland or Canada, however, it does indeed make a difference. This is why many traditional distilleries prefer to invest in the more expensive, air-dried casks.

It is an open secret that the sherry strongly influences the flavor of a whiskey in a first-fill cask, which is why the second usage of a sherry cask is considered to be ideal. A possible third filling of a cask is another option; however, in that case, the sherry hardly leaves any traces in the matured whiskey.

Cask Filling and Storage

CASK FILLING

As mentioned before, the middle cut of the distillate is collected in a receptacle, then transferred to the casking station. Malt whiskey spirit has an alcohol content of approximately 70 percent. In years long past, experimentation proved that maturation progresses only slowly with such a high alcoholic content. The solution was to combine the spirit with water; the best results are achieved at a concentration of 63.5 percent. If the whiskey is watered down further, that is, if the alcohol content is lower than 63.5 percent, the whiskey that results after maturation is too weak. Another disadvantage of additional cutting is that it generates a greater volume of liquor: more casks require more storage space, which forces up production costs.

After the distillate has been cut to just the right strength, the whiskey is casked. In most distilleries this happens at predefined intervals. Smaller distilleries, for example, might have a weekly casking schedule. Casks formerly used for Bourbon and sherry are used most often, but occasionally they may be wine casks (e. g., port wine casks). The latter play an important part more often when it comes to finishing. Sherry casks are most frequently the butt type (500 liters/132 gallons) or the rounder-bellied puncheon (545 liters/144 gallons). Bourbon casks are likely to be barrels, and hold approximately 200 liters (53 gallons). In Scotland, barrel casks are often taken apart and rebuilt: five barrels can be turned into four hogshead casks (250 liters/66 gallons).

STORAGE

The storage of the oak casks is of utmost importance for the development of a whiskey's character and color. The use of oak wood is required by law, as is the minimum maturation time: in Scotland the minimum maturation is three years, while it is only two years in Kentucky. However, most whiskies age significantly longer than that. Depending on the climate, maturation time can vary widely. A Kentucky Bourbon matures in about a year's time

Before being filled into casks for maturation, the fine spirit is cut with water until it has an optimal alcohol content of around 63.5% by volume.

less than, say, a Scotch whisky. One more remark on the subject of wood: oak was not chosen on a whim. Experiments with other types of wood, such as chestnut, did not lead to satisfactory results.

The wood, the cask size and the type of beverage previously stored in the cask all influence the flavor of a whiskey. But that is not all: the design of the warehouse and its geographic location play an important role, as well. Each

The great oak casks at the Gelfarclas Distillery can hold up to 130 gallons (500 l) of whiskey. Rolling those casks is heavy labor that requires a practiced hand.

The Glenfiddich Distillery has a typical Scottish warehouse in which casks are stacked in three layers. The low ceiling and thick walls ensure a relatively constant temperature.

warehouse has its unique microclimate, and each distillery has certain preferred warehouses. In fact, experts claim that storage determines 60 to 80 percent of a whiskey's flavor.

In general, a distinction is made between three types of warehouses. First are the traditional dunnage warehouses, stone or brick buildings that are most common in Scotland. They have thick walls in order to counteract fluctuations in outdoor temperature as much as possible, and their earthen floors keep humidity levels at the required high level. Casks are stacked in no more than three layers to ensure that they are all exposed to the same temperature.

Nowadays, however, racked warehouses are more common than dunnage warehouses. In a racked warehouse, up to twenty-four layers of casks can be stacked on top of each other. Because of the racks' height, the temperature surrounding the casks can vary widely. In the USA, racked warehouses are often constructed with thin metal walls and are free-standing on hills in order to take full advantage of climatic conditions. Below the roof of such a warehouse, the temperature can reach 104°F/40°C during summer. The lower rows

of casks are exposed to less fluctuation of temperature. In the past, the casks were actually rotated, with great effort, to counteract this; today, only a few distilleries continue this practice. The more frequent procedure now is to simply cut the whiskey matured in the higher levels of casks with the contents of the lower ones in order to give the final product a consistent character. It has become clear that the microclimate has an influence on a whiskey's character, but does not affect its quality.

The third type of warehouses is relatively new and manages without racks entirely. Instead, the casks are stacked on palettes. When one palette is full, another palette is stacked on top and so on.

The porous wood of the casks allows whiskey to breathe. In Scotland, it loses approximately 2 percent of its alcohol content per year, a loss that is lovingly referred to as the "angels' share." In the USA this value can be as high as 3 percent, especially from casks from the lower, cooler rows; the higher temperature in the middle and upper layers causes more water to evaporate, which in turn leads to higher concentration of alcohol. In extreme cases, the whiskey's alcoholic strength can be as much as 75 percent.

FINISHING

In recent years, a new feature has entered discussions of whiskey storage: finishing. Finishing is actually less about bringing the whiskey production process to completion than it is about perfecting or rounding off a whiskey's flavor during maturation. A secondary period of maturation can add new aromas, complexity and depth. Casks that have held wine are most often used for this purpose. Following the primary maturation, the whiskey is recasked in these containers and continues to mature for a few months, or sometimes as long as a year or two. Only after the whiskey has received this special treatment is it ready for the market.

In terms of wood management, a wide range of casks are suitable for secondary maturation: sherry, port, Bordeaux, Cognac, Calvados, Marsala, rum, Madeira, Shiraz, Chardonnay, Burgundy or Sauterne casks are just a few of the possible choices. Islay malt casks have also been used, and sometimes the whiskey is even filled into brand new casks. The whole subject is hotly debated.

Once the whiskey has been cut with water, the only further addition that is permitted after maturation is caramel color, which gives the whiskey just the right hue. However, there are traces of residue in any cask, which play an important role in maturation and the development of a whiskey's characteristic flavor. Purists would no doubt point out that, strictly speaking, any additives beyond caramel color are not permitted. A more liberal view holds that the character of a whiskey (its aroma, flavor and color) results from the interplay of the raw materials used (variety of grain, water, etc.), the manufacturing process and the maturation period. This view implies that since second-fill casks are used for maturation anyway, there cannot be any objections to used casks for a final finishing period thereafter. Another hotly debated subject is the use of casks that previously contained malt whiskies from another region: is Balvenie Islay Cask already a blended whiskey? At this time, there is no definite answer to this kind of question, but it is to be expected that in the long term legal regulations will be developed.

Bottling and Filtering

THE BOTTLING OF A SINGLE MALT after the maturation period is usually not carried out by the distilleries themselves, as it once was. Today, most distilleries don't even have their own bottling stations. There are exceptions to the rule, of course, including Glenfiddich, Springbank and Bruichladdich. In general, however, distilleries contract with independent bottling plants, which provide the services of bottling, labeling and sealing whiskies.

Preparations for this step for the most part still takes place in the distillery. In the case of cask-strength single cask bottlings, the individual casks are selected and taken directly to the bottler. If the whiskey is to be reduced to drinking strength (40, 43 or 46 percent). it first needs to be cut with spring water, whereby the alcoholic strength must remain above 40 percent. If the whiskey is not a single cask bottling, various casks are chosen and mixed in a large cask or vat in a process called vatting. Vatting also involves bringing the alcohol content of the whiskey down to drinking strength. When just the right flavor has been achieved, distilleries have the option of adding plain caramel (E 150) for coloring. With single malts, this practice is controversial; it is mostly employed with blends. Purists demand that the color of a whiskey should be natural as well, since whiskey is supposed to be a natural, organic product, after all. Many people believe that caramel coloring

The Bruichladdich Distillery is one of the few remaining in Scotland that still has its own in-house bottling station.

influences the flavor. This is not the case, though. It is used in such minute quantities that it could not possibly cause a change in flavor. Eventually, the whiskey is transported to the bottler by truck.

At the bottling station, the whiskey is frequently cold filtered just before bottling in order to achieve a perfectly transparent whiskey without any fine particles. Cold filtration involves bringing the undesirable particles into a solid state so they can be removed more easily. Some of those particles can be important aroma carriers, which may result in a change of flavor. This is why distilleries such as Glenmorangie, Bruichladdich or Ardbeg have decided to abandon cold filtration.

Unlike wine, a whiskey will not continue to mature once it has been bottled. It is important to store whiskey bottles upright to prevent the alcohol from affecting the cork. Bottles should also be protected from direct sunlight. The best place to store whiskey at home is in a cupboard with solid doors and at room temperature. Bottles that are nearly empty should be finished as soon as possible, since the substantial amount of oxygen in the bottle can strongly influence the whiskey. Other than that, whiskey can be stored for a long time.

Bottling of Maker's Mark whisky in Kentucky. Once it has been filled into the characteristic full-bellied bottles, the distillery's famous label is applied.

Opposite: Stacked casks in a cooperage in the Speyside region, ready to be used in local distilleries.

Blending

BLENDING IS THE MIXING OF various whiskies, usually somewhere between twenty and fifty different kinds, in order to achieve a constant and characteristic product. In the case of Scotch blends, the proportion of malt whiskey can range from 5 to 70 percent; the remaining share is grain whiskey. With Irish whiskies, of course, pure pot still whiskey is usually one of the ingredients. The proportions of the various kinds of whiskey determine the quality of the resulting blend. In the USA, it is uncommon for distilleries to exchange or buy full casks; all of the whiskies used for blends are produced in-house. However, it is permitted to add up to 2.5 percent of what is referred to as blender on top of all the various kinds of whiskey. Wine or sherry are often used as blender, which adds new nuances of flavor to the blended whiskey and thus further depth to its character. This process is not be confused with finishing (see page 40). In Canada, it is even legal to blend the spirits before maturation, a practice known as pre-blending. In Japan, because the small number of distilleries makes it impossible to obtain a variety of casks for blending, whiskey is often imported, primarily from Scotland.

Many of the well known blends have been in existence for several generations. It is absolutely crucial that the high quality, the flavor and the color of a particular label remain consistent over the years. Obviously, the whiskey industry is subject to the vagaries of the market, and some

Becoming a master blender is a lengthly endeavor. It takes approximately ten years for experts to acquire the experience necessary to "nose" a perfect blend.

whiskies are simply no longer available. Distilleries close down and new ones are started, while others that have gone out of operation start up production again. This makes it necessary to plan ahead and secure a large supply of the whiskies needed for a particular blend, and if a certain whiskey is no longer available, substitutes have to be found. Since the overall blend needs to have the same taste and color, it is not uncommon for one whiskey to be replaced by five others.

The people in charge of blending the final product are the master blenders. They collect a wide range of samples in their laboratories in order to make appropriate selections. They also have access to up-to-date inventories of all the whiskies currently available on the market for the production of blends.

Becoming a master blender (sometimes also referred to as "noses," since they use only their sense of smell to assess the whiskies, without tasting them) is no easy enterprise. As a rule, quality checks and tastings do not take place until the blend is finished and ready for bottling, so there is no margin for error. Master blenders usually have professional experience of twenty,

Prior to the actual blending, the contents of individual, carefully selected casks are filled into big tubs and mixed.

thirty or even forty years under their belts. Early in their education, they have to hone their sense of smell and learn how to handle an incredible range of aromas. It becomes apparent rather quickly, during the first year or two of the apprenticeship, whether or not someone has a knack for this profession. There is scientific evidence that women have an edge when it comes to describing flavors and nuances of taste, which makes it rather surprising that in spite of this, most master blenders are men. After about five years of training, an experienced blender is able to distinguish between different whiskies with a high degree of certainty. Even so, it takes approximately ten years to complete the entire apprenticeship and become certified as a master blender.

The early morning hours are generally the best time for nosings. The blender's nose is in perfect shape early in the day, so this is the preferred time of day for composing blends.

When just the right mixture has been identified, any missing casks have to be purchased. Once

obtained, these are poured into stainless steel tanks at the blending station (see illus. opposite below). After that the spirits are filled into a blend cask, and all the varieties of whiskies are precisely mixed in perfect proportion. Finally, the finished blend is cut down to drinking strength with distilled water. The mixing is performed either with compressed air or, more traditionally, with stirrers. If the coloring is not quite perfect, it is still possible to make slight adjustments by adding caramel color, but the blender will usually try to achieve the desired color back in the laboratory. Sometimes, the blends are recasked and stored for another one or two years.

Blends are often labelled with predicates such as "standard," "premium" or "deluxe." In general, the proportion of malt whiskey is highest in deluxe blends. If the age of a blended whiskey is printed on the label, it refers to the youngest whiskey contained in the recipe. If the blend states twelve years, for instance, this means that the youngest whiskey contained must be twelve years old.

Blends combine whiskies from as many as fifty different distilleries. Each blender has his or her own well-kept secret.

THE BRANDS
OF THE WORLD

Whisk(e)y originated in Ireland and Scotland, but the treasured drink has long found many fans on every continent. This chapter presents an overview of the world's best distilleries and the wonderful variety of whiskies.

SCOTLAND

SCOTLAND

Scotland is the world's foremost producer of whisky (here without the "e"): there are more distilleries in this small country than in the rest of the world combined. This is in part due to the country's history, but it is also a testament to the Scots' passion for and dedication to their national beverage. By now, Scotch whisky has triumphed in markets around the globe.

FOR WHISK(E)Y CONNOISSEURS, this country in the northwestern reaches of Europe is definitely worth a visit. Anyone who has been to Scotland once will feel compelled to return. The wildly romantic scenery, the friendly and helpful character of the Scottish people and the wide range of sightseeing attractions are appealing to anyone. Of course, whisky fans will also enjoy seeing the many distilleries, where one can learn something new at every visit. Visitors will have the greatest opportunities to tour distilleries during the main tourist season, from Easter until mid-September. Some are open to the public almost year-round; the only time when it is not possible is during the "silent season," when operations shut down so any necessary maintenance work can be done. It is advisable in any case to inquire before visiting, since a considerable number of distilleries are not open to the public at all, or will only accept guests who have made an appointment in advance.

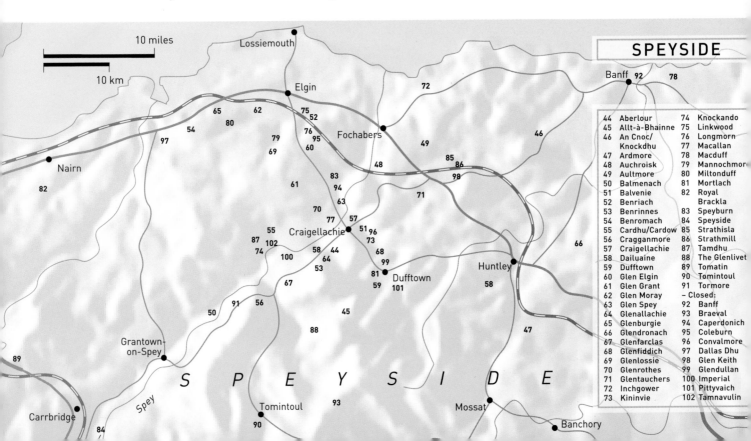

SPEYSIDE

44	Aberlour	74	Knockando
45	Allt-à-Bhainne	75	Linkwood
46	An Cnoc/	76	Longmorn
	Knockdhu	77	Macallan
47	Ardmore	78	Macduff
48	Auchroisk	79	Mannochmor
49	Aultmore	80	Miltonduff
50	Balmenach	81	Mortlach
51	Balvenie	82	Royal
52	Benriach		Brackla
53	Benrinnes	83	Speyburn
54	Benromach	84	Speyside
55	Cardhu/Cardow	85	Strathisla
56	Cragganmore	86	Strathmill
57	Craigellachie	87	Tamdhu
58	Dailuaine	88	The Glenlivet
59	Dufftown	89	Tomatin
60	Glen Elgin	90	Tomintoul
61	Glen Grant	91	Tormore
62	Glen Moray		– Closed:
63	Glen Spey	92	Banff
64	Glenallachie	93	Braeval
65	Glenburgie	94	Caperdonich
66	Glendronach	95	Coleburn
67	Glenfarclas	96	Convalmore
68	Glenfiddich	97	Dallas Dhu
69	Glenlossie	98	Glen Keith
70	Glenrothes	99	Glendullan
71	Glentauchers	100	Imperial
72	Inchgower	101	Pittyvaich
73	Kininvie	102	Tamnavulin

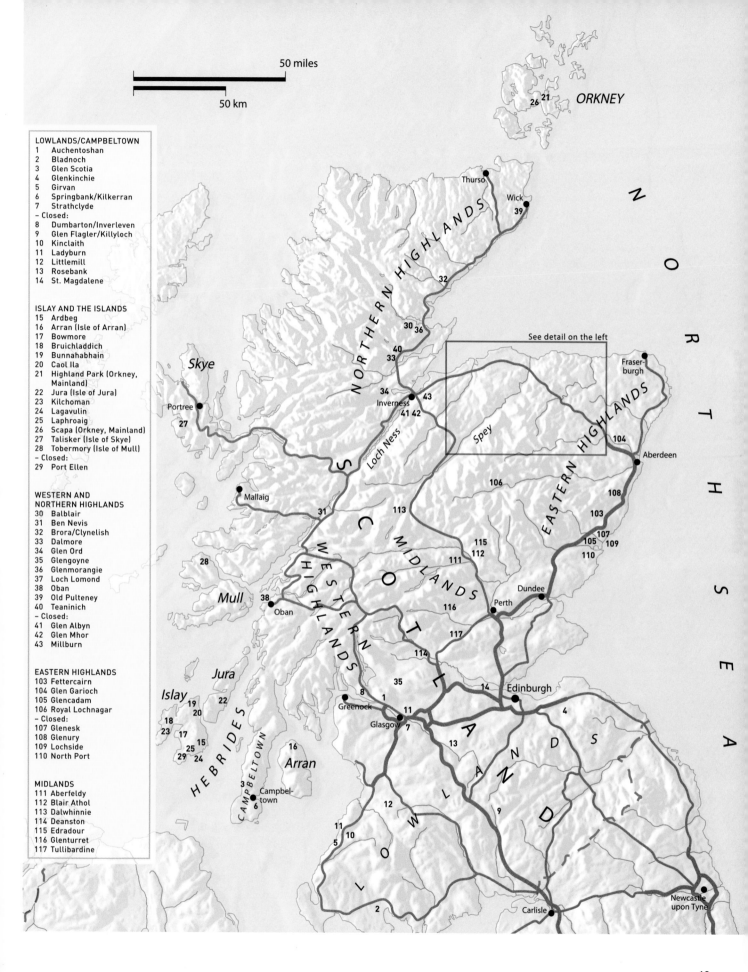

50 miles

50 km

ORKNEY

26 21

THURSO

WICK
39

N
O
R
T
H

NORTHERN HIGHLANDS

32

30 36

40
33

Skye

34

43

Portree
27

Inverness
41 42

Fraser-
burgh

Spey

104

EASTERN HIGHLANDS

Aberdeen

Loch Ness

See detail on the left

106

108

Mallaig

31

113

103

S
C
O
T
L
A
N
D

107
105   109
110

115
112

111

WESTERN HIGHLANDS

28

Mull

38

Oban

MIDLANDS

116

Dundee

Perth

117

114

Jura

22

35

8

1

14   Edinburgh

Islay

19
20

18
23   17

Greenock

11

4

25   15
29   24

Arran

16

Glasgow
7

13

L
O
W
L
A
N
D
S

HEBRIDES

3

Campbel-
town

6

12

9

11
5   10

2

Carlisle

Newcastle
upon Tyne

N
O
R
T
H

S
E
A

History

The origins

It probably was Gaelic people from Ireland who first introduced whisky to Scotland during the fifth or sixth century. The first historical record that refers to whisky was written by a monk named John Cor, who in 1494 received orders from King James IV (1488–1513) to acquire "eight bolls of malt" (over 2600 lbs/1200 kg) for the production of *aqua vitae* (water of life). James IV did not see whisky as a mere beverage; he also wished to find out about its medicinal benefits. In fact, only barbers, who provided medical and surgical services at the time, were allowed to sell it.

In 1503, James IV married Margaret Tudor, the daughter of King Henry VII of England. After Henry's death, the powerful Henry VIII inherited the throne. It seems that the alcohol must have gone to James IV's head: he dared to attack England while Henry VIII was commanding an expedition in France. This led to one of the worst defeats in Scottish history and to the death of James IV in the Battle of Flodden Field. Henry VIII, on the other hand, had a fallout with Pope Clement VII in 1534 and unceremoniously declared himself the supreme head of the Anglican Church in the Act of Supremacy. Since the Scots wanted to retain their Catholic faith, Henry took revenge on them by having his commander in chief, the Earl of Hertford, destroy the Melrose, Kelso, Jedburgh and Dryburgh monasteries, not least in order to prevail over the church in Scotland. Additional monasteries were destroyed as a result of the Reformation in 1559. When the monks were forced to take up regular professions, their long tradition of knowledge of the production of strong spirits, which they had kept closely guarded for a long time, was spread to the common people. Many small farmers who could barely meet their land-lease payments began to make whisky out of their surplus barley. This kind of secondary occupation was, of course, entirely illegal.

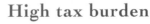

King James IV of Scotland died in the Battle of Flodden Field in 1513.

High tax burden

In January 1644, the Scottish parliament passed a law imposing a tax on alcohol; money was needed in order to go to war with King Charles I, who refused to recognize the rights of the parliament. When King Charles II returned from exile in 1660 after the end of Oliver Cromwell's reign as Lord Protector, this tax was abolished. In 1707, the Scottish parliament was integrated with the English parliament (Westminster) by the Act of Union. London wanted to prevent any unilateral actions by the Scottish in the future.

In 1713, a newly introduced malt tax met with resistance among the oppressed Scots. Evading payment of this tax was considered a matter of honor and was attempted with all kinds of tricks. The many illegal distilleries and whisky smugglers acquired a kind of heroic status. In 1736, two men widely known to be smugglers were sentenced to be executed in Edinburgh. At that time there were approximately 400 illegal distilleries in operation in Edinburgh alone. When one of the two smugglers managed to escape, John Porteous, then captain of the city ward, had the other smuggler executed in the most atrocious way. The execution was followed by protests that resulted in nine people being shot and another twelve badly injured. The captain's luck was no better: he was later hanged by the rebels.

These rebellions made clear just how much discontent about the English government there was among the Scots. The Jacobites, a group of Catholic followers of the exiled King James II, unsuccessfully tried to free themselves from the yoke of English rule in several wars. Bonnie Prince Charlie, Scottish national hero, suffered the worst defeat at Culloden, when the son of James II tried to regain the Scottish crown. He always made sure that his forces had a steady supply of whisky. Before the decisive battle, however, food and whisky were not delivered in time, which meant the soldiers were not properly fortified when they entered the battle. They fought the troops of the English government, led by William Augustus, the Duke of Cumberland, who were invigorated by brandy. Brandy was much less expensive than whisky at the time, because it was not taxed. With this defeat, all hope for Scottish independence was extinguished. The victorious English even went so far as to banish bagpipes and kilts in 1746. Innumerable stills at farm distilleries in the Highlands were destroyed, and in 1781, private distilling was banished entirely.

Nonetheless, to paraphrase Robert Burns, "whisky and freedom" meant a lot to the Scots, so they tended to ignore the ban. A fierce struggle ensued between the distillers and smugglers, on the one hand, and the official forces on the other. At times, smugglers even collaborated with customs and excise officials: not averse to accepting whisky as a bribe, officials would provide hints as to where and when unannounced inspections could be expected. The "water of life" was most often transported via hidden trails in the difficult terrain of the Highlands down to the Lowlands.

The 1823 whisky tax and its consequences

Things could not go on like that indefinitely. Lord Gordon, a clever landowner, proposed a law that would drastically reduce taxes on whisky, while prescribing a minimum size for still necks in order to eliminate the private and illegal farm distilleries. Moreover, the proposal envisioned a yearly fee of £10 per legal license and still. The law was passed in 1823. Adoption was initially slow, but the positive consequences for the legal distilleries soon became apparent. At the same time that transport routes were extended thanks to the recent invention of the train, the distilleries' output was increasing. It was even quite common for whisky to be transported by ship. The *uisge beatha* (water of life) that was produced in the legal distilleries proved to be of much higher quality than the moonshiners' version. Moreover, production in larger quantities led to relatively low production costs. In this way, "official" whisky slowly but steadily established itself.

Thanks to Robert Stein's and Aeneas Coffey's invention of the column still (also known as a Coffey or patent still), a distilling procedure that allowed for the continuous distillation of whisky had become available. The Lowlanders used this type of still to produce grain whisky, which was the basis for the first blends created by pioneers such as Andrew Usher around 1850. Blended whiskies, mixtures of malt and grain whiskies, were easier and less expensive to produce than pure malt, and it was easier to maintain a consistent quality.

The Scots also profited from another fact: in nineteenth-century France, the vine pest destroyed vineyards in entire regions. Consequently, brandy stocks were thinning out and prices were skyrocketing. Since brandy was particularly popular in England, a substitute had to be found. Many people switched to whisky, and thus the triumph of blends began. Soon, blended whiskies had superseded the pure malt and Irish whiskies;

Jacobite memorial at Glenfinnan. This is where Bonnie Prince Charlie met with allied clan chiefs in 1745.

the latter stuck to their own traditional distilling procedures and were not yet offering any blends.

Opposite: A pub on the whisky island of Islay dispenses a wide array of the region's specialties. The water of life tastes even better in its natural surroundings ...

Pattison and Prohibition

In 1898, the Scottish whisky industry suffered a severe blow. The Pattison company acquired casks of whisky in great quantities, keeping them in their own storehouses in Leith to use for the production of blends at a later time. Pattison was soon turned into a stock company, returns were on the rise, and the company continued to expand. Many new distilleries were established that signed guaranteed delivery contracts with Pattison. However, this only went well until the output of whisky started to exceed the demand for it. Financial failure ensued, the banks denied further loans, and the Pattison owners were sentenced to prison time for fraud. The Pattison bankruptcy dragged many distilleries into ruin as well.

Glenfiddich's William Grant turned out to be a pioneer in those days. He decided to avoid dependency on other companies altogether and took the wholesale trade, the export business and the blending itself in his own hands. He established a whisky shop in Glasgow and opened an export office soon thereafter. Subsidiaries in Canada and the USA were founded to safeguard the company's future and to increase the popularity of Scotch whisky all over the world.

At the time, Prohibition played a big role in the USA. The national ban on alcohol took effect in 1920 and would last for thirteen years. This led to some major losses in Scotland as well, in particular for most of the distilleries in the Campbeltown region, which depended almost completely on exports to America. The black market in the USA, however, was thriving, and during Prohibition Scotch simply made its way to America via more indirect routes. When Prohibition was repealed in 1933, both Scottish and Canadian whiskies were so firmly established that regional brands almost didn't stand a chance against the foreign competition.

The renaissance of malt

In the early 1960s, William Grant & Sons played a pioneering role by putting single malts back on the map. Initially met with mockery by the industry, this willingness to embrace innovation turned out to be highly profitable. Today, Grant's Glenfiddich is the most widely drunk single malt in the world. Independent bottlers contributed to the vitalization of the single malt market by introducing a great number of single malts that had never been available as private bottlings before.

Smaller, private distilleries tried out various innovations, ranging from wood finishing to experiments with organic barley. Today, the variety of products on the Scotch whisky market is unrivalled, and the increase in sales in recent years has been remarkable.

The Mortlach Distillery in 1898. Today, this gigantic facility mainly produces whiskies for the Johnnie Walker blend.

LAPHROAIG
SINGLE ISLAY MALT
SCOTCH WHISKY
10
Years Old
ESTABLISHED 1815
BRUICHLADDICH
ISLAY SINGLE MALT
SCOTCH WHISKY
10
Ardbeg
SINGLE ISLAY MALT
SCOTCH WHISKY
TEN
NON CHILL-FILTERED
ISLE OF
JURA
SINGLE MALT
40% vol
JOHNNIE WALKER
1820
35
SOLO
35
SOLO
35
METRIX
35
ml

LOWLANDS/CAMPBELTOWN

"Anybody who hates dogs and loves whiskey
can't be all bad."

ATTRIBUTED TO W. C. FIELDS

THE LOWLANDS AND CAMPBELTOWN are located in the very south of Scotland. There are only a few distilleries still operating in these regions.

LOWLANDS

The Lowlands border directly on England in the south and the Highland Line to the north. This virtual border, once drawn by the British parliament, stretches from Greenock to Dundee. The malt distilleries in this area have always been few, not least because the flat landscape did not allow many options for whisky to be distilled secretly (or illegally) during the heydays of moonshining. At the same time, this region boasts the greatest number of industrial grain distilleries. Unfor-

tunately, their mass-product image has negatively affected the reputation of the local malt whiskies.

The Scottish capital of Edinburgh is located in the center of the Lowlands. With a population of 450,000, it is the country's second biggest city, second only to Glasgow. Edinburgh is also the cultural center of Scotland. Modern times have caught up with the venerable city, whose status was given a boost with the establishment of the Scottish parliament there after certain legislative powers were successfully transferred from London in 1999.

While whisky connoisseurs visiting Edinburgh will not find a distillery, they are sure to appreciate the Scotch Whisky Heritage Centre, which offers

a varied tour through the past and present of whisky production methods. Another highlight is the headquarters of the Scotch Malt Whisky Society. Other than that, there are no more than three distilleries still in operation to be found in the Lowlands. However, with demand for milder whisky brands on the rise in recent years, this market may very well see some growth.

CAMPBELTOWN

The small town of Campbeltown is located in the south of the Kintyre Peninsula. The area surrounding this town used to be a thriving whisky region in its own right during the early twentieth century. Of the approximately thirty distilleries in operation back then, only three remain.

Thanks to its sheltered location, Campbeltown was long a stronghold of illegal whisky distillation. When it became possible to distill whisky legally by obtaining a license, distilleries sprang up like mushrooms. Due to the conveniently located harbor nearby, exports to the USA soon became the region's main source of income. This source, however, ran dry overnight with the advent of Prohibition. Another reason for the downturn was that the oily whisky style favored here was unpopular among blenders, who preferred the lighter Speyside whiskies. The quality of Campbeltown whiskies deteriorated, and they disappeared almost entirely from the whisky scene.

Top: The Forth Rail Bridge, which connects Edinburgh with the Fife Peninsula, is considered a masterpiece of engineering. Bottom: The Kintyre Peninsula was once a center for transatlantic trade. Today, most of the boats moored here are fishing boats.

Opposite: Trossachs National Park was the first national park established by the Scottish government.

Auchentoshan

AUCHENTOSHAN	
OWNER	Morrison Bowmore Ltd.
ESTABLISHED	1817
MEANING OF NAME	Corner of the field
STATUS	In production
ANNUAL PRODUCTION	1.8 million liters/ 475,000 gallons

THE WHITEWASHED BUILDING of the Auchentoshan Distillery is located on the outskirts of Glasgow, in between the Killpatrick Hills and the Clyde River.

Whisky distillation in Auchentoshan has a long tradition that dates back to 1800, although the distillery's license was first granted only in 1823. In 1875, the distillery was rebuilt for the first time. During World War II, it was bombed and severely damaged by German air forces; burning whisky actually flowed into the Clyde River that night. The facility was not reconstructed until after World War II, in 1948. The next modernization took place in 1974, and ten years later, in 1984, the distillery was acquired by the Morrison group. Today Auchentoshan is the last of the twenty-some distilleries that used to produce malts in Glasgow and its surroundings. It is one of the few distilleries that still employ the triple distillation method that is traditional in this region. In 2005, a feature was added to the Auchentoshan Distillery that is of particular interest to whisky connoisseurs: a brand-new visitors center not only introduces an interested audience to whisky production methods, but also offers tastings.

With their light and dry taste, Auchentoshan's whiskies are quite typical of those distilled in the Lowlands region.

WHISKY
Auchentoshan Three Wood, 43% ABV, official bottling
Color: Lovely, transparent amber

TASTING NOTES
The nose of this whisky is very sweet, at times perhaps even reminiscent of brown sugar, with hints of prunes and red currants. The flavor retains this fruitiness, which is even slightly intensified by lemon, hazelnut and cinnamon. The finish is fruity and fresh, with a long-lasting sweetness.

The triple-distilled Auchentoshan whisky is stored in heavy casks.

Bladnoch

BLADNOCH, THE SOUTHERNMOST distillery in Scotland, is located near a small village of the same name near Wigtown. The little brook that supplies the distillery with water, yet again of the same name, flows into the Solway Firth, an inlet that constitutes the border between Scotland and England. The origins of the Bladnoch Distillery date back to 1817, when the business started out as a farm distillery. It remained in the hands of the family that founded it, the McCleelands, until 1938, when ownership changed for the first time. The distillery was closed down in 1993 by its owner, United Distillers (UD). In 1995, the present owner, Raymond Armstrong, visited Scotland in search of a vacation home, and this was his original intention when he acquired the distillery's premises. He eventually reconsidered, however, changed his plans, and decided to reactivate the distillery, even though his sales contract stipulated a cap on whisky production at a certain level. Visitors can even book a whisky seminar that teaches the basics of whisky distillering in several days.

Bladnoch is a whisky that is typical of this region, light and fresh. Currently, it is hard to come

BLADNOCH	
OWNER	Raymond Armstrong (Northern Ireland)
ESTABLISHED	1817
MEANING OF NAME	Old Gaelic name of a river (meaning unknown)
STATUS	In production
ANNUAL PRODUCTION	100,000 liters/ 26,400 gallons

by, and can be obtained almost exclusively through Diageo, the former owner, or through independent bottlers. This situation will likely change with the new bottlings.

WHISKY
Bladnoch, 10 years old, 43% ABV, Flora & Fauna
Color: Very light straw

TASTING NOTES
This straw-colored whisky yields a nose of citrus fruits with a hint of sherry; the latter is also apparent in the flavor, complemented by a hint of malt. The finish is medium, with a highly characteristic dryness.

Small brooks and lush, green hills are characteristic of the scenery around Wigtown. The Bladnoch Distillery is nearby.

Glen Scotia

GLEN SCOTIA

OWNER	Glen Catrine Bonded (Loch Lomond Distillery Co. Ltd.)
ESTABLISHED	1835
MEANING OF NAME	Valley of the Scots
STATUS	Seasonal production (summer months)
ANNUAL PRODUCTION	80,000 liters/ 21,000 gallons

THE GLEN SCOTIA DISTILLERY is on High Street in the northern district of Campbeltown.

The distillery was established in 1835, a few years after Springbank began production. It was acquired in 1919 by West Highland Malt Distillers (WHMD). People tried to ward off the impending economic crisis in Campbeltown, which had started to unfold even then, by increased whisky production. This effort, unfortunately, came at the cost of a loss in quality. Five years later, the group had to file bankruptcy. Duncan MacCallum, a former WHMD manager, continued on his own, but had to shut down the distillery in 1928 as a result of Prohibition, and remained out of operation until 1933. In 1930, MacCallum committed suicide by drowning in Loch Campbeltown, and locals claim that his ghost has haunted the distillery ever since. Others say that everything that could go wrong at the distillery has done so ever since his death. Following this episode, Glen Scotia

belonged to Hiram Walker for a short time before it was sold to A. Gillies in 1955, whose manager also owned the Littlemill Distillery. The facility was closed again from 1984 until 1990. The following owner, Gibson International, had to file bankruptcy in 1994, after which the distillery was acquired by Glen Catrine Bonded, a subsidiary of Loch Lomond Distillery Co. Ltd., which bought the stock but did not resume distilling.

As of 1999, Glen Scotia has been in production: the Springbank staff produce around 21,000 gallons (80,000 l) of whisky each summer. This is a fresh and salty whisky with a distinct maritime influence.

WHISKY
Glen Scotia, 12 years old, 40% ABV
Color: Golden yellow

TASTING NOTES
Long term, the twelve-year-old will replace the fourteen-year-old whisky, which can occasionally still be found on the market. The twelve-year-old Scotch retains the familiar fresh, salty and well-balanced nose. The flavor has hints of peat smoke and a pleasant spiciness. The finish is very long and further accentuates these flavors.

Present-day Campbeltown is a quiet fishing village. Back in the days, this port shipped large quantities of whisky to the USA.

Glenkinchie

THE VILLAGE OF PENCAITLAND is located about 15 miles (25 km) outside of Edinburgh, and is home to the Glenkinchie Distillery. Glenkinchie has become a popular attraction for Edinburgh locals, which explains why their labels bear the words "The Edinburgh Malt." The Lammermuir Hills are nearby, and the area is well known for the high quality of the barley grown there.

The origins of the Glenkinchie Distillery date back to the year 1835, when the facilities were still in use as a farmhouse. It was not before 1914, after acquisition of the premises by SMD under the management of John Haig, that the distillery started permanent production of whisky on a larger scale. Similar to Rosebank, Glenkinchie remained in production during World War II. Today, the buildings also house a museum, which was most recently expanded and modernized in 1997. Among many other attractions, this museum has a fully operational, 30-foot (10-m) miniature model of the distillery.

Glenkinchie whisky is light and spicy, with more complex flavors than are typical of the Lowlands. It is among the classic malts.

GLENKINCHIE	
OWNER	UDV (Diageo)
ESTABLISHED	1837
MEANING OF NAME	Valley of the Kinchie
STATUS	In production
ANNUAL PRODUCTION	1.6 million liters/ 423,000 gallons

WHISKY

Glenkinchie Distillers Edition, 1990 vintage, 43% ABV
Color: Sunny gold

TASTING NOTES

This whisky is Amontillado sherry cask aged, which is quite evident in its aroma. On the palate it has a nutty, sweet note, combined with a very light floweriness, and the sherry flavors are further emphasized. The finish is long and dry. At first tasting, Glenkinchie will likely not be recognized as a Lowland.

The red brick buildings of the Glenkinchie Distillery near Edinburgh have the appearance of an industrial factory.

Grain Distilleries Girvan · Strathclyde

GIRVAN

OWNER	William Grant & Sons
ESTABLISHED	1963
MEANING OF NAME	Short river
STATUS	In production
ANNUAL PRODUCTION	ca. 68 million liters/ 18 million gallons

THE GIRVAN GRAIN DISTILLERY is located near the small, quiet coastal town of the same name. It was established in 1963 by William Grant & Sons. The Grants intended for this project to make them somewhat more independent from their competitors. The state-of-the-art production facilities yield well over 15 million gallons (60 million l) of spirit annually. For grain whisky production, Girvan employs column stills. The distillery is also used for the production of other strong spirits, including gin and vodka.

WHISKY
Girvan, 1964, 48% ABV
Color: Amber

 TASTING NOTES
The sweet aroma is dominated by flavors of banana and butterscotch. A little bitter on the palate, this whisky is reminiscent of Bourbon.

STRATHCLYDE

OWNER	Pernod Ricard
ESTABLISHED	1927
MEANING OF NAME	Valley of the River Clyde
STATUS	In production
ANNUAL PRODUCTION	40 million liters/ 10.6 million gallons

THIS GRAIN DISTILLERY is in the center of Glasgow's Gorbals district. Although it is located on the banks of the River Clyde, it draws its water supply—as does the entire city—from Loch Katrine in the Trossachs.

The distillery was built by the beer brewers Seager Evans in 1927, who began to take an interest in whisky at that time. The industrial complex itself is known as Long John. The Kinclaith malt distillery used to be located on the same premises, but was demolished to make room for an extension building. After some time, it was sold to the Whitbread company, and was subsequently acquired by Allied Distillers, who in turn merged to become Allied Domecq. Allied Domecq was eventually acquired by the large French conglomerate Pernod Ricard in 2005.

WHISKY
Strathclyde, 33 years old, 1973/ 2007, 56.5% ABV, Duncan Taylor
Color: Bright amber

 TASTING NOTES
This thirty-three-year-old has a sweet aroma with strong caramel notes. Its flavor is fruity, with a distinct oak note resulting from the long ageing process. Very smooth on the tongue. The finish is long, with a slightly oily texture.

Springbank/Kilkerran

The Springbank Distillery produces three different malts: Springbank, Longrow and Hazelburn.

THE SPRINGBANK DISTILLERY is located in the city of Campeltown in the south of the Kintyre Peninsula. To reach it, turn into Longrow Street just before the A 83 road ends.

The distillery was officially established in 1828, probably three years after the founding family had built the Riechlachan Distillery on the same site. It had its start as a moonshining business, but an official license was soon acquired. The distillery is family-owned by the Mitchells to this very day. Little has changed at this company since the beginning of the twentieth century, one difference being that the on-site malthouse was reno-vated and put back into use in the 1990s. The barley is planted and harvested in Campel-town exclusively for use by the distillery. Spring-bank is arguably the only distillery left in Scotland today in which all the processes of whisky pro-duction are carried out manually in their entirety, including an in-house bottling station. In order to utilize the capacity of the facilities to the full, an independent bottler,

Cadenhead, was acquired in 1969. In 2004, the family opened an additional distillery, also in Campbeltown. That is Kilkerran, which is already selling limited editions of bottles to connoisseurs; those whiskies, however, will not be delivered before 2014. The Kilkerran Distillery, which is located right next to the Springbank Distillery, was originally called Glengyle. This name cannot be used any longer because there is a vatted malt of the same name. Glengyle remained in pro-duction only until 1925 and remained out of operation until 2004. Renovations were initiated from 2001 onward, and at that time the facility was designated as a historic building. The name Kilkerran itself is steeped in history. It is derived from the Gaelic name of the first Celtic settlement that was located here: *Ceann Loch Cille Chiarain.*

This whisky preserves the typical, highly complex Campbeltown style, and most people consider it to be the most traditional malt in all of Scotland. The distillery is known for having revived several classics, including the Longrow (heavily peated) and the Hazelburn, which was bottled in 2006. The triple-distilled Hazelburn will be rather mild.

WHISKY
Springbank 100 Proof, 10 years old, 57% ABV, official bottling
Color: Gold

TASTING NOTES
This whisky has an exceptionally sweet aroma, with the slightest suggestion of smoke. The flavor is very fruity, with a little sherry. The finish is a veritable explosion of flavors, with a strong smoky and spicy note.

SPRINGBANK	
OWNER	J. + A. Mitchell
ESTABLISHED	1828
MEANING OF NAME	Spring on a hill
STATUS	In production
ANNUAL PRODUCTION	125,000 liters/ 33,000 gallons

Dumbarton/Inverleven

DUMBARTON/INVERLEVEN

OWNER	Pernod Ricard
ESTABLISHED	1938
MEANING OF NAME	Fortress of the Britsh
STATUS	Closed

THIS LARGE DISTILLERY COMPLEX is in Dumbarton, directly on the River Leven. The conspicuous red brick building can be seen from afar.

This business was established in 1938 with the primary purpose of producing whisky for Ballantine's. In addition to grain whisky production, a malt distillery was in operation at Inverleven, producing for the same blend. Apart from the two pot stills, there was a Lomond still (a combination of a pot still and a column still). The facilities were shut down in 1991. Unfortunately, no privately bottled single malt was ever released. Gordon & MacPhail and Cadenhead, however, have put some bottlings on the market; some of them are still available at the time of writing.

Dumbarton Castle, thought to be the oldest in Scotland, was built atop volcanic basalt rock.

Eventually, the production of grain whisky ceased as well, in 2002, when the distillery's owner, Allied Domecq, decided to pool production with Strathclyde, another Glasgow-based grain whisky distillery that is part of the group.

WHISKY
Inverleven, 1985, 40% ABV, Gordon & MacPhail
Color: Bright straw

 TASTING NOTES
This whisky has a nose of peaches and strawberries, complemented by spices, a note of malt and a hint of vanilla. It is spicy on the palate, with notes of cedar wood and white pepper. The finish is dry, again with flavors of fruits and spices.

Glen Flagler/Killyloch · Kinclaith

GLEN FLAGLER/KILLYLOCH

OWNER	Inver House
ESTABLISHED	1965
MEANING OF NAME	Valley of the Flagler
STATUS	Closed

THE GLEN FLAGLER DISTILLERY was housed in a former paper mill.

The distillery took up production in 1965, but was closed already in the mid-1980s. This is where Killyloch whisky was produced, which was withdrawn from the market in the early 1970s. The company caused another stir in the 1990s when Signatory brought a small edition of both malts to the market.

Both whiskies had a distinct Lowland character, with Glen Flagler being the spicier of the two.

WHISKY

Glen Flagler, 1973, 30 years old, 46 ABV
Color: Gleaming gold

 TASTING NOTES

The light nose of this Glen Flagler recalls fizzy orange drink and has notes of malt and flowers. Its flavor is smooth and nutty. The medium finish brings out the nut flavors again.

KINCLAITH

OWNER	Pernod Ricard
ESTABLISHED	1957
MEANING OF NAME	Head of the River Clyde
STATUS	Demolished

THIS DISTILLERY used to stand on the premises of the Strathclyde grain whisky distillery in the center of Glasgow. Sadly, Kinclaith was only in existence for a very short time.

It was built by the beer brewers Seager Evans in 1957. The company was owned by an American firm at the time, Schenley. Among other assets, Schenley also owned the Strathclyde grain distillery. The Kinclaith malt distillery was built with Schenley money on the same premises. The Americans made further investments as well, for example in Tormore. However, Kinclaith had to close down as early as 1975, when the owners withdrew from Scotland. The British brewery corporation Whitbread took over the helm and

expanded the grain distillery, but the malt distillery had to make way for this extension. The grain distillery was subsequently sold to Allied Distillers, which later became Allied Domecq and was eventually taken over by the Pernod Ricard group in 2005.

WHISKY

Kinclaith, 35 years old, 1969, 54% ABV, Signatory Vintage
Color: Amber

 TASTING NOTES

The nose of this signatory bottling is sweet, full and pleasant. The body of the whisky is light, and it is very fruity on the palate, with substantial complexity. The finish reveals some oak and a peppery, spicy note.

Ladyburn · Littlemill

LADYBURN

OWNER	William Grant & Sons
ESTABLISHED	1966
MEANING OF NAME	Brook on a hill
STATUS	Demolished

THE LADYBURN MALT DISTILLERY stood in the Girvan complex in Ayrshire. The village of Girvan is directly on the coast.

Like almost all the malt distilleries that were erected on the site of a grain distillery, Ladyburn's life was but a short one: its four pot stills were in production for a mere ten years, from 1966 until 1975, when the distillery was completely demolished by the owner at the time, William Grant & Sons. Allegedly, a few casks still remain in the warehouses.

The Ladyburn single malt was put on the market only a single time. Another twenty-year bottling was produced solely by Cadenhead. Legend has it that the rest was divided among the employees.

WHISKY
Ladyburn 1973 Vintage Single Cask, 50.4% ABV
Color: Greenish gold

 TASTING NOTES
The nose is dominated by a fine aroma of honey, fruit peel and a hint of oak. The whisky is very smooth on the palate, with sweet notes of vanilla and peach. The finish is dominated by dry oak.

LITTLEMILL

OWNER	Loch Lomond Distillery Co. Ltd.
ESTABLISHED	1772
MEANING OF NAME	Little mill
STATUS	Closed (burnt down)
ANNUAL PRODUCTION	800,000 liters/ 211,000 gallons

THE LITTLEMILL DISTILLERY was in Bowling, on the north bank of the Clyde River. Its water supply did not come from the Clyde, but from the Kilpatrick Hills, which are already part of the Highlands. The distillery itself, however, was located in the Lowlands.

Officially, the origins of the distillery date back to 1772, though there is reason to assume that distillation was taking place on the site as early as 1750, which makes Littlemill one of the oldest Scottish distilleries, together with Strathisla and Glenturret. Littlemill has seen many changes of ownership and shutdowns. Most recently, it was acquired from bankruptcy proceedings by Glen

Catrine Bonded Warehouse and has been run under the name of Loch Lomond Distillery Co. Ltd. Some of the buildings have been demolished, while others were protected as historic buildings, foiling a plan to convert the distillery into apartments. In the end, things turned out differently. After it was planned to erect a new stillhouse in the malthouse and to reopen the distillery as a museum, the remaining buildings caught fire in 2004, allegedly caused by playing children.

WHISKY
Littlemill, 12 years old, 40% ABV
Color: Bright red-gold

 TASTING NOTES
This whisky has a fruity aroma with a hint of peat smoke. It tastes delightfully round, with a slight oiliness. The finish is long and heavy.

Rosebank · St. Magdalene

ROSEBANK

OWNER	British Waterway Board
ESTABLISHED	1840
DERIVATION OF NAME	The banks of the channel were once overgrown with roses, hence the name.
STATUS	Closed; some buildings converted to apartments and a restaurant.
ANNUAL PRODUCTION	320,000 liters/ 84,500 gallons

THE ROSEBANK DISTILLERY stands alongside the Forth Clyde canal on the outskirts of Falkirk, near the remains of the Antonine Wall erected by the Romans to protect themselves from attacks by the Celts and the Picts. Rosebank was established in 1840 by James Rankine and despite hefty protests, was closed down in 1993 by its owner, United Distillers. Preference was given to the more picturesque Glenkinchie Distillery, which attracted a greater number of tourists. Attempts to resume production in 1997 were unsuccessful because the required funds could not be raised. As of press time, some buildings are in the process of being converted to apartments, and others have already been demolished.

This whisky is widely thought to be the finest Lowland.

WHISKY
Rosebank Mission Range, 17 years old, 1989/2006, 55.3% ABV
Color: Gold

TASTING NOTES
This whisky has light, flowery aromas of chamomile, grass, apricot, peach and orange flowers. It is light, sweet and creamy on the palate, with a long-lingering fruitiness. The finish is sweet, fruity fresh, with notes of herbs, slightly dry, and almost ethereal.

ST. MAGDALENE

OWNER	DCL/UDV (Diageo)
ESTABLISHED	1765
STATUS	Closed, partly converted to apartment houses

THE ST. MAGDALENE DISTILLERY stood in the small town of Linlithgow. Ruins of the castle of the same name, where Mary Queen of Scots was born, can still be found and are even a popular tourist attraction nowadays.

The site where the distillery was built during the eighteenth century had formerly been home to a leper hospital (in the twelfth century) and then a monastery. According to some sources, the distillery was founded in the year 1765, while others suggest that the first official record of an owner, Adam Dawson, only goes back to 1798. Either way, this distillery was also forced to shut down operation in 1983. Some of the buildings have been converted to luxury apartment houses, but others are protected as historic buildings. The pagoda towers and the name, painted in large white letters, still bear testimony to the distillery's past.

This highly aromatic whisky was heavily peated during the malting process, making it not particularly typical of the region.

WHISKY
St. Magdalene, 19 years old, 1979, 63.8% ABV, Rare Malts
Color: Deep gold

TASTING NOTES
This highly aromatic whisky is reminiscent of malt and licorice. On the palate, its flavor echoes the malt and licorice notes. The finish is unusually strong and peaty.

Islay and the Islands

"Whisky is liquid sunshine."

GEORGE BERNARD SHAW

THE HEBRIDES ON THE WEST COAST of Scotland and the Orkney Islands far to the north are popular travel destinations, not only because of their spectacular scenery—including secluded bays, bizarre rock formations, deserted peat bogs and picturesque small harbor towns—but also because this is where the most typical of all the Scotch single malts are produced.

ISLAY

Islay is the southernmost of the Hebridean Islands, and it undeniably holds a special place in the world of whisky. The island, which is a mere 20 miles (32 km) long and 9 miles (15 km) wide, is home to no fewer than nine active distilleries. In fact, it is considered an independent region by

many whisky connoisseurs. At least some parts of the facilities of two further distilleries have also survived, such as the warehouses, and in one case a kiln. In its glory days, Islay boasted up to twenty-six distilleries. Nowadays, the island's population of approximately 3,300 make their living primarily from distilling, fishing, sheep breeding and tourism.

The word Islay (pronounced "eye-la") was originally the name of a Norwegian princess. The Norwegian influence on the Hebrides, however, was by no means as harmless as the name of a king's daughter might suggest: the Normans tyrannized the residents of the island for centuries. The Kildalton Cross, one of the most impressive Celtic crosses in Great Britain, can be found

near the Ardbeg Distillery. The Normans once destroyed a monastery on that site and killed the abbot, along with many other people. Only a few centuries later, when the pagan Normans had been Christianized as well, would they allow themselves to be buried in the same cemetery. Further interesting sights on the island include the Round Church in Bowmore. Legend has it that it was built in a round shape so the devil could not hide in any corners. There also is an excavation site of a medieval fortress that was built by Finlaggan, Lord of the Isles. Visiting the island is particularly interesting for geologists, since the rock formations near Bruichladdich are considered some of the oldest in the world.

Like many other regions in Scotland, Islay is also known as a birds' paradise. Approximately 10,000 white-fronted geese and twice that number of barnacle geese overwinter here. Ornithologists and nature lovers can also observe some very rare species, such as the corn crake.

ARRAN

Many consider the island of Arran to be Scotland in a nutshell. Just like the larger Scotland, the island itself is structured into a northern part with mountains and lakes and a southern part with scenery featuring soft hills and wide meadows.

Since 1995, there has once again been a good reason for whisky connoisseurs to visit this island.

Top: The Island of Skye charms visitors with deserted moors, bizarre rock formations and breathtaking steep coasts.
Bottom: The Round Church in Bowmore, here with its cemetery, is one of the most original buildings on Islay.

Opposite: The often photographed colorful houses along Tobermory's waterside promenade on Mull.

After a period of 150 years during which no whisky was produced here, the Arran Distillery near Lochranza took up production a little more than a decade ago.

JURA

Jura is separated from the mainland only by a strait. Once one arrives on the island, a narrow street in the southeast leads up to the only settlement, the village of Craighouse. This is where the Isle of Jura distillery is located. Continuing along that street further to the north one reaches the small cottage in which George Orwell lived for a period of time while he was writing his best-selling novel, *1984*.

Nowadays, fewer than 200 people make their home on the island. The name Jura, which is of Norwegian origin and means "red deer," is not coincidental: approximately 6,000 red deer inhabit the island. The Paps of Jura can be seen from the neighboring island of Islay, and on a clear day, even from Northern Ireland. These mountains with their three peaks are a popular destination among mountaineers. The word "paps" is old Gaelic for "breasts."

MULL

The island of Mull is one of the most often visited of the Hebrides islands. The approximately 2,700 locals make their living mostly from tourism and cattle or sheep breeding.

The Carsaig Arches, a group of basalt rocks that have been shaped by the sea in the course of time, are located in the south. Their bizarre arches, caves and tunnels are one of the island's major sightseeing attractions. Up north, there is the main village of Tobermory, known for its colorful houses alongside the harbor. It is considered the most picturesque harbor town on the Hebrides. Whisky connoisseurs will be interested in the distillery of the same name.

SKYE

Skye, 50 miles (80 km) long and between 3 and 25 miles (5–40 km) wide, is the largest of the Hebrides. It can be reached conveniently by car thanks to a bridge that connects it to the mainland.

In terms of scenery, Skye is spectacular in many respects. There are the Cuillins Hills in the south, a mountain range with peaks up to 3,300 feet (1,000 m) high, and its wildly romantic landscapes alternate with valleys carpeted with flowers. On the Trotternish Peninsula in the north, an impressive rock formation known as the Old Man of Storr can be admired. In the northwest, Dunvegan Castle attracts many visitors.

For whisky connoisseurs, there is only one distillery to visit at the moment: Talisker. A second one is currently under construction—a new chapter in the history of whisky is soon to begin.

ORKNEY

The Orkney Islands (sixty-seven islands in total) are located in the far north of Scotland. Only seventeen of these islands are inhabited, and the total number of inhabitants is a mere 19,000. But the steep coasts of the Orkney Islands are home to the largest number of seabirds in all of Great Britain. The Orkneys are actually located at the same latitude as St. Petersburg in Russia; however, due to the Gulf Stream, it hardly ever becomes genuinely cold here. At the same time, this year-round moderate climate also means that a summer day rarely gets any warmer than 60 °F (16 °C).

The islanders owe their name to the Vikings, who called the group of islands "orkneyjar," meaning "island of the seals." Kirkwall, the capital, has approximately 7,000 inhabitants and is located on the island of Mainland. This lovely town is considered one of the most important attractions in Scotland. It is particularly well known for the St. Magnus Festival of the cultural arts, which takes place every year in June.

Skara Brea in the west of Mainland, the oldest settlement in Great Britain, is worth a visit as well. It dates back to the year 3100 BCE and remained populated for approximately 500 years before it was covered completely by drifting sand. In 1850, a violent tempest uncovered many ruins of this stone age settlement, and these are currently accessible to visitors. A trip to the prehistoric Maes Howe tomb, which dates back to the period around 2700 BCE, is no less interesting.

Whisky connoisseurs will find Kirkwall particularly interesting because this is where Highland Park is located. A little further south, near Scapa Flow Bay, is the Scapa Distillery, which has always stood somewhat in the shadow of its neighbor to the north.

Opposite: The Old Man of Hoy, a butte located on the Orkneys, braves North Atlantic storms.

Ardbeg

ARDBEG	
OWNER	Glenmorangie plc (LVMH)
ESTABLISHED	1815
MEANING OF NAME	Small hill
STATUS	In production
ANNUAL PRODUCTION	950,000 liters/ 251,000 gallons

ARDBEG IS THE FIRST DISTILLERY that comes into view when one arrives on the Isle of Islay by ferry. The distillery's whitewashed buildings with the prominent logo, located directly on the south coast, cannot be missed.

Legend has it that moonshiners were producing whisky on the site where the distillery is located today before it was officially established in 1815. Two years after the foundation of the business, the distillery was acquired by the McDougall family, who sold it to Hiram Walker in 1977. From that point onward, the business has gone downhill. Only four years later, the distillery was shut down. Allied bought it in 1989 and resumed production for a further seven years. However, they decided against using the in-house malthouse because it did not have any fans for the chimney, which resulted in a pronounced peat flavor. After the distillery had to

shut down once again, Glenmorangie came to the rescue and renovated the buildings. Although the question of whether the malthouse should be reinstated has still not been settled, the distillery has been in production again since the Glenmorangie acquisition and has been managed by Stuart Thomson ever since the reopening. The in-house coffeehouse, by the way, is an insider's tip; it is said to serve excellent food. Glenmorangie was bought by the luxury goods group LVMH in 2005.

Ardbeg is one of the smokiest and peatiest of all whiskies. The six-year Very Young has split experts into two camps: some find it too robust and not mature enough, while others appreciate it exactly for this unique character.

WHISKY
Ardbeg Ten, 10 years old, 46% ABV
Color: Pale straw yellow

TASTING NOTES
The ten-year-old is particularly popular. Fans of smoky malts appreciate it for its smoky aroma, which is complemented by a strong note of salt water, for its moderately heavy body, and the slightly sweet flavor that comes on strong and bursts into a strong, iodine finish.

View of the Sound of Islay with the white buildings of the Ardbeg Distillery in the foreground.

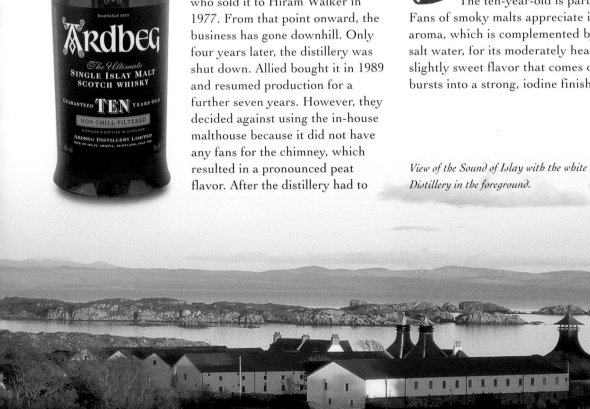

Arran

A WAYS OUTSIDE OF LOCHRANZA, on the A 841 highway in the north of the Isle of Arran, the Arran Distillery lies nestled into a small valley. The valley is called Glen Eason Biorach, which roughly means "valley of the small waterfall." On a clear day, the distillery can be seen from the ferry and from the Kintyre Peninsula.

The island was without any distillery at all for about 150 years. In 1992, the idea was born to build a new distillery. This was realized and the facility took up production in 1995, one year after the planned opening. A pair of eagles had been breeding on the distillery's premises, making it necessary to delay completion for environmental reasons. One exceptional feature of the Arran Distillery is that all buildings have pagoda roofs.

Harold Currie, the founder, came up with a special approach to fund the endeavor. In an exceptional promotional effort, he sold promissory notes to interested parties, who, after the required maturation time, received whisky in return. The owners are particularly proud of the visitors center, which was inaugurated in 1997 by Queen Elizabeth II herself. The arrival of Her Majesty, who entered the harbor of Lochranza with her yacht, was celebrated as a special occasion.

This whisky is smooth and creamy, yet spicy. It has a slightly flowery note and a fine hint of peat smoke. The first limited edition was put on the market after only three years (i.e., the legally required minimum maturation time). A variety of different seven- and eight-year wood finishes have been in circulation for some time now: Calvados, Marsala, port, rum and cognac. The ten-year-old Arran was finally presented on September 21, 2005.

ARRAN	
OWNER	Isle of Arran Distillers
ESTABLISHED	1995
MEANING OF NAME	Place of peaked mountains
STATUS	In production
ANNUAL PRODUCTION	750,000 liters/ 198,000 gallons

Since 1995, the Isle of Arran has had its own distillery once again. Its two pot stills produce a spicy, creamy whisky.

WHISKY

Arran, 10 years old, 46% ABV, official bottling
Color: Mature, golden barley yellow

TASTING NOTES

The distillery's first ten-year-old, which is finally available on the market now in addition to the successful Finish series, has a distinctly sweet nose of oranges and nut, which is echoed on the tongue. The whisky is smooth, has a medium-heavy body, and finishes on sherry notes.

Bowmore

BOWMORE

OWNER	Morrison Bowmore Distillers Ltd. (Suntory)
ESTABLISHED	1779
MEANING OF NAME	The big reef
STATUS	In production
ANNUAL PRODUCTION	1.7 million liters/ 450,000 gallons

Built directly seaside is the impressive Bowmore Distillery, which now belongs to the Japanese firm Suntory.

THE BOWMORE DISTILLERY is located in the town of the same name on Islay. It was built right next to the harbor in the bay of Loch Indaal.

This gorgeous, whitewashed distillery was established in 1779, which makes it Islay's oldest. Former owners Sheriff & Co. sold it to Stanley P. Morrison in 1963, which was later renamed Morrison Bowmore. In 1989, the Japanese Suntory group acquired 35 percent of the company, before taking it over completely in 1994. The same group also owns two other Scotch distilleries, Auchentoshan and Glen Garioch.

Remarkably, Bowmore produces approximately 50 percent of its malt in-house, and that in a very cost- and energy-saving way, thanks to a special pipe system that recaptures heat. The excess heat is even used to warm a swimming pool that was installed in an old warehouse. Only a few feet away is a schoolhouse, also with a pagoda roof, which has been mistaken for the distillery by many a tourist.

Compared to all the other distilleries on the island, Bowmore uses a particularly large number of sherry casks. Approximately one-third of the whisky produced here matures in sherry casks. Bowmore is less intense than the malts from the south of the island, but it also has a strong peat note caused by the high concentration of peat

absorbed by the water, which is rich in iron and also carries aromas of reed, moss and ferns. Since the warehouses are located directly on the coast, some of them below sea level, it should come as no surprise that this whisky is salty. Similar to the other whiskies from the south, Bowmore is complex on the palate. The best known version is arguably Black Bowmore (named after its color), bottled three times in 1993, 1994 and the 1995 Final Edition. Black Bowmores have achieved cult status and are traded at horrendous prices. Only a chosen few will ever get to taste this particular whisky. However, Bowmore offers a wide and varied selection of much more affordable whiskies in proprietary bottlings.

WHISKY

Bowmore Enigma, 12 years old, 40% ABV
Color: Light golden yellow

 TASTING NOTES

The salty, smoky nose is echoed on the palate and complemented by notes of sherry, seaweed, heather and spices. The finish is long, as expected, and adds a touch of salt.

Opposite: Whisky casks have been rolled through the gates of the Bowmore Distillery since 1779. Bowmore is considered Islay's oldest distillery.

BOWMORE DISTILLERY

Bruichladdich

BRUICHLADDICH

OWNER	Bruichladdich Distillery Company Ltd.
ESTABLISHED	1881
MEANING OF NAME	Spot on the shore
STATUS	In production
ANNUAL PRODUCTION	500,000 liters/ 132,000 gallons

THE VILLAGE OF BRUICHLADDICH with the distillery of the same name (sometimes lovingly referred to as "Laddie") is located opposite Bowmore, on the northern shores of Loch Indaal. Until recently, this was Scotland's westernmost distillery, until the Kilchoman Distillery opened a few miles west of Bruichladdich during the summer of 2005.

The brothers Robert, William and John Gourlay Harvey established the Bruichladdich Distillery in 1881. It was converted only six years later and remained in production until 1928, after which it fell idle for eight years. During the following years, the distillery saw many changes of ownership. Between 1940 and 1949, it belonged to the American group National Distillers. In 1957, it was acquired by AB Grant and was sold to Invergordon in 1968. 1975 saw the renovation of the facilities and an extension by two stills, bringing the total number of stills to four. In 1994, the distillery was taken over by Whyte & Mackay (JBB), who closed it down shortly thereafter. The story continues in the year 2000, when the independent bottler Murray McDavid (together with Gordon Wright and Simon Coughlin) and some investors bought the distillery for approximately £6.5 million and brought it back to life. Jim McEwan, who had worked for Bowmore under the previous owner, was contracted as the master distiller.

At first, there was a lot of renovation work to do, but since May 2001, Bruichladdich has been distilling whisky again. One of their bottlings is Port Charlotte, named after some distillery ruins located about a mile from Bruichladdich; its warehouses are still in use today. Bruichladdich is Scotland's fastest-growing distillery thanks to the many innovative ideas of Jim and his staff of forty. They use organic barley, they boldly create interesting new products, they produce the whisky with the highest phenolic content, and they offer a "Whisky Academy" to customers, which provides a five-day introduction to the art of distilling whisky.

The privately managed, highly innovative Bruichladdich Distillery is located on the northern shores of Loch Indaal.

WHISKY

Bruichladdich 2nd Edition, 15 years old,
46% ABV, no chill filtration
Color: Pale golden yellow

TASTING NOTES
The Sauternes notes come through
clearly in the nose, complemented by hints of
nougat, vanilla and sherry. On the palate, the
malt and the slightly sweet wine complement
each other perfectly. The finish allows all these
flavors to emerge fully.

*In the five-day introductory course offered by Bruichladdich, the
basics of pot stills and distillation techniques are taught.*

YELLOW SUBMARINE

The Bruichladdich Distillery produces many different whiskies.
The private, small structure of the company allows for quick and
flexible reactions. One of Bruichladdich's special editions, undoubtedly
their most original whisky, has a particularly interesting story
behind it. It goes like this:

An Islay local, a fisherman named
Baker, was out on the sea, pulling
lobster pots on board his boat to
check them. While doing so, he
noticed a yellow object floating in the
water. He first thought it was a buoy
attached to a fishing net, but on
closer inspection the object turned
out to be a 6.5-foot (2-m) Royal Navy
minesweeper. The remotely operated
object bearing the Royal Navy seal
was drifting aimlessly in the ocean.
The fisherman alerted the local coast
guards, who found the news delightfully amusing and enquired if Baker
had already drunk his share of whisky
that day. However, when the fisherman continued to insist, the coast
guard eventually contacted the Navy—
who denied having lost track of any
such object. Thus, the unknown
yellow object was salvaged and
brought to land, of which the Royal
Navy was informed again. The

underwater diving vehicle, a product
of a French manufacturer, had an
estimated value of approximately half
a million pounds.

Several days passed before the
Royal Navy admitted having lost the
HMS Penzance minesweeper in an
exercise. However, it took several
months before the Navy bothered to
pick up the lost vehicle. So as to avoid
causing a sensation, the HMS Blythe,
which was in charge of picking up the
minesweeper, planned to do so very
early in the morning. However, word
was already out by that time, and half
the island was up early in the morning
to appropriately welcome the soldiers.

In the meantime, Mark Reynier and
his staff at Bruichladdich had already
marketed a fourteen-year-old whisky
that they dubbed Yellow Submarine in
commemoration of the incident and,
of course, the famous Beatles song.
The Yellow Submarine edition was

introduced to the market in September 2005.

In any event, the commander of the
Royal Navy crew in charge of the
collection was presented with six
bottles of this special whisky, which
was limited to 12,000 bottles. The
French manufacturer of the minesweeper bought 1,000 bottles as a
marketing gag.

Bunnahabhain

BUNNAHABHAIN

OWNER	Burn Stewart Distillers Ltd.
ESTABLISHED	1881
MEANING OF NAME	Mouth of the brook
STATUS	In production
ANNUAL PRODUCTION	1 million liters/ 265,000 gallons

THE BUNNAHABHAIN DISTILLERY is located on the Sound of Islay, even further north than Caol Ila. It can only be accessed via a narrow, winding 7-mile (11-km) road. Driving on that stretch can be quite an adventure, especially for trucks. The road, which was constructed specifically for the distillery, turns off just before Port Askaig.

Founded in 1881, the distillery remained the property of its builder, Highland Distillers (today the Edrington Group), until 2003. Due to its isolated location, special housing for staff was built next to the production facilities at the time the distillery was constructed. One of the buildings used to house a school and another was a grocery store. Burn Stewart bought the distillery in 2003, thus saving it from being shut down.

All Bunnahabhain whiskies bear the logo of a saluting helmsman, a gesture of reverence for the song *Westering Home*, which is popular on Islay. The whisky itself does not have much to do with the complex, smoky malts that are typical of the south coast. It is very soft, light and fruity, with only the slightest suggestion of peat. The water used in distillation comes directly from limestone and is conveyed to the distillery via pipelines, and thus does not pick up any peat or other aromas.

WHISKY

Bunnahabhain, 12 years old, 40% ABV
Color: Amber

 TASTING NOTES
The nose is very fresh and is strongly reminiscent of sea air. The flavor is light with a hint of nutty, malty, sweet aromas that first unfold completely in the finish. This whisky is thus particularly suitable as an aperitif.

On a clear day, the north coast of Islay offers a marvelous view of the range of hills on the neighboring island, Jura.

Caol Ila

CAOL ILA
DISTILLERY
ISLAY MALT SCOTCH WHISKY
AGED 12 YEARS
75cl. BULLOCH LADE & CO.LTD. 40% vol.
GLASGOW, SCOTLAND

CAOL ILA	
OWNER	UDV (Diageo)
ESTABLISHED	1846
MEANING OF NAME	Sound of Islay
STATUS	In production
ANNUAL PRODUCTION	3.5 million liters/ 925,000 gallons

THE CAOL ILA DISTILLERY is tucked into a small bay within sight of the neighboring island of Jura, near Port Askaig. It is only accessible via the one road that leads down to the coast. The current of the Sound of Islay, from which the distillery derives its name, is quite dangerous at this site.

The building was erected in 1846 and was acquired by Bulloch, Lade and Co. in 1863. In 1930, the distillery was taken over by DCL. DCL became part of UD and later of UDV, which makes it part of the Diageo spirits corporation. The boats used to moor directly at the distillery, and the whisky was shipped overseas directly from here. Nowadays, trucks transport the bottled whisky to the ferry, which takes it to the mainland. In the 1970s, the distillery was completely modernized and a new stillhouse with six stills was added. A wide row of windows opens up a view of the nearby Paps of Jura peaks from inside the distillery.

For a long time, Caol Ila single malt was only available through independent bottlers, unless one happened to taste it directly at the distillery or bought it in Italy, where it was also sold. It was only the Faun & Flora series released by Diageo that made it more widely available. Due to its popularity, Caol Ila was recently added to the circle of Classic Malts.

WHISKY
Caol Ila, Signatory Vintage 1991, 12 years old, 43% ABV
Color: Very pale yellow

TASTING NOTES
The nose has an extremely strong note of peat smoke, which is complemented on the palate by a sweet note of sherry. The smokiness is reaffirmed in the finish. The flavor is completed by sea air and a touch of salt. Caol Ila is a light to medium-heavy whisky that goes particularly well with smoked salmon.

The Caol Ila Distillery in 1954. Back then, boats docked directly at the distillery's pier to pick up whisky to be shipped overseas.

Highland Park

HIGHLAND PARK	
OWNER	The Edrington Group
ESTABLISHED	1798
STATUS	In production
ANNUAL PRODUCTION	2 million liters/528,000 gallons

HIGHLAND PARK, the northernmost distillery in Scotland, is situated on Mainland, the main island of the Orkney archipelago. More specifically, it is located on a hill in the southern outskirts of the capital of Kirkwall.

According to the present-day owners, Highland Park was founded in 1798. Historical records, however, prove that David Robertson, the founder, had already started distilling three years earlier. In 1898, the distillery was acquired by James Grant, whose father had previously been a successful manager for Glenlivet. To this day, the distillery's license is made out to this family, even though the company was sold to Highland Distillers as early as 1935, who in turn belong to the Edrington Group. The distillery still uses their in-house malthouse and employs strictly traditional production methods.

Caol Ila has a strongly smoky character with notes of heather and malt, generated by the use of regional peat for malting. This peat is very young, which is why it is mixed with heather. Highland Park is undoubtedly one of the

Many whisky connoisseurs consider Highland Park to be one of the absolutely top-notch single malts.

finest single malts available. It has depth, a rounded character and a long finish. It is available in many different variations. Whisky connoisseurs appreciate it as a fine all-rounder, and it enjoys an impeccable reputation even among the most knowledgeable whisky experts.

WHISKY

Highland Park, 18 years old, 43% ABV, official bottling
Color: Amber

TASTING NOTES

The aromatic smoke, complemented by a sherry note and a hint of oak, is immediately noticeable in the nose. The whisky is full-flavored on the palate, where honey and peat develop. The full complexity becomes apparent in the long finish, which nonetheless remains soft.

Jura

The distillery, located in Craighouse on Jura, resumed production in 1963.

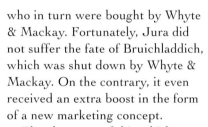

JURA	
OWNER	Whyte & Mackay
ESTABLISHED	ca. 1810
MEANING OF NAME	Red deer
STATUS	In production
ANNUAL PRODUCTION	800,000 liters/ 211,000 gallons

ONLY A SOUND SEPARATES the Isle of Jura from the Scottish mainland. The island, known for the Paps of Jura mountain range, is only accessible via a ferry from the Isle of Islay in the southwest. The Isle of Jura Distillery is located in Craighouse, the only settlement on this island.

The distillery was erected around 1810, or at least this is the date from which clear records of legal activities exist. Less-than-legal distillation had taken place prior to that. James Ferguson and his sons were distilling here during the nineteenth century, but he demolished the facilities when he could no longer reach an agreement with the owner of the land. Following World War I, nothing much happened until a plan was born to reactivate the distillery in 1958. Two island locals started the project in order to create new jobs on the island. They succeeded in winning support from Mackinlay MacPherson (today Scottish & Newcastle). W. Delmé Evans, who had already been in charge of planning Tullibardine and Glenallachie, was contracted for the construction and the distillery resumed operation in 1963. In 1985, it was acquired by Invergordon Distillers,

who in turn were bought by Whyte & Mackay. Fortunately, Jura did not suffer the fate of Bruichladdich, which was shut down by Whyte & Mackay. On the contrary, it even received an extra boost in the form of a new marketing concept.

The character of this whisky cannot be compared to the whiskies from Islay, the neighboring island. Jura is often referred to as "the Highland from the Island." It is hardly peated at all. Superstition is an exception, a relatively light, oily and dry malt that has a soft yet salty note, and which is usually enjoyed as an aperitif.

WHISKY
Isle of Jura Superstition, 45% ABV, official bottling
Color: Amber

 TASTING NOTES
Superstition has a slight aroma of peat smoke, complemented by sweet notes of honey and marzipan. Honey and peat smoke are gently echoed on the palate. The flavor is completed by a spicy note, which can be perceived in Jura's pleasurably sweet finish, as well.

Jura whisky is hardly smoked at all. It is more reminiscent of a Highland malt than a typical island whisky.

Kilchoman

KILCHOMAN

OWNER	Anthony Wills
ESTABLISHED	2004
MEANING OF NAME	St. Coman
STATUS	In production, no whisky on the market at the time of writing
ANNUAL PRODUCTION	50,000 liters/ 13,200 gallons

KILCHOMAN, SCOTLAND'S SMALLEST distillery, is located in a small town of the same name near the sandy beaches of Machir Bay in the west of the Isle of Islay. While Edradour is a contender for the title of smallest distillery, Kilchoman is definitely the westernmost of them all. Visitors planning a trip to Kilchoman have to turn into a very narrow road shortly before Bruichladdich and then continue for another twenty minutes or so to reach the distillery.

Kilchoman was built in 2004 in the style of a farm distillery of the kind that used to be so common in earlier times. Production started in 2005, but the company soon experienced a major setback when the kiln, which contained a malt silo, burnt down and had to be rebuilt. The renovation work wasn't completed until October 2006, at which time production could be started up again. In order to generate some revenue during the time until the first five-year-old whisky will be ready for bottling and sale in 2010, Kilchoman is selling casks that can be bottled after maturation, as well as small sample bottles. Moreover, the distillery hopes to attract many visitors with their visitors center. Like Bruichladdich and Bladnoch, they offer a five-day workshop they call "The Whisky Experience."

The Kilchoman spirit still. At the moment, their whisky is only available as samples. The first single malt will be introduced on the market in 2010.

Lagavulin

LAGAVULIN IS THE MIDDLE of the three distilleries on Islay's south coast. It is just over a mile from Ardbeg and about two miles southwest of Laphroaig. The ruins of the Dunyvaig Castle, where the Lords of Islay of the McDonald clan used to live, are within sight.

The exact year of founding cannot be determined with certainty, but it is thought to be 1816. Ten or so illegal distilleries are said to have been in operation in the immediate area in the mid-eighteenth century, but from 1837 onward, Lagavulin was the only distillery in the area. In 1867, it was acquired by James Logan, who left it to his nephew, Peter Mackie, in 1889. Mackie had already completed his apprenticeship at Lagavulin, and later built up White Horse Distillers from this business.

Since Lagavulin and Laphroaig had always been big rivals, it was Peter Mackie's ambition to produce a phenolic whisky similar to the neighboring distillery's. To this purpose, he built a second distillery on the same premises in 1908, called the Malt Mill. That distillery used the Lagavulin mash tuns, but had its own pot stills and malting floors. Malt Mill remained in production until 1962. Today, its former malthouse is a visitors center.

During the White Horse era, Lagavulin's whisky was used

LAGAVULIN	
OWNER	UDV (Diageo)
ESTABLISHED	ca. 1816
MEANING OF NAME	The hollow where the mill stands
STATUS	In production
ANNUAL PRODUCTION	2.3 million liters/ 608,000 gallons

exclusively for the White Horse blend. Nowadays, though, more than 80 percent of production is used for the single malt, which has become very popular since Diageo, the current owner, began marketing Lagavulin as one of the six Classic Malts of Scotland. In recent times, production has hardly been able to keep up with the enormous demand.

Lagavulin whisky is staggeringly complex, very smoky, peaty and highly sophisticated. It is generally perceived to be quite dry.

WHISKY
Lagavulin, 16 years old, 43% ABV
Color: Deep amber gold

TASTING NOTES
The sixteen-year-old is Lagavulin's most popular. It has a nose of smoke, interspersed with sherry notes, both echoed on the palate. The flavor adds notes of salt and grass that are complemented by a highly characteristic peat flavor in the finish.

The Dunyvaig Castle ruins in Lagavulin Bay offer a lovely view of the distillery.

Laphroaig

LAPHROAIG	
OWNER	Fortune Brands
ESTABLISHED	1815
MEANING OF NAME	Beautiful hollow by the broad bay
STATUS	In production
ANNUAL PRODUCTION	2 million liters/ 528,000 gallons

AS ITS GAELIC NAME SUGGESTS, this distillery is located in a beautiful bay. Laphroaig is the westernmost of the three distilleries in the south of Islay. Like the others, it is accessible via a narrow road winding up to it from Port Ellen.

According to its label, Laphroaig was established in 1815. There are some people, however,

The distillery's warehouses are located directly adjacent to the sea, the source of Laphroaig's salty seaweed flavor.

who claim it was only founded five years later. Its existence can be established with certainty in the year 1826. The distillery was built by Donald Johnston, who, according to legend, fell into a cask of whisky in 1847 and drowned in it. The business remained family-owned until 1954, when ownership was transferred to Bessie Williamson, the secretary, who had been an employee of the distillery for many years. She sold the business to

Long John in 1967, but continued to conduct business herself until she retired in 1972. In 1975, Laphroaig was acquired by Whitbread, which was part of the Allied Distillers group. Most recently, in 2005, it was bought by Fortune Brands.

One thing that makes Laphroaig special is the fact that they have taken up in-house floor maltings again, producing more than 10 percent of the malt at the distillery.

Laphroaig used to have an especially apt advertising slogan: "You love it or you hate it." This certainly hits the nail on the head. There really only are those two camps, and many whisky connoisseurs will remember at least one discussion on this subject with other fans of whisky. Laphroaig has a strong medicinal flavor that makes it unique. Its character has been unflatteringly compared to gauze, disinfectant and mouthwash.

WHISKY
Laphroaig, 10 years old, 57.3% ABV
Color: Pale golden yellow

TASTING NOTES
The pronounced phenolic nose and medium body of the ten-year-old cask-strength Laphroaig go over well with whisky connoisseurs. Recent Laphroaigs have been slightly sweet compared to older ones, but they retain the salty and tarry notes of seaweed. The finish is medicinal and peaty and continues the tar and phenol notes. This is an enormously complex whisky that leaves a strong impression, whether favorable or not.

Scapa

SCAPA

OWNER	Pernod Ricard
ESTABLISHED	1885
MEANING OF NAME	Boat (derived from Old Norse)
STATUS	In production
ANNUAL PRODUCTION	1 million liters/ 265,000 gallons

THE SCAPA DISTILLERY is on Mainland in the Orkney Islands, south of Kirkwall, right on the coast of the Scapa Flow. This place may be familiar to those interested in military history: it was the chief naval base of the British Royal Navy during both World Wars. German U-boats repeatedly tried to enter Scapa Flow.

The Scapa Distillery was built on the site of a former mill by John T. Townsend and Macfarlane in 1885. The original owners, however, did not pay much attention to it. For a long time Scapa was overshadowed by its neighbor, Highland Park, which has always done an excellent job of marketing its own distillery. In 1954, Scapa was acquired by Hiram Walker & Sons. This firm subsequently went through a series of acquisitions and mergers, becoming Allied Domecq in the process and eventually joining the Pernod Ricard group in 2005. In 1994, the distillery was temporarily shut down.

Between 1997 and 2004, production continued due to the work of Highland Park employees; Highland Park was allowed to use some of the Scapa warehouses in return. Since 2004, the distillery has been in full production again. At the time of writing, it is being rebuilt and renovated. The last renovations took place in 1954 and 1956, when Hiram Walker & Sons rebuilt most of the recently acquired distillery in a more functional way, leaving only some of the old warehouses intact. In 1956, another Lomond still was added for the production of Ballantine's, which comes from the same company.

This is a salty, oily whisky with hints of seaweed, spicy chocolate and a characteristic heathery peatiness.

WHISKY

Scapa, 14 years old, 40% ABV, official bottling
Color: Pale gold

TASTING NOTES

The nose is robust and sweet, but also reminiscent of orange and dried fruit. The flavor reveals the typical heather note, which is complemented by a sweetness of honey and spices. The lingering, dry finish rounds off this highly interesting whisky.

Of the original Scapa distillery, only a few old warehouses survive. The rest of the plant has been demolished and rebuilt.

Talisker

TALISKER

OWNER	UDV (Diageo)
ESTABLISHED	1831
MEANING OF NAME	Sloping rock
STATUS	In production
ANNUAL PRODUCTION	1.5 million liters/ 396,000 gallons

THE CNOC NAN SPEIREAG SPRING supplies the Talisker Distillery, located in the far west of the Isle of Skye right on the shores of Loch Harport, with its intensely peaty water.

Talisker was built in 1831 in the town of Carbost. It is named after the farm's owner, who was probably the original founder. For a few years it was owned by Roderick Kamp, who would later buy Macallan. The distillery was extended in 1900, and from 1925 onward it belonged to the DCL. Triple distillation was practiced until 1928, which explains the unusual constellation of five stills. After that year, Talisker switched to double distillation. In November 1960, a fire destroyed the stillhouse and other facilities. Luckily, the warehouses were spared from the fire. After some extensive renovation, the business was able to resume production in August 1962. A long series of mergers eventually led to the distillery becoming part of UDV; Talisker is thus currently owned by the Diageo group.

This is a highly complex and unconventional whisky. Its distinct peppery flavor adds to its exceptionally warming spiciness. The sensory impressions that result from drinking Talisker are often described with the phrase "explodes on the palate." Since it has been promoted as one of the Classic Malts of Scotland, it has become widely available, though no longer through independent bottlers.

WHISKY
Talisker, 18 years old, Limited Edition, 45.8% ABV, official bottling
Color: Golden yellow

TASTING NOTES
This limited edition whisky smells fruity, with notes of prunes and a hint of orange, caramel and a touch of smoke. The flavor is slightly sweet at first and then develops into a more robust body, with a slight hint of smoke and toffee. The medium finish adds a characteristic spiciness of chili peppers.

The Talisker Distillery stands in a very picturesque spot on the shores of Loch Harport, Isle of Skye.

Tobermory

THE TOBERMORY DISTILLERY is the only distillery on the Isle of Mull. It is located on the outskirts of a small fishing village of the same name, right next to a waterfall. Tobermory, with its colorful houses along the docks, is one of the most often photographed spots in Scotland.

Tobermory has a highly eventful history. It was first established around 1795, at about the same time as the Oban Distillery. For some time, both distilleries belonged to the same owner, John Hopkins & Co. As early as the nineteenth century, Tobermory had to be shut down several times. Ownership changed in 1916, when it was acquired by DCL, who discontinued production in 1930. This hiatus lasted for forty-two years, until the distillery was reopened in 1972 under the new name of Ledaig. It was subsequently extended to four stills, but had to shut down once again after only a short period of production. Even the warehouses were closed down, sold off and converted into apartment buildings. In the meantime, a visitors center had been set up, which even contained a cheese shop. The distillery's eventful history continued until 1993, when Burn Stewart acquired it and finally assured some continuity. Ever since then, the distillery has been using two stills. Since the warehouses are no longer available, the casks are stored at Deanston, which belongs to the same company.

This whisky is available either unpeated as Tobermory, or in a peated version called Ledaig. With earlier bottlings, this distinction is not always as clear, and the quality varies widely. Since there

TOBERMORY	
OWNER	Burn Stewart Distillers Ltd.
ESTABLISHED	ca. 1795
MEANING OF NAME	Well of the Virgin Mary
STATUS	In production
ANNUAL PRODUCTION	1 million liters/ 265,000 gallons

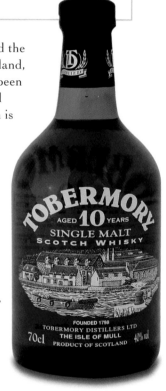

are no longer warehouses on-site and the casks are now stored in central Scotland, the seaside character has obviously been lost. Tobermory has a dry, sweet and malty flavor. The new Ledaig, which is creamy and slightly oily, reveals a noticeable peat note.

WHISKY
Tobermory, 10 years old, 40% ABV, official bottling
Color: Golden yellow

TASTING NOTES
In spite of its smoky aroma, Tobermory is apparently produced entirely from unpeated barley. The peat smoke is already noticeable on the nose, and it develops a hint of maltiness in combination with the slightly sweet note on the palate. The finish is pleasantly smooth and dry.

Port Ellen

PORT ELLEN	
OWNER	UDV (Diageo)
ESTABLISHED	1825
STATUS	Closed, partly demolished

Opposite: The fascinating scenery of Islay, which features such bizarre phenomena as the Needle near Port Charlotte, attracts many visitors.

THE REMAINS OF THE ORIGINAL distillery can still be seen in the Port Ellen Bay on Islay, even though the only buildings still standing are the warehouses, the kiln and some of the auxiliary structures. Behind these stands the impressive Port Ellen malting, which was built in 1973 and supplies several distilleries on Islay with malt. The distillery has only enjoyed significant popularity since its shutdown, and the remaining stores of whisky are sold at correspondingly high prices.

But to start at the outset: Port Ellen was established in 1825 and acquired five years later by John Ramsey. He was ahead of his time and accomplished a lot of pioneering work in the world of whisky production. Legend has it, for instance, that he invited both Robert Stein (developer of the patent still) and Andreas Coffey (Coffey still) to Port Ellen to let them experiment with their new distillery procedures for the first time at Port Ellen. Ramsey is also said to have been the first to use a spirit safe, which later became a legal requirement.

Ramsey was also a very prudent businessman. He exported whisky to America, having it shipped right from his doorstep. In 1929, his descendants sold the distillery to W.P. Lowrie & Co. and to the better-known John Dewar & Sons, both subsidiaries of DCL, the largest corporation. However, the distillery had to be shut down for a long period and was not able to resume production until 1966. Prior to that it was renovated, and two additional stills were added to the existing pair. Eventually, in 1983, Port Ellen was closed for good. Parts of the distillery were demolished. The remaining facilities, some of which are among the oldest industrial buildings in Scotland, are protected as historic buildings and owned by Diageo.

Similar to Talisker, Port Ellen has a peppery note and a characteristic salty, smoky aroma. Since it has become publicly known that the distillery will never resume production, demand for this whisky has risen continually.

WHISKY
Port Ellen, 25 years old,
1978 vintage (4th release),
56.2% ABV, official bottling
Color: Light amber

 TASTING NOTES
The nose of this Port Ellen is definitely less smoky than its predecessors; it has a stronger fruity component and a light note of oak wood. The smoke is found again on the palate, nicely balanced by oak wood and complemented by honey and a touch of spiciness. The finish reveals a pronounced note of vanilla and honey, and highlights the smoke and oak flavors once more.

Whisky was once shipped to America directly from the distillery's own pier.

WESTERN AND NORTHERN HIGHLANDS

"I love to sing, and I love to drink scotch.
Most people would rather hear me drink scotch."

GEORGE BURNS

THE SETTING OF HIGH MOUNTAINS, a great many lakes and numerous islands scattered along the coastline all combine to make the Highlands a truly spectacular region of Scotland.

WESTERN HIGHLANDS

The Atlantic Ocean lies to the west of the Western Highlands, with the Inner Hebrides not far off the coast. In the south, the Highlands share a border with the Lowlands, geographically separated by one of two geological faults that divide Scotland in three parts. A little north of the divide is the Campsie Fells, a chain of hills that is slightly

higher than 1,650 feet (500 m) above sea level at its highest point.

Fort William and Oban are the two largest towns in the region, and Ben Nevis, the highest mountain in Great Britain, is located near Fort William. Even though Ben Nevis is a moderate 4,406 feet (1,343 m) high, ascending it requires good hiking gear. Anyone planning a hiking trip in this region should also be prepared for the quickly changing weather to thwart their plans. Moreover, Ben Nevis is shrouded in fog nine days out of ten. Most visitors ascend from the west; while this trail is long and stony, it is the least steep. The route via

the steep northeast face should only be attempted by experienced mountaineers. A short way west of Fort William is Glenfinnan, site of the Jacobite memorial commemorating the spot where Bonnie Prince Charlie met with the Cameron Clan in 1745, raising forces in order to prepare for the Jacobite rebellion against English government troops. One of Scotland's most beautiful lakes, Loch Shiel, is nearby. Fans of the Harry Potter movies will recognize the place, too: the steam train to Hogwarts was filmed riding across the impressive Glenfinnan railway viaduct.

The other important center in this region, the village of Oban, is one of Scotland's most frequented tourist resorts. While Oban has a mere 8,000 inhabitants, it has a lot to offer. In summer, it is the launching point for ferries to the various Hebrides, which is why this little town in its picturesque location on the Firth of Lorn is also known as the "Gateway to the Isles." The town's landmark is an unusual one: McCaig's Tower, a building inspired by a Roman collosseum, was commissioned by John McCaig, a wealthy banker, in 1895. McCaig wanted to erect a memorial for himself and his family, but also to fight the high unemployment rate in the region. Construction was never completed, but the walls now surround a public garden. The harbor area, with its many inviting shops and fish restaurants, is perfect for taking leisurely strolls or enjoying a superb meal.

Top: The small town of Oban, located on the Firth of Lorn, attracts visitors especially during summer.
Bottom: Wick, formerly the herring capital, got its name ("bay" in English) from the Norwegians, who were influential in this region in medieval times.

Opposite: The 1,250-ft (380-m) Glenfinnan viaduct is set against a backdrop of breathtaking Highland scenery.

And right in the center of it all, alongside the harbor, is the Oban Distillery, which is a favorite destination for visitors.

Loch Lomond is one of many the popular, interesting and rewarding destinations for a trip in this area. The Loch Lomond Distillery, incidentally, is not located on this namesake lake, but a little further away in the small industrial town of Alexandria.

NORTHERN HIGHLANDS

The area north of the town of Inverness is the Northern Highlands. The Black Isle Peninsula is located a little above Inverness; its name is derived from the rich, black soil there, which provides particularly fertile ground for growing barley. This is why some distilleries that use locally grown barley, such as Glen Ord and Teaninich, are located here. The major harbor town on the Black Isle, Cromarty, used to be a flourishing center of trade and industry during the eighteenth century. One of its main industries was rope-making.

Continuing northward along the east coast, one passes through the austere and sparsely populated region of Sutherland. Most of the inhabitants of Sutherland were resettled to the eastern coast against their will because the space inland was

Opposite: Steep cliffs and lush, green meadows: the rugged east coast epitomizes northern Scotland.

needed for raising sheep. Many of them left, emigrating to Australia, Canada and the USA. Continuing along the coast on the A9 road, one drives by almost all of the distilleries in the region. Dunrobin Castle, one of the most popular and often visited castles in Scotland, is located on this route, as well. It has been owned by the Earls of Sutherland since the thirteenth century, and is situated in a marvelous park with a number of beautiful gardens. Nowadays, a large part of the castle is open to visitors.

The small village of John o' Groats is located at the northern tip of Scotland; it is the settlement farthest to the northeast on the British mainland. The name John o' Groats derives from a fifteenth-century Dutchman, Jan de Groot, who acquired the ferrying license for the Orkney Islands. Today you have to go a little further west, to Scrabster, to take a ferry to the Orkneys; or drive southward a short way from John o' Groats to reach the small fishing town of Wick. In this less tourism-centered town is the region's northernmost distillery, Old Pulteney. During the nineteenth century, Wick was a center of the fishing industry, and was tranformed into the European herring capital for six weeks during the summer months each year. Around 1840, there were times when the town had more than a thousand active fishing boats, and many inhabitants of the Highlands found work in the fishing industry or associated processing industries. In order to quench the workers' thirst for whisky, a distillery was built in town. World War I brought the busy hustle and bustle to a sudden end when the Royal Navy confiscated the small fishing fleet. Since the boats were never returned to their original owners after the war, high unemployment ensued. In order to counteract alcohol abuse among the unemployed, the sale of alcohol in Wick was prohibited without further ado, a law that remained in effect until 1939. Nowadays, the region's excellent whisky can once again be enjoyed in the local pubs.

The present appearance of Dunrobin Castle, with its majestic parks and gardens, is the result of renovations that took place between 1845 and 1851.

Balblair

BALBLAIR	
OWNER	Inver House (InterBev)
ESTABLISHED	1790
MEANING OF NAME	Settlement in the plains
STATUS	In production
ANNUAL PRODUCTION	1.3 million liters/ 343,000 gallons

THE BALBLAIR DISTILLERY is a neighbor of the Glenmorangie Distillery, both on the old A9 road between Dornoch Firth and Edderton.

By its own account, the distillery was established in 1790, which makes it the second-oldest in Scotland. The oldest surviving buildings, however, only date back to 1871. Those structures, together with the brick chimney, contribute a great deal to the charm of this small distillery. Robert Cummings revived the facility post-World War II but sold it to Hiram Walker in 1970. After their subsequent acquisition by Allied Distillers, the distillery was bought by the current owner, Inver House, which had previously acquired Old Pulteney. Balbair whisky has always been an important ingredient of Ballantine's; only recently, under new ownership, has it been made available as a single malt. In 2001, Inver House became a 100% subsidiary of Pacific Spirits UK, which in turn was acquired by Thai

International Beverage Holdings Ltd. (InterBev) in 2006.

This is a light, slightly peated, solid and dry whisky that is suitable as an aperitif. The slight peat taste may well originate from the water, which flows first through the pine forests of Beinn Dearg (a mountain peak) and then through dry peat fields on its way to the distillery.

WHISKY
Balblair, 16 years old, 40% ABV, official bottling
Color: Amber

 TASTING NOTES
The nose of this sixteen-year-old whisky is very fresh and light. On the palate, it reveals a light note of peat, with a slightly sweet hint of citrus aromas. The finish is very fresh again, surprisingly complex and, once again, slightly sweet.

The Balblair Distillery has a picturesque setting in a valley, set against the backdrop of the rugged Northern Highlands scenery.

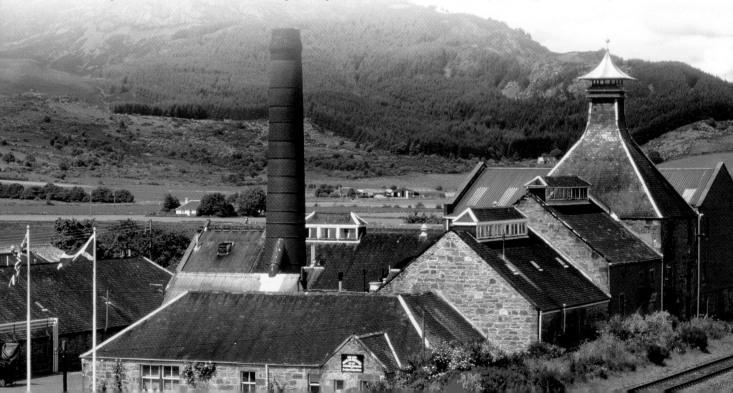

Ben Nevis

BEN NEVIS IS THE HIGHEST MOUNTAIN in Great Britain. At the foot of the mountain, north of Fort William and directly on the A82, is the Ben Nevis Distillery.

In 1825, this distillery was established by John MacDonald, who was also known as "Long John" due to his impressive height. There is also a blend that carries this same name, but it no longer has anything to do with the MacDonald clan. At some point around 1920, the distillery was sold to Seager Evans Ltd. Since then, the business has experienced many changes in ownership. In 1981, it was sold to Whitbread, who even started operating a fifth still in order to produce Blend Dew of Ben Nevis. This fifth still, however, was demolished at a later date. The Whitbread Group shut down the distillery in 1986, but retained the rights to the Long John brand. In 1989, Ben Nevis was sold again, this time to the Japanese company Nikka, which remains the owner to this day. Nikka has installed an interesting visitors center in order to attract greater numbers of tourists. Currently, Blend Dew of Ben Nevis is once again in production, among other products. Nikka was also able to secure the rights to the Glencoe brand.

This is a robust, very fruity, oily and often dry whisky. Ben Nevis is the kind of

Ben Nevis whiskies are matured in sherry, wine and Bourbon casks.

BEN NEVIS	
OWNER	Ben Nevis Co. (Nikka)
ESTABLISHED	1825
MEANING OF NAME	Terrible mountain
STATUS	In production
ANNUAL PRODUCTION	2 million liters/ 528,000 gallons

whisky that is best enjoyed as a nightcap, just before going to bed.

WHISKY
Ben Nevis, 10 years old, 46% ABV, official bottling
Color: Pale amber

TASTING NOTES
The nose of this whisky is nutty and oily. It is difficult to distinguish other aromas. The flavor reveals pleasant notes of citrus, a distinct note of oak and a wide range of other influences. The long finish is reminiscent of toasted coffee.

Brora/Clynelish

BRORA/CLYNELISH	
OWNER	UDV (Diageo)
ESTABLISHED	1819
MEANING OF NAME	Brora: River of the bridge
	Clynelish: Slope of the garden
STATUS	Brora: Closed
	Clynelish: In production
ANNUAL PRODUCTION	3.5 million liters/
	925,000 gallons

THE BRORA AND CLYNELISH DISTILLERIES are right next to each other and near the famous Dunrobin Castle.

The history of the two distilleries can hardly be separated, which is why they share one heading. Brora was established under the name of Clynelish in 1819 by the Duke of Sutherland, then owner of Dunrobin Castle. The duke was also responsible for the ruthless expulsion of farmers from their valleys. He deemed these Highland Clearances necessary in order to maximize the use of the land for sheep breeding.

As early as 1930, the distillery belonged to DCL, which means that it now belongs to Diageo. In 1967, the new Clynelish Distillery was built on the same premises as a modern, functional building; the old distillery was shut down for a short period. When it reopened, both distilleries produced under the name of Clynelish, but only for a short while. Within the year, the old Clynelish Distillery was renamed Brora, which obviously caused some confusion on the market.

Looking back, former employees now say that the old whiskies were heavier and peatier, and thus more similar to Islay whiskies. Brora was shut down for good in 1983. Only the warehouses are still used, partly by the neighboring Clynelish Distillery. The old buildings also house a visitors center. It seems that Diageo has no ambitions to reactivate the distillery, even though the demand for Brora has risen significantly in recent years.

WHISKY
Brora, 30 years old, 56.6% ABV, official bottling
Color: Intense amber

 **TASTING NOTES**
The aroma is extremely complex and slightly salty and smoky. The flavor is quite mild. The smoky note is echoed on the palate and is complemented by a hint of oil. With a little water, the salty aspects reappear in the flavor. The long finish adds a light note of pepper.

Following the Highland Clearances, many former tenant farmers found work at the Clynelish Distillery after it opened in 1819.

Dalmore

THE DALMORE Distillery, established in 1839, is located near the town of Alness in a secluded spot close to the fertile north shore of Cromarty Firth.

Dalmore started out as a typical farm distillery and was family-owned by the Mackenzies for almost 100 years. The Mackenzies were friends of James Whyte and Charles Mackay, whose popular blend also contains Dalmore whisky. The family's coat of arms bears the head of a deer, and it can still be found on the whisky's label. In 1960, the family business merged with the friends mentioned before and became Whyte & Mackay, who remain the owners to this day. The design of their two stills is highly unusual: the wash still has a conically-shaped head, and the spirit still has a water-cooled copper cladding.

This is a voluminous whisky with a fruity aroma of orange marmalade. It has a malty flavor and a distinct sherry note due to its maturation in sherry casks. In some countries, the single malt is readily available as a twelve-year-old version, in others as a twenty-one-year-old malt. Special thirty- and fifty-year vintages ended up in a very high price range and are almost unaffordable at the time of writing. The Dalmore Cigar Malt, created especially for cigar smokers, made quite a stir when it was introduced.

DALMORE	
OWNER	Whyte & Mackay Ltd.
ESTABLISHED	1839
MEANING OF NAME	Big valley
STATUS	In production
ANNUAL PRODUCTION	3 million liters/ 793,000 gallons

WHISKY

Dalmore, 21 years old, 43% ABV, official bottling
Color: Dark amber with a reddish tint

TASTING NOTES

Compared to its twelve-year-old cousin, this twenty-one-year-old malt is considerably more complex. The nose immediately gives away a striking, fruity sherry note. Further nosing reveals aromas of chocolate, nuts and candied or dried fruits. On the palate, sweet malt and some oak emerge. The dried fruits and chocolate are echoed again. The finish has a slightly smoky note, with a pleasurable, velvety mouthfeel.

Whisky is not the only thing produced in the Cromarty Firth region: several platforms produce oil.

Glen Ord

GLEN ORD	
OWNER	UDV (Diageo)
ESTABLISHED	1838
MEANING OF NAME	Valley of the rounded hill
STATUS	In production
ANNUAL PRODUCTION	3 million liters/ 793,000 gallons

The distillery's enormous maltings supply a large number of other distilleries with malt.

THE GLEN ORD DISTILLERY is located in the town Muir of Ord, southwest of the Black Isle Peninsula and surrounded by extensive barley fields. It used to have a somewhat infamous reputation for its illegal distillation activities.

Officially, Glen Ord was founded in 1838, and it has changed hands many times since then. It was acquired by John Dewar & Sons in 1923, and just one year later became part of the DCL.

Through a series of mergers, the distillery finally ended up in the owner-ship of UDV and its parent corporation, Diageo. In 1966, the facilities were modernized for the first time. Two years later, the gigantic Glen Ord Maltings were built, which supply many other distilleries with malt. Saladin boxes previously installed continued to be used.

It is only recently that Glen Ord has attained a certain renown. Prior to that, the many name changes— from Muir of Ord to Ord and Glenordie to Glen Ord—made it difficult for consumers to develop any loyalty. In 2005, Diageo started paying more attention to Glen Ord, beginning with an increased advertising budget for the brand.

Glen Ord is a flowery whisky with a rose character, spicy, malty and with a dry finish. It is popular as a drink after a meal. The proprietary bottlings generally have a very distinct Olorosy sherry character.

WHISKY

Glen Ord, 12 years old, 43% ABV, official bottling
Color: Golden amber

 **TASTING NOTES**

This is indeed a smooth whisky, yet robust, with a hint of peat, a little smoke and notes of flowers. On the palate it is well-balanced, slightly syrupy and dry, with a light note of sherry. The medium finish brings out a slightly spicy note.

Some of the Glen Ord Distillery's buildings date from the first half of the nineteenth century.

ORD DISTILLERY

Glengoyne

GLENGOYNE DISTILLERY IS 12 miles (20 km) north of Glasgow, near the town of Killearn, at the foot of the Campsie Fells. Its buildings are in an idyllic setting, nestled into a forested valley at the transition between the Highlands and the Lowlands. Glengoyne is considered the southernmost of the Highlands distilleries. The whitewashed buildings are grouped around a small pond fed by a lovely waterfall. Glengoyne is certainly one of the most beautiful distilleries in Scotland.

During the eighteenth and nineteenth centuries, illegal distillation was practiced here, since exporting whisky from the Highlands was prohibited. Initially, when the distillery was officially established in 1833, it was called Burnfoot. When the Lang Brothers acquired the business in 1876, they renamed it Glen Guin, Gaelic for "valley of the wild geese." In 1905, the distillery received its current name, Glengoyne. The Lang brothers used their whisky for a number of blends, such as Lang's Blend, Famous Grouse and Cutty Sark. In the 1960s, they became part of Robertson & Baxter, which in turn belonged to the Edrington Group. In 2003, the distillery was sold to Ian Macleod, an independent bottler. Since May 2006, Glengoyne also has a new visitors center welcoming whisky connoisseurs.

Glengoyne whisky is slightly sweet, very elegant and completely free of smoke or peat flavors due to the fact that the Campsie Fells water has no contact with peat at any time. In addition, peat-free malt is used exclusively. Glengoyne is also said to have aromas of apple. It is rather dry, and is often served with dessert.

WHISKY
Glengoyne, 17 years old, 43% ABV,
official bottling
Color: Golden yellow

TASTING NOTES
This medium-heavy whisky, with gleaming orange to golden-yellow color, has a malty, fruity nose with notes of cedars and oak, which are echoed on the palate. In well-aged versions, these flavors are complemented by notes of nuts and apples. The finish is very long.

GLENGOYNE	
OWNER	Ian Macleod
ESTABLISHED	1833
MEANING OF NAME	Valley of the wild geese
STATUS	In production
ANNUAL PRODUCTION	1.2 million liters/ 317,000 gallons

One of the big pot stills at the Glengoyne Distillery.

Nothern Highlands

Glenmorangie

GLENMORANGIE

OWNER	Glenmorangie plc (LVMH)
ESTABLISHED	1843
MEANING OF NAME	Valley of tranquility
STATUS	In production
ANNUAL PRODUCTION	4 million liters/ 1.06 million gallons

THE GLENMORANGIE DISTILLERY is located along the Inverness–Wick railway, directly on the A9 highway and Dornoch Firth, just north of the town of Tain. It has a long and turbulent history. Historical records show that illegal brewing and distilling took place on the Morangie farm as early as the beginning of the seventeenth century and into the eighteenth century. In 1843, the brewery was converted into a legal distillery. Esteemed whisky chronicler Alfred Barnard visited in 1887; in his book he described Glenmorangie as the most primitive distillery he had ever seen.

Shortly after Barnard wrote this, however, the facilities were renovated and heating was installed, a first in any distillery. The oldest buildings that survive today date back to that time. The company listed as owner of the facilities since 1918 or 1921 (sources are contradictory), Macdonald & Muir, was renamed Glenmorangie plc in 1997. In addition to Glen Moray, the Ardbeg Distillery also belongs to the same group. In 2004, the corporation took the entire whisky industry by surprise when the company, including all its subsidiaries and labels, was sold to the luxury goods corporation LVMH (Moët Hennessy Louis Vuitton) for £300 million. Glenmorangie was one of the first distilleries to release its whisky as a single malt, and is considered a pioneer of wood finishing. The distillery has the highest stills of any in the indus-

In Scotland itself, no whisky is sold more often than Glenmorangie.

try, and has its own spring, which supplies it with very hard water that is rich in minerals.

This is a light whisky. Being in close proximity to the ocean results in a smooth malt with a gentle salt note, complemented by fruits and spices. Glenmorangie's wood management allows for a great number of variations and thus a wide range of different whiskies. Their courage has been rewarded with success: Glenmorangie is the most popular whisky in Scotland.

WHISKY
Glenmorangie Cellar 13, 10 years old, 43% ABV, official bottling
Color: Very light golden yellow

TASTING NOTES
Even though a wide range of wood finishes are available, we chose to taste a different, unique malt: the Cellar 13. Warehouse 13 allegedly provides the very best conditions for maturation, and thus a special edition of the ten-year-old was produced. It smells strongly of vanilla, with subtle honey and light butter notes. The vanilla note is repeated on the palate. This is a highly complex whisky, and the nearness of the ocean comes through strongly in the flavor. The finish is slightly dry and complex.

Loch Lomond

CONTRARY TO WHAT ITS NAME ssuggests, Loch Lomond Distillery is not near the lake of the same name, but in an industrial area in the town of Alexandria, which is located on the River Leven at the very border of the Highlands.

The distillery was founded in 1965/66 by Duncan Thomas of the USA. In 1984, then owner ADP had to shut it down due to the difficult economic times and sold it to Glen Catrine Bonded Warehouse one year later. In 1993, an additional grain distillery was built on the same premises. Apart from the traditional pot stills, Loch Lomond has column stills to produce grain whisky and a Lomond still. This variety allows for great flexibility; more than half a dozen types of spirits can be produced at this facility.

The whiskies are all quite different. The two most widely known malts are sold under the names of Inchmurrin and Old Roshdhu, but there are also whiskies once again being marketed under the distillery's own name, Loch Lomond.

Loch Lomond uses malt from various maltings, including the smoky malt produced by Port Ellen. The Inchmurrin is said to have a note of eucalyptus. This gives it a slightly medicinal character that

LOCH LOMOND	
OWNER	Loch Lomond Distillers Co. Ltd.
ESTABLISHED	1814
MEANING OF NAME	Lake of Lomond
STATUS	In production
ANNUAL PRODUCTION	10 million liters/ 2.64 million gallons

does not, however, cancel out its smooth and slightly oily nature. Loch Lomond tastes of caramel and has a fine note of mint. The younger bottlings (twelve years), in particular, are slightly more fruity.

WHISKY

Loch Lomond, 21 years old, 40% ABV
Color: Golden

TASTING NOTES

The twenty-one-year-old has a delicate nose of flowers. The long oak cask maturation shows in the flavor, which adds a malty sweetness of honey. The finish is nice and long, and brings out a whiff of smoke.

Loch Lomond attracts not only whisky connoisseurs, but also a great number of water sports enthusiasts.

Oban

OBAN

OWNER	UDV (Diageo)
ESTABLISHED	1793
MEANING OF NAME	Small bay
STATUS	In production
ANNUAL PRODUCTION	700,000 liters/ 185,000 gallons

WHEN THE OBAN DISTILLERY was founded in close vicinity to the harbor, the actual town of Oban did not yet exist. The town started to grow and expand around the distillery, which made it impossible to extend the production facilities within town at a later stage.

The Oban Distillery was established in 1793 by the Stevenson family, though the stone buildings that survive date back only to around 1880. During the early nineteenth century, the distillery was closed for some time. In 1923, the facilities were acquired by John Dewar & Sons, who in turn sold it to the DCL soon after. In the process, the license was transferred to a subsidiary, John Hopkins & Co. Today the distillery is owned by UDV and its parent corporation, Diageo. In the 1930s and 1960s, production was put on hold, even though the facilities had just been modernized in 1960. Since space restrictions made it impossible to expand within town, Oban still only has two stills. This

limitation also affects storage: the casks cannot mature exclusively in the adjacent warehouses. On top of all this, the spring that supplies Oban with water is quite far away. Oban whisky is bottled in a large plant in Leven.

Oban is slightly peaty, with a whiff of ocean air and seaweed. It has a smooth texture and reportedly goes well with seafood. It has been released as a twelve-year-old single malt, and a fourteen-year-old version has been included in the Classic Malts series.

WHISKY
Oban, 14 years old, 43% ABV, official bottling
Color: Deep gold to amber

TASTING NOTES
This slightly smoky yet fruity and sweet whisky has a nose of toasted malt. The flavor again brings out the sweetness and adds notes of spices to the malty, fruity undertones. The finish is mild yet remarkably long and dry, with a whiff of salt.

View of the buildings of the Oban Distillery, directly on the harbor in the town of Oban.

Old Pulteney

THE OLD PULTENEY DISTILLERY is located in the heart of the town of Wick, a little south of the harbor and near the coast.

For a long time, Wick was considered the European herring capital. In order to quench the numerous dockworkers' and fishermen's thirst for whisky, the town needed a distillery. Eventually, James Henderson established Old Pulteney in 1826. The business was family-owned until the 1920s. Around that time, however, the town was devastated by unemployment and a strict ban on alcohol was imposed, prohibiting the sale of whisky from 1922 until 1939.

The distillery received its name from Sir William Pulteney, who had founded parts of the village and the harbor in 1810. "Old" was added to the name because this whisky is said to mature unusually quickly, making it taste "old" after a short period of time. After a few changes in ownership, the company became part of the DCL, who purchased it from John Dewar & Sons. Due to the prohibition, DCL shut down the distillery from 1930 until 1951. The next owner sold the business to Hiram Walker after four years, and in 1995, Old Pulteney became the property of the present owner, Inver House. Up until then, this whisky was mostly used for the production of blends, including Ballantine's, and was not particularly widely known. It was Inver House that released a single malt as an official bottling. In 2001, the company became a 100 percent subsidiary of Pacific Spirits UK, which in turn was acquired by the Thai corporation International Beverage Holdings Ltd. (InterBev) in October 2006.

OLD PULTENEY	
OWNER	Inver House (InterBev)
ESTABLISHED	1826; In production
ANNUAL PRODUCTION	3 million liters/ 793,000 gallons

This whisky is salty and fresh, with a whiff of ocean air and seaweed. Some bottlings are slightly peated and generally have a malty-sweet undertone.

WHISKY
Old Pulteney, 17 years old, 46% ABV, official bottling
Color: Amber

TASTING NOTES
The nose of this whisky is fruity, reminiscent of apples and pears, with a slight undertone of oak. It has a full body, with notes of vanilla and flowers and a remarkably long finish.

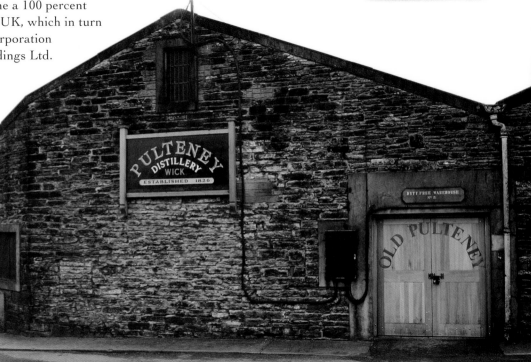

Thanks to Old Pulteney, whisky plays an important role in the former fishing town of Wick.

Teaninich

TEANINICH	
OWNER	UDV (Diageo)
ESTABLISHED	1817
MEANING OF NAME	The house in the moor
STATUS	In production
ANNUAL PRODUCTION	3 million liters/ 793,000 gallons

THE TEANINICH DISTILLERY is in Alness, directly on Cromarty Firth and not far from the much more renowned Dalmore Distillery.

Teaninich was founded by landowner Captain Munro in 1817. It has been owned by the DCL since 1905, and therefore belongs to the UDV group today. As early as 1899, the distillery was modernized and extended, followed by further refurbishments in the 1960s and 1970s. By 1972, the complex included ten stills in two stillhouses. Unfortunately, both of them were shut down in 1985, and only the large stillhouse—known as "A side"—resumed production five years later. The distillery and its whisky have never been particularly widely known, since Teaninich has primarily been used in blends, including Haig Dimple and VAT 69. Stillhouse B remains closed.

Although Teaninich is mostly used for blends, some official bottlings have been released, for instance for the Rare Malts series. Some independent bottlings are available, as well. Teaninich has a leafy, quite robust and voluminous character.

WHISKY

Teaninich, 10 years old, 43% ABV, Flora & Fauna
Color: Pale golden

 TASTING NOTES

The nose is dominated by citrus fruits and has a very light and sweet character. The lightness is confirmed on the palate with a hint of spiciness. The finish is long and dry. Overall, this malt is particularly suitable as an aperitif.

The Teaninich Distillery, which used to operate up to ten stills, has produced some of the lesser known whiskies in the region.

Glen Albyn · Glen Mhor · Millburn

OWNER	UDV (Diageo)
ESTABLISHED	1846, 1892, 1807
MEANING OF NAMES	Glen Albyn: White valley
	Glen Mhor: Great valley
	Millburn: Mill stream
STATUS	Part demolished, partially rebuilt

THESE THREE DISTILLERIES once operated in Inverness and belonged to the giant firm Diageo. In the 1980s they were closed, officially because they did not produce particularly high-quality whisky. While the quality of Glen Albyn's whiskies may have varied, Glen Mhor had a striking heaviness, and Millburn whiskies were known for their honey-sweet character. For these reasons, there is actually quite some demand for the latter two.

GLEN ALBYN

Glen Albyn stood directly on the shore of the Caledonian Canal, next to the Glen Mhor Distillery.

The distillery was established in 1846, based on an old brewery, at the initiative of the mayor of Inverness, James Sutherland. Fire struck the plant as early as 1849, and Glen Albyn had to be shut down for three months for renovations. It was

closed again in 1855, until it was slightly modernized by Grigor/Gregory & Co. in 1884. In 1920, the distillery was acquired by Mackinlays & Birnie Ltd. Charles Mackinley also owned the nearby Glen Mhor Distillery; under his management, Glen Albyn saw its most successful days. In 1972, it was sold to DCL, which shut it down and had it demolished eleven years later. Today, a shopping mall is located on the premises.

GLEN MHOR

Glen Mhor was located on the western outskirts of the village of Inverness, across from Glen Albyn.

The distillery was built by John Bernie in 1892. Bernie, together with his partner James Mackinlay, later acquired Glen Albyn as well. In 1972, Glen Mhor and its neighboring distillery were sold to DCL. Again, it shared Glen Albyn's fate when it was shut down in 1983 and had to make way for a shopping mall.

WHISKY
Glen Mhor, 28 years old, 1976 vintage, 51.9 % ABV
Color: Green-gold

TASTING NOTES
On the tongue, this complex, fresh Highland malt reveals notes of lemon juice and white pepper. It is sweetly dry, with a soothing, minty finish.

MILLBURN

This distillery was located on the eastern outskirts of Inverness, near a railway line.

A man named Welsh established the distillery in 1807. Back in those days, it was one of the first legal distilleries anywhere in Scotland. Several changes in ownership took place, and Millburn even had to close down from 1851 until 1876. There is some confusion about who the owner was at the time. Be that as it may, the distillery was rebuilt in 1876 and acquired by Andrew Haig & Co. soon thereafter.

In 1921, Millburn came into ownership of the Booth gin company. Shortly after that change of hands, in 1922, a fire broke out. Thanks to the quick reaction of soldiers stationed in nearby barracks, serious damage was prevented and most of the whisky inventory could be saved, though the distillery had to be renovated. Millburn was sold to DCL in 1937. In 1985, it was shut down for good and sold to Beefeaters four years later, who converted the buildings into a restaurant and a hotel. Beefeaters also owns a building at the Rosebank Distillery, which was also closed and replaced by a restaurant.

SPEYSIDE

"A good gulp of hot whisky at bedtime—it's not very scientific, but it helps."

SIR ALEXANDER FLEMING

SPEYSIDE IS A CORE REGION in the Highlands that spreads out from the River Spey; in fact, Speyside extends far beyond the Spey River area. The distilleries located along the Livet, Fiddich, Avon, Lossie, Findhorn and Deveron Rivers, for instance, are all considered Speyside distilleries, as well. Since the area is not a geopolitical unit, precise borders have never been established. As a result, there are some cases in which it may be a matter of debate whether a particular distillery should be considered part of one region or another. This said, sixty-three of the ninety distilleries currently active in Scotland are located in Speyside.

Why are there so many distilleries in this area? In the past, because the entire region was relatively accessible, it provided a safe haven for the mostly illegal distilleries. Later, when the railway had been built and the streets improved, the infrastructure was in place to make Speyside attractive to investors. The regions also fulfills all of the preconditions necessary for whisky production: water, peat and barley are all plentiful here. Finally, the Glenlivet Distillery boosted this development when, in 1823, it was the very first distillery in Scotland to acquire a license. Impressed by Glenlivet's success, other distilleries added "Glenlivet" to their names. Glenlivet whisky

enjoyed such an excellent reputation that the region itself was even referred to as Glenlivet for a long while; it only received its present name, Speyside, at a later stage.

Most distilleries are concentrated in and around some of the larger towns, such as Elgin, Rothes, Keith and especially Dufftown, the secret whisky capital: no other town has more distilleries. Even two centuries ago, there was a saying: "Rome was built on seven hills, Dufftown stands on seven stills." This refers to the distilleries Balvenie, Convalmore (demolished), Dufftown, Glendullan (closed), Glenfiddich, Mortlach and Parkmore (demolished). Nowadays, the saying doesn't quite fit: Kininvie and Pittyvaich (also demolished by now) were added established thereafter. The town boasts several other historic buildings worth seeing, such as Mortlach Church, which dates back to 566. The bell tower in the center of Dufftown used to house an illegal distillery. The tower clock, which became famous as "the clock that hanged MacPherson," came to Dufftown from Banff. In 1700, MacPherson, a kind of a Scottish Robin Hood, was supposed to be hanged. On the day of the execution, the sheriff of Banff had the clock set an hour ahead in order to beat a pardon that was on its way. Because of this extra hour, the execution had already taken place by the time the official message made it to Dufftown.

Top: Gordon & MacPhail run a delicatessen in Elgin that is a great favorite among whisky enthusiasts. Gordon & MacPhail are also independent bottlers and distillery owners.
Bottom: The magnificent ruins of the Gothic cathedral, begun in 1224, in the former bishop's see of Elgin.

Opposite: The Speyside region, home to many distilleries, derives its name from the River Spey, Scotland's longest river.

Aberlour

ABERLOUR

OWNER	Pernod Ricard
ESTABLISHED	1879
MEANING OF NAME	Loud confluence
STATUS	In production
ANNUAL PRODUCTION	3.5 million liters/ 925,000 gallons

THE ABERLOUR DISTILLERY is situated in an exceptionally favorable location directly on the A95, at the foot of Ben Rinnes, and not far from the Lynn of Ruthie waterfall.

While the distillery states 1879 as the year of its founding on its labels, a distillery is said to have existed on the same premises in 1826, and it was known by the same name. After a major fire, the facilities had to be rebuilt almost entirely in 1898. Most of the buildings still standing today date back to that period. In 1945, the distillery was acquired by Campbell Distillers and immediately refurbished. In 1973, it was extended to four stills, and one year later Campbell Distillers was taken over by the Pernod Ricard spirits group, which has remained the owner to the present day. In spite of the distillery's convenient location, a visitors center was only opened in recent years.

This whisky has a nutty and soft character with a spiciness reminiscent of nutmeg. It is most often served with dessert or as a digestive. Most Aberlour bottlings are highly aromatic with an undertone of sherry.

WHISKY

Aberlour, 12 years old, 40% ABV, official bottling
Color: Deep red amber

TASTING NOTES
The nose brings out a slight smokiness and a hint of butter. The pleasantly heavy body adds a very sweet note of sherry and some undertones of honey. Furthermore, there are flavors of nuts and a hint of oak. The finish is medium, with a touch of ginger, very warming and increasingly dry.

Over the decades, the Aberlour Distillery has been continuously modernized and extended. Since 1973, the complex has included four stills.

Allt-à-Bhainne

THE ALLT-À-BHAINNE DISTILLERY is located on the southern slope of Ben Rinnes, near the small town of Dufftown in the southwest.

It was built in 1975 by Chivas Brothers (which belonged to Seagram) at the same time they established Braes of Glenlivet. The original intention was to build five distilleries, but this ambitious project was never finished. The architects designed a very modern distillery that still fits in well with the landscape. Pagoda roofs were even added, though they are purely decorative. The entire production process is fully computer controlled. Since Allt-à-Bhainne does not have any warehouses of its own, the spirit is transported to Keith in tank trucks immediately after distilling. The distillery was extended in 1989. While it only has two stills, together they have a capacity of up to one million gallons per year.

Alt-à-Bhainne whisky is flowery, slightly sweet, with a light spicy note. It is particularly suitable as an aperitif. However, it is used exclusively for the Chivas Regal blend, which is why there has never been an official bottling. It has only been available through a select few independent bottlers.

ALLT-À-BHAINNE

OWNER	Chivas Brothers (Pernod Ricard)
ESTABLISHED	1975
MEANING OF NAME	Brook of milk
STATUS	In production
ANNUAL PRODUCTION	3.8 million liters/ 1 million gallons

WHISKY
Allt-à-Bhainne, 1991, 43% ABV, Gordon & MacPhail, Connoisseurs Choice
Color: Pale yellow

TASTING NOTES
The nose immediately reveals the fruity-sweet and spicy aromas. On the palate, there is a noticeable element of pepper and an undertone of cedar wood. The medium finish is pure and clear.

Allt-à-Bhainne is one of the most modern distilleries in Scotland and produces large quantities of blends. As a single malt, Allt-à-Bhainne is only available through independent bottlers.

An Cnoc/Knockdhu • Ardmore

AN CNOC / KNOCKDHU

OWNER	Inver House (InterBev)
ESTABLISHED	1894
MEANING OF NAME	The hill/Black hill
STATUS	In production
ANNUAL PRODUCTION	1.2 million liters/ 317,000 gallons

THE KNOCKDHU DISTILLERY is located near Huntly, at the base of cone-shaped Knock Hill.

The distillery's buildings were erected in 1893/94 by DCL, which owned Knockdhu until 1987. Knockdhu was inactive from 1931 until 1933 and again during World War II. Production resumed and continued for fifty years, but was stilled one more time in 1983. Four years later, Guiness (and thus United Distillers) acquired the facility. Only in 1989 did Inver House resume production under the new management.

ARDMORE

OWNER	Fortune Brands
ESTABLISHED	1898
MEANING OF NAME	Great height
STATUS	In production
ANNUAL PRODUCTION	3 million liters/ 793,000 gallons

THE ARDMORE DISTILLERY stands right next door to the Kennethmont train station, south of Huntly, on the rail line connecting Aberdeen and Inverness. Since the distillery is located on the outskirts of Speyside, it is sometimes considered part of the eastern Highlands.

Ardmore took up operations in 1898 under William Teacher & Sons. Then as now, Ardmore primarily produced whisky for the Teacher's Highland Cream blend, as it does under the present owner, Fortune Brands. The stillhouse was extended to include four stills in 1955, and since 1974 has had eight stills. Part of the distillery is still fueled with coal. Ardmore is also one of few distilleries with its own in-house cooperage.

The malt was named An Cnoc, the Gaelic word for hill, due to concern that customers might confuse Knockdhu whisky with products from the Knockando Distillery. Today, Knockdhu whisky can be found almost exclusively under the name An Cnoc, which was added to the heading on this page as a compromise, as the distillery continues to be Knockdhu.

WHISKY
An Cnoc, 1991, 46% ABV, official bottling
Color: Golden yellow

TASTING NOTES
The aroma reveals notes of vanilla and caramel, with undertones of wood. The flavor is very fruity and, surprisingly, brings out a suggestion of peat smoke. The finish is medium-long and very pleasant.

This is a malty whisky, reminiscent of cream, with an oily body. So far, it has only been released through independent bottlers, but this is expected to change soon.

WHISKY
Ardmore Heavily Peated, 11 years old, 1994/2005 vintage, 60.8% ABV, Specialty Drinks Ltd.
Color: Golden yellow

TASTING NOTES
In the nose, clear smoke and a pleasant note of wood unfold. The smokiness is repeated on the palate, complemented by a certain spiciness, which in turn is balanced by a buttery sweetness. There are also slightly fruity undertones. The short finish is pleasant and ends on a light note of smoke.

Opposite: The Knockdhu Distillery, bathed in rare Scottish sunshine on a peaceful day, unaffected by name or brand confusion.

Auchroisk

AUCHROISK	
OWNER	UDV (Diageo)
ESTABLISHED	1974
MEANING OF NAME	Ford on the red river
STATUS	In production
ANNUAL PRODUCTION	3 million liters/ 793,000 gallons

THE AUCHROISK DISTILLERY is located near the tiny settlement of Mulben, which is near Keith on the Burn of Mulben.

Auchroisk was built in 1974 after a Justerini & Brooks manager located a previously undiscovered spring. The water quality was so exceptional that he was able to convince the executive board to buy the property in order to establish a distillery there. Auchroisk whisky is primarily used in the making of J&B blends, but it is also available as a single malt. Following the Grand-Met and Guinness merger, Auchroisk is now owned by UDV/Diageo.

This is a slightly peated whisky with a sophisticated sherry note.

WHISKY

Auchroisk, 10 years old, 43% ABV, Flora & Fauna
Color: Pale gold

TASTING NOTES

The nose of this whisky is quite fruity, slightly sweet, and reminiscent of berries and white grapes. The flavor is smooth and sweet, dominated by nuts and figs. The finish is relatively short and dry, with the slightest hint of smoke.

This distillery, located on the Burn of Mulben, is relatively young. It was designed to echo the compound architectural style of older distilleries.

Aultmore

THE VENERABLE Aultmore Distillery can be found a short way north of Keith.

Aultmore was founded in 1896 by Alexander Edwards, who had already inherited the Benrinnes Distillery from his father. Edwards also established Craigellachie and bought the Oban Distillery. In 1923, however, he had to sell Aultmore to John Dewar & Sons, which in turn was acquired by DCL two years later. Distillers Company Ltd. added two more stills, bringing the total to four. DCL merged with the Guinness subsidiary United Distributors in 1987, and when the Diageo group acquired UD, antitrust laws made it necessary to sell Aultmore. When the dust settled, it ended up in the ownership of Bacardi.

AULTMORE

OWNER	Dewar & Sons (Bacardi)
ESTABLISHED	1896
MEANING OF NAME	Big stream
STATUS	In production
ANNUAL PRODUCTION	2.2 million liters/ 580,000 gallons

TASTING NOTES

After a hiatus of ten years, an official bottling was finally released again. The aroma is very light, flowery, with a sweet and fruity undertone. The flavor strongly emphasizes the fruitiness; one is tempted to think it might contain stewed plums. The finish is medium-long and dry.

The character of this whisky is very fresh, with strong notes of herbs and spices. It is usually quite dry and popular as an aperitif. Unfortunately, there are only a few single malt bottlings available; Aultmore produces primarily for Dewar's blend.

WHISKY

Aultmore, 12 years old, 40% ABV, official bottling
Color: Golden yellow

Most of Aultmore's whisky is used for Dewar's blend, but a single malt is also available.

Balmenach

BALMENACH	
OWNER	Inver House (InBrew)
ESTABLISHED	1824
MEANING OF NAME	The farm in the middle
STATUS	In production
ANNUAL PRODUCTION	2 million liters/ 530,000 gallons

THE BALMENACH DISTILLERY is in the heart of the Speyside region, between Grantown-on-Spey and Bridge of Avon, near the A95 road.

The distillery was officially established in 1824 as one of the first to receive a distilling license. It was founded by the McGregors, who are related to two well-known writers: Sir Robert Bruce Lockhart (his 1951 book *Scotch* features this distillery) and Sir Compton McKenzie, whose bestselling book *Whisky Galore* was even turned into a movie. One of the founding brothers, James McGregor, had experience working as an illegal master distiller with the Tomintoul Distillery. After James' death in 1870, his widow continued to run the business at first. Unfortunately, necessary maintenance and renovations did not take place, and the facilities became visibly dilapidated. During World War I Balmenach remained closed. In 1922, it was acquired by a group of blenders (James Watson, Peter Dawson and MacDonald Green), who were bought out by DCL in the 1930s. In 1963, a Saladin box was installed to replace the floor maltings. In 1991, the new owner, UD, released the first single malt in the Flora & Fauna series. Two years later, however, they shut

Balmenach down. Inver House acquired the distillery in 1997 and resumed production soon after. Interestingly, though, the new owner has not yet issued a single malt.

The character of this whisky is slightly peaty, with strong elements of flowers and herbs. The whiskies that are not sherry matured can be enjoyed as aperitifs; the others are better as digestives. Apart from being in the Flora & Fauna series, it has been made available through independent bottlers.

WHISKY

Balmenach, 1988/2002 vintage, 40% ABV, Gordon & MacPhail, Connoisseurs Choice
Color: Very pale amber

TASTING NOTES

The nose is flowery, sweet, with notes of honey and an undertone of heather. The sweetness is emphasized on the palate; a slightly spicy flavor of tobacco leaves and a touch of smoke emerge. The medium-long finish is dry and brings out a sherry note.

Life at the family-owned Balmenach Distillery was described in a novel by Robert Bruce Lockhart.

Balvenie

ON THE OUTSKIRTS of the secret whisky capital of Dufftown, the Balvenie Distillery can be found directly next door to its bigger neighbor, Glenfiddich.

William Grant and his sons built the distillery in 1892. It remains family-owned to this day, together with the Glenfiddich and Kininvie Distilleries, by William Grant & Sons. The name Balvenie is derived from the nearby Balvenie Castle. The New Balvenie Castle, formerly a manor house, was used as a source of stones when the distillery was built. The first stills, incidentally, were bought second-hand from Lagavulin and Glen Albyn. Today the distillery has eight so-called Balvenie stills, a type of still with a bulge between the neck and the still pot; there are, however, other distilleries that also employ stills with a similar shape. The ownership situation and the proximity to Glenfiddich allow for certain synergetic effects: Balvenie uses waste heat from Glenfiddich for heating its own stills. Both distilleries receive their water from the same spring (Robbie Dubh); William Grant bought the entire property in his lifetime in order to ensure that the spring and the stream would

BALVENIE	
OWNER	William Grant & Sons
ESTABLISHED	1892
MEANING OF NAME	Beathan's farm
STATUS	In production
ANNUAL PRODUCTION	5 million liters/ 1.3 million gallons

never be contaminated or run dry due to the demands of other building projects. David Stewart, master blender of William Grant & Sons, was the first to put into practice the idea of wood finishing, initiating a trend that continues to this day.

This malt has the strongest honey element of any malt whisky. It matures well; most bottlings are medium-heavy, with hints of exotic fruits. The twenty-one-year-old Balvenie is a legend: it matures in Bourbon casks before being finished in port wood casks for another six to twelve months. Unfortunately, it is only available in very limited quantities.

WHISKY
The Balvenie Double Wood, 12 years old, 40% ABV, official bottling
Color: Dark amber

TASTING NOTES
The Double Wood has established itself as a constant star among malt connoisseurs. The nose brings out characteristic aromas of oranges, balanced by sherry. The sweet sherry note develops fully on the palate, complemented by a touch of nuts and some cinnamon. The finish is very pleasant and long.

The famous Balvenie stills are known for their characteristic shape.

Benriach

BENRIACH

OWNER	The Benriach Distillery Company Ltd.
ESTABLISHED	1898
MEANING OF NAME	Speckled mountain
STATUS	In production
ANNUAL PRODUCTION	2 million liters/ 528,000 gallons

In the past, Benriach whisky used to be transported by train, which conveniently stopped directly at the distillery.

THE BENRIACH DISTILLERY is located south of Elgin, next to the Longmorn Distillery.

Benriach was built in 1898, during the height of the whisky boom, and taken over the same year by the neighboring Longmorn Distillery. Only two years later, the bankruptcy of the major producer Patisson led to a downturn for Benriach as well, and the distillery had to be shut down. It was not until 1965 that the Glenlivet Group reactivated it. In 1978, the entire Glenlivet Group was acquired by the Seagram Corporation of Canada. 1994 saw the release of a single malt; previously, Benriach had only been available from individual bottlers. A 2001 merger with Chivas Brothers turned Benriach over to the ownership of Pernod Ricard, which owned more distilleries than the management deemed necessary, once again leading to the closure of Benriach. Finally, in 2004, the long hoped-for solution was found: Billy Walker (formerly director of Burn Stewart) and two South African businessmen, Wayne Keiswetter and Geoff Bell, came to the rescue and acquired the distillery along with all of its inventory, which includes bottlings that date back to the mid-1960s. The Benriach Distillery Company was established specifically for this purpose.

Benriach whiskies are quite varied. Some are dry and rather smooth, but there is also a heavily peated, smoky and oily version that has a certain

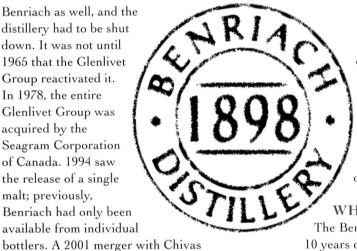

complexity, yet still tends to the dry. Since November 2006, some fifteen-year-old wood finishes (sherry, rum, Madeira and port) have been introduced on the market.

WHISKY
The Benriach Curiositas, 10 years old, 40% ABV, official bottling
Color: Amber

 TASTING NOTES

The peat smoke, unusually strong for a Speyside whisky, is immediately noticeable. It is complemented by aromas of fruits, flowers and heather. The flavor is well balanced and adds a bittersweet note of peat smoke and a touch of oak. The medium finish continues the smoke and oak tones.

Benrinnes

THE BENRINNES DISTILLERY is near Aberlour, at the foot of the mountain of the same name.

The distillery was founded next to a farmhouse, which still stands, in 1826. Back then, it carried the name of a nearby waterfall: Lyne of Ruthie. Just three years after opening, the river burst its banks and the resulting flood destroyed most of the buildings, which had to be rebuilt from scratch. In 1842, a new owner, John Innes, renamed the distillery Benrinnes. It was acquired in 1845 by William Smith, but he had to file for bankruptcy in 1864. The next owner, Davie Edward, would later also establish Cragellachie. Benrinnes was sold in 1922 to by John Dewar & Sons, who in turn merged with DCL three years later. During the years 1932 and 1933 and from 1943 until 1945, the distillery was shut down. Operations started up again in 1951 and the facility was expanded in 1955. In 1964, Saladin boxes were added for more convenient production of malt; unfortunately, though, these were demolished in 1984 due to cost concerns. The number of stills was doubled in 1966, and in 1978, the production process was changed to the triple distillation method Benrinnes uses to this day, which is highly unusual for the Speyside region. There were no official bottlings for a long time; UD was the first to remedy this. At present, Benrinnes is owned by the Diageo group.

This whisky has an intense flavor, creamy and smoky, with a touch of toffee and vanilla.

BENRINNES	
OWNER	UDV (Diageo)
ESTABLISHED	1826
MEANING OF NAME	Promontory hill
STATUS	In production
ANNUAL PRODUCTION	1.6 million liters/ 423,000 gallons

WHISKY
Benrinnes, 15 years old, 43% ABV, Flora & Fauna
Color: Mahogany

TASTING NOTES
The nose of this single malt is surprisingly smoky. It is certainly not as smoky as an Islay malt, but for a Speyside whisky, the fine note of smoke is exceptionally noticeable on the palate. Other than that, it is pleasantly fruity. The finish is long and continues the smoky element while bringing out intense spice notes.

A picture from the past: the venerable Benrinnes Distillery continues to use triple distillation, a most unusual technique for a Speyside distillery.

Benromach

BENROMACH	
OWNER	Gordon & MacPhail
ESTABLISHED	1898
MEANING OF NAME	Shaggy (or spiky) mountain
STATUS	In production
ANNUAL PRODUCTION	200,000 liters/ 53,000 gallons

THE BENROMACH DISTILLERY is located in the northern outskirts of Forres.

The distillery was founded in 1898 by Duncan MacCallum, then owner of the Ben Nevis Distillery, and F.W. Brickman, a spirits merchant. When the whisky boom came to a sudden end, Benromach was shut down after Brickmann had to file bankruptcy for his own company. Benromach was acquired in 1911 by the London-based Harvey McNair & Co., and production was resumed early in 1912. After the First World War, John Joseph Calder bought the distillery in 1919. 1925 saw another shutdown, and 1937 the acquisition by Associated Scottish Distillers Ltd. (ASD), who in turn were taken over by National Distillers of America a year later. In 1974, the current owner, DCL, had some renovations made, but stopped production again in 1983. The present owners, Gordon & MacPhail, bought the distillery in 1993. They had made several bottlings of Benromach in the past, and the acquisition was a dream come true for them. They carried out extensive renovations for almost five years before Benromach's reopening was celebrated in the presence of no less a celebrity than Prince Charles, exactly one hundred years after its founding.

This is a highly energetic whisky with lingering undertones of flowers and frequently a slight hint of cream. It is popular for dessert or as a digestive.

The smallest of the Speyside distilleries was revived by the independent whisky bottlers Gordon & MacPhail in the 1990s.

WHISKY
Benromach Traditional, 40% ABV, official bottling
Color: Straw yellow

 TASTING NOTES
The malt, which is slightly peaty and smoky at the malting stage, is not particularly noticeable on the nose. Elements of citrus fruits and a little honey are more prominent. The flavor brings out a little more of the peat smoke and adds distinct malt and pepper tones. This single malt is relatively dry, with a pleasantly long, syrupy finish, again complemented by an undertone of malt.

Cardhu was an illegal distillery before it received its license. Ever since the late nineteenth century, this distillery has been home to the Johnnie Walker brand.

Cardhu/Cardow

THE CARDHU DISTILLERY stands on the north shore of the River Spey, between Upper Knockando and Cardow near the B 9102.

Cardhu was established in 1811 by Helen Cummings. Together with her husband, she at first ran the distillery as an illegal business. The official license was granted in 1824. Back then, they distilled their whisky on their farm in Cardow. Helen Cummings's inventiveness allowed her to evade the despised English customs officials time and time again. In 1874, her daughter-in-law had a new building erected on the site where the distillery stands today. Even back in 1893, Johnnie Walker was the most important Cardhu brand. The distillery has been owed by UDV since 1997, making it part of the Diageo corporation. Cardhu was called Cardow until 1975, when it received the name it bears today.

CARDHU / CARDOW

OWNER	UDV (Diageo)
ESTABLISHED	1824
MEANING OF NAME	Black rock
STATUS	In production
ANNUAL PRODUCTION	1.9 million liters/ 502,000 gallons

WHISKY
Cardhu, 12 years old, 40% ABV, official bottling
Color: Amber

TASTING NOTES
Since demand for this single malt is extremely high in Spain, Cardhu sells almost its entire output to Spain. In the rest of the world, most whisky retailers have to import Cardhu directly. Cardhu's aroma is very delicate, with a hint of smoke. On the palate, it is malty-sweet and nicely balanced. The long finish continues the slight sweetness and adds some peat.

Cragganmore

CRAGGANMORE	
OWNER	UDV (Diageo)
ESTABLISHED	1869
MEANING OF NAME	Big rock
STATUS	In production
ANNUAL PRODUCTION	1.2 million liters/ 317,000 gallons

A beautiful wrought iron sign announces the entryway to the small Cragganmore Distillery.

HIGH ABOVE THE RIVER SPEY, the Craggan-more Distillery is situated in a hollow in between Aberlour and Grantown-on-Spey.

The distillery was built by John Smith in 1870. Before Smith decided to go into business for himself he had gained experience at Macallan, Glenlivet and Glenfarclas. From the start, his malt was in high demand. The downside to this great demand, however, was that it was used almost exclusively for blends. In spite of its success, Cragganmore has always been a small distillery. It has seen several changes in ownership (from White Horse Distillers to DCL to UD), and like many other distilleries, is currently owned by UDV, which makes it part of the Diageo group.

The character of this whisky is highly complex (which is certainly due in part to the unusually shaped stills), tart and dry and highly aromatic. It is particularly suitable as a digestive.

WHISKY

Cragganmore, 12 years old, 40% ABV, official bottling
Color: Gold

 TASTING NOTES
The complexity of this whisky shows on the nose: it is dry and smells of herbs. On the palate, it is slightly smoky, malty and develops a full body. The long finish continues the smoke, complemented by a slightly sweet and malty undertone.

The Cragganmore Distillery has maintained its charm throughout the centuries.

Craigellachie

THE CRAIGELLACHIE DISTILLERY is situated in the heart of the Speyside region, southeast of the town of the same name, in between Dufftown, Aberlour and Rothes. Nearby, the Fiddich River flows into the Spey. Less than a mile away toward Dufftown is the famous Speyside Cooperage.

Craigellachie was built in 1891. The founding members included Peter Mackie, whose name is inseparably associated with White Horse Distillers and the world-famous White Horse blend. After his death, Cragellachie was acquired by DCL in 1927 and came into the ownership of UD in 1987. In between, in 1965, it was refurbished. Following the merger with Diageo, the successor, UDV, sold the distillery in 1997. It was acquired by Dewar's (and thereby Bacardi) together with Aberfeldy, Aultmore and Royal Brackla.

Tradition and modernity meet in the fully computer-controlled Craigellachie Distillery, in the heart of Speyside.

CRAIGELLACHIE

OWNER	Dewar & Sons Ltd. (Bacardi)
ESTABLISHED	1891
MEANING OF NAME	Rocky mountain
STATUS	In production
ANNUAL PRODUCTION	2.8 million liters/ 740,000 gallons

This is a relatively sweet whisky, malty and nutty, frequently also with notes of fruits and smoke. It can be found through independent bottlers and is particularly suitable as a digestive.

WHISKY
Craigellachie, 1989 vintage, 43% ABV, Gordon & MacPhail, Connoisseurs Choice
Color: Straw yellow

TASTING NOTES
The aroma is slightly smoky, with a malty sweetness. On the palate, this sweetness as well as the smoke are echoed and complemented by a flavor of nuts. The finish is very long and continues the smoky element.

Dailuaine

DAILUAINE	
OWNER	UDV (Diageo)
ESTABLISHED	1851
MEANING OF NAME	Green valley
STATUS	In production
ANNUAL PRODUCTION	2.5 million liters/ 660,000 gallons

NESTLED INTO A HOLLOW between the Ben Rinnes and the River Spey, near Carron and Aberlour, is the Dailuaine Distillery. It is not far from the Imperial Distillery.

Dailuaine was established in 1851 by William Mackenzie on the same land where it stands today. The design for the facility, drawn up by architect Charles Chree Doig, included the first pagoda roof to grace a distillery. The early years saw many changes in ownership within the family, first from the founder to his wife, then to their son, Thomas. In 1898, Dailuaine became part of the Dailuaine-Talisker Distilleries Ltd.; via the DCL, it came into the possession of UD, and thereby of Diageo. Twice the facilities had to be rebuilt due to fires that had ravaged the distillery, in 1917 and in 1959. Following the second disastrous fire, the owners extended the number of stills from four to six. Conveniently, Dailuaine had a railway connection of its own. This was practical not only for transportation of whisky and raw materials, but also of workers and employees. Today, only parts of the railway are in operation. In the past, however, the distillery even owned its own steam engine. Dailuaine is one of the lesser known brands; their whisky is used almost exclusively for Johnnie Walker blends.

This whisky usually tastes quite fruity, with notes of fresh apples and a touch of smoke and nuts. An official bottling has been released in the Flora & Fauna series, and it has also been available from some independent bottlers.

WHISKY

Dailuaine, 16 years old, 43% ABV, Flora & Fauna
Color: Very dark amber

 **TASTING NOTES**

This single malt is very dry on the nose, with a slight hint of sherry, which becomes stronger on the palate, if with less of the characteristic sweetness. Other than that, this oak-flavored whisky tastes light and mild. The finish is surprisingly long, smooth and mild.

Dailuaine, located on the River Spey, produces primarily for the Johnnie Walker blend. Single malt editions have been bottled in small quantities.

Dufftown

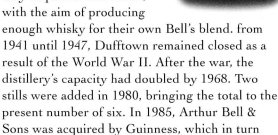

ON THE OUTSKIRTS of the small town that shares its name, which is Scotland's secret capital of whisky, and on the River Fiddich stands the Dufftown Distillery.

The distillery was founded by Peter MacKenzie in 1896. Prior to that, the old stone buildings on the grounds had housed a mill. In his day, MacKenzie was particularly successful with his blends, especially in the USA. Due to Prohibition, however, he was forced to sell the distillery to Arthur Bell & Sons in the 1920s. Bell & Sons bought the facilities at the same time they acquired Blair Athol, with the aim of producing enough whisky for their own Bell's blend. from 1941 until 1947, Dufftown remained closed as a result of the World War II. After the war, the distillery's capacity had doubled by 1968. Two stills were added in 1980, bringing the total to the present number of six. In 1985, Arthur Bell & Sons was acquired by Guinness, which in turn came into the ownership of the Diageo group.

This whisky has a dry, malty and quite aromatic character with light, nutty elements. In recent years it has become even lighter, and the grassy notes have become more pronounced. It is only suitable as an aperitif and is used especially for the Bell's and Johnnie Walker blends. Some official bottlings are on the market; Dufftown has been released in the Flora & Fauna series, for instance. Other than that, there have been some single malts from independent bottlers.

WHISKY

Dufftown, 15 years old, 43% ABV, Flora & Fauna
Color: Amber

An illegal distillery was once hidden behind the walls of the famous bell tower right in the center of Dufftown.

DUFFTOWN	
OWNER	UDV (Diageo)
ESTABLISHED	1896
MEANING OF NAME	Named after town founder, James Duff
STATUS	In production
ANNUAL PRODUCTION	3.5 million liters/ 925,000 gallons

 TASTING NOTES

The dryness is immediately noticeable on the nose, accompanied by malty undertones. The dryness continues on the palate and one notes a syrupy element with a hint of rubber. The finish is again extremely dry, yet smooth.

Glen Elgin

GLEN ELGIN

OWNER	UDV (Diageo)
ESTABLISHED	1898
MEANING OF NAME	Little Island
STATUS	In production
ANNUAL PRODUCTION	1.8 million liters/ 475,000 gallons

THE GLEN ELGIN DISTILLERY is located outside the town of Elgin, along the road to Rothes, in the immediate vicinity of the Longmorn Distillery.

Construction of the Glen Elgin Distillery began in 1898, during the heyday of the Scotch industry, and was completed after a two-year construction period. Thereafter, no further distilleries were built in Speyside for sixty years. Glen Elgin was only acquired by White Horse Distillers later, when White Horse obtained a license from its then-owner, SMD, a subsidiary of DCL. As a result of a great number of mergers, Glen Elgin is now part of the large Diageo group. In 1964, the facilities were modernized and the number of stills extended to four.

This whisky has a distinctive honey character and is sweet. Most bottlings have a flowery aroma and tend to be dry. Like Craigellachie and Lagavulin, Glen Elgin is also used for the White Horse blend. During the past couple of years, it has not only been available as a twelve-year-old official bottling, but was also released several times by independent bottlers.

WHISKY

Glen Elgin, 12 years old, 43% ABV, official bottling
Color: Deep gold

 TASTING NOTES
The aroma is sweet and smells of marzipan, almonds and fruits. The sweet note continues on the palate, yet at the same time it is quite dry and slightly spicy. The well-balanced finish brings out the dryness again.

Casks of 1992 Glen Elgin, a whisky that in the past was used exclusively for blends. Nowadays, it is available as a single malt again.

Glen Grant

THE GLEN GRANT DISTILLERY is tucked into a side street off the main road on the outskirts of the quaint town of Rothes.

The distillery was founded by the brothers John and James Grant in 1840. They had already owned another distillery in a different location, and apparently they were also particularly successful smugglers. This was not without a certain irony, given that James was actually a lawyer, but it seems not to have troubled him in the least. In 1898, they built Caperdonich, yet another family-owned distillery, just opposite Glen Grant. They eventually merged with George and J.G. Smith in 1953, becoming The Glenlivet & Glen Grant Distilleries. Longmorn joined the group in 1970, as did the Chivas Brothers (then under Seagram) in 1977, when the name was changed to Chivas & Glenlivet Group. Today, Chivas is owned by Pernod Ricard. Since Glen Grant has always enjoyed an excellent reputation, marketing their whisky as a single malt from a very early stage, the company is very proud of being number two on the global market today, second only to Glenfiddich. Since the group also produces a wide range of excellent, well-known blends, however, the majority of the whisky is still used for blending. Late in 2005, Glen Grant was sold to Campari for a record price of 150 million Euros ($208 million).

This whisky is generally rather light, since it matures almost exclusively in Bourbon casks. Its flavor is reminiscent of herbs, with certain elements of nuts, which makes young bottlings suitable as aperitifs. Older versions are often finished in sherry casks; those are best enjoyed after a meal. Apart from the official bottlings, several series have been released by independent bottlers.

This Glen Grant Distillery building asserts itself like a little castle.

GLEN GRANT	
OWNER	Campari
ESTABLISHED	1840
MEANING OF NAME	Grant's valley
STATUS	In production
ANNUAL PRODUCTION	5 million liters/ 1.3 million gallons

WHISKY
Glen Grant, 25 years old, 40% ABV, Gordon & MacPhail
Color: Mahogany

 TASTING NOTES
Sherry is immediately noticeable in the aroma, accompanied by caramel and apple. A sherry flavor is also dominant on the palate, complemented by nut and grain flavors. The finish is rather dry.

Glen Moray

GLEN MORAY	
OWNER	Glenmorangie Plc (LVMH)
ESTABLISHED	1897
MEANING OF NAME	Valley of the seaside village
STATUS	In production
ANNUAL PRODUCTION	1.85 million liters/
	490,000 gallons

THE GLEN MORAY DISTILLERY is located west of Elgin on the banks of the River Lossie. It stands virtually on the border of the Speyside region in an area known for growing barley, in the Lossie River valley.

Glen Moray was converted into a distillery in 1897. Prior to that, as in the case of the Glenmorangie Distillery, the buildings had housed a brewery. Even though Glen Moray

This whisky is dry, and its character is defined by barley elements. Most bottlings also have a fruity tone, and a grassy note is frequently present. As in the case of Glenmorangie, Glen Moray's sister distillery, Glen Moray is finished with various woods and sold in a number of variations. The wine-cask finished whiskies, in particular, enjoyed a great reputation, but they are completely sold out by now. On the mass market, the malt has firmly established itself. In Great Britain, Glen Moray is already number five. The twelve-year-old recently appeared in a chain of German grocery stores at a very affordable price, triggering a discussion about whether Glen Moray was thereby degrading its good reputation.

WHISKY

Glen Moray, 16 years old, 40% ABV,
    official bottling
    Color: Amber

WELCOME TO THE HOME OF

ELGIN CLASSIC

GLEN MORAY

SINGLE MALT WHISKY

Finest Quality Malt Whisky since 1897

TASTING NOTES

This Glen Moray has a distinct aroma, with a whiff of spices and apples. The flavor adds a slight note of smoke, some oak tones and toffee. The long finish is noticeably smoky once again.

managed to survive the big whisky crisis, it still had to be shut down in 1910. In 1923, the distillery was acquired by Macdonald & Muir, and was later incorporated into Glenmorangie plc, which is presently owned by the French group Moët Hennessy Louis Vuitton (LVMH). In 1958, the number of stills was extended to four and the facilities were modernized; from 1958 until 1977, a Saladin box was used for malting.

Glen Moray has become number five among Great Britain's most popular single malts.

Glen Spey

THE GLEN SPEY DIS-TILLERY stands along the main road in the center of the town of Rothes. It is arguably the most famous of the town's five distilleries.

James Stuart built this distillery in 1880. It was acquired only seven years later by Gilbey, whose core business was actually gin production. Gilbey, in turn, came under the ownership of IDV in 1962, and was subsequently renovated under IDV management in 1970. The refurbishment included an extension of the stills to four. After a series of mergers, the distillery eventually became part of the UDV group, which belongs to Diageo.

Glen Spey whisky is produced mainly for J&B blends, and the eight-year-old official bottling is very difficult to find; it is only offered through independent bottlers every once in a while. The whisky's character is light, grassy, nutty and slightly peaty. It is perfect as an aperitif.

GLEN SPEY	
OWNER	UDV (Diageo)
ESTABLISHED	1878
MEANING OF NAME	Valley of the Spey
STATUS	In production
ANNUAL PRODUCTION	2 million liters/ 528,000 gallons

TASTING NOTES

The aroma leaves a certain element of cookies, complemented by chocolate and some coconut. On the palate, the syrupy note of citric fruits transforms into a spicy-dry flavor. The long finish continues on the spice notes.

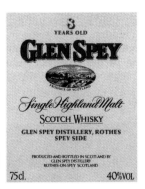

WHISKY
Glen Spey, 12 years old, 43% ABV, Flora & Fauna
Color: Golden yellow

All the local distilleries are within walking distance of the sophisticated Rothes Glen Hotel.

Glenallachie

GLENALLACHIE

OWNER	Campbell Distillers (Pernod Ricard)
ESTABLISHED	1967
MEANING OF NAME	Valley of the rocky place
STATUS	In production
ANNUAL PRODUCTION	3 million liters/ 793,000 gallons

This relatively young distillery produces almost exclusively for the blends of Clan Campbell, House of Lords and White Heather.

ALONG THE A95 ROAD toward Grantown-on-Spey, approximately two miles from Aberlour, a small road veers off to the left that leads up to the Glenallechie Distillery, which is nestled among green meadows.

The distillery was originally built by W. Delmé Evans for Mackinlay McPherson, and production began in 1967. Prior to that, Mackinlay McPherson had been running the Isle of Jura and Tullibardine Distilleries. In 1985, Glenallachie temporarily came into the ownership of Invergordon, though no whisky was produced during that period. After four years, Invergordon sold the distillery to Campbell Distillers, which already belonged to Pernod Ricard at the time. Pernod Ricard, still a small group back then, was able to almost double their overall production with this acquisition.

Almost all the whisky produced at Glenallachie is used for Clan Campbell, House of Lords and White Heather blends, which explains why there are no Glenallechie single malt official bottlings currently available. Invergordon did release a proprietary bottling, but this version has become quite rare. There have been occasional releases by independent bottlers.

This malt's delicate, subtle and light-yet-complex character makes it particularly suitable as an aperitif.

WHISKY

Glenallachie, Gordon & MacPhail, Connoisseurs Choice, 1992 vintage, 43% ABV.
Color: Straw

TASTING NOTES

Glenallachie bottlings are very rare. This bottling has a nose with aromas of malt and dry grass, complemented by a light sweetness. On the palate, this whisky is peppery, with a hint of charred oak, accompanied by flowery aromas and a slight sweetness of honey. The finish is spicy.

The ultramodern, computer-controlled Glenburgie Distillery is kept running smoothly by precisely two workers.

Glenburgie

THE GLENBURGIE DISTILLERY is a short way outside of Alves, a town that lies between Elgin and Forres.

The founding date is often given as 1810, though there are no historical records to confirm this. The only thing that is known for certain is that the distillery was named Kilnflat between 1829 and 1871, and that it belonged to William Paul during all those years. After 1871, there was an almost continual series of changes of ownership. The distillery remained silent from 1871 until 1878 and from 1925 until 1935. From 1930 onward it belonged to Hiram Walker, who had the distillery renovated from the ground up before resuming production. They used most of the whisky for Ballantine's blends. The business was later acquired by Allied Domecq, which in turn has belonged to the Pernod Ricard group since July 2005. In 1958, two Lomond stills were added and, as at other Allied distilleries, a new malt, Glencraig, was added to the program. The two Lomond stills, however, were demolished in 1981 and replaced by two regular stills.

To this day, most of the malt production of Glenburgie goes into blends such as Ballantine's, which is why it is difficult to find an official

GLENBURGIE	
OWNER	Chivas Brothers (Pernod Ricard)
ESTABLISHED	1810
MEANING OF NAME	Valley with the fortress
STATUS	In production
ANNUAL PRODUCTION	Not specified

bottling. Gordon & MacPhail, Signatory and a few independent bottlers have released several series. Glenburgie's whisky is best served as an aperitif. It can be oily, but it is very fruity and has a distinct note of herbs.

WHISKY

Glenburgie, 10 years old, 40% ABV, Gordon & MacPhail
Color: Dark amber

TASTING NOTES

The aroma of this malt is fresh and fruity, with citrus fruits dominating. It is slightly sweet, with a waft of hay. On the palate, a voluminous, sweet malt element is dominant, complemented by a light undertone of oak. The finish is very short and sweet, continuing the light oak note.

Glendronach

GLENDRONACH	
OWNER	Pernod Ricard
ESTABLISHED	1826
MEANING OF NAME	Valley of the brambles
STATUS	In production
ANNUAL PRODUCTION	300,000 liters/ 80,000 gallons

To this day, the Glendronach Distillery employs traditional production methods. Some of the pot stills are still fired by coal, and the barley comes from local grain fields.

THE GLENDRONACH DISTILLERY is located in between Banff and Huntly, near the town of Forgue, east of the A97 road.

The distillery was built as early as 1826 and used to belong to a son of Glenfiddich owner William Grant from 1920 to 1960. Later it came into the hands of Wm. Teacher & Sons, which also owned the nearby Ardmore Distillery and was one of the industry's largest family-owned whisky businesses at the time. As opposed to Ardmore, the production methods at Glendronach are very conservative. The barley supply comes from the immediate region, the washbacks are made of wood, and at least some of the pot stills are still fired by coal. The warehouses even have earthen floors like in the old days. In 1976, the venerable family business was sold to Allied Distillers, whose parent corporation, Allied Domecq, announced that the distillery was going to be shut down in 1996. Fortunately, production was resumed in 2004. Since a takeover in 2005, it has been part of the Pernod Ricard group.

This whisky's character is fresh and smooth, with sweet notes of butterscotch and caramel complemented by a pleasant maltiness. Ageing in sherry casks results in an intense sherry element. Glendronach is preferably served after a meal. There used to be an eight-year-old matured in Bourbon casks, a twelve-year-old matured in sherry casks, and a 1976 vintage eighteen-year-old. The only bottling from the Allied Distillers era still available is a fifteen-year-old. Glendronach is available from independent bottlers.

WHISKY
Glendronach, 12 years old, 40% ABV, official bottling
Color: Amber

 **TASTING NOTES**
This whisky has an intense nose of vanilla and caramel, followed by fruits including pears. It also has a strong nutty undertone. On the palate, it is very smooth and silky with malty sherry notes. The light and tingling finish continues the nuts theme.

Tranquility: there is no place for hustle and bustle in whisky production. Time is an essential factor in the quality of the product.

Glenfarclas

Glenfarclas has been run by the same family since 1865, over what is by now five generations.

GLENFARCLAS	
OWNER	J. & G. Grant
ESTABLISHED	1836
MEANING OF NAME	Valley of the green grass
STATUS	In production
ANNUAL PRODUCTION	3 million liters/ 793,000 gallons

THE GLENFARCLAS DISTILLERY is right near Ballindalloch Castle, directly on the A95 highway.

According to official records, the distillery was built by Robert Hey in 1836, though other sources mention the years 1835 and 1844. What is certain, though, is a change of ownership in 1865, when Glenfarclas was acquired by the Grant family (they are not related to the Glenfiddich Grants). At the time, John Grant bought the distillery with the intention of leasing it to John Smith. Five years later, however, John Smith quit in order to establish Cragganmore. Instead, John Grant and his son George took over the business. Pattison was chosen as a partner in order to provide funding for necessary renovations. This whisky giant's highly public bankruptcies took a heavy toll, but Glenfarclas managed to survive the rough times. In 1960, the distillery was extended to four stills, and to six in 1976. The family started opening the complex to the public at an early stage. As early as 1973, they established a visitors center—a pioneering idea at the time. Their success proved them right: the investment in a visitors center was followed by a significant increase in sales. Today, Glenfarclas malt enjoys an excellent reputation among blenders. It is a first-rate Scotch that is near the top of the wish list of any blender, and it is also available as a single malt in different versions. The company is family-owned to this day, and by now has been run by the Grants for no fewer than five generations.

This whisky's character is complex, full and malty. It has a noticeable note of sherry, and is most often served after a meal.

WHISKY
Glenfarclas 105, 60% ABV, official bottling
Color: Deep golden

 TASTING NOTES
This approximately eight-year-old single malt has gained an enthusiastic following among whisky connoisseurs. Without water, its flavor is intense and full; when water is added, it is rather mild. The aroma is dry, yet malty-sweet. On the palate, the boisterous momentum and the malty note are continued, and there is a hint of oak. The finish is long and dry, yet warming.

Glenfiddich

GLENFIDDICH	
OWNER	William Grant & Sons
ESTABLISHED	1887
MEANING OF NAME	Valley of the deer
STATUS	In production
ANNUAL PRODUCTION	10 million liters/
	2.65 million gallons

THE GLENFIDDICH DISTILLERY is located in the whisky capital Dufftown in the Fiddich Valley.

The distillery was founded in 1886/87 by William Grant. The Grant family built it themselves with the help of an architect. When the large blending firm Pattison went bankrupt in 1898, Glenfiddich was seriously affected; Pattison, the former model company, had been one of the most important purchasers of the Grant family's whiskies. Eventually, the family decided to produce their own internationally-marketed blend—and the idea panned out. Unlike so many other distilleries that did not survive Pattison's bankruptcy, Glenfiddich

managed to continue and was successful. With competition growing ever fiercer in the face of many mergers into large corporations, Glenfiddich, which remains a small family business to this day, took the industry by surprise in 1963, when it was the first distillery to introduce a new single malt. This step was met with incomprehension at the time, but the Grants were proven right: thanks to their untiring marketing, signature triangular green bottle, stag's head logo and great flexibility, the business has not only become world-famous, but is actually the number one single malt with a world market share of more than 26 percent.

Young Glenfiddich whisky is fruity and therefore appropriate as an aperitif. With longer maturation, it develops a chocolate flavor and one reminiscent of raisins; old Glenfiddich bottlings are thus better served as a digestive.

WHISKY
Glenfiddich, Caoran Reserve, 12 years old, 40% ABV, official bottling
Color: Golden

 TASTING NOTES
Caoran is Gaelic for peat ember. The smoky aroma stems from a finishing period in Islay casks that were previously filled with a smoky malt. In addition, the nose of this Glenfiddich has a very sweet aroma of oranges and sherry. It is very full and fruity on the palate, with a light, peaty note of smoke. The finish is creamy and continues the light smoke theme.

In 1963, Glenfiddich once again introduced a single malt on the market, and went on to write whisky history.

Opposite: One of the twenty-eight stills at Glenfiddich, still in the same size and shape as in William Grant's days.

Glenlossie

GLENLOSSIE	
OWNER	UDV (Diageo)
ESTABLISHED	1876
MEANING OF NAME	Valley of the Lossie
STATUS	In production
ANNUAL PRODUCTION	2.2 million liters/ 580,000 gallons

THE GLENLOSSIE DISTILLERY is to be found south of Elgin in the valley of the River Lossie. The Mannochmore Distillery, which was built later than Glenlossie, is on the same premises. There is a also a railway nearby.

Glenlossie was established in 1876 by John Duff. Due to the convenient railway connection and because this whisky was popular with blenders, the business flourished from the start. In 1919 it was acquired by SMD, whose subsidiary, John Haig & Co., was placed in charge of running the business. In 1962, the distillery was extended to six stills, and the Mannochmore Distillery was built on the same property in 1971. In 1987, when DCL came under the ownership of UD, Glenlossie released its first single malt. Today the distillery belongs to the Diageo group.

Glenlossie whisky is grassy, malty and very flowery. It is popular as an aperitif. Smoothness and suppleness are further characteristics associated with Glenlossie.

WHISKY
Glenlossie, 10 years old, 43% ABV, Flora & Fauna
Color: Sherry

TASTING NOTES
The sweet and fruity aroma is accompanied by undertones of coconut and tobacco, as well as the slightest hint

Glenlossie is located on the same property as the newer Mannochmore Distillery. In contrast to its younger sister distillery, Glenlossie's history goes back to 1876.

of heather. The flavor is homogenous, slightly oily and mellow. The finish is subtly malty, with a slight dryness and a touch of spices.

Apart from producing whisky for the Cutty Sark blend, the Glenrothes Distillery has started to release some single malts again.

Glenrothes

THE GLENROTHES DISTILLERY is located on a side road off the main road, slightly hidden, on the outskirts of Rothes.

Glenrothes was founded in 1879 by William Grant & Co. This William Grant, however, should not be confused with the Grant family that established Glenfiddich. Today the distillery is owned by the Edrington Group. After an explosion in 1903 destroyed the buildings, the distillery had to be rebuilt from scratch. In 1922, there was another catastrophe: one of the warehouses burnt to the ground and 2,500 casks were destroyed by the fire.

After yet another incident, but also because of high demand, the distillery was renovated in 1963. During the reconstruction, Glenrothes was extended from four to six stills. In 1980, a new stillhouse with eight stills was built.

GLENROTHES	
OWNER	Edrington Group
ESTABLISHED	1879
MEANING OF NAME	Valley (of the Earl) of Rothes
STATUS	In production
ANNUAL PRODUCTION	5.9 million liters/
	1.55 million gallons

The whisky was not available on the market as a single malt for a long time. Nowadays, official bottlings can be easily identified by the unique bottle and label.

WHISKY

Glenrothes Vintage, 12 years old, 1992 vintage, 43% ABV, official bottling
Color: Golden yellow

TASTING NOTES

The aroma is pleasantly smooth and fruity with a bit of licorice. On the palate, a sherry note is complemented by oak and some orange. The medium-long finish is spicy.

Glentauchers

GLENTAUCHERS	
OWNER	Pernod Ricard
ESTABLISHED	1898
MEANING OF NAME	Valley of the wind
STATUS	In production
ANNUAL PRODUCTION	1.9 million liters/ 502,000 gallons

THE GLENTAUCHERS DISTILLERY is in Mulben, in between Keith and Rothes.

The distillery was built by James Buchanan & Co. in 1898. In 1925, it became part of DCL. It was successfully renovated in 1965; the facilities were extended to include six stills at that time. In 1983, however, a year of crisis for the Scotish whisky industry as a whole, Glentauchers had to shut down. It did not resume production until 1989, after having been sold to Allied. After a series of mergers, the business ended up under the ownership of the Pernod Picard group in 2005.

Glentauchers whisky is rather dry and has a malty sweetness. It was released mainly by independent bottlers. Jim Murray's paperback edition of *The Complete Guide to Whisky* features Glentauchers as one of his five personal favorites.

WHISKY

Glentauchers, 1990/2005 vintage, 40% ABV, Gordon & MacPhail
Color: Amber

Vintage 1975
Single Highland Malt Scotch Whisky

TASTING NOTES

The nose of this slightly smoky malt has a pronounced sherry note, which is complemented by herbs and sweet malt. The strong sherry note is continued on the palate and in the distinct finish.

One of the reasons the Glentauchers Distillery was built in this particular spot was the convenient location near both a street and a railway line.

Inchgower · Kininvie

INCHGOWER

OWNER	UDV (Diageo)
ESTABLISHED	1824
MEANING OF NAME	Field (or island) of goats
STATUS	In production
ANNUAL PRODUCTION	2.3 million liters/ 608,000 gallons

THE INCHGOWER DISTILLERY is located on the A98 road between Fochabers and Buckie, in the furthest reaches of the Speyside region.

The distillery began production in 1871. Its founder, Alexander Wilson, had previously run the Tochineal Distillery, which, however, turned out to be too old and too small for him. The main reason, of course, was that the lease for his former distillery had been increased to twice the original amount. Thus, he decided to build Inchgower. In 1936, the Buckie city fathers bought the distillery from Wilson for a mere £1,000, then sold it to Bell & Sons two years later. The license is issued in the name of Bell & Sons to this day, even though they became part of UD in 1985, and therefore Diageo.

This whisky is used first and foremost for the Bells' blend. As a single malt, it was first bottled as a twelve-year-old, and belongs to the Flora & Fauna series. Every once in a while, there are new releases by independent bottlers.

WHISKY
Inchgower, 27 years old, 1976, 55.6% ABV, Rare Malts
Color: Gold

TASTING NOTES
The nose brings out a waft of hazelnut and some smoke, accompanied by a hint of fruits. This whisky is very pleasant and complex on the palate, with a little malt, citrus fruits, wood and green hazelnuts. The finish is relatively short, with a subtle element of wood, malt and even a little coffee.

KININVIE

OWNER	William Grant & Sons
ESTABLISHED	1990
MEANING OF NAME	End of the beautiful plain
STATUS	In production
ANNUAL PRODUCTION	4.4 million liters/ 1.2 million gallons

ON THE OUTSKIRTS OF DUFFTOWN, in the valley of the River Fiddich, the Kininvie Distillery can be found on the extensive property that is also home to the Glenfiddich and Balvenie Distilleries. Kininvie's mash tun is housed in a Balvenie building, even though the two distilleries are not connected by any pipes and operate entirely independent of each other.

On July 18, 1990, Janet Sheeds Robert of the William Grant & Sons family was on hand to personally open the third active distillery on the site.

Convalmore, a fourth distillery, has since ceased production. Kininvie was built in order to meet steadily increasing requirements for the production of Grant blends, since the demand for Glenfiddich and Balvenie single malts had been skyrocketing, leading to a shortage of whisky for the blends.

The date for a first release of a single malt from the youngest of the family's distilleries has been a matter of speculation for a long time. A number of high-ranking visitors have been fortunate enough to taste Kininvie straight from the cask.

In 2006, finally, Hazelwood 105 was bottled on the occasion of the 105th birthday of Janet Sheeds Roberts, granddaughter of the business founder William Grant and founder of this distillery in 1990. This first-fill sherry cask single malt is fifteen years old and has 52.5 percent ABV. However, it was only distributed among the staff, which is why no tasting notes can be provided.

Knockando

KNOCKANDO

OWNER	UDV (Diageo)
ESTABLISHED	1898
MEANING OF NAME	Little black hill
STATUS	In production
ANNUAL PRODUCTION	1.9 million liters/ 502,000 gallons

THE KNOCKANDO DISTILLERY is on the left bank of the River Spey, tucked away in a little valley not far from the Tamdhu Distillery.

The distillery was built by John Thomson during the whisky boom year of 1898. It only survived the crisis triggered by the Pattison bankruptcy because it was acquired by Gilbey in 1904. In 1962, following the merger of Gilbey and J&B to become IDV, the official owner's name changed once again. The license was made out to Justerini & Brooks until 1977; Justerini & Brooks were also responsible for the 1969 renovation, during which Knockando was extended to four stills. Nowadays the distillery is owned by the Diageo group, which still uses the whisky for the J&B blend. Releases from independent bottlers are quite rare in this case, but official bottlings are easy to come by.

The character of this whisky is very elegant and smooth. It is popular as an aperitif.

WHISKY

Knockando, 12 years old, 1991 vintage, 43% ABV, official bottling
Color: Light gold

🛢 TASTING NOTES

On the nose, the fruity note is immediately noticeable. It is accompanied by a hint of spices and a touch of vanilla. On the palate, a distinct malt tone materializes, and the vanilla note found on the nose is continued. Further flavors include spices and hazelnuts. The increasingly dry finish is surprisingly smooth and has a slight undertone of caramel.

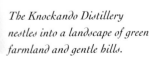
The Knockando Distillery nestles into a landscape of green farmland and gentle hills.

Linkwood

THE LINKWOOD DISTILLERY is located a little south of Elgin.

Linkwood took up production in 1821 and was rebuilt from scratch in 1871. From 1933 onward, it belonged to DCL. The official license holder was the subsidiary John McEwan until 1992, when everything was signed over to UD, which is now UDV and its parent corporation, Diageo. Some 100 years after the reconstruction, an additional stillhouse was added. In 1962, distillery manager Roderick McKenzie oversaw another renovation and had the stills exchanged. He was only willing to resume production after the spiders had woven their webs in the same spots again. Apparently, McKenzie was worried that any change would negatively impact the whisky. He may have had a point: the new stillhouse does not produce a whisky as distinctly individual as the original Linkwood product. When the casks are stored for maturation, however, no distinction is made between those from stillhouse A and stillhouse B.

This whisky is very flowery. Some bottlings are peaty and hearty with a dry maltiness. Linkwood is also often said to have aromas of cherries or rosewater, which makes it an excellent companion for fruit cakes. Those whiskies matured in sherry casks take on distinct sherry flavors. Ever since

the McEwan era, there have been official bottlings in different versions, including releases in the Flora & Fauna series. Cadenhead and Signatory have regularly released bottlings as well. Linkwood whisky is also used in the Abbot's Choice and Chequer's blends.

WHISKY
Linkwood, 12 years old, 43% ABV,
Flora & Fauna
Color: Straw yellow

TASTING NOTES
The slightly sweet nose is reminiscent of vanilla and comes with a hint of smoke. The flavor has a strong note of flowers, with elements of roses and cedar wood. The finish is long and sweetish.

LINKWOOD	
OWNER	UDV (Diageo)
ESTABLISHED	1821
STATUS	In production
ANNUAL PRODUCTION	2.6 million liters/685,000 gallons

A highly aromatic, rather smoky malt is produced in the six Linkwood pot stills.

Longmorn

LONGMORN	
OWNER	Chivas (Pernod Ricard)
ESTABLISHED	1893
MEANING OF NAME	Chapel (or place) of the holy man
STATUS	In production
ANNUAL PRODUCTION	3.5 million liters/ 925,000 gallons

THE LONGMORN DISTILLERY is on the main road that leads from Elgin to Rothes, not far from the Benriac Distillery.

Longmorn was founded by John Duff in 1895, who selected a spot not far from a former chapel, as suggested by the distillery's name. This is probably also the source of a local story that avows the well there will never run dry. When bankruptcy forced Duff to sell, Longmorn was first acquired by the nearby Benriach Distillery. After the merger of Glenlivet and Glen Grant in 1970, Longmorn was renovated and expanded, first to six stills, and finally to eight, which were fired by coal until 1993. Following a takeover by Chivas Brothers and the subsequent acquisition of that group by Pernod Ricard, Longmorn single malt has become increasingly available.

Longmorn whisky is complex and malty, which has earned it a loyal following among connoisseurs.

WHISKY
Longmorn, 15 years old, 45% ABV, official bottling
Color: Dark amber

TASTING NOTES
This malt has a powerful aroma, very malty and fruity, with a slight note of flowers and oil. On the palate it continues the malt theme, complemented by pleasantly sweet and fresh flavors. The finish is very long and remains pleasantly on the sweet malt note.

Longmorn whisky develops to its full potential in the presence of a neighboring small chapel.

Macallan

The sherry casks that Macallan uses exclusively are specially made for them in Jerez, Spain.

MACALLAN	
OWNER	The Edrington Group
ESTABLISHED	1824
MEANING OF NAME	Son of Allan
STATUS	In production
ANNUAL PRODUCTION	5.5 million liters/
	1.5 million gallons

THE MACALLAN DISTILLERY is situated in a park, on a small hill overlooking the River Spey near Craigellachie. The offices and the visitors center in the old Easter Elchie manor house are right in the middle of the park, while the facilities of the distillery proper are just outside it.

Macallan was built in 1824. It was bought by Roderick Kemp in 1892, who had recently sold his share in Talisker. In order to increase sales while preserving the character of the whisky, between 1965 and 1975 the number of stills was increased from six to twenty-one. During the 1980s, Allan Shiach, a direct descendant of the Kemps, was responsible for a highly successful marketing strategy for Macallan single malt. Shiach also enjoyed a successful second career as a screenwriter. In fact, his life's work can be explored at the distillery's visitors center. Writing under the pseudonym Alan Scott, he was the author of many successful screenplays, including *Don't Look Now*. The Macallan Distillery remained family property of the Shiachs until 1996. As time passed, however, it became more and more difficult to resist a takeover, especially since a 25 percent share had been sold to Suntory and a 1 percent share to Rémy during an earlier rocky period. These 26 percent of shares were bought by Highland Distillers, leading to a perfect sales opportunity.

The consequences of the takeover were not as negative as had been feared. The new owners were aware that they had acquired a gem, and did not try to force any changes. Instead, they looked for other means to increase sales. In November 2006, a new visitors center was opened, in which the story of the special oak casks, whisky maturation, and everything else that contributes to the unique Macallan flavor is showcased. Macallan has all their casks made exclusively in Jerez, Spain, where they are first filled with Gonzalez Byass sherry. Once the sherry has matured, the casks are delivered to Macallan. This distillery also offers overnight accommodations on the premises. The renovation of the entire complex cost no less than £1 million.

This whisky stands out for its impressive richness and complexity, with a lovely, well-balanced aroma. It has the typical Speyside malt note of flowers and, thanks to the Oloroso casks, a slight sherry flavor. It is preferably served as a digestive, although there are recent releases that are appropriate as aperitifs.

WHISKY
Macallan Fine Oak, 12 years old, 40% ABV, official bottling
Color: Mahogany

TASTING NOTES
This pleasantly fine, light malt is suitable for newcomers in spite of the complexity and fullness of its aroma. It is smooth on the nose, with elements of fruits and vanilla. The flavor is spicy, very well-balanced; the fruity and malty undertone is present on the palate again and is complemented by a hint of oak. The medium-long finish is increasingly sweet, leaving one with a very pleasant final impression.

Macduff

MACDUFF	
OWNER	William Lawson Distillers Ltd., John Dewar & Sons Ltd. (Bacardi)
ESTABLISHED	1962
MEANING OF NAME	Son of Duff
STATUS	In production
ANNUAL PRODUCTION	2.4 million liters/ 635,000 gallons

Macduff operates five pot stills. It was the first distillery to use mash tuns made of metal.

THE MACDUFF DISTILLERY is located near the coast on the outskirts of Banff, a little north of the River Deveron.

It was built rather recently, only in 1962, by Glen Deveron Distillers, a consortium of four investors (Leslie Kaufman, George Crawford, Brodie Hepburn and Marty Dykes). A mere ten years later, however, in 1972, this group sold Macduff to William Lawson Distillers, a subsidiary of Bacardi. This was significant, because it represented the very beginning of Bacardi's involvement with the whisky business. The name of the distillery hearkens back to the Duff House settlement, which is located on the opposite side of the River Deveron. In 1966, an extra still was added to the two existing pot stills; 1968 saw the extension to four stills; and eventually, in 1990, a fifth still was added. This final extension made it necessary to rebuild the stillhouse to accomodate the most recent addition. The millhouse was renovated in 2000. The Macduff Distillery also operates its own small in-house cooperage.

Official bottlings are sold under the name Glen Deveron. Independent bottlers, however,

label the whisky under the name of the distillery, Macduff. Macduff whisky has a malty sweetness and is often slightly fruity.

WHISKY
Glen Deveron (Macduff), 10 years old, 1996 vintage, 40% ABV, official bottling
Color: Amber

TASTING NOTES
This straightforward Macduff single malt is sold under the name Glen Deveron. Its aroma is malty and fruity and has a pronounced note of wood. On the palate, the fruity note develops further, now accompanied by nuts. The rather short finish is pleasantly mild.

Mannochmore

SPEYSIDE
SINGLE MALT *SCOTCH WHISKY*

MANNOCHMORE

distillery stands a few miles *south* of Elgin in *Morayshire*. The nearby *Millbuies Woods* are rich in birdlife, including the Great *Spotted* Woodpecker. The *distillery* draws process *water* from the Bardon Burn, which has its *source* in the MANNOCH HILLS, and *cooling water* from the Gedloch Burn and the *Burn of Foths*. Mannochmore *single MALT WHISKY* has a *light, fruity* aroma and a *smooth, mellow taste*.

AGED **12** YEARS

43% vol   Distilled & Bottled in *SCOTLAND*. MANNOCHMORE DISTILLERY, Elgin, Moray, Scotland.   70 cl

MANNOCHMORE	
OWNER	UDV (Diageo)
ESTABLISHED	1971
MEANING OF NAME	Tall monk
STATUS	In production (seasonal)
ANNUAL PRODUCTION	2.6 million liters/ 685,000 gallons

SOUTH OF ELGIN AND on the same premises as the Glenlossie Distillery is the Mannochmore Distillery.

The history of Mannochmore dates back to 1971, when John Haig & Co., then a part of DCL, ordered a distillery to be built right next to Glenlossie. Designed with six pot stills, Mannochmore was from the beginning intended to produce more than 265,000 gallons (1 million liters) per year. The actual output was considerably lower than those high expectations, even though the whisky was very popular with blenders. During the 1983 whisky crisis, Mannochmore had to be shut down, but production was resumed in 1989 under UD, the successor to DCL. The major reason for reopening Mannochmore was that the neighboring Glenlossie Distillery had to be closed for extensive renovations. Mannochmore was stilled again in 1995, even though both distilleries were operated by the same staff. Only two years later, production resumed on a seasonal basis. The distillery is currently owned by the Diageo group, which continues limited production.

Mannochmore whisky is similar to the whisky of the neighboring

Glenlossie Distillery, but slightly less complex. It is slightly oily, fruity, with notes of flowers and sometimes of peat. Most bottlings are rather dry. A twelve-year-old was released in the Flora & Fauna series. A special designer whisky named Loch Dhu, which was almost black, caused a stir on the whisky market when it was first released, but it was not a commercial success. Some of the bottlings by independent bottlers, on the other hand, including Signatory, Gordon & MacPhail and Cadenhead, sell quite well. Signatory also released bottlings matured in sherry casks made of South African wood, among them a rare cask-strength malt. Every once in a while, entirely new bottlings enter the market.

WHISKY
Mannochmore South African Sherry, 11 years old, 1991 vintage, 43% ABV, Signatory
Color: Straw yellow

TASTING NOTES
The aroma of this malt is exceptionally fruity, sweet, with notes of apples and vanilla. On the palate, it is slightly oily and very sweet, gentle and soft. The finish is again sweet and dry.

Miltonduff

MILTONDUFF

OWNER	Chivas Brothers (Pernod Ricard)
ESTABLISHED	1824
MEANING OF NAME	Black mills
STATUS	In production
ANNUAL PRODUCTION	3.5 million liters/ 925,000 gallons

THE MILTONDUFF DISTILLERY stands southwest of the town of Elgin, not far from the ruins of Pluscarden Abbey. According to legend, the monks who lived there were already distilling *uisge beatha* ("water of life") as a side enterprise to their beer brewery.

The distillery was founded in 1824 as the first legal business of Andrew Pearey and Robert Bain. Since 2005 it has belonged to beverage giant Pernod Ricard. As was the case with many other distillery concerns, two Lomond stills were added in 1964 in order to produce Mosstowie whisky.

Where the monks of Pluscarden Abbey once made their spirits is now the Miltonduff Distillery.

They were not used for very long and were disassembled in 1981. In 1974–1975 the complex was completely renovated, including the addition of a new stillhouse and mash house, increasing the number of washbacks from eight to eighteen.

Miltonduff whisky rates very high with blenders. The single malt is an ingredient in both Ballantine and Teachers Scotch. Bottled as a single malt, this fine whisky is only rarely available.

WHISKY

Miltonduff, 10 years old, 40% ABV
Gordon & MacPhail
Color: Amber

 **TASTING NOTES**
The aroma is scrumptious vanilla with light peat. The flavor is somewhat flowery, with the vanilla note continuing and the smoky note coming through at the end. The finish is rather strong, with a dash of nuttiness.

Mortlach

THE MORTLACH DISTILLERY is located on the outskirts of Dufftown, not far from Mortlach Kirk, one of the oldest churches in Scotland, which is said to have been built in 566. The distillery itself also stands upon the crossroads of history: in 1010, Scottish King Malcolm II defeated the Danes on this very spot.

The distillery was founded early on. It was built in either 1832 or 1823—no one knows for sure anymore. In comparison to most others, Mortlach has gone through relatively few changes of ownership. For a brief time it belonged to J.&J. Grant of Glen Grant. In 1854 it was sold to George Cowie, who kept it in the family for many years. His name can still be found on the door of what was once his office. The company was eventually taken over by DCL and, like so many other distilleries, wound up as part of the UDV and Diageo empires.

Mortlach whisky has always been very popular with blenders. It is an important element in Johnny Walker, among many other brands. In the early years, it never occurred to its owners to bring out a single malt bottling, but fortunately, Gordon & MacPhail would frequently have it on offer in their specialty shop in Elgin. It is only in recent years that multiple bottlings have been produced in-house. The label on its ten-year-old malt, interestingly, still bears the name of George Cowie & Sons as manufacturers.

One of the truly complex single malts, Mortlach whisky is very flowery, fruity and malty. In addition, it is usually deeply smoky and peaty. Many bottlings have an additional pleasant note of sherry.

MORTLACH	
OWNER	UDV (Diageo)
ESTABLISHED	1823
MEANING OF NAME	Spoon-shaped valley, great green hill
STATUS	In production
ANNUAL PRODUCTION	2 million liters/ 528,000 gallons

WHISKY

Mortlach, 16 years old, 43% ABV, Flora and Fauna
Color: Mahogany

TASTING NOTES

The aroma is lightly smoky alongside light orange notes. Despite the lightness, the nose is persistent and intense. On the palate the flavors are very nutty, pleasant and minimally salty. In the finish, the nutty influences are occasionally accompanied by a return of the light smokiness.

An image from olden days. As late as the 1950s, the casks for maturation of the whisky were still being made in the Mortlach Distillery's own coopery.

Royal Brackla

ROYAL BRACKLA	
OWNER	Dewar & Sons (Bacardi)
ESTABLISHED	1812
MEANING OF NAME	Place of the fallen trees
STATUS	In production
ANNUAL PRODUCTION	2.6 million liters/ 685,000 gallons

The Brackla Distillery received its royal license in 1835 and since then has been entitled to call itself Royal Brackla.

THE ROYAL BRACKLA DISTILLERY is located in Cawdor, due south of Nairn. Nearby is the famous castle, also called Brackla, where Macbeth is said to have lived. There is also a brook of the same name, from which the distillery draws its water supply.

Captain William Fraser founded the distillery in 1812. The honorific "Royal" was awarded in 1835 because William IV was particularly fond of the whisky made by Brackla. Queen Victoria must have liked it, too: she extended the privilege. Royal Brackla was the first of only three distilleries that are still permitted to use that title today.

Following many changes of ownership, at first still within the family, John Bisset & Co. Ltd. purchased the company in 1926. In 1943 it was sold to a subsidiary of DCL, and soon after that to UDV. In 1998 it was sold to comply with anti-monopoly laws, this time to Bacardi, which owns Royal Brackla today.

The distillery was shut down during the Second World War. Its owners completely renovated the facility in 1965–1966, expanding the complex further in 1970 from two stills to four. Between 1985 and 1991, production at the distillery was stopped once again.

Under its previous ownership, the whisky produced by Royal Brackle was used almost solely for the Johnny Walker Gold Label blend. Currently, it is primarily found in Dewar's White Label. It was once part of UD's Flora & Fauna series, and was later bottled as a Rare Malt.

Barcardi uses Royal Brackla whisky mainly in blends, with single bottlings only available from the independents Gordon & MacPhail, Cadenhead or Signatory. Royal Brackla single malt is fairly fruity and relatively dry, often with a sharp finish.

WHISKY
Royal Brackla, The Coopers Choice, Single Cask, 15 years old, 1984/2000 vintage, 57.9% ABV, The Vintage Malt Whisky Co. Ltd.
Color: Lovely golden yellow

TASTING NOTES
The aroma is rather light and fruity with the sweet notes of vanilla and licorice. The flavor on the palate is quite sharp, with strong oak influences tempered by sweetness. The finish is long and warming, with strong woody elements.

Speyburn

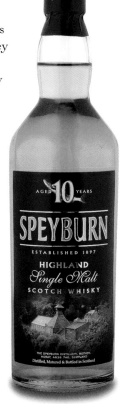

SPEYBURN DISTILLERY is beautifully situated in a valley near Rothes. From the old road to Elgin, one has a view over the entire distillery.

Speyburn's founder company was a subsidiary of John Hopkins & Co. The distillery dates to 1897, the year in which Queen Victoria celebrated her sixtieth jubilee. Every effort was made to complete construction and start production during the jubilee year. Thanks to the workers' tremendous efforts, exactly one cask could be produced in the icy cold of winter before the year was out. In 1916, Hopkins merged with DCL, and the license was transferred to John Robertson & Sons. Speyburn whisky had always played a large role in their Yellow Label blend. UD, the successor of DCL, bottled Speyburn as a single malt in their Flora & Fauna series, then sold the distillery in the early 1990s to Inver House, which still owns it today.

SPEYBURN	
OWNER	Inver House (InterBrew)
ESTABLISHED	1897
MEANING OF NAME	Spey bay
STATUS	In production
ANNUAL PRODUCTION	1.2 million liters/ 317,000 gallons

Speyburn whisky is full of character, flowery and heathery.

WHISKY
Speyburn, 10 years old, 40% ABV, official bottling
Color: Golden yellow

TASTING NOTES
The aroma of this quite mild malt has light flowery notes paired with a hint of hay, heather and honey. In the balanced taste, heather and other new herb notes come to the fore, accompanied by a malty sweetness. The malt returns fresh and sweet in the finish.

The plants growing all around the distillery seem to make their way into the taste of Speyburn whiskies.

Speyside

SPEYSIDE	
OWNER	Speyside Distillery Co. Ltd.
ESTABLISHED	1990
MEANING OF NAME	Spey region
STATUS	In production
ANNUAL PRODUCTION	600,000 liters/ 158,500 gallons

There are many lovely, traditional buildings tucked between the mountain slopes near the village of Kingussie.

THE SPEYSIDE DISTILLERY stands at the confluence of the rivers Tromie and Spey, on the B970 highway four miles from the village of Kingussie. Close by is the original Speyside Distillery, the first to carry the name of this famous whisky-producing region.

The Speyside Distillery was founded fairly recently. In the 1950s, whisky blender George Christie wanted to start his own company here, as had long been his dream. It was not until 1964, though, that the impressive, gabled stone distillery was completed. Driving past the original distillery, one has the impression that it has been standing for a hundred years, instead of forty or so. Even more unusual is the date when whisky actually began to flow here for the first time. Due to myriad crises in the whisky industry, it was 1990 before whisky from Speyside Distillery came on the market. In the end, it only happened at all because the Swiss investor group Scowis bought into the Christie family operation. Three years later, the first bottle of Drumguish, named after a local village, was ready for sale. So little was produced that after three years, the first

Speyside single malt could only be sold to those who had helped with construction of the distillery. In 2000, the management of Speyside Distillery, now the Speyside Distillers Co., bought out the Swiss investment firm, including the bottling facility in Broxburn.

Drumguish whisky is rather oily with a light peat note, flowery and hazelnut-nutty. The Speyside single malt is similar to Drumguish, but without the turfy, smoky notes. The finish is characterized by vanilla flavors. Speyside single malt is best enjoyed as an aperitif. The ten- and twelve-year-old versions have been on the market for quite some time, and the latter has received a number of awards.

WHISKY
Speyside, 12 years old, 40% ABV, official bottling
Color: Amber

🛢 TASTING NOTES
The most recent 12-year-old single malt from this young distillery was released in 2006. Its aroma recalls roasted barley, but is still very delicate and balanced. The flavors are silky-creamy, complemented by a light turfy smoke and hazelnut notes. The medium-length finish leaves behind gentle traces of caramel or vanilla.

Strathisla

STRATHISLA DISTILLERY is on the outskirts of the village of Keith near a small river named Isla, from which its name is derived.

Monks were already brewing beer here in the thirteenth century, using the same hard water, which is almost devoid of peat. The distillery has been in operation since 1786, when it was known as Milltown (It was later renamed Milton). In 1876, the first in a series of catastrophes struck when a fire damaged the main building. Eleven years later, it was destroyed by an explosion. By then, the distillery was known by its current name, Strathisla, but was renamed again. Ruin seemed certain in 1949 when the London speculators who owned it were convicted of tax fraud. When their assets were auctioned off, Chivas Brothers, at that time owners of Seagram, were the high bidders. They restored the name of Strathisla, boosted it to the top distillery in their group, and generally gave the brand the tender loving care it had been missing.

Despite its expansion to four stills, Strathisla whisky is still produced by traditional methods.

STRATHISLA

OWNER	Chivas Brothers (Pernod Ricard)
ESTABLISHED	1786
MEANING OF NAME	Broad valley of the Isla
STATUS	In production
ANNUAL PRODUCTION	2.5 million liters/ 660,000 gallons

The remaining original buildings were left standing, making this distillery complex one of the most beautiful in Scotland. After an extended period of mergers and company takeovers, Strathisla came under the ownership of Pernod Ricard in 2005.

Strathisla whisky is dry and fruity. It is best enjoyed as a digestive.

WHISKY

Strathisla, 12 years old, 43% ABV, official bottling
Color: Deep, strong gold

TASTING NOTES

This malt has a strong aroma with a gentle sweetness and additional light smoky note. It is notably mild on the palate, with the turf notes returning along with the malty sweetness and a touch of nuts. The finish is long and strong, with nut and tender smoke notes returning.

Strathisla, with its fieldstone buildings and small water wheel, is without a doubt one of the most beautiful distilleries in Scotland.

Strathmill

STRATHMILL	
OWNER	UDV (Diageo)
ESTABLISHED	1891
MEANING OF NAME	Mill in a (broad) valley
STATUS	In production
ANNUAL PRODUCTION	1.7 million liters/ 450,000 gallons

Strathmill whisky is chiefly used in the J&B blend, appearing only rarely as an individually bottled single malt.

THE STRATHMILL DISTILLERY, like Strathisla, stands near the small Isla River on the outskirts of the village of Keith. There is a cooperage nearby, as well as a third whisky distillery.

Keith was once a central milling village where flour was produced from grain brought to market from the surrounding areas. It is no surprise that Strathmill Distillery is on the site of the former mill that gives it its name. When the distillery was officially founded in 1891, however, it was named Glenisla, after the river. Well back in time, around 1823, the same building had already seen use as a distillery, but in 1837, the complex was converted back into a milling operation. In 1895 the Glenisla Distillery was sold to W & A Gilbey for £9,500. That company merged with Justerini & Brooks in 1962, becoming IDV. Further mergers led to the distillery becoming part of UDV, and later Diageo. In 1968, two additional stills were built, bringing the total number to four. For many years, a sign declaring this to be "Home of Dunhill" hung near the entrance, reminding visitors that the malt produced here was an important component of the Dunhill blend. At some point, sadly, the Dunhill sign was replaced with a standard J&B logo, as J&B is the blend in which Strathmill malt is most commonly found today.

Strathmill whisky is employed almost exclusively in its own unique blends, making it one of the lesser known single malts. Former owner Gilbey produced a few single bottlings, and it can be found in the Flora & Fauna series today. Every now and then, an independent single malt bottling comes on the market. The whisky is for the most part very fruity with a note reminiscent of nutmeg. For this reason it is best served with dessert.

WHISKY
Strathmill, 12 years old, 43% ABV,
Flora & Fauna series
Color: Golden yellow

TASTING NOTES
This malt, very rich and heavy, is not at all typical of those produced in the Speyside region. The aroma is dry, malty and nutty. Sherry appears late, and reappears later on the palate, complemented by vanilla and caramel notes. The finish is medium-long and amazingly soft.

Tamdhu

THE TAMDHU DISTILLERY lies between the villages of Knockando and Cardhu along the Speyside Way, a former railroad line.

The distillery was founded in 1897 to serve as a supplier for blended whisky brands. The location was chosen because of its proximity to the railway line, which simplified transport from the factory to the blenders. Only one year after its founding, Tandhu was forced to shut down, one of many distilleries ruined by the Pattisons' collapse. It did not remain closed for long, however. That very same year it was bought by its current owners, the

Highland Distillers, which has since changed names to become the Edrington Group Ltd. The whisky was first produced primarily for the blend The Famous Grouse, and more recently (since 1997) for the Dunhill blend. The well-maintained distillery gets its raw materials, both the grain and the peat, from the immediate area, and production methods remain highly traditional. It still has Saladin boxes, in which all the grain needed for production is malted, which is quite uncommon these days. Tamdhu produces so much malted grain that it supplies nearby distilleries as well. At one time, the distillery ran a visitors center in the old train station, which has unfortunately since closed. The reason given was that Tamdhu lay at the very end of the Whisky Trail, and many of

Tandhu is in a valley between the villages of Knockando and Cardhu. The distillery is able to procure all its raw materials from this fertile area.

TAMDHU	
OWNER	The Edrington Group
ESTABLISHED	1897
MEANING OF NAME	Dark hill
STATUS	In production
ANNUAL PRODUCTION	4 million liters/ 1.06 million gallons

the visitors arrived having already sampled a great deal of whisky, in a rather excitable state. The female distillery employees complained of harassment, forcing the company management to shut down the visitors center.

WHISKY
Tamdhu, 18 years old, 43% ABV, official bottling
Color: Amber

TASTING NOTES
For this whisky, only malt from the distillery's own malting operation, which is dried by a peat fire, was used. In spite of this, it is only minimally smoky. Instead, it has a very fruity aroma, with a little ginger. Its flavor is sweet and soft, with a hint of honey and a little oak. The finish is lightly spicy and pleasantly soft.

The Glenlivet

THE GLENLIVET

OWNER	Chivas (Pernod Ricard)
ESTABLISHED	1824
MEANING OF NAME	Valley of Livet
STATUS	In production
ANNUAL PRODUCTION	6 million liters/ 1.58 million gallons

This is the only distillery with official license to add "the" to its name in order to distinguish itself from all the other distilleries in the Livet Valley (Glen Livet in Scottish).

THE GLENLIVET DISTILLERY is in the valley of the River Livet, near the point where the Livit and Avon converge and the valley gives way to rolling hills.

George Smith founded this distillery in 1824 after trying for some time to get an official license. His son supported him in this effort, and took over the enterprise upon this father's death. Prior to 1824, the region was well known as a hotbed of illegal whisky distilling. In 1858, The Glenlivet moved to its present location, into buildings that still stand today. The distillery building itself is known as Minmore. The company was sold to Glen Grant in 1953. Some twenty years later, Longmorn and Hill, Thomson & Co. were added to the group, which called itself Glenlivet Distillers. The North American beverage giant Seagram took over the entire operation in 1977.

The Glenlivet whisky has characteristics that many associate with the River Livet itself: clear,

The Glenlivet Distillery lies in a high valley between the soft rolling hills of the upper Livet River. At one time there were as many as 200 illegal distilleries in this valley alone.

flowery, fine and elegant. It is particularly pleasing as an aperitif.

WHISKY
The Glenlivet, 18 years old, 43% ABV, official bottling
Color: Amber

 ## TASTING NOTES

Thanks to its many nuances, warmth and intensity, The Glenlivet single malt is unique. Its aroma includes light notes of peat smoke with a little oak wood and a light sweetness in the background. The flavors on the palate are sweet, nutty and floral. Its long finish brings the return of the flowery sweetness, coming to an ever so slightly bitter conclusion.

Tomatin

THE TOMATIN DISTILLERY lies at the northern foot of the Grampian Mountains, just off the A9 highway. It is 1033 feet (315 m) above sea level, which in Scotland is quite a substantial elevation.

The distillery was built during the whisky boom year of 1897, and like so many others, shut down the same year in the wake of the Pattisons' collapse. It re-opened in 1909 and was greatly expanded in 1956 and 1962. Tomatin whisky was soon an integral element in many famous blends. In 1974, demand was so high that the distillery was expanded once more. Boasting no fewer than twenty-four stills, it was honored with the super-lative "Greatest Distillery in Scotland." The plant was also very profitable. Its size, however, would soon be the very thing that nearly brought it to ruin. Its savior was the Japanese consortium Takara Shuzo & Co. and Okura. At the time, the Tomatin Distillery was the first Scottish company to be fully owned by a Japanese concern. Okura eventually ended its partnership with Takara Shuzo for financial reasons, and Takara Shuzo remains the sole owner today. The distillery complex now produces only a sixth of its maximum capacity during its heyday. The enormous ware-houses, capable of storing 10.6 million gallons (40 million l) of whisky, are only partially filled. The majority of Tomatin's production is shipped in bulk directly to Japan, where it is blended with a local grain whisky.

Tomatin whisky is a good choice for beginning whisky drinkers who, after sampling light single malts, are ready to move on to something stronger. It is best enjoyed after a good meal because it is

The Valley of Findhorn is home to Scotland's largest malt distillery. Today, unlike in this 1965 photo, the giant warehouses are only partially filled.

TOMATIN	
OWNER	Takara & Co Ltd.
ESTABLISHED	1897
MEANING OF NAME	Juniper bush
STATUS	In production
ANNUAL PRODUCTION	9 million liters/ 2.4 million gallons

full of flavor, but not particularly complex, slightly spicy and has a well-rounded malt note.

WHISKY

Tomatin, 12 years old, 40% ABV, official bottling
Color: Amber

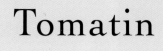 **TASTING NOTES**

The aroma of this single malt is consistently spicy, with herbal and nutty influences. The flavor on the palate is malty-sweet and fruity, with apple and peach being the most noticeable. Caramel notes and a return of the nuttiness complete the assemblage. The very intense flavors return at the finish, supple-mented by a mild smokiness.

Tomintoul

TOMINTOUL	
OWNER	Angus Dundee Distillers plc
ESTABLISHED	1964
MEANING OF NAME	Barn on a hill
STATUS	In production
ANNUAL PRODUCTION	3 million liters/ 793,000 gallons

LOCATED IN A WILDLY ROMANTIC setting on the edge of a forest, the Tomintoul Distillery is also quite near the River Avon. It does not draw its water from the river, however, preferring to use the crystal clear Ballantruan Spring. Starting out from the village that shares its name—the highest elevated town in the region—it is a drive of around eight miles to the Tomintoul Distillery.

The distillery began production only in 1964. It was owned variously by W. & S. Strong and Hay & MacLeod. In 1972, the distillery was sold to Scottish & Universal Investment, who had purchased Whyte & Mackay in the same year. Whyte & Mackay took over the principal duties of ownership, although the parent firm ended up under the control of Invergordon. It was Invergordon that coordinated distribution of the single malt. Despite already having endured so many changes of ownership and management within such a short time, the distillery was sold yet again in 2000 to Angus Dundee Distillers plc, a privately owned London firm. Today, the distillery has four pot stills producing its whisky.

Tomintoul whisky has the lightest aroma of all the single malts from the region. It is grassy, often with fruity notes, and is wonderful served as an aperitif.

WHISKY
Tomintoul, 16 years old, 40% ABV, official bottling
Color: Amber

 TASTING NOTES

This 16-year-old malt is more balanced than the 10-year-old. With a greater sherry influence, it is also sweeter. The aroma is very malty-soft, with a hint of light peat smoke. This returns, together with the sweetness, on the palate. The finish is very clean and medium long.

Tomintoul is part of the Malt Whisky Trail that travels a 155-mile (250-km) route through Speyside, with stops at a good many distilleries along the way.

Opposite: View of Loch Avon from the Cairngorn Plateau. Tomintoul is not far from the River Avon.

Tormore

TORMORE

OWNER	Pernod Ricard
ESTABLISHED	1958
MEANING OF NAME	Big hill
STATUS	In production
ANNUAL PRODUCTION	3.4 million liters/ 898,000 gallons

THE TORMORE DISTILLERY stands just below the Cromdale Hills along the A95 highway between Aberlour and Grantown-on-Spey.

The historicizing style of the actually quite modern distillery building is hard to miss: it resembles a nineteenth-century distillery down to the last detail. It may come as a surprise to learn that it was built as recently as 1960. Its architect, Sir Albert Richardson, designed the complex for the owners at the time, Long John International, to include an artificial lake, one so lovely and inviting that few tourists pass up the chance to take a few photos in front of it. Complete with a quaint bell tower, the entirety of Tormore is simply marvelous. Sadly, there is still no visitors center.

The whisky is bold, nutty, lightly sweet and well-rounded. Unfortunately, it is only very rarely available as a single malt bottling, since the distillery was meant from the very beginning to serve the Long John blend.

WHISKY
Tormore, 12 years old, 40% ABV, official bottling
Color: Light amber

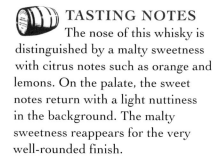 **TASTING NOTES**
The nose of this whisky is distinguished by a malty sweetness with citrus notes such as orange and lemons. On the palate, the sweet notes return with a light nuttiness in the background. The malty sweetness reappears for the very well-rounded finish.

With its small well, bell tower and green roof, Tormore Distillery is certainly one of the loveliest in Scotland.

Banff · Braeval

BANFF

OWNER	UDV (Diageo)
ESTABLISHED	1824
MEANING OF NAME	Poetic name for Ireland
STATUS	Demolished

THE BANFF DISTILLERY stood less than two miles west of the village of the same name.

The distillery was probably built around 1863, though other sources suggest there are records of it dating back to 1824. In any case, Banff once supplied the British House of Commons with whisky, and it has survived a number of catastrophes. In 1877, the distillery burnt in a tremendous blaze. During the Second World War, on August 16, 1941, it was bombed by the German Luftwaffe. The distillery had belonged to SMD as of 1932, which means that like so many others, Banff Distillery ended up as part of the beverage

giant Diageo. The final stroke of bad luck occurred in 1983, when another fire sealed its fate. Diageo shut it down and dismantled the distilling equipment. There are nevertheless still a few bottles in circulation from its final years of production. In addition, casks of the malt turn up every now and then, which are sold by independent bottlers.

WHISKY
Banff, 12 years old, 1981 vintage, 57.1% ABV, Rare Malts series
Color: Glistening gold

 TASTING NOTES
This whisky immediately wins one over with the tantalizing aroma of hazelnuts. The taste brings to mind a vanilla wafer. The finish is middle long, with hints of oat biscuits, nuts and ginger preserves.

BRAEVAL

OWNER	Pernod Ricard
ESTABLISHED	1973
MEANING OF NAME	Steep cliff
STATUS	Closed
ANNUAL PRODUCTION	3.8 million liters/ 1 million gallons

THE BRAEVAL DISTILLERY lies in a valley called Braes of Glenlivet. The distillery once had the same lengthy name as the valley, but changed it so as not to be confused with The Glenlivet Distillery. Both distilleries belong to the same company. Braeval stands directly beneath a mighty mountain ridge. A stream that flows into the Livet runs beneath the property.

The distillery was built by Chivas (Seagram) in 1973–1974 and already expanded one year later. In 2001 it was closed, but kept in good condition

with all its equipment in place and in good working order so that it could begin production again on short notice. In 2005, the Braeval Distillery became part of Pernod Ricard after it acquired Braeval's parent company, Allied Domecq.

WHISKY
Braeval Deerstalker, 10 years old, 40% ABV
Color: Honey gold

 TASTING NOTES
The aroma of this light whisky is strongly malty. The palate flavors add a note of grapefruit. The finish is very pleasant, with vanilla influences.

155

Caperdonich · Coleburn

CAPERDONICH

OWNER	Pernod Ricard
ESTABLISHED	1898
MEANING	Secret spring
STATUS	Closed

CAPERDONICH IS JUST ONE of several distilleries in the small village of Rothes that have permanently closed their doors.

The Caperdonich Distillery was founded in the 1898 boom year by J. & J. Grant. Built just opposite the Glen Grant complex, the new distillery was originally named Glen Grant Nr. 2. Alas, it did not survive the Pattison's debacle, and was shut down only three years later. The facility was silent until 1965, when Chivas stepped in and reactivated it. The distillery was expanded to include four stills and was completely modernized. As of 1977 it belonged to Seagram, which itself ended up as part of Allied Domecq. After just three months of production in 2001, the distillery

was shut down for good in the following year. Since then, the facility has been silent. In 2005 it was acquired by Pernod Ricard following its purchase of Allied.

The whisky is smoky, very dry, with a flavor that suggests dried fruit, such as raisins. Since the distillery mainly produced whisky for blends, there has only been a single official bottling, a special edition sold only in Italy. There have been occasional bottlings by Gordon & MacPhail, Cadenhead and Signatory.

WHISKY
Caperdonich, 1980 vintage, 46% ABV, Gordon & MacPhail, Connoisseurs Choice
Color: Golden amber

 **TASTING NOTES**
The aroma of this whisky is fruity, reminiscent of dates. On the palate it is oily and mild, with a note of hazelnut liquor. The finish is short and restrained.

COLEBURN

OWNER	UDV (Diageo)
ESTABLISHED	1897
MEANING	Brook on the corner
STATUS	Closed

THE SHUTTERED COLEBURN DISTILLERY sits in a valley running roughly along the A491 highway between Elgin and Rothes. Just opposite the complex are railroad tracks where trains ran until 1966.

The distillery was founded in 1897 by John Robertson & Sons, who were already famous for their Yellow Label whisky. In 1916, the Clynelish Distillery Co. took over, and in 1925, the DCL. The license was then transferred to J & G Steward, producer of the popular Usher blend. In 1985, Coleburn was shut down for good. UD, successor to UCL, allowed its license to lapse in 1992. At the

end of 2004, there was discussion about plans to revamp the complex as a concert hall, hotel and shopping center.

The only original single malt bottling was released in 2000 as part of the Rare Malts series. It has been up to the independent bottlers to issue the malt in special editions, despite the fact that tracking down Coleburn Distillery casks has proved very difficult, making the single malt a genuine collector's item. The whisky itself is very fruity, semi-dry and oily.

WHISKY
Coleburn Connoissieurs Choice, 30 years old, 1972 vintage, 40% ABV, Gordon & MacPhail
Color: Amber

TASTING NOTES
This rare bottling comes from a refill hogshead cask. The aroma, flavor and dry finish are all characteristically fruity.

Convalmore · Dallas Dhu

CONVALMORE

OWNER	William Grant & Sons
ESTABLISHED	1893
MEANING OF NAME	Big Conval Mountain
STATUS	Closed

THE CONVALMORE DISTILLERY is in the Fiddich River valley, directly above the Balvenie Distillery and at the entrance to the village of Dufftown.

The distillery was founded in 1894, and by 1906 was part of the beverage empire of James Buchanan. He experimented with column stills until 1916, but reverted to pot stills thereafter. In 1925, the distillery was taken over by DCL. It remained closed during the Second World War, and in 1985 was shut down for good. In the end, UD sold Convalmore to William Grant & Sons, owners of the neighboring Balvenie Distillery. Since then,

the new owners have used the Convalmore buildings as warehouses.

The whisky was mainly used in Black & White and Lowrie's blends. The owners only produced one single malt bottling, in 1977, as part of the Rare Malts series; they also appeared infrequently from an independent bottler. This whisky was fruity, full-bodied and malty, best enjoyed as a digestive.

WHISKY
Convalmore, 28 years old, 57.9% ABV, official bottling
Color: Intense gold

 TASTING NOTES
This single malt has a very flowery and fruity aroma. Its complex taste includes citrus fruit complemented by soft malt notes. The finish is long, warm and nutty, with the hint of citrus returning.

DALLAS DHU

OWNER	UDV (Diageo)
ESTABLISHED	1898
MEANING OF NAME	Meadow by the black waterfall
STATUS	Closed, converted into a museum

DALLAS DHU IS NOT FAR outside of Forres along the A940 highway toward Grantown-on-Spey, somewhat hidden behind a small forest.

The distillery was built in 1898 and managed by Wright & Greig, who also owned the Roderick Dhu blend. In 1929, Dallas Dhu fell under the control of DCL, and it had to be rebuilt in 1939 after extensive fire damage. It was shut down for good in 1983 after rumors spread that its water source was contaminated. In 1986 it passed into the hands of Historic Scotland, which restored the distillery and reopened it in 1988 as a museum. In 1992, the new owner, UD let its liquor license lapse. Had they maintained it, the distillery-museum might have been able to resume production some day.

The whisky was produced primarily for the Roderick Dhu and Benmore blends. The single malt was bottled as part of the Rare Malts series, as well as in a cask-strength 24-year-old limited Millennium Edition bottling. There were also regular releases by independent bottlers. The whisky is very silky and honey-sweet with rich, chocolate notes. It is best enjoyed as a digestive.

WHISKY
Dallas Dhu, 1982/2005, 40% ABV, Gordon & MacPhail
Color: Straw yellow

 TASTING NOTES
It has a characteristic aroma of barley, quite spicy with woody nuances. The flavor emphasizes the barley again, supplemented by citrus fruits and a light smokiness. Its slightly sharp finish is on the dry side, with a soft touch of malt.

Glen Keith · Glendullan

GLEN KEITH

OWNER	Chivas Brothers (Pernod Ricard)
ESTABLISHED	1957
MEANING	Wooded valley
STATUS	Closed

THE GLEN KEITH DISTILLERY stands on the banks of the Isla River not far from its sister facility, Strathisla, in the village of Keith.

Glen Keith was constructed on the site of an old grain mill in 1957. Seagram, its owner at the time, built giant warehouses to be used by all nine of its distilleries for storage, preparation and blending. In 1970, Glen Keith was expanded to include five stills. A Saladin box for on-site malting was added in 1976, and a sixth still was installed in 1983. Nevertheless, production ceased in 2002 following the 2001 takeover by the Pernod Ricard group.

The single malt has twice appeared on the market as a 10-year-old, twice as an official

bottling, and occasionally as a special edition sold by independent bottlers. The whisky was most commonly used in the Chivas Regal, 100 Pipers and Passport blends. Glen Keith whisky is malty and slightly sharp with a hint of ginger.

WHISKY
Craigduff, 32 years old, 1973 vintage, 49.9% ABV, Signatory Vintage
Color: Intense gold

 ### TASTING NOTES
This single malt named Craigsduff sparked quite some conversation and debate. It was discovered that it comes from Glen Keith, not Strathisla, and was aged in sherry casks. It is lightly smoky. The sherry asserts itself, but not so much as to conceal the definitive malty character of this whisky.

GLENDULLAN

OWNER	UDV (Diageo)
ESTABLISHED	1897
MEANING	Valley of Dullan
STATUS	Closed

GLENDULLAN WAS ONE of the seven original distilleries in Dufftown.

Williams & Sons, blenders from Aberdeen, founded Glendullan in 1897. They provided whisky for King Edward VII, among others, an honor that served as an excellent marketing tool for many years. The distillery was sold in 1919, ending up as part of DCL in 1926. The facility was modernized in 1962. Nine years later, however, a brand new distillery with eight stills was built right next door. It quickly took over most of the production from

Opposite: Small roads meander through the lovely landscape around the former whisky capital of Dufftown.

Glendullan, but the two distilleries continued to work side by side as Glendullan A and B until 1985. At that time, the older one was closed and turned into a maintenance shop for the rest of the company. That workshop is still in use, although the newer distillery has also since closed.

The whisky was used in blends like Dewar's, Bell's, Black & White, Old Parr and Johnnie Walker. Single malt from the old distillery was considered fuller and herbier; that from the newer one was light, fruity, dry and somewhat oily.

WHISKY
Glendullan, 12 years old, 43% ABV, Flora & Fauna series
Color: Pale gold

 ### TASTING NOTES
Glendullan has a highly complex aroma with a variety of exotic fruit notes. The taste is fruity and lightly nutty. The finish is very aromatic with hints of dark chocolate.

Imperial

IMPERIAL	
OWNER	Pernod Ricard
ESTABLISHED	1897
STATUS	Closed
ANNUAL PRODUCTION	1.6 million liters/423,000 gallons

THE IMPERIAL DISTILLERY is in the town of Carron, near Abelour, directly on a former railroad line. The Speyside Way, an idyllic wagon track through the region, used to run along the levee next to the tracks.

Thomas Mackenzie founded the distillery in 1897, the year of Queen Victoria's sixtieth Jubilee. The name "Imperial" was chosen to honor the occasion. Its architect was Charles Doig, who had designed the famous pagoda in Kew Gardens. The air came out of the enterprise early, as it became caught up in the Pattison's collapse and was forced to close just three years later in 1900. In 1915, a consortium led by James Buchanan, John Dewar and John Walker took over the company, reopening it for production in 1919. It came under the control of DCL in 1925, and from 1926 to 1954 only the malting floors were in use. In 1955, the complex was modernized and expanded to four stills. After it was shut down again in 1985, it was reopened in 1988 following its purchase by Allied. By 1998, it was once again in production, but was finally shut down for good in 2000. The buildings and grounds now belong to Pernod Ricard.

Every spring, a vast number of toads make their way to the old stillhouse. They arrive via the rear entrance and hop right through the building, heading out the main entrance. The owners handle this odd situation with aplomb, patience and good humor. A much greater problem is posed by the four enormous stills, each of which has a capacity of around 9,500 gallons (36,000 l). Their size alone makes them relatively inflexible. As the saying goes, either make a lot of Imperial, or none at all.

The single malt has only appeared as an official bottling once, although independent bottlers occasionally produce a special edition on their own. Whisky expert Michael Jackson has named Imperial one of the most undervalued single malts from the Speyside region. During its time under Allied ownership, the whisky was mainly used in blends such as Black Bottle, whose logo is still displayed on the sign outside the distillery's entrance.

This whisky's style is very sweet and strong, sometimes with an element of smoke.

WHISKY

Imperial Cognac Wood Finish, Private Collection Series, 1991 vintage, 40% ABV, Gordon & MacPhail
Color: Straw yellow

 **TASTING NOTES**

The first impression is the powerful scent of sweet cognac, an aroma that only strengthens in the mouth, where it lingers, sweet and pleasant. The finish is medium-long, with a surprising sharpness at the conclusion.

In the end, the Imperial Distillery was done in by its sheer size. It was shut down in 2000, probably for good.

Pittyvaich · Tamnavulin

PITTYVAICH

OWNER	UDV (Diageo)
ESTABLISHED	1975
MEANING OF NAME	The farm with the cow barn
STATUS	Demolished

PITTYVAICH ONCE STOOD on the grounds of the Dufftown Distillery, which included a farm. The name Pittyvaich probably stems from this.

Arthur Bell & Sons founded the distillery in 1975 with the goal of producing large quantities of whisky to be sold to blenders. It was the eighth distillery built in Dufftown, making obsolete the local proverb: "Rome was built on seven hills, Dufftown stands on seven stills." After Bell was taken over by Guinness in 1985, UD let the license lapse, shutting down the distillery in 1993. Thereafter it was only used for specific purposes, such as distilling gin. Later, under Diageo, the Pittyvaich

stills were used to experiment with different types of barley and distilling techniques. In 2002, Pittyvaich was closed for good and demolished.

While owned by the Bells, the whisky was never bottled as a single malt. Independent bottlers such as MacArthur, Cadenhead and Signatory have since issued special editions. Intially, the whisky was known for its fine, peaty aroma. Later, as part of the Flora & Fauna series, the single malt was more distinguished for its sherry notes.

WHISKY
Pittyvaich, 12 years old, 43% ABV,
Flora & Fauna series
Color: Deep amber

 TASTING NOTES
The nose has a fine, strong note of sherry. The flavor is vibrant, fruity with a little malt. The long finish is dry and aromatic.

TAMNAVULIN

OWNER	Whyte & Mackay Ltd.
ESTABLISHED	1966
MEANING	Mill on the hill
STATUS	Closed

THE TAMNAVULIN DISTILLERY is located in the village of Tomnavoulin. The names of the village and distillery are pronounced the same, if not written exactly the same way. This was one of the distilleries that could have called itself "Glenlivet," since it too lies in the valley along the Livet Rivet. The water for the whisky came not from the river, but from an underground spring.

The Tamnavulin Distillery was built in 1966, right next to a magnificent water mill once in service of the local wool manufacturing industry. The distillery itself is a sober industrial complex first put into production by Invergordon. One year later, Whyte & Mackay purchased the facility, shutting it down in 1994. Since 1995 all that

remains is the visitors center inside the old mill building, preserving a few local jobs.

The owners brought out several single malt bottlings, for example a twelve-year-old that is still available on the market thanks to the large number of barrels in storage at the time the distillery was shut down. Independent bottlers have also issued it as part of their special edition series.

WHISKY
Tamnavulin, 12 years old, 40% ABV,
official bottling
Color: Pale amber

 TASTING NOTES
This is a very aromatic malt whisky, lightly sweet with a hint of peat smoke. The herbs and heather typical of the region are also present. Lemony notes emerge as well on the palate, along with the light influence of wine and black currant blossoms. The finish is dry.

THE EASTERN HIGHLANDS

"The water was not fit to drink. To make it palatable, we had to add whisky."

SIR WINSTON CHURCHILL

THE THINLY SETTLED Grampian Mountains occupy one portion of the Eastern Highlands, and the North Sea forms their eastern border. A car traveling along the A90 highway from Dundee passes by many of the distilleries in this region, among them Glencadam in the village of Brechin, and Fettercairn, located 12.5 miles (20 km) further along in the village of the same name.

The Eastern Highlands region offers a number of other attractions for visitors, as well. Dunnottar Castle is one of the most-photographed sites in Scotland. The ruins of this imposing citadel are perched atop a steep cliff that rises from the sea. Bathed on three sides by churning waves, this point was once considered unconquerable. Nearby is the quaint, romantic fishing village of Stonehaven. A number of lovely hiking paths branch out from the town, winding their way along small bays and along the top of imposing cliff faces.

Just north of Stonehaven is Scotland's third biggest city: Aberdeen. The city blossomed into an economic center in the 1970s following the discovery of oil off its coast below the North Sea.

Aberdeen's upswing thanks to "black gold" also had a positive impact on a number of other industries and businesses, permitting the city to expand continually ever since. Prior to the oil boom, Aberdeen was already a center of regional trade and an important overseas transportation hub. The historical development of North Sea shipping can be followed in the exhibits in the city's excellent Maritime Museum. What Aberdeen no longer has is an operational whisky distillery of its own.

Leaving Aberdeen and heading to the west on the A93 highway leading to the Grampian Mountains you will reach Royal Lochnagar, the only distillery that remains active in the western part of this region. The famous Balmoral Castle, summer residence of the British royal family, is not far from there. The castle was purchased in 1848 by Queen Victoria, and completely renovated inside and out by her consort, Prince Albert. Balmoral is magnificently nestled in the valley of the River Dee, surrounded by large tracts of forest. The nearest village is Braemar, famous as the location of the Braemar Highland Games, also know as the Braemar Games, visited by enthusiasts from all over the world, not least because the royal family itself has been known to attend. The games begin on the first Saturday in September, bringing together athletes specializing in traditional Scottish sports like caber tossing for the Highlands equivalent of the Olympic Games.

Top: The lonely, bare landscape of the Grampian Mountains has been thinly settled territory every since the Highland Clearances drove out most of its inhabitants.
Bottom: The Merat Cross at the end of Union Street in Aberdeen.

Opposite: The picturesque setting of Dunnottar Castle makes it one of the most breathtaking ruins in Scotland.

Fettercairn

FETTERCAIRN	
OWNER	Whyte & Mackay Ltd.
ESTABLISHED	1824
MEANING OF NAME	Forested hill
STATUS	In production
ANNUAL PRODUCTION	1.5 million liters/ 396,000 gallons

THE FETTERCAIRN DISTILLERY is located just east of the Cairnmorn Mountains in an area well known for its fertile fields.

When the Excise Acts were passed in 1823 — a law that legalized whisky distilling in exchange for a low one-time fee and a stable rate of taxation — Fettercairn was one of the first distilleries to apply for a license under the new regulations. In 1860, what is known as the Spirits Act was introduced. This law took into account the needs of distillers, permitting the export of bottled spirits and abolishing the tax on malt. This series of events seems to have encouraged Fettercairn's owner at the time, Gladstone, a brother of the British Prime Minister, to focus on the production of whisky. The distillery was nearly burned to the ground in 1887 in a catastrophic fire. Large parts of the facility had to be rebuilt from the ground up. Fettercairn was shut down from 1926 to 1939, but resumed production under the ownership of Train & MacIntyre, a subsidiary of National Distillers of America. In 1966, the entire complex was renovated and expanded to four pot stills. In 1973, Fettercairn was sold to Whyte & Mackay, who still own the distillery today. Only 4 percent of the total whisky produced is bottled as single malts; the vast majority flows into the parent company's blended brands. The owners have in the meantime opened a visitors center and part of the facility to the general public.

The whisky is slightly earthy, nutty and is said to have a bit of rubber aftertaste. The aroma is exceptionally well balanced. The single malt is marketed under the name Old Fettercairn.

WHISKY

Fettercairn 1824, 12 years old, 40% ABV, official bottling
Color: Dark amber

TASTING NOTES

This light twelve-year-old whisky is excellent as an aperitif. The aroma reveals notes of vanilla and caramel. On the palate there is a nutty flavor, but the whisky maintains its lightness. In the mouth it is soft, sweet and creamy. The finish is smooth, with just a touch of sweetness.

The foothills of the Grampian Mountains form a backdrop for the Fettercairn Distillery, which has been in operation here since 1824.

Glen Garioch

GLEN GARIOCH

OWNER	Morrison Bowmore Distillers (Suntory)
ESTABLISHED	1797
MEANING OF NAME	Steep-sided valley
STATUS	In production
ANNUAL PRODUCTION	350,000 liters/ 92,500 gallons

The granite façade of Glen Garioch. In 1995, the distillery was about to be shut down when production began again.

EAST OF KENNETHMORE in the village of Oldmeldrum is where one can find the Glen Garioch Distillery. Most experts consider it to be within the Eastern Highlands, though many maps place it in the Speyside region. Their borders are far from fixed.

The distillery points to the year 1797 as its founding date, although this can no longer be proven with any accuracy. It is certain that it was in operation before 1800, making it one of the oldest distilleries anywhere. Its founder was Thomas Simpson. Over the course of the cen-turies the distillery weathered frequent changes of ownership. A. W. Sanderson, for example, the producer of the Vat 69 blend, was in charge for a time, after which Booth's Distillers took over. In 1937, Glen Garioch was purchased by SMD, which shut down produc-tion in 1968 as a result of questions about the quality of the distillery's water supply. Two years later, it was sold to Stanley Morrison, who located a new spring and returned Glen Garioch to production a year later with the addition of a third still, followed in 1973 by a fourth. The facility was also supplied with floor maltings, much like those found at the Bowmore Distillery, which was owned by the same company. Heat generated by the production process was drawn off and used to heat a greenhouse that is unfortunately no longer in existence. The prototype

was once again the Bowmore facility, where the excess heat had been used to heat a nearby swimming pool. The on-site malting using peat ensured that Glen Garioch whisky was always particularly peaty. In 1995, it looked as if this venerable distillery had reached the end when Morrison's son sold the company to the Japanese whisky giant Suntory, which had already been a part owner of Glen Garioch. The distillery's doors were closed and Glen Garioch was put up for sale. When no buyers stepped forward, the Japanese decided to invest in the distillery themselves, bringing it into production once again in 1997.

The whisky once had a stronger peat flavor than it does today, with spicy and flowery notes. More recently it has become popular as an aperitif. Older bottles, in contrast, are better enjoyed as digestives.

WHISKY

Glen Garioch, 15 years old, 43% ABV, official bottling
Color: Dark amber

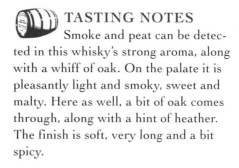 ### TASTING NOTES

Smoke and peat can be detec-ted in this whisky's strong aroma, along with a whiff of oak. On the palate it is pleasantly light and smoky, sweet and malty. Here as well, a bit of oak comes through, along with a hint of heather. The finish is soft, very long and a bit spicy.

Glencadam

GLENCADAM	
OWNER	Angus Dundee Distillers
ESTABLISHED	1823
MEANING OF NAME	Valley of the wild goose
STATUS	In production
ANNUAL PRODUCTION	1.3 million liters/ 343,000 gallons

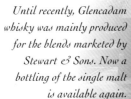

THE GLENCADAM DISTILLERY stands on the edge of the town of Brechin near the River Esk. The distillery does not use water drawn from the Esk, but from Loch Lee, some 30 miles (50 km) away, which is the river's source. The water has to be pumped to the distillery.

Glencadam is one of the lesser known of Scotland's many distilleries. It was probably already in production in 1823, although the date is controversial. Hiram Walker took over in 1954, making it part of the Allied Domecq empire. Its whisky was primarily produced for Stewart's Cream of the Barley, a blend produced by the company Stewart & Sons of Dundee, which also belonging to Allied. In 2003 ownership changed again, and Glencadam currently belongs to Angus Dundee Distillers.

The whisky is unusually creamy, with a light trace of berries. It is best served as a dessert whisky or just after a meal.

Until recently, Glencadam whisky was mainly produced for the blends marketed by Stewart & Sons. Now a bottling of the single malt is available again.

Glencadam is only seldom available as an official single malt bottling, such as the Limited Edition or a fifteen-year-old. It is more readily obtained through an independent bottler like Gordon & MacPhail, which issues a Glencadam single malt at more or less regular intervals.

WHISKY
Glencadam, 15 years old, 40% ABV, official bottling
Color: Very dark amber

TASTING NOTES
Glencadam Distillery finally released a proprietary single malt bottling in 2006. The nose of this whisky is extremely dry, with a spicy scent somewhat reminiscent of cinnamon. The flavor is fruity, recalling raisins and coconut, with a creamy caramel-like sweetness. The medium-long finish is somewhat medicinal.

Royal Lochnagar

THE ROYAL LOCHNAGAR DISTILLERY is quite close to the royal castle of Balmoral. Driving along the A93 highway from Ballater to Braemar, there is a road that branches off and leads to the castle. Following the road further brings one directly to the distillery, at the foot of a mountain that shares its name.

John Begg founded Royal Lochnagar in 1845. Since his distillery was operating under an official license, Begg constantly came into conflict with the illegal distilleries that were still common in the area. He soon found a powerful patroness in Queen Victoria. She was enthusiastic about everything to do with the Scottish highlands, so much so that she purchased Balmoral Castle in spite of the fact that it was so close to a distillery. In the same year, Begg invited Queen Victoria, Prince Albert and their children to visit the facility, serving them some of his whisky at the end of the tour. It pleased the royal couple so well that Lochnagar was named a supplier to the crown, enabling it to add the prefix "Royal" to its name. In 1916, the distillery was sold to DCL, eventually becoming part of he Diageo beverage empire. In the 1970s, the "Royal" was briefly withdrawn after the distillery fell out of favor with Prince Philip, Duke of Edinburgh. The problem seems to have been resolved in the meantime, as Royal Lochnagar is once again the official label. The resolution may have had something to do with Prince Charles, who greatly enjoys spending time at Balmoral. He wrote a children's book titled *The Old Man of Lochnagar*, painted many watercolors of the Lochnagar area, and was a regular visitor to the distillery.

The whisky is medium-bodied, malty and fruity with a hint of smoke and some spiciness. It has

ROYAL LOCHNAGAR	
OWNER	UDV (Diageo)
ESTABLISHED	1845
MEANING OF NAME	Loud lake
STATUS	In production
ANNUAL PRODUCTION	430,000 liters/ 114,000 gallons

been available as a twelve-year-old single malt bottling for a relatively long time. Also available are a Selected Reserve—each bottle is numbered and it is quite expensive—and a Rare Malts series edition. Royal Lochnagar is seldom available through independent bottlers.

WHISKY

Royal Lochagar, 12 years old, 40% ABV, official bottling
Color: Pale amber

 **TASTING NOTES**
The aroma reveals itself as very full and pleasant with a sour-fruity character. On the palate, the flavor the fruity flavors develop into a lovely malty sweetness, with a faint suggestion of smoke. The finish is soft and long.

Royal Lochnagar, which is not far from Balmoral Castle, is an official supplier to the crown.

Glenesk · Glenury

GLENESK

OWNER	UDV (Diageo)
ESTABLISHED	1897
MEANING OF NAME	Valley of the River Esk
STATUS	Demolished

THE GLENESK DISTILLERY AND MALTINGS lay west of the village of Montrose, close to the North Esk River.

The distillery was founded in 1897 under the name Highland Esk, which was changed to North Esk after two years, and changed several times more over the next several years. The property was once the site of a flax mill, parts of which were simply rebuilt and converted for their new function. The distillery was shut down during the First World War and only reopened as a subsidiary of National Distillers of America in 1938. From that point on, however, the distillery only produced grain whisky, marketed under the name Montrose. In 1964 it was sold to SMD along with William Sanderson & Sons, which changed its

name to Hillside and converted the facility back to the production of malt whisky. SMD used the whisky primarily for the blend Vat 69. In 1968, the Glenesk maltings were added, producing malt on an industrial scale in enormous malt drums. The distillery was given its final name, Glenesk, in 1980, just five years before it was closed. The maltings are still in production, supplying many of the regional distillers with malt.

WHISKY
Glenesk, 1985/2000, 40% ABV,
Gordon & MacPhail,
Connoisseurs' Choice series
Color: Rich gold

 TASTING NOTES
The whisky has a soft, harmonious aroma with toffee notes. This first impression is reinforced by the wonderfully soft flavor of malt and a bit of apricots, as well as the long-lasting, slightly sweet finish.

GLENURY

OWNER	DCL (Diageo)
ESTABLISHED	1825
MEANING OF NAME	Valley of Ury
STATUS	Closed, renovated

THE GLENURY DISTILLERY derives its name from a small valley in the Ury district. It is south of Aberdeen, very close to the fishing village of Storehaven and the River Cowie.

Glenury can trace its beginnings to 1825, when it was founded by Captain Robert Barclay. This extraordinary man was a farmer and sheep breeder as well as a world-record holder in running. During his tenure as a member of parliament, he became such good friends with a certain member of the royal family that when the friend later ascended the throne as King William IV, he granted Glenury

permission to add the title "Royal" to its label. The distillery was modernized in 1966, only to be shut down in 1985 by DCL, its owner at the time. Its license has since been allowed to lapse.

WHISKY
Glenury Royal, 50 years old,
42.8% ABV, official bottling
Color: Golden amber

 TASTING NOTES
This whisky's sweet aroma is reminiscent of rosewood, incense, nutmeg and a little cheese rind. The flavors caress the palate with a pleasing sweetness, like a sugar cookie, along with a hint of woodiness. The finish is molasses-like, with tannin content.

Lochside · North Port

LOCHSIDE

OWNER	Allied Lyons
ESTABLISHED	1957
STATUS	Demolished

THE LOCHSIDE DISTILLERY stood on the same property as the once-famous James Deuchar Ltd. brewery in Montrose.

Joseph Hobbs, who already owned the Ben Nevis Distillery, opened the Lochside facility for production in 1957. Having purchased the property, he had the brewery buildings refitted for the production of both malt and grain whisky. In 1973, the distillery was sold to the Spanish DYC consortium. This move caused just as much of an uproar as the first purchase of a Scottish distillery by a Japanese company a few years later. The Spaniards kept everything running much as it always had, although they discontinued production of grain spirits in order to focus on the malt whisky. Only a small portion of the product was exported to Spain. It was soon revealed that

Hiram Walker, and thereby the beverage giant Allied Domecq, stood behind the Spanish firm. In the early 1990s it became known that the company wanted to put the rather run-down distillery up for sale. No one within the firm was particularly interested in sustaining it, and the facilities had never been renovated or modernized. When no buyers stepped forward, as in many similar cases, the distillery was shut down. In 1992 its stills were even dismantled and its warehouses demolished.

WHISKY
Lochside, 1991, 43% ABV,
Gordon & MacPhail,
Connoisseurs' Choice series
Color: Pale gold

 **TASTING NOTES**
The whisky's sweet camphor aroma merges with a malty note. The taste is sweet and spicy with a return of the malt. The finish is relatively dry.

NORTH PORT

OWNER	UDV (Diageo)
ESTABLISHED	1820
STATUS	Demolished, property now occupied by a shopping center

THE NORTH PORT DISTILLERY was located in Brechin, near the still active Glencadam facility.

A local family founded the distillery under the name of Townhead in 1820. Three years later it was renamed Brechin after the town. At some point the name was changed a final time, to North Port. In the 1920s it came into the possession of DCL, which shut it down from 1928 to 1937. Mitchel Brothers, a subsidiary of DCL, took over management of the distillery. They concentrated their efforts on a vatted brand called Glen Dew, never releasing a proprietary single malt bottling. In the 1970s the distillery was modernized one last

time, only to close its doors forever in 1983. In 2002, it was sold to a consortium that demolished all the buildings to make space for a modern shopping center that stands in their place. Today, there is nothing left to remind visitors of the North Port Distillery.

WHISKY
North Port-Brechin, 1981, 43% ABV,
Gordon & MacPhail,
Connoisseurs' Choice series
Color: Straw

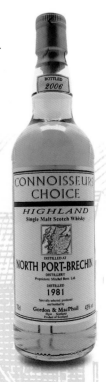

TASTING NOTES
The aroma of this whisky is sweet and fruity, with cinnamon and a hint of ginger. The flavor is sweet and smoky on the palate, with malty notes and once again a hint of fruits. The finish is somewhat smoky, with the fruitiness returning.

MIDLAND VALLEY

What whiskey will not cure,
there is no cure for.

IRISH PROVERB

THE MIDLAND VALLEY, also called the Central Lowlands, is that part of Scotland that lies between the Highlands and the Southern Uplands, though geographically speaking, it still belongs to the Highlands. The Grampian Mountains occupy a large portion of the eastern Midland Valley and continue into the Eastern Highlands.

There are only a few distilleries still operating in the Midland Valley, and all of them are near the A9 highway. (Aberfeldy, Edradour and Glenturret are just a few minutes off the highway on small roads.) Setting out from Inverness, the first distillery one reaches is the highest in elevation: Dalwhinnie.

The next sight along the highway is the famous Blair Castle at Blair Atholl, a few miles from the village of Pitlochry. This famous castle—very

complex in structure and regularly whitewashed—has been rebuilt numerous times during its 700-year history. Today it is a museum with impressive interior furnishings, as well as a number of historic paintings on permanent exhibit. Also on display are gloves and a pipe that belonged to Scottish national hero and pretender to the crown of Britain, Bonnie Prince Charlie. It is said that he spent two nights here trying to rouse support for the Jacobite rebellion. Queen Victoria also lived here for a while, with the private army of the sixth Duke of Atholl serving as her bodyguard. She later gave them their colors as an official regiment known as the Atholl Highlanders.

The single most important event in the world of whisky takes place annually at Blair Castle, in the

festive ballroom, at that! Here, whisky enthusiasts from all over the world are honored for their service to the Scottish whisky industry, a select group of "Keepers of the Quaich". Not just anyone can join: new recruits must be recommended by at least two members. A committee then decides whether the candidate should be accepted into the circle of more than 1,400 worldwide members.

Not far from the castle is the beautiful village of Pitlochry, which survives almost entirely from tourism. It is home to the Blair Athol Distillery and the small Edradour Distillery, not far away, draws over 100,000 visitors each year! The village itself is also worth seeing, in particular its famous "salmon ladder." This is a series of ponds, one higher than the next, built to help the salmon get past the otherwise insurmountable barrier of the hydroelectric dam at Loch Faskally and make their way back to the streams where they spawn.

Somewhat further south is the village of Aberfeldy and the distillery of the same name. Near the town of Crieff, visitors can embark on "The Famous Grouse Experience" tour offered by the Glenturret Distillery, maybe even stopping for a bite to eat in its restaurant. Tullibardine, another distillery, is located just outside Perth in the small town of Blackford.

Top: Wade's Bridge near Aberfeldy is one of forty bridges built by General George Wade's army during the years of the Jacobite uprising.
Bottom: A break in the Highland Games, which take place annually near Pitlochry, is accompanied by a wee dram of the local whisky.

Opposite: The Hotel Atholl Palace is located on the grounds of a beautiful estate park near the village of Pitlochry.

Aberfeldy

ABERFELDY	
OWNER	Dewar's (Bacardi)
ESTABLISHED	1896
MEANING OF NAME	Mouth of the Feldy River
STATUS	In production
ANNUAL PRODUCTION	2 million liters/ 528,000 gallons

THE ABERFELDY DISTILLERY is in the village of the same name on the River Tay. This idyllic little town of fewer than 2,000 inhabitants is fairly high up in the Grampian Mountains.

The Perth-based whisky traders John Dewar & Sons founded Aberfeldy in 1896, and in 1925 merged with DCL. A new stillhouse was built in 1972, expanding the distillery's capacity to four pot stills. For financial reasons, however, in-house malting was discontinued. When DCL was taken over by Guinness, Aberfeldy Distillery came under the umbrella of UD, which once again took up the license originally issued to John Dewar & Sons. As a result of the mergers and the founding of the Diageo conglomerate, anti-trust and monopoly officials in America and at European Union headquarters in Brussels decided that Dewar's, along with four distilleries (including Aberfeldy), had to be sold. Why did it need to be sold? Because Dewar's White Label had become the best-selling blended whisky in the USA, completely dominating the American market, as it still does. Thus, in 1998, the Aberfeldy Distillery, along with Dewar's, was sold to Bacardi, which still owns it today. Bacardi opened a visitors center on the site in 2000.

The whisky is very strong, oily and fruity. As a single malt it is best as a digestive. Since its former owner UD included it in the Flora & Fauna series, it has been easier to get hold of a bottle. This whisky has such a strik-

ing character that it is easy to distinguish its flavors in the Dewar's White Label blend, for which it is primarily manufactured.

WHISKY
Aberfeldy, 12 years old, 40% ABV, official bottling
Color: Amber

 TASTING NOTES

The aroma of Aberfeldy whisky is surprisingly smoky, with a light honey scent unfolding until it is well developed. On the palate, the smokiness returns, at first very fine, then increasingly strong and spicy. The finish is long, with a sweet conclusion.

This venerable distillery now belongs to Barcardi.

Blair Athol

THE BLAIR ATHOL DISTILLERY stands just south of Pitlochry alongside the A9 highway. Especially in the warmer months, when most of the building is covered in ivy and flowering climbing plants, the main building is a real gem. The region around Blair Athol has plenty of interesting sites, and is certainly part of the reason the distillery is visited by thousands of tourists every year.

In 1798, a building already stood where the distillery is now. Visitors admiring the sturdy fieldstone construction certainly might think that Blair Athol could date back that far, but that is not the case. After Arthur Bell & Son bought the complex—along with the Dufftown Distillery— in 1933, they had a completely new facility built in 1949. Ever since then, Blair Athol whisky has been produced primarily for the Bell's blend. After the company was sold to Guinness, which later merged with UD, Blair Athol Distillery became part of the giant Diageo group. It is often falsely assumed that the distillery is somehow connected to nearby Blair Castle in the town of Blair Atholl, but the town spells its name with a second "l" and the castle has nothing to do with whisky production. Even the famous Scottish whisky liqueur, Atholl Browse, comes from a different house, namely that of Gordon & MacPhail.

BLAIR ATHOL	
OWNER	UDV (Diageo)
ESTABLISHED	1798
MEANING OF NAME	Plain or moor of Athol
STATUS	In production
ANNUAL PRODUCTION	1 million liters/ 264,000 gallons

Although it is primarily produced for Bell's, Blair Athol has also been sold as a single malt. Although its body is not particularly complex, the sherry notes are rich. The whisky is spicy, nutty and reminiscent of shortbread.

WHISKY
Blair Athol, 12 years old, 43% ABV, Flora & Fauna series
Color: Polished mahogany

 TASTING NOTES
It has a light, sweet aroma with minimal smoke and a hint of orange. The taste is again sweet, but balanced and warming, at times reminiscent of nuts. The finish is long, with a pronounced, light sweetness and discreet smokiness.

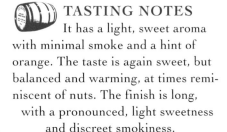

Ivy and wild grapes climbing up the facade of the Blair Athol Distillery add a lovely splash of color.

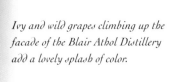

Dalwhinnie

DALWHINNIE	
OWNER	UDV (Diageo)
ESTABLISHED	1897
MEANING OF NAME	Assembly place
STATUS	In production
ANNUAL PRODUCTION	1.3 million liters/ 343,000 gallons

The visitors center at Dalwhinnie is open all year round, offering an interesting perspective on the history and production methods of the distillery.

THE DALWHINNIE DISTILLERY is the highest in Scotland, standing at an elevation of 1,083 feet (330 m) above sea level. It is located on the edge of the town of the same name, directly on the railway line between Glasgow and Fort William and within sight of the A9 highway, one of Scotland's major transportation arteries. The weather in the Scottish mountains is markedly cooler than in the rest of the country, and it is not uncommon for the distillery to be snowed in. The Dalwhinnie workers are also responsible for a small meteorological station that collects data for the National Weather Service.

The distillery was founded in 1897 under the name Strathspey, despite the fact that the Spey River is nowhere near Dalwhinnie. It belonged to an American group for a short time before it was sold to DCL in 1926, which hoped to use the whisky in the Black & White blend bottled by James Buchanan & Co. Today, the license is still in the name of Buchanan. Dalwhinnie's has in the meantime changed hands from DCL to UD to UDV to the beverage conglomerate Diageo. UD added the whisky to its Classic Malts series, somewhat mysteriously calling it "Northern Highland Whisky" on the label. This could be corrected, and the adjective "northern" was omitted from further bottlings.

The whisky has a light peaty style, somewhat sweet with a leaning toward heather honey. It is relatively clear, reminiscent of fresh cut grass. It is best enjoyed as an aperitif.

WHISKY
Dalwhinnie, 20 years old, 1986/2006, 56.8% ABV, official bottling
Color: Bright amber

TASTING NOTES
The nose is very distinctive and ripe. It starts out spicy and smelling of herbs, then moves into sweeter orange, peach and holiday cakes. When cut with water, the flavors become even more complex, with an additional light note of smoke. Smoke is also present on the palate, which is boldly complex and warming, starting off sweet, then becoming drier over time. Spice and orangey aromas emerge over time. The finish is medium to long, reminiscent of ripe fruit.

Deanston

THE DEANSTON DISTILLERY is not far from the small town of Doune, just north of the famous "line" that separates the Highlands from the Lowlands of Scotland. Doune, once famous for its pistol factory, is today visited primarily because of its castle, where *Monty Python and the Holy Grail* was filmed. The town lies on the River Teith, which supplies Deanston with its water.

Although Deanston Distillery was officially founded in 1965/66, it can still look back on a long history. Richard Arkwright, one of the fathers of the Industrial Revolution, built the imposing building where the distillery is housed today as a cotton mill in 1785. When the factory was expanded in 1836, the water of the Teith was already in service driving the mill wheel. The owners noted the consistently high quality of that water and converted the mill into a distillery in 1965. In 1972, Invergordon purchased the complex, leading to the golden age of the Deanston Distillery. Unfortunately, the boom years were followed by hard times, and Invergordon was forced to sell again in the 1980s. With the ever increasing interest in single malt whiskies at the close of the twentieth century, Deanston was sold to Burn Stewart in 1991, and production began anew. Since then, Deanston single malt has been more readily available. In autumn 1998, the distillery was expanded and outfitted with

The clear, sparkling water of the River Teith supplies the Deanston Distillery.

DEANSTON	
OWNER	Burn Stewart Distillers Ltd. (CL World Brands)
ESTABLISHED	1965
MEANING OF NAME	Hill fort
STATUS	In production
ANNUAL PRODUCTION	3 million liters/ 793,000 gallons

additional equipment so that gin and vodka could be distilled at the same site. The whisky is light and a little nutty with a distinct, malty sweetness. For many connoisseurs, it has more qualities of a Lowland malt than of a Highland variety.

WHISKY
Deanston, 12 years old, 40% ABV, official bottling
Color: Golden yellow

TASTING NOTES
The whisky has a very light, oily aroma with a clear note of oak. It is notably stronger on the palate than the nose would lead one to expect. Additional flavors include lemon, malt and an intensive spiciness. The intense oak of the nose returns in the finish.

Edradour

EDRADOUR	
OWNER	Signatory (Andrew Symington)
ESTABLISHED	1825
MEANING OF NAME	Between two rivers
STATUS	In production
ANNUAL PRODUCTION	900,000 liters/ 238,000 gallons

THE EDRADOUR DISTILLERY LIES IN the hamlet of Balnauld, hidden in a small valley above the town of Pitlochry.

The distillery was founded under the name Glenforres in 1825, but the present facility was not constructed until 1837. Over the following century, the distillery changed hands many times before it was purchased in 1933 by William Whitely & Co., a subsidiary of the American group J.G. Turney & Sons.

In 1982, the Pernod Ricard group took over the helm of Edradour. Four years later, the first official bottling of its ten-year-old single malt was released, but unfortunately, due to a lack of marketing strategy, it was only available at the distillery itself. Everything changed in the middle of 2002 when the distillery once again came into Scottish hands. Andrew Symington, owner of the independent bottler Signatory Vintage, fulfilled a personal dream. It took him all of five minutes to negotiate the purchase of Edradour from its French owners. Shortly after the sale, there was a series of strong thunderstorms in the area that caused both local rivers to flood, putting half the distillery, including the visitors center, under water. The facility could only be reopened after extensive restoration and repair. It was a good six months before Symington made his next strategic move: he hired Iain Henderson, formerly of Laphoraig, as his production manager. Henderson quickly got things up and running, making changes that greatly improved the quality of the whisky. He offered special wood finishes and experimented with a strongly peat-influenced whisky, among others. Today, the majority of Edradour whisky, up to 90 percent, is marketed as single malt. The distillery employs just three people to produce about 800 gallons (3,000 l) a week. In the summer, though, the sheer number of visitors requires hiring as many as twenty guides: some 100,000 people pass through these sacred halls each year.

This whisky, always strong, has been greatly altered by the use of varying wood finishes (Marsala, Madeira, port, Chardonnay, Sauternes, Bordeaux and Burgundy casks have been used) since 2002. A peaty Ballechin was added to the selection in late 2006. Edradour also produces a fine cream liqueur similar to Bailey's Irish Cream.

WHISKY

Ballechin Burgundy Matured,
46% ABV, official bottling
Color: Medium-dark amber

TASTING NOTES This strongly peated single malt is something very special, in part because it is a limited edition of only 6,000 bottles, but also because it is the very first whisky of its kind. The intense peat smoke unfolds in the nose accompanied by a light licorice note. On the palate one tastes a strong spiciness paired with a lighter sweetness and a hint of sandalwood. The finish is very long and intensively smoky.

Opposite: Formerly a cooperative, Edradour is one of Scotland's smallest—and at the same time, prettiest—distilleries.

Glenturret

GLENTURRET

OWNER	The Edrington Group
ESTABLISHED	1775
MEANING OF NAME	Turret River valley
STATUS	In production
ANNUAL PRODUCTION	400,000 liters/ 106,000 gallons

THE GLENTURRET DISTILLERY is on the western outskirts of the village of Crieff in the Turret River valley.

Along with Strathisla and Littlemill, Glenturret is among the very oldest distilleries in Scotland. By 1717 mash was being produced here illegally, and the current distillery dates back to 1775. This is the year featured on the label today, staking Glenturret's claim to being the country's oldest distillery. Whether or not this is true is no longer easily clarified. What Glenturret can claim with pride is that the oldest buildings in the compound, which truly were built in 1775, are still in use. The historic-style visitors center was built in 1981.

From 1929 to 1959, the facility was shut down. In 1959, James Fairlie bought it with an eye toward returning single malt whiskies to their former (and present) glory. By making quality his first priority, Fairlie was able to win over whisky lovers the world over and secure a reputation for his brand. Toward that end, he enlisted the Cointreau distillery and later Highland Distillers as partners. Today, Glenturret, along with several local restaurants owned by the same firm, are among Scotland's top attractions, visited by hordes of tourists each year. No distillery has attracted more visitors: more than two million have crossed its threshold since 1981.

After James Fairlie's death, his son Peter had quite some influence over Glenturret's further development. When Macallan was taken over by Highland Distillers, Peter Fairlie worked him way up to become Glenturret's marketing director. A whisky liqueur was even named "Fairlie's" in honor of the family and all their contributions to the brand. None of this has done Peter Fairlie all that much good, actually. He was let go by Highland Distillers in 1999, much to the dismay of the rest of the whisky industry. The history of Glenuturret has served as a warning about the negative consequences of too many mergers and consolidations. After leaving Glenturret, Peter Fairlie became

The moorhen, also known as a grouse, keeping watch over the courtyard of the Glenturret Distillery makes it very clear that this is the home of The Famous Grouse.

an independent bottler, founding his own company.

Glenturret whisky is esteemed most highly as an important part of The Famous Grouse blend, the number one blend in Scotland, and Glenturret's single malt bottlings take second place. The single malt is very complex, fresh, flowery and dry. The younger bottles are best as aperitifs; the older are preferred as digestives.

WHISKY
Glenturret, 10 years old, 40% ABV, official bottling
Color: Pale amber

TASTING NOTES
The aroma that rises into the nose is a wonderfully sweet sherry note with a little smokiness and malt. The malt is continued on the palate, along with a creamy sherry and slightly peppery sharpness. The finish is medium-long and again a little creamy.

TOWSER'S STORY

In addition to its whisky, Glenturret is also known for its cat, Towser, who managed to make her way into the *Guinness World Records* book. Mice have a special liking for malt, and so nearly every distillery has cats in order to keep the rodent population under control. Towser was far and away the best mouser ever. Through her long life—and she lived almost twenty-four years, from 1963 to 1987—she is said to have "taken out" 28,899 mice and other rodents, a record no other cat has come close to matching.

By the time Towser died, she was already a legend. A statue of Towser was erected on the grounds of the distillery ten years later in her honor.

It is said that Towser also loved the local whisky, and happily slurped it up at any opportunity, whenever there was a little bit of "run-over" at cask filling time.

A granddaughter of Towser, named Amber, was the exact opposite of her famous ancestor. She apparently never once managed to kill a single mouse before she died in 2004. This news inspired the Cats Protection organization to begin a nationwide

Since 1997, this little statue has stood in the courtyard of Glenturret Distillery in honor of the great huntress, Towser.

search for a more suitable successor. This animal welfare organization places up to 60,000 stray cats per year in new homes with carefully selected owners. Every Scottish branch of the group—including those in Arborath, Cardyke, Dundee, Forfar and Perth—joined in the search to find a cat for

Glenturret that could live up to Towser's achievements and reputation. Given Towser's record-breaking mousing ability, this was, of course, nearly impossible. The finalists were Brooke, Domino, Frances, Hanna, Holly, Jet Li, Maggie, Lola, and two cats named Dylan. A committee made up of the Cats' Protection organization and the Glenturret distillery workers couldn't choose just one, so the Dylan from the Forfar region, a white and ginger male, and Brooke are now Glenturret's official felines.

Other distilleries have also had famous cats at work in their malthouses. Barley, for example, was a champion mouser at Highland Park. Over the past few years, however, food safety regulations have been strengthened and hygiene has become a greater priority, making the small mouse-hunting felines less welcome than they have been in the past. Another factor is that the storage facilities are frequently no longer located in the same place as the distilling operation. Cats are therefore encountered less and less often wandering across a distillery's courtyard, on the hunt for mice.

TULLIBARDINE DISTILLERY
2004
UISGE BEATHA
CASK NO.373
BLACKFORD
2004
GUSTAFSSON
BLACKFORD
TULLIBARDINE DISTILLERY
2004
FRASERROSS STO
CASK NO. 370
BLACKFORD
TULLIBARDINE DISTILLERY
2003
ROBERT & GORDON
CASK NO. 19
BLACKFORD
2003
CASK NO. 20
BLACKFORD
TULLIBARDINE DIST
PROVAN
BLACKFORD

Tullibardine

THE TULLIBARDINE DISTILLERY is located in Blackford, near the golf courses of the famous, five-star luxury hotel Gleneagles. Blackford is also known for Highland Springs brand mineral water. The crystal-clear water used at the distillery, which is on the same spot where an ancient brewery once stood, stems from a spring deep in the Ochil Hills.

Tullibardine was not founded until 1949, by the engineer William Delmé Evans. Evans was also the architect of the Glenallachie and Jura distilleries. In 1947 he purchased the venerable brewery in Blackford and set about converting it into a distillery. The brewery was one of the oldest in Scotland: it had supplied beer to King James IV as early as 1488. Indeed, the distillery's gift shop and cafe are named "1488" in honor of this history. It is thought that beer was brewed on this site, and using water from the same source, as early as the twelfth century.

In 1953, Evans sold the Tullibardine Distillery to Brodie Hepburn, who sold it to Invergordon in 1971. The new owner expanded the facility from two to four stills. The years 1991–1994 were the heyday of the unfriendly takeover. Whyte & Mackay, under the control of their parent company, American Brands, bought out Tullibardine. As had happened to so many other distilleries, the new owners immediately shut down production. In 2003, the year in which its founder, Evans, died, ownership changed again. This time, Tullibardine became the property of a consortium of whisky connoisseurs. After being closed for nine years, the stills were again in production by December 2003. A year later, the gift shop opened its doors and the distillery could once again welcome visitors from all over the world.

Younger bottlings of this easy-drinking whisky are very mild, soft, citrusy, malty and sweet,

Opposite: In 2003, a consortium of whisky connoisseurs purchased the Tullibardine Distillery in Blackford.

TULLIBARDINE

OWNER	An investment group including Gary Grant, David Myles and John Black
ESTABLISHED	1949
MEANING OF NAME	Bardine hill
STATUS	In production
ANNUAL PRODUCTION	1.5 million liters/ 396,000 gallons

making them excellent as an aperitif. As the whisky ages it becomes drier and nuttier, with an increasingly more potent and oilier body.

WHISKY
Tullibardine Vintage, 1988, 46% ABV
Color: Golden yellow

TASTING NOTES
The nose of this whisky is fresh and light, with a whiff of vanilla. On the palate, the vanilla note comes through stronger, mildly sweet and reminiscent of white chocolate. The 1988 vintage is decidedly stronger than the 1993. The finish is wonderfully long and pleasantly warming.

The Tullibardine Distillery was established in 1947 in buildings that used to house a beer brewery with a long tradition.

IRELAND

The Emerald Isle with its hospitable people is always a rewarding destination for whiskey fans, even though there are currently only three distilleries actively producing pure pot still, blended and malt whiskies. These few production plants nevertheless offer an impressive range of around thirty different Irish whiskies. In addition, there are also a few distilleries that no longer produce new whiskey, some of them not for decades, but still have numerous casks stored in their remaining warehouses.

AS FAR AS WHISKEY IS CONCERNED, the Irish, like the Scots, can look back on an eventful history. The luck of the Irish was not always with them, and in addition, some serious mistakes were made that had great impact on future developments. Once a world leader in the whiskey sector, today the Irish once again have to make serious efforts to increase awareness and appreciation of Irish whiskey beyond the shores of their island. The Prohibition period in the United States, in particular, plunged the Irish whiskey industry into a deep crisis. In recent years, many brands that were once major players in the whiskey business are being revitalized. A century ago they were able to achieve extraordinary successes, only to disappear suddenly from the limelight. Their fervent desire to rekindle connections with those past achievements is only understandable. And so it is that over the past few years, the remaining distilleries of Cooley, Midleton and Old Bushmills have released a veritable flood of new products, some of which are truly noteworthy. Once again, *uisce beatha*, the water of life, the Gaelic name for whiskey, is on the march in Ireland. Cheers! Or as the Irish say, *Sláinte*!

According to legend, the Giant's Causeway in County Antrim served the giant Finn MacCool as a kind of footpath to reach his lady-love on the Scottish island of Staffa.

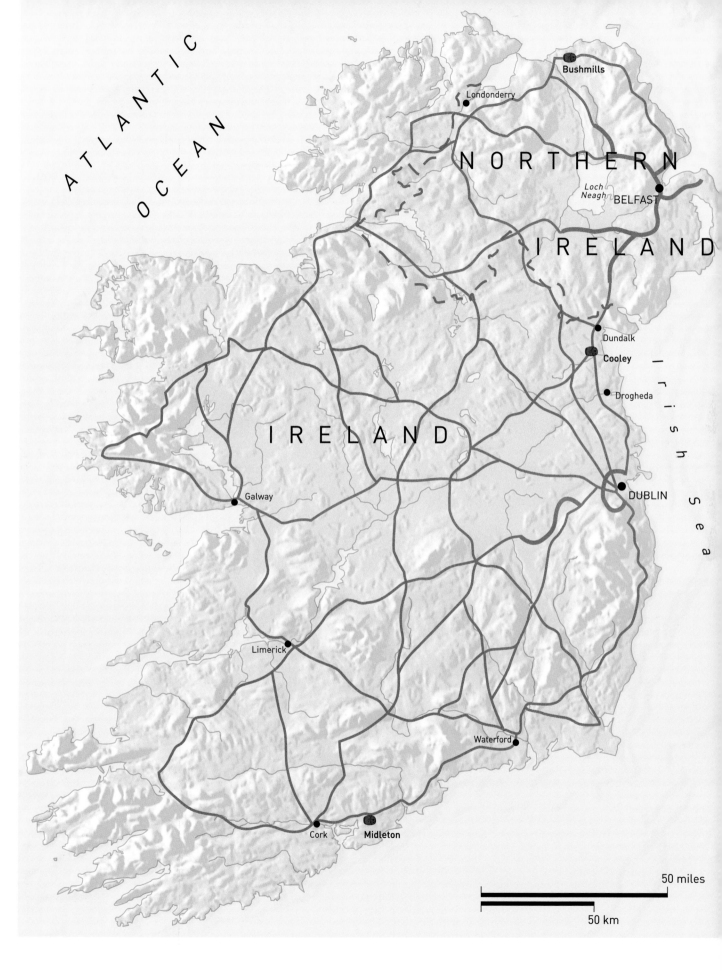

ATLANTIC OCEAN

NORTHERN IRELAND

Bushmills

Londonderry

Loch Neagh

BELFAST

IRELAND

Dundalk

Cooley

Drogheda

Irish Sea

Galway

DUBLIN

Limerick

Waterford

Cork   Midleton

50 miles

50 km

History

The inventors of whiskey

Experts are generally in agreement: whiskey originally came from Ireland. Unfortunately, there is no hard evidence to prove that beyond all doubt. In fact, the first historically documented evidence comes from Scotland, to the great delight of Ireland's whiskey-producing competitor. And so the somewhat superfluous argument over the right of one country or the other to claim the invention of whiskey as its own continues unabated. Years ago, Jim Murray, the well-known whiskey connoisseur, once again looked closely at the matter. He carried out detailed research and tried to prove in his book, *Classic Irish Whiskey*, that all references to "aqua vitae" actually referred to brandy and not to whiskey.

According to legend, it was Christian monks who, in the fifth century, brought equipment for producing medicines and perfumes to Ireland, but also to Scotland. For the Irish, there can be no doubt that it was St. Patrick himself, the nation's patron saint, who gave impetus to these activities. Although monks are said to have been the first to distill liquids as clear as water, there is no evidence that anyone knew how to produce an alcoholic drink by means of distillation, at least not during St. Patrick's lifetime. Perhaps this knowledge came to Ireland from Italy. Farmers soon adopted the art of distillation from the monks. Just like their Scottish neighbors, the farmers also processed some of their grain to "water of life" in order to earn extra income to pay for the lease of the land they farmed.

As early as 1556, and again in 1620, the Irish government made efforts to warn people of the danger that excessive consumption of alcohol posed to their health. Public health warnings, such as those that are required on every pack of cigarettes today, are therefore no modern invention. The increased consumption of alcohol, which for many ended in total dependency and great financial distress for entire families, finally forced the government to take action. In 1661, on Christmas Day of all days, it imposed a painfully high tax on whiskey, but only succeeded in achieving the same results as in Scotland: from that point on, whiskey was mainly distilled illegally and smuggled across the country.

If one is to believe Irish myths and legends, St. Patrick himself, their patron saint, concerned himself with producing whiskey.

From moonshine to whiskey boom

There was now taxed "parliament whiskey" on the one hand, and *poitín*, the illegally distilled alcohol of the common people, on the other. A good proportion of the population distilled and smuggled and used all kinds of ingenious tricks to avoid paying the onerous taxes. As in Scotland, it took about 150 years before the first laws were finally enacted, in 1822 and 1823, that paved the way for the legal production of whiskey. From then on, a license was required.

Individual licenses, however, had also been granted prior to passage of these laws. And so the Irish are proud to be the home of the world's oldest licensed distillery. In 1608, King James I of England and Ireland granted Sir Thomas Phillips the privilege of being allowed to distill whiskey in the Bushmills area. The distillery that currently bears this name, however, was first established in 1784, and is therefore younger than Kilbeggan or a number of Scottish distilleries such as Glenturret, Littlemill and Bowmore. Nevertheless, the founding year of 1608 is still recorded with pride on the Bushmills label.

The comparatively light pure pot still, which is given its unmistakeable flavor by the addition of unmalted barley, went down well with customers. In England and the USA, it even outstripped Scotch whisky in popularity and enabled large Irish firms such as John Jameson, William Jameson, John Power and George Roe to amass great fortunes. These four combined forces in 1878 to publish the book *Truths about Whisky* (note the spelling). It describes exactly what makes a good whiskey, and warns against inferior and adulterated spirits. The whiskey boom had admittedly given rise to many a black sheep, who brought products of inferior quality onto the market, thereby threatening whiskey's good reputation. This was already the first indication that Irish whiskey was going downhill, although the whiskey producers can certainly not be blamed for it.

The decline of Irish whiskey production

Many reasons can be given for the collapse of the Irish whiskey industry. For one, Ireland had its own temperance movement, which raised its warning finger and branded alcohol as the devil's work. At its head was a certain Father Matthew, who preached complete abstinence. His words fell upon so many open ears among the deeply religious Irish that between 1838 and 1844 the number of pubs fell from 21,000 to 13,000.

In addition, Scottish blends came onto the market. The process of continuous distillation,

perfected by Robert Stein and Aeneas Coffey, an Irish excise officer from Dublin, brought about the breakthrough for the production of grain whiskey. However, contrary to what one would expect due to Coffey's country of origin, it was the Scots who profited from this innovation rather than the Irish. In Scotland, the grain whiskey needed for the blends was produced in great quantity. With the new process, blended whiskey became considerably cheaper as well as lighter than the pure pot still. In practically no time at all, it spread throughout the world and overtook Irish whiskey as the world's market leader. Only when it was for all intents and purposes much too late did the Irish also begin to produce blends, and in the process they neglected the Irish pure pot still that had formerly brought them renown. When the Irish blends finally appeared on the market, they were merely a further variation of the already established Scottish blended whiskies.

The passage of the Eighteenth Amendment in the USA dealt the next blow to an already ailing industry. The nearly fourteen years of Prohibition, from 1920 to 1933, harmed not only American whiskey producers, but also those in Ireland. The Irish were far too God-fearing, and in particular law-abiding, to simply carry on; their scruples prevented them from illegally smuggling whiskey into the USA. The Scots, by contrast, and to an even greater degree the Canadians, showed no inhibitions in importing whiskey into the USA, to some extent through third countries (primarily in the Caribbean).

Old Bushmills prides itself on being the world's oldest distillery. Distillation was already taking place in the Bushmills area of County Antrim as early as 1608.

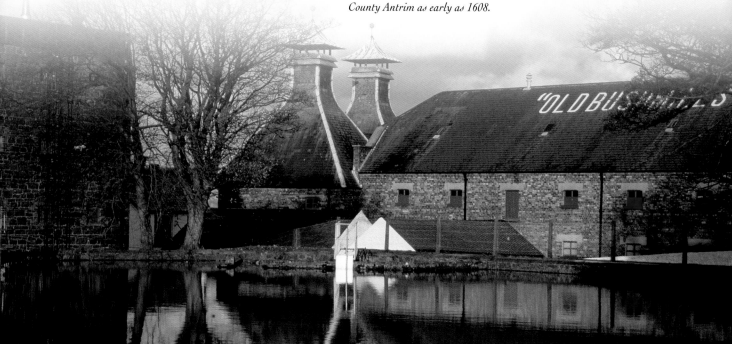

And so Irish whiskey disappeared from the American market completely. Most Americans, however, never knew anything about the lack of fresh supplies from Ireland. There were plenty of Americans, but first and foremost the gangsters, who produced the cheapest of whiskey in their own illicit distilleries and sold it as Irish whiskey. Trust in the "fusel from Ireland" thereby sank rapidly. It sank so low, in fact, that after Prohibition came to an end, Irish firms had practically no chance of re-establishing their whiskies on the market due to its image.

But it was not just on the American market that things went downhill. Following the Easter Rising of 1916, the English occupying forces imposed a trade embargo, which cut off important export markets such as Australia and New Zealand. In the meantime, many Irish distilleries had gone bankrupt, and those that remained in business made life difficult for one another during the 1950s. Since they were barely capable of supplying the home market, they finally came to their senses and realized that there really was more strength to be found in unity. To begin with, the Cork Distillers Company was formed, consisting of four distilleries in the area around Cork. Then, in 1966, came the major merger of Cork Distillers, John Powers and John Jameson to form the Irish Distillers Group (IDG). Bushmills joined this large group in 1972. From then on, things began to improve again.

Many poor farmers left their homeland and emigrated to America during the Irish Famine. Some of them continued the Irish whiskey tradition in the New World.

In 1975, the IDG built a completely new distillery, which was designed in such a way as to allow the production of all possible whiskies. With this step, all the group's prior distilleries, with the exception of Bushmills, were closed and later turned into museums. In 1987, IDG was the object of a takeover battle between John Teeling and Pernod Ricard. The French company won and brought Irish whiskey back on the road to success thanks to its large distribution network.

Without further ado, Teeling, who like most proud Irishmen could not make peace with the concern being delivered into foreign hands, established Colley, the third distillery that is still producing today. Of course, it first required a tremendous amount of effort to build up and consolidate the enterprise. But success came with time, and Pernod Ricard (IDG) showed a great deal of interest in a takeover. The Irish monopolies commission, however, was able to prevent it. And in 2006, IDG even had to sell off the Bushmills distillery to Diageo. Diageo actually owns more whiskey distilleries than any other company in the world. Pernod Ricard's higher volume of whiskey production was cited as grounds for granting approval for the move. Doesn't that make a nonsense of anti-monopoly legislation?

Irish Whiskey versus Scotch Whisky

The two countries are often compared to one another, and they are both widely considered to be whisk(e)y producers par excellence. The first difference between them, however, can already

be found in the spelling: the standard spelling in Irish is "whiskey," as the Americans also write, while the Scots spell it "whisky" without an "e." This was not always so. The spelling in Ireland was actually quite arbitrary until the beginning of the last century, sometimes with an "e" and sometimes without.

In addition, Irish pure pot still, which helped Irish whiskey achieve its worldwide fame, was manufactured by a different production process than Scotch. In addition to malt, the Irish also added a measure of unmalted barley during mashing. This "discovery" was originally a necessary economizing measure due to the imposition of a tax on malt by the English occupying powers. But the process proved to be of value not only financially, but also very much as far as taste was concerned. Its lighter body distinguished Irish whiskey from the heavier Scottish malt whiskies. There then came the triple distillation method that more and more distilleries practiced in order to improve the quality of their whiskey, as well as the construction design of the pot stills, which were much larger than their Scottish counterparts, and still are today. A further distinctive feature of Irish whiskey is that no peat was used to dry the malt, but exclusively wood or coal. Today peat is used only sporadically, as for example with Cooley's Connemara.

The Temple Bar is in a district of Dublin also called Temple Bar, the leisure and entertainment hub of the Irish capital.

Active distilleries

There were twenty-eight legal distilleries active around 1880, a time when the Irish whiskey industry was still flourishing. They were described by English author Alfred Barnard in 1887 in his book *The Whisky Distilleries of the United Kingdom*. Barnard recorded that several were still using the process of double distillation, which disproved the general preconception at the time that "only" triple distillation was used in Ireland.

Even after the merger of the major companies such as Jameson and Power to form IDG, no feeling of "together we are strong" arose. And this did not change with the construction of the super-distillery in Midleton, which could produce from one distillery the entire range of the Irish individualists already described by Barnard.

Another chapter in the history of Irish whiskey began when Irish businessman John J. Teeling set up the Cooley Distillery. His place in history will be secure beyond doubt should he succeed in breathing new life into the Kilbeggan Distillery, which also belongs to Cooley. Diageo's Old Bushmills Distillery is the third member of the trio of Irish distillers.

Cooley

COOLEY	
OWNER	Cooley Distillers plc
	(largest shareholder: John Teeling)
ESTABLISHED	1987
STATUS	In production
ANNUAL PRODUCTION	5 million liters/1.3 million gallons

Production volume at the Cooley Distillery has risen consistently since 1987. Around 20,000 barrels of whiskey can now be matured in the Riverstown warehouse.

THE COOLEY DISTILLERY is located in Riverstown near Dundalk in County Westmeath, not far from the border with Northern Ireland. The formerly state-owned spirit factory, which dates back to before the Second World War, lies somewhat hidden behind a row of fir trees and gives a rather somber impression despite recent renovation work.

The distillery was established as recently as 1987 by the charismatic businessman John Teeling. He had aimed to buy up the IDG but was beaten to the finish line by the French concern Pernod Ricard, which put an end to his plans. Instead, together with a group of investors he was able to buy the Cimicei Distillery from the state for £12,000. In the past, this distillery had primarily produced potato spirit for Smirnoff's vodkas. Since at the time this facility did not include any storage warehouses necessary for maturing whiskey, Teeling additionally bought the Kilbeggan Distillery, and with it a number of brands such as Inishowen, Locke, Millar, Tyrconnell and Watt. At the time, it was owned by the Locke

Cooley's Greenore was awarded the International Wine and Spirits Competition's gold medal.

family and was only open for viewing as a museum. Today a warehouse with a capacity of around 20,000 barrels stands in Riverstown.

How Teeling came to whiskey is itself an interesting story. He earned his doctorate in business administration at Harvard at the beginning of the 1970s, carrying out research into the whiskey sector in Ireland in the process. As a result, he came to the conclusion that Ireland had the world's best whiskey, and the world's worst marketing. At the time, this could not be denied, at least not the second point. Thanks to his sound marketing skills, he began to introduce measures for promoting sales immediately after he acquired the distillery. In particular, he renamed the company Cooley, after the nearby mountain range, which was far easier to remember than the previous name.

In order to be able to react more flexibly and also to produce malt whiskey, the group also acquired the pot stills that had been used at the long-closed Comber Distillery in Belfast, as well as the mash tun of the old Scottish Moffat Distillery.

To finally gain income for the business, after the minimum ageing period of three years, Teeling released Tyrconnell on the market, a product that received good reviews from the critics. This naturally awakened the interest of the competition: the IDG wanted to buy up Cooley, but was prevented from doing so by the monopoly authorities. That was not enough, however, to put the distillery on solid ground financially. Teeling therefore signed distribution agreements with UD and in particular with Invergordon. These are no longer valid, but at the time they were essential in order to enable the company to sell its whiskey for blends and thereby ensure that money flowed into the company's coffers. The blends were mainly sold to several British retail chains, such as Tesco, Sainsbury and Marks & Spencer.

Meanwhile, the company has managed to gain a very respectable share of the worldwide market for its products. This has been in large part due to innovative whiskies such as the Connemara, a peated single malt; the Greenmore, a single grain whiskey; as well as the blends Kilbeggan, Locke's, and the house brand Celtic, launched in honor of the Scottish soccer club Glasgow Celtic—to name just a few of the company's many labels. John Teeling has impressively proved to the whiskey world that with vision it is still possible to be commercially very successful in Ireland without the backing of a large concern.

WHISKEY
Connemara Peated Single Malt
40% ABV
Color: Strong golden-yellow

TASTING NOTES
The aroma reveals the influence of peat smoke, paired with lovely, fruity lemons. The whiskey comes across as amazingly complex. On the palate, the smoke is augmented by a little sweetness from the malt. Some miss the salty aroma of the sea familiar from Islay malts, while others cherish precisely this distinction. It has a long-lasting aftertaste with a nice lingering note of peat smoke.

John Teeling's good ideas and innovative business concepts have succeeded in establishing the Cooley brand on the market.

Midleton

MIDLETON

OWNER	IDL (Pernod Ricard)
ESTABLISHED	1825
STATUS	In production
ANNUAL PRODUCTION	20 million liters/5.3 million gallons

THE SMALL SOUTHERN IRISH TOWN of Midleton, which grew up around a Cistercian abbey founded in the twelfth century by French monks from Burgundy, lies approximately 15 miles (24 km) from Cork.

A small fork in the road near the town's church leads to Midleton's original distillery. Although it was built within viewing distance of the old buildings, the new facility is a less charming, more modern industrial complex, somewhat hidden behind the old distillery and a stand of poplar trees on the hill.

The distillery was founded in 1825 by the three Murphy brothers. The same family currently runs a brewery in nearby Cork, among other things. The Murphys were able to build the distillery shortly following the relaxation of regulations on the taxation of alcohol, as was the case in Scotland, as well. Like Old Bushmills, this distillery has weathered all the ensuing ups and downs in the course of the history of Irish whiskey. At the

end of the nineteenth century, Midleton banded together with other distilleries in the Cork area to form the Cork Distillers Company, thereby setting in motion a process similar to that which could be observed in Scotland. After surviving all the reverses of the industry unscathed, it finally merged with the Jameson and Powers distilleries in 1966 to form Irish Distillers Limited, or IDL for short. Due to a lack of space, particularly within Dublin, the idea was born of centralizing production for all the member distilleries on one site. Midleton appeared to be the ideal location. The production capacity of the existing distillery was too small, however, and so a completely new and modern industrial construction was built near the old distillery in 1975. A highly complex plant was installed in order to continue producing all the different whiskies of the old distilleries. The heart of the distillery consists of four pot stills as well as six column stills. The pot stills are not as large as the enormous onion-shaped copper kettles in the old distillery, but nevertheless have a significantly larger capacity than any to be found in Scotland.

This tremendous size also has its drawbacks: you have to produce a lot of whiskey to make it

Today, the pretty buildings of the old Midleton Distillery are home to the Jameson Heritage Centre.

The master distillers and their families used to live in this old cottage of the Midleton Distillery.

really worthwhile operating the stills. All ten of the stills are located in one building and stand closer together than anywhere else. This construction design makes the distilling equipment the most flexible in the world.

MALT WHISKEY

Midleton's production process also differs somewhat from that of other distilleries. The number of pot stills alone is surprising. Midleton normally uses a three-fold distillation process, as is generally the case in Ireland. Four kettles are used for this, two of which serve as wash stills. The fact that this setup generates whisky with a widely varying alcohol content is also quite unusual. The percentage volume already varies during the first distillation. The wash stills produce a raw spirit with an alcohol content of between 22 and 50 percent. Between 50 and 78 percent is achieved during the second heating, and the final distillation produces a fine spirit with an alcohol content of between 63 and 85 percent.

GRAIN WHISKEY

The six column stills (also called Coffey or patent stills) that are used for distilling grain whiskey through the process of continuous distillation, are once again used for a triple distillation. Three column stills are used here in Midleton for this purpose, which means that two sets of three stills are always in operation parallel to each other. The first column produces a raw spirit that already contains about 70 percent alcohol. Then something unusual happens during the second distillation: water is mixed in to remove undesirable types of alcohol and fusel oils. This results in the alcohol level dropping to around 20 percent. During the third and final distillation things really get going: at 94.5 percent, the interim product approaches the state of pure alcohol. After ageing, however, the alcohol content is 63 percent.

In Midleton, grain whiskey is mainly produced from corn—which is evident from the two giant corn silos right in front of the distillery—but they also occasionally use wheat or barley. A certain amount of barley is necessary anyway in order to provide the enzymes that are necessary for producing alcohol.

The majority of Irish blended whiskey is produced in Midleton's column stills. This is because Old Bushmills produces only malt whiskey, and because the other competition, Cooley, is still a very young distillery that makes whiskey almost exclusively for its own house brands.

Midleton also produces malt whiskey in addition to the pot still whiskey, if only not to leave this field the sole prerogative of Bushmills. All the brands that belong to IDG today are produced in Midleton. Whiskies used for other brands are also produced here, including some for Old Bushmills, although it no longer belongs to the French concern. Diageo is currently keeping a very low profile and will really have to consider whence the grain whiskey for blends should come in the future. Whiskey for the company's own brands is bottled in its own bottling plant in Dublin.

Prior to bottling, the whiskey is matured in the twenty-five warehouses in Midleton. Typically, there are more than 30,000 barrels stored in each individual warehouse. A few of the old distillery's warehouses are also still used to store the precious commodity.

Some of the whiskey is matured in Spanish sherry barrels. Whiskey from these barrels usually ends up in the standard products of the Jameson brand. The larger part of the whiskey, however, is aged in Bourbon barrels from the Wild Turkey or Heaven Hill Distilleries in the USA; even former Jack Daniel's barrels have been put to use. Wood finishing has also found its way to Midleton: Madeira, port, wine and marsala barrels are all used, in addition to new oak casks.

Midleton was also one of the first distilleries to introduce storage on pallets. The filled barrels are positioned lengthwise until a pallet is full. Then the pallets are layered on top of each other, one after another. This method makes it possible to stack up high towers to save space. These vast storerooms obviously have a very industrial appearance and no longer have anything to do with the charm of the dark, often damp and compact warehouses that are especially strongly associated with Scotland.

The beautiful, historic buildings of the original distillery were converted in 1975 into a wonderful museum and opened to the public. Although it is

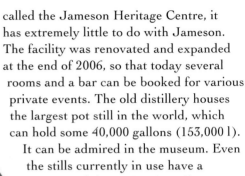

called the Jameson Heritage Centre, it has extremely little to do with Jameson. The facility was renovated and expanded at the end of 2006, so that today several rooms and a bar can be booked for various private events. The old distillery houses the largest pot still in the world, which can hold some 40,000 gallons (153,000 l).

It can be admired in the museum. Even the stills currently in use have a capacity of almost 20,000 gallons (75,000 l), which is a large amount in comparison with Scottish stills.

As already mentioned, the Midleton facility produces a wide variety of brands. But even under its own name, the distillery offers a number of various whiskies. There are even some that were still distilled in the old plant, including Old Midleton Whisky (note the spelling of whisky without an "e") and a twenty-six-year-old, pure pot still, port-cask-aged released to mark the 175th anniversary. The Midleton Very Rare, a blend that is hand-signed by the distillery manager, comes from the new distillery.

WHISKY

Midleton Very Rare, 1990 vintage, 40% ABV, Irish blend
Color: Golden yellow

 TASTING NOTES
As with so many Irish blends, the nose reveals a pronounced citrus note augmented by the scent of toffee. These are joined on the palate by a slightly sweet malt taste. An additional trace of spice is also characteristic. This blend has a medium-long finish with a soft, lingering fruity note.

Opposite: The copper kettle that can be admired in Midleton's distillery museum is claimed to be the world's largest pot still.

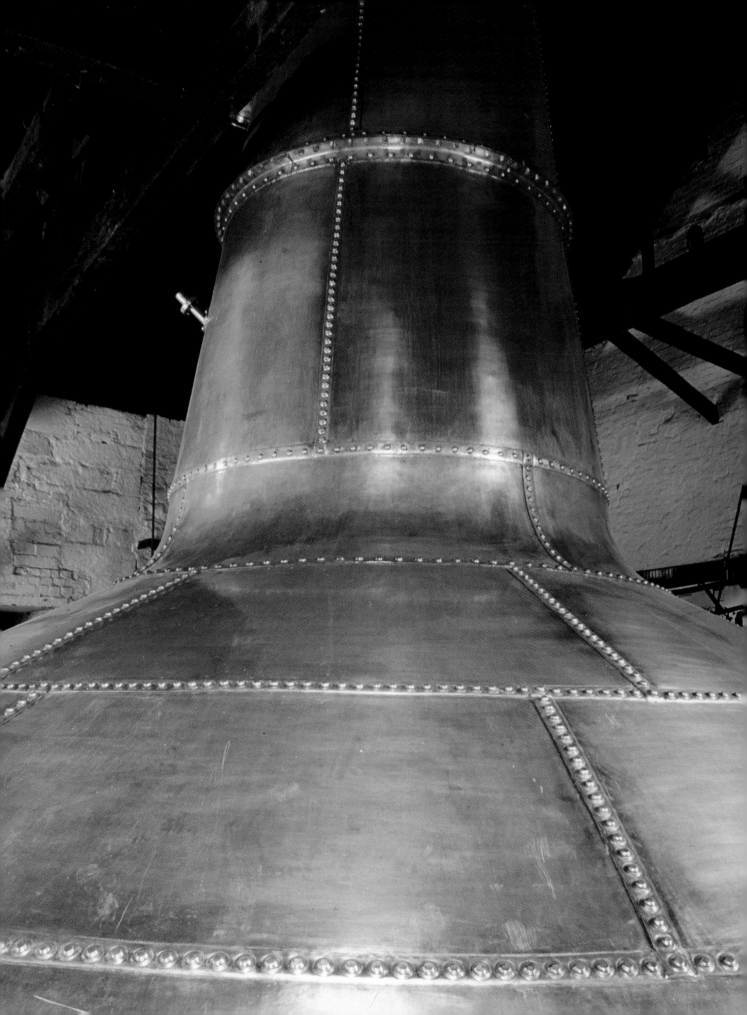

Old Bushmills

OLD BUSHMILLS

OWNER	Diageo
ESTABLISHED	1608
STATUS	In production
ANNUAL PRODUCTION	3 million liters/793,000 gallons

Some of the whiskey made by Old Bushmills Distillery is matured in Bourbon and sherry casks, which are later "married" in port wine barrels.

THE OLD BUSHMILLS DISTILLERY lies just outside the town of Bushmill in the Northern Irish county of Antrim. The distillery buildings are built on a low hill to the east of town and are more reminiscent of a small hamlet. Up to 150 people work here during the summer months. It is just about two miles to the coast, and from there only 25 miles (40 km) to Scotland. On a clear day, it is sometimes possible to see as far as the Scottish island of Islay or the Kintyre Peninsula.

Opinions differ as to the exact date of the distillery's founding. A license for distilling whiskey had been granted in the Bushmills area as early as 1608. The present owners believe this must have belonged to their predecessors, but in fact, it could actually have belonged to the neighboring Coleraine Distillery, which has since closed. All that is known for sure is that Thomas Phillips, the governor of King James I, issued a permit for distilling that was valid for a large area of County Antrim. It can be concluded from the name and several other clues that at least one of the buildings was formerly a watermill.

Distilling first took place in the buildings around 1743—at first illicitly. In the nineteenth century, the year 1784 was stated as the founding year on the Bushmills label. It can thus be assumed that part of the present facility dates from that time. This early history cannot be precisely reconstructed because a fire devastated the distillery in 1885, destroying all documentation. In addition, the administration and bottling plant in Belfast were bombed by German aircraft during the Second World War, irrevocably destroying further records.

After the war, the buildings were reconstructed in Scottish style. At that point, the owner made the decision to produce only malt whiskey, and to use a process of triple distillation; previously, the distillery had been committed to pure pot still.

Following a number of changes of ownership—including both Seagram and the beer brewer Charington, among others—the distillery became part of IDG in 1972. From 1987, it belonged to the Pernod Ricard concern, but had to be transferred to the Diageo group in 2006 in order to fulfill the requirements of the monopolies commission.

Ownership of the Coleraine Distillery was transferred to the owner of Old Bushmills as early as 1930, after they had previously considered each other to be major competitors. And so it was that grain whiskey from Coleraine came to be used for Bushmills' blends.

It disappeared from Bushmills blends again in the mid-1980s, when distillation at the Coleraine Distillery was abandoned entirely as a result of the move to the new, collective production site at Midleton.

The large number of stills at Old Bushmills is not surprising, considering that triple distillation is the rule here. Four wash stills and five spirit stills fill the somewhat cramped distillation house, all of which have long, narrow necks. The wash stills produce the typical 20 to 22 percent alcohol during the first distillation process. The second distillation is then considerably more complex: the weaker contingent, here called weak feints and containing only between 30 and 32 percent alcohol, is reserved and distilled again with the next batch. The stronger liquid (strong feints) runs through three of the spirit stills in the third distillation, is brought to a strength of 83 percent and, as fine spirit, filled into barrels. The third distillation also leaves a weaker contingent that is once again distilled with a 70 percent liquid from the second distillation.

Old Bushmills' present blends are produced almost exclusively on-site. Many contain a large proportion of malt whiskey, around 80 percent, and the grain whiskies used today come from the Midleton Distillery. In recent years, Bushmills has finally resumed production of single malts as well. Since the takeover by Diageo, however, it is uncertain what will happen with the blends in the future. It is assumed in the longer term, the grain whiskey will no longer come from Midleton. The next few years will show what alternatives there are.

WHISKEY
Bushmills Three Wood, 16 years old, 40% ABV
Color: Bronze

TASTING NOTES
As the name suggests, this malt whisky is aged for about sixteen years in Bourbon casks, or occasionally in oloroso sherry barrels. They are then "married" in port wine barrels. This wine asserts itself in the nose, but still leaves room for dried fruit, raisins and vanilla on the palate. The port wine once again comes into its own in the finish: dry, but sweet, with a hint of dark chocolate.

Water from the St. Columba River is stored in a reservoir. Old Bushmills whiskey draws its water from this pool.

Jameson

JAMESON	
OWNER	IDL (Pernod Ricard)
ESTABLISHED	1780
STATUS	Closed

TODAY, ONLY A MUSEUM REMAINS as a reminder of the famous Jameson Distillery that once stood in Bow Street in Dublin.

According to official information, the distillery was founded by John Jameson in 1780; no more precise documentary records exist, however, to prove this with certainty. Jameson originally came from Scotland and was related by marriage to that country's Haig whisky dynasty. His son, John, married the daughter of Robert Stein, the inventor of continuous distillation. John ran the business on Bow Street and was able to sell enormous numbers of barrels. In 1902, the distillery was turned into a public company. The Jamesons were known to strive for good quality and realized the importance of maturation early on. At that time, whiskey tended to be stored for only a short time and drunk young. The Jamesons are also considered the trailblazers of ageing in sherry barrels. In 1966, Jameson merged with Powers and Cork Distillers to form IDG. The distillery was closed and production took place at Powers, once its biggest competitor. When the new distillery was built in Midleton in 1975, Powers

closed its doors as well, and production was transferred there completely. The old buildings decayed with time, and were even in danger of collapsing. The old ruins were finally restored in 1998 and have been the home of a museum ever since. It was closed once again in 2006 in order to carry out a 3.5 million euro expansion of the premises, including restaurants, bars, special tasting rooms, a shop and further buildings. This renovation was concluded, naturally, on March 17, 2007: St. Patrick's Day.

The most popular whiskey in Ireland was only launched as a private brand in the 1960s. Prior to that, it had only been sold by the cask to other bottlers. Today it is the only Irish whiskey found in the list of the top 100 spirits. In 1999, the first fifteen-year-old pure pot still whiskey appeared on the market. The visitors center also offers an exclusive twelve-year-old Jameson Distillery Reserve.

WHISKEY
Jameson, 12 years old, 40% ABV, Irish blend
Color: Golden yellow

 TASTING NOTES
This twelve-year-old blend from the house of Jameson is the elder brother of Ireland's most-sold whiskey. Appreciable sherry notes, as well as vanilla, characterize the aroma. On the palate, the twelve years of ageing are evident in the strong, full-bodied and sweet sherry flavor, augmented by dried fruits. In the pleasantly long finish, sherry once again comes to the fore with a note of vanilla.

The Old Jameson Distillery in Dublin dates back to 1780. A visitors center was opened in in the building in 1997, where one can learn everything there is to know about whiskey production.

Kilbeggan

The little stream of Brusna still turns the distillery's millwheel. The distillery reopened in 2007 following a period of use as a warehouse and a museum.

KILBEGGAN DISTILLERY LIES in the town of the same name in County Westmeath, to the east of Dublin. The large waterwheel, still turned by the Brusna stream as in past centuries, is highly visible from the Dublin to Galway road.

Whiskey was first produced here in 1757, and Kilbeggan and Bushmills make a great show of vying for the title of the country's oldest distillery. In those days, the distillery was bore the name of the little river of Brusna. According to records, the distillery initially only had one still at its disposal, and as a result, had to distill its alcohol three times in the same still. John Locke took over the lease to the distillery in 1843. The Locke family eventually bought the distillery outright, and between 1860 and 1880 invested a lot of money in its expansion. Most of the buildings, as well as some of the production plant, still date from this time. Unfortunately, the family was forced to sell the distillery after the Second World War. It was not long before criminals came up with the idea of selling the contents of the warehouses on the black market. Later it briefly belonged to a German owner, who was also only interested in

KILBEGGAN	
OWNER	Cooley Distillers plc (largest shareholder: John Teeling)
ESTABLISHED	1757
MEANING	Small church
STATUS	Resumed in 2007
ANNUAL PRODUCTION	Planned: 250,000 liters/ 66,000 gallons

the inventory and sold it off. Production was brought to a halt once and for all in 1953, and the distillery was even used as a pig sty for a while. Thanks to the citizens of Kilbeggan, the distillery did not deteriorate completely, and a nice museum was established within the old walls. In 1987, it was acquired by John Teeling, who needed warehouse space for his Cooley whiskies. Teeling has restored Kilbeggan, and production resumed in March 2007 using the pot still that dates from 1901. A production volume of around 66,000 gallons (250,000 l) is envisaged in the first year.

Teeling has already brought several whiskies onto the market in honor of the Locke family through Cooley, including its signature blend, Kilbeggan. This blend was specially created by Scottish master blender Jimmy Lang of Chivas. A special bottling of Old Super Premium Kilbeggan Irish Whiskey, aged for fifteen years, was released to celebrate the opening of the new Kilbeggan Distillery.

WHISKEY

Kilbeggan, 40% ABV, Irish blend
Color: Pale gold

TASTING NOTES

Lemony scents immediately rise to the nose. On the palate, the citrus notes in the sweet flavor are joined by a light note of roasted malt. The finish is well-balanced and dry.

Powers

POWERS	
OWNER	IDG (Pernod Ricard)
ESTABLISHED	1791
STATUS	Closed

THE POWERS DISTILLERY, named after John Power, who owned it from 1809 onward, was on John's Lane, near the Liffey. Its biggest competitor at the time, the Jameson Distillery, could be found on the opposite bank of the river. However, none of their whiskies have been produced in Dublin since the merger of the two companies.

Powers Distillery was founded in 1791 by James Power. His son, John, who was actually knighted, had the name changed to John Power & Son in 1809. The company developed splendidly and became the number one producer for the Irish market, ahead of its rival Jameson. At the time, Jameson concentrated mainly on the export market. Powers stood out for its innovative methods of production and was the first distillery to bottle its own whiskey. It also introduced a miniature bottle, the "baby power." The distillery enjoyed an excellent reputation in regards to quality, and was able to celebrate many successes.

The plant was renovated in Victorian style following an expansion of the company in 1871. The complex created at that time still shapes Powers' appearance in Dublin.

However, following the merger

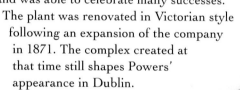

to form IDG and the resulting construction of the new Midleton Distillery, production in Dublin was stopped, as was the case with Jameson. Today, the three pot stills remain as reminders of a great past. The lovely buildings are now home to the National College for Art and Design.

WHISKEY
Powers Gold Label, 40% ABV, Irish blend
Color: Golden yellow

 ### TASTING NOTES
This gritty blend contains a high proportion of potent pure pot still whiskey, which is somewhat mellowed by the grain whiskey content. The nose has a hint of toasted wood with a pinch of spice. On the palate, these aromas are augmented by slightly oily notes as well as sweet ones. The finish proves to be of medium length and balanced.

The pretty Victorian buildings of the former Powers Distillery today house the National College for Art and Design.

Tullamore

THE TOWNSHIP OF TULLAMORE lies in the heart of Ireland, in County Offaly. It was once considered the center of Irish whiskey production. The distillery of the same name was built directly on the banks of the Grand Canal, which in turn was long the most important transport route for the whiskey.

Today, only one warehouse remains standing, which houses the Tullamore Heritage Centre with its museum, shop, pub and restaurant. The pot stills were dismantled as early as 1953 and removed to the museum in Kilbeggan. What remains is a collection of various old mementos of the past.

Everything began in 1829 when Michael Molloy founded the Tullamore Distillery. Before his death, he bequeathed it to his nephew, Bernard Daly. But it was only the later owner, Daniel E. Williams, who managed the great breakthrough. Adding "DEW" to the brand name proved to be a stroke of marketing genius. DEW just happened to be his personal initials, and this play on words, of which the Irish are very fond, was perfected with the advertising slogan "Give every man his Dew" (due). Success was immediate. Tullamore Dew became the country's best-known whiskey and also achieved great success in the export market. In those days a pure pot still whiskey was produced through three-fold distillation and aged in sherry and port barrels. But following the success of Scotch blends, Tullamore also changed to producing blends. This happened in 1947 when the grandson of D. E. Williams returned from the USA. The business quickly went downhill commercially despite the distillery's pioneering efforts with blends. The blend brought no great success; neither did the liqueur Irish Mist.

The old walls of the Tullamore Distillery today house a Heritage Centre and museum.

TULLAMORE	
OWNER	Cantrell & Cochraine (BC Partners)
ESTABLISHED	1829
MEANING OF NAME	Big hill
STATUS	Closed

The distillery was therefore sold to John Power & Sons in 1954, which later joined IDG. In 1993, the brand was sold to Cantrell & Cochraine, which at the time still belonged to Diageo and Allied Domecq. In 1999, it was finally taken over by BC Partners.

WHISKEY
Tullamore Dew, 12 years old, 40% ABV, Irish blend
Color: Pale golden yellow

TASTING NOTES
This whiskey has a complex aroma, as do most blends with an unmistakable pot still character. A sweet sherry note becomes apparent on the palate. Its astonishingly long finish has a slightly spicy effect.

Green Spot

MANY NAMES AND BRANDS were forgotten for a while in the wake of the mass demise of Irish distilleries in the period between the First World War and the Prohibition years in the USA. In recent years, however, the remaining active distilleries and several independent companies have bought the rights to old brands and breathed new life into them. This concept has, in part, been highly successful. But even prior to that, there have been companies that have marketed whiskey made specially for them, as the few examples below show.

GREEN SPOT

A RARITY IN MORE WAYS THAN ONE: in the first place, because only 6,000 bottles of Green Spot are filled annually, and also because it is the last whiskey to be produced for a wine and grocery merchant. The Mitchell & Son company is still doing business on Kildare Street in Dublin. Year in, year out, many devotees of this blend make a pilgrimage to Kildare Street to secure their bottle of Green Spot. From the early 1920s onward, the whiskey was distilled in the Jameson Distillery. Today, naturally, it comes from the distillery in Midleton.

WHISKEY

Green Spot, 40% ABV, Irish blend
Color: Somewhat pale gold

TASTING NOTES

This seven- to eight-year-old blend has a very lightly minty and refreshing aroma. On the palate it is gently sweet, somewhat spicy, becoming stronger over time. The finish is malty and slightly reminiscent of mint, soft and lingering, rounding off the sense of freshness.

Most Irish pubs, like Ryan's in Dublin, shown here, have a wide range of whiskies on hand.

Redbreast · Tyrconnell

REDBREAST

THIS PURE POT STILL WHISKEY is also known as "The Priest Bottle" since it is supposed to have pleased the palates of many a clergyman. Redbreast first appeared on the market in 1939. The whiskey was produced in Dublin by Jameson, but the Gilbey Company aged it in their own sherry casks, then bottled and marketed the resulting product. It already enjoyed an excellent reputation at the time. After the Jameson Distillery had closed its gates, Gilbey continued to deliver Redbreast until the mid 1980s. In the end, these whiskies were ultimately considered to be over-matured.

A few years ago, IDG breathed new life into Redbreast. Unfortunately, this exceptional and typically Irish pure pot still whiskey has not yet met with great success. According to some unpleasant rumors, the marketing company did not pay this whiskey the necessary attention that it actually deserved. There is also a blended whiskey sold under the same name.

WHISKEY

Redbreast, 12 years old, 40% ABV, pure pot still whiskey
Color: Bright bronze

 TASTING NOTES
Connoisseurs consider this pure pot still whiskey to be one of the best that Ireland has to offer. The nose contains complex aromas of dried fruit with banana and apple. They are augmented by notes of vanilla and nuts, for example, almonds. Sherry and further fruits, such as pears and apricots, can be noticed in the flavor. The finish is bombastically long, with renewed sherry and raw barley.

TYRCONNELL

IN FORMER TIMES, the company of A. A. Watt produced a whiskey under the name Tyrconnell. A. A. Watt owned the Abbey Street Distillery in Londonderry, Northern Ireland, up until 1925. Watt achieved fame as the country's first distillery to possess a Coffey (or column) still, which was installed in 1833 by none other than its inventor, Aeneas Coffey. The distillery was long considered to be the country's largest and was able to achieve a high volume of sales in the USA. But Prohibition sealed Watt's fate. Iriscot took over the inventory and blended the whiskey with Scottish whisky until the brand was finally withdrawn from the market in 1970.

Cooley resurrected the A. A. Watt name by resuscitating the Tyrconnell brand and launching a double distilled malt whiskey. With this exceptionally good marketing campaign, success for the Cooley Distillery, then a very young business, was not long in coming.

WHISKEY

Tyrconnell, 40% ABV, Irish single malt
Color: Golden yellow with a tinge of green

 TASTING NOTES
This double distilled single malt (made only from malted barley) has a very fruity nose that brings to mind apples and pears. There is also a light citrus note. Malt and lemons come to the fore in the slightly oily taste. One notices the short ageing period, but this does not prevent it from having a smooth, medium-long finish.

EUROPE

EUROPE

Almost every European country has a proud tradition of spirits such as brandy or schnapps. The recent whiskey boom has stirred interest among many distillers to produce whiskey, too. In some cases this is simply a matter of extending a product range, but more often than not, it is motivated by the sheer joy of trying something new, and passion for creating a fine spirit.

WHILE IT CANNOT BE DENIED that the majority of whiskies consumed all over the world are produced in Scotland, the USA, Canada and Ireland, the skill and ingenuity of European distilleries should not be underestimated. Some of them imitate their (mostly Scottish) role models to such a degree of perfection that they are hardly distinguishable from Scotch single malts, both in quality and in taste. Others undertake bold experiments, such as oat whiskies.

The following pages present some interesting European businesses and their products. Some of the whiskies are only available regionally and in limited quantities. When planning to visit a European distillery, it is generally a good idea to make prior reservations by phone. There might even be an opportunity to talk shop and chat with a master distiller over a dram.

Some of these distilleries have only been founded recently, and thus have not yet released their first whiskies. Because the European companies have adopted the spelling "whisky," that will be used on the following pages.

The popular Holstein distilling equipment is in use in many distilleries throughout Europe, including the Jelínek Distillery in the Czech Republic, shown here.

200 miles

200 km

SWEDEN

NORWAY

Bergen

Oslo

Mackmyra

Stockholm

Göteborg

North Sea

DEN-
MARK

Copen-
hagen

B
a
l
t
i
c

RUSSIA

Danzig

SCOTLAND

Edin-
burgh

NORTH
IRELAND

IRELAND

Belfast

Dublin

GREAT

Penderyn

Cardiff

BRITAIN

London

St. George's
Distillery

NETHER-

Amsterdam

LANDS

Brussels

BELGIUM

Hamburg

GERMANY

Berlin

POLAND

Warsaw

Zielona Góra

Frankfurt

CZECH

Prague

REPUBLIC

Jelínek

Krakow

SLOVAKIA

Warenghem

Distillerie
des Menhirs

Paris

Blaue Maus

Strasbourg

Munich

Slyrs

Holle

Swissky

SWITZERLAND

Reisetbauer

Waldviertler
Roggenhof

AUSTRIA

Budapest

HUNGARY

FRANCE

Bordeaux

Bilbao

drid

Andorra

Barcelona

Marseille

Milan

Venice

SLO-
VANIA

Zagreb

CROATIA

BOSNIA-
HERZEGOVINA

Belgrade

Sarajevo

SERBIA

MONTE-
NEGRO

ITALY

Ajaccio

Rome

Adriatic

Mediterranean

AIN

Germany

Grüner Hund (Green Dog) whisky is produced by Robert Fleischmann in the village of Eggolsheim in Upper Franconia, on the Regnitz River.

LEGEND HAS IT that German attempts at producing whiskies date back to 1913. Before World War II, the distinguished guests at big hotels were often served Scotch whisky. Some of these hotels even had their own brands, such as the Adlon Hotel in Berlin. In general, however, whisky was entirely unheard of among the general population. It only became popular with a wider audience around 1958, when A. Racke began to produce the Racke Rauchzart blend made from imported Scottish malt and grain whisky distilled from locally grown crops. This blend was originally called Red Fox, but had to be renamed following protests from Scotland. The change of name made no difference at all to the blend's success, and by 1969 it was the most popular whisky in Germany, having sold approximately 3 million bottles. In fact, Scotch whiskies and American Bourbons did not start to outsell Racke Rauchzart until the 1970s. Racke has turned its focus increasingly to wine, and abandoned the spirit industry entirely in October 2006.

The first German single malt was released in 1996, by Eggolsheim-based Robert Fleischmann, with the catchy name Piraten-Whisky (Pirate's Whisky). Slyrs, produced in Upper Bavaria, has recently caused a stir, as well. A company called Gruel produces a single grain whisky in Swabia, and the Rabel firm makes a rather smoky, mild whisky. Holger Höhler is a whisky producer in the state of Hesse, and hotelier Volker Theurer distills his own whisky in Tübingen. Reiner Mösslein, a Franconian winery, makes a whisky that matures in French oak casks for five years.

BLAUE MAUS

OWNER	Robert Fleischmann
ESTABLISHED	1923
STATUS	In production

THE FAMILY-OWNED Robert Fleischmann business is based in Eggolsheim-Neuses, near Forchheim. The company was established in 1923 and has been managed by Robert Fleischmann since 1973. In 1984, their first single malt was released, some of which is still stored in the company's cellars. This whisky was originally intended to be served in the in-house bar, which is designed like a dockside bar. Robert Fleischmann's passion for seafaring is well-known, and is the source of the whiskies' names. Piraten-Whisky (Pirate's Whisky), for example, was presented to the public in 1994 after it had been distilled in 1986 and matured in oak casks for eight years. It was labeled "pur malt," which caused some confusion as to whether Piraten-Whisky was merely a vatted malt. It is unclear whether the missing "e" in "pur" was a misprint, or intended to stress that Piraten-Whisky is a German single malt. For legal reasons, only small quantities can be produced, so only a few casks are put on the market each year. The individual vintages have been given names such as Blaue Maus (Blue Mouse), Schwarzer Pirat (Black Pirate), Spinnaker, Grottentaler and Grüner Hund (Green Dog).

WHISKY
Grüner Hund, 40% ABV,
1992 vintage, official bottling
Color: Dark amber

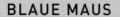 **TASTING NOTES**
This single malt has notes of almonds and a hint of flowers in the nose, especially at the outset. Almonds are echoed on the palate, roasted this time, with some slightly bitter notes and a pleasantly sweet hint of malt. The medium-long finish is nicely warming.

A BEER BREWER by training, Florian Stetter founded his own whisky distillery at Lake Schliersee in Upper Bavaria in 1997. Two years later, in 1999, he produced the distillate for Slyrs, his first whisky modeled on Scotch. This Bavarian whisky is made of pure barley malt and Alpine mountain water, then matured in American white oak casks for at least three years. A spirit still typically used by schnapps distillers is used for the distillation. The first Slyrs was bottled in 2002, with an alcoholic content of 43 percent, and introduced on the market.

The name, incidentally, is derived from the nearby Benedictine Schliersee Monastery, which was established here in 779. The distillery, which is actually called Lantehammer, was founded as early as 1928. When Lantehammer started to produce whisky, however, some conflict arose between that firm and the Franconian whisky distiller Robert Fleischmann. Lantehammer took pleasure in advertising its whisky as Bavaria's first and only, even though Robert Fleischmann had been quicker. While relations between the Franconians and the rest of Bavaria may not always be perfectly harmonious, Franconia is nonetheless located within the limits of the Free State of Bavaria. Slyrs is now marketed as the first and only whisky of the administrative district of Upper Bavaria.

As one might expect in the beautiful mountain landscape of the Lake Schliersee region, Slyrs produces primarily fruit schnapps. Their whisky, however, adds something special to the range available on the market.

SLYRS / LANTENHAMMER

OWNER	Florian Stetter
ESTABLISHED	1928
STATUS	In production

WHISKY
Slyrs, 2003 vintage, 43% ABV, official bottling
Color: Golden yellow

TASTING NOTES
This Upper Bavarian single malt has elements of vanilla on the nose, complemented by aromas of honey and marzipan. On the palate, it develops a full-bodied flavor of barley and sweet syrup. The perfectly timed finish continues the malted barley and adds a slightly oily accent.

Austria

EARLY IN THE 1990s, Branger Bräu released a Tyrolean Malt. Since its maturation time was only one year, however, it could not be marketed as a whisky. Shortly thereafter, Johann Haider presented his Waldviertler Whisky. Wolfram Ortner, a former World Cup ski racer who was forced to retire from skiing due to an injury, opened his own schnapps distillery and coffee roastery and soon started distilling whisky, as well. Ortner's whiskies are usually sold in packages with nice glasses and cigars. The Weidenauer Distillery is mainly known for its exotic whiskies, including oat and spelt whiskies.

REISETBAUER

OWNER	Julia and Hans Reisetbauer
ESTABLISHED	1995
STATUS	In production

THE REISETBAUER DISTILLERY'S single malt whisky is produced in the village of Axberg, near the city of Linz. Hans and Julia Reisetbauer have established their reputation with their fruit spirits; after all, their farmhouse is surrounded by approximately 6,000 Williams Christ pear trees. In addition, since 1995 Reisetbauer has also been producing a single malt that matures for about seven years. In order to differentiate themselves from their competitors, Reisetbauer uses both Chardonnay casks and very special casks used for Trockenbeerenauslese ("dry grapes, select picking") wine. The whisky is bottled both at 43% ABV and as a cask strength 56% ABV version.

WHISKY
Reisetbauer Single Malt Whisky, 56% ABV, 1997 vintage, official bottling
Color: Very bright amber

 **TASTING NOTES**
This single malt has aromas of toasted hazelnuts and herbs. On the palate it is pleasantly malty and slightly spicy, with a hint of smoke. The mild finish subtly echoes the malt and the touch of smoke.

WALDVIERTLER ROGGENHOF

OWNER	Monika and Johann Haider
ESTABLISHED	1995
STATUS	In production

AUSTRIA'S FIRST WHISKY that is entitled to be labeled a whisky, due to its three-year cask maturation, comes from the Waldviertel region, arguably Austria's weakest area economically. The region does offer everything needed for whisky production, however, from plentiful grain to some of the best and purest water all over the world to the Manhartsberger oak trees used to make casks. Monika and Johann Haider produce five kinds of whisky: pure barley single malt whisky, pure rye malt whisky, and a rye whisky labeled Waldviertler Roggenwhisky J.H. (*Roggen* means rye), made with 40 percent rye and 60 percent barley. The pure malt and pure rye whiskies are also distilled with a darker malt, sold as "Karamell" and "Nougat," respectively.

WHISKY
Waldviertler Gersten-Malz-Whisky (pure malt), cask strength, 54% ABV, official bottling
Color: Amber

TASTING NOTES
This single malt has a distinct aroma of oak and a note of malt. The oak note is noticeable again on the palate, where it is complemented by a slightly oily touch. The pleasant finish adds a hint of caramel.

Switzerland

DISTILLING GRAIN WAS ILLEGAL in Switzerland following World War I until 1999. The first distiller to pioneer production of Swiss whisky was the schnapps distiller Ernst Bader, and many more followed. Edi Bieri, located in the village of Baar, produces Swissky, the most widely-known Swiss whisky. Ruedi Käser, whose distillery is situated in Fricktal, had already made a name for himself with fruit brandies, schnapps and wine before he started distilling whisky. He founded Whisky Castle as an extension of Käser's Schloss, a gourmet emporium.

BRENNEREI-ZENTRUM BAUERNHOF

OWNER	Edi Bieri
ESTABLISHED	2002
STATUS	In production

EDI BIERI'S DISTILLERY, where Swissky is produced, is near the small town of Baar in the canton of Zug. Bieri created Swissky in cooperation with a brewery in Baar and its manager, Kurt Uster. The malt comes from Bamberg, Germany, which is known for its smoked malt. In 2003, Bieri took his mobile distillery (which is available to rent) to visit hotelier Claudio Bernasconi, who owns the world's largest whisky bar, housed in the Waldhaus am See hotel in St. Moritz. Within three days, Bieri had created St. Moritz Whisky.

WHISKY
Swissky, 40% ABV, official bottling
Color: Golden yellow

TASTING NOTES
This is a very young whisky with a fresh, malty aroma that has a hint of apples. On the palate, there are clear notes of sweet malt and a touch of oil. The nicely smooth finish adds a note of oak and barley malt.

WHISKY-BRENNEREI HOLLE

OWNER	Ernst Bader
ESTABLISHED	1999
STATUS	In production

ERNST BADER is the pioneer among Swiss distillers. He has been producing his own whisky on his farm in the village of Lauwil since 1999.

Ernst Bader distills his whisky on his own farm.

WHISKY
Holle Single Malt, 5 years old, 42% ABV, matured in Chardonnay casks, official bottling
Color: Amber

TASTING NOTES
The aroma has a touch of malt and Chardonnay grapes. The flavor is slightly fruity, pleasantly sweet and comes with a nice prickling sensation on the tongue. The short finish is mild and slightly sweet.

France

FRANCE IS ONE of the world's largest whisky markets. Cognac, Armagnac and pastis have gone increasingly out of fashion and have been losing market shares for years. More and more distilleries have started producing their own whiskies, many of which, such as Menhirs and Warenghem, are located in Brittany, a region that has a climate similar to that of Ireland and Scotland.

DISTILLERIE DES MENHIRS

OWNER	René Le Lay
ESTABLISHED	1921
STATUS	In production

THE DISTILLERIE DES MENHIRS, established in 1921, is family owned to this day. Like most French distilleries, it is located in Brittany, near the town of Quimper.

Most of what Distillerie des Menhirs produces is apple spirits, but since it is located in a region known as a buckwheat growing area, the idea was born to create a buckwheat whisky. It was soon put into practice: Eddu Silver, a malt whisky made from malted buckwheat and matured in French oak casks for four years, was presented in 1999. It was followed by the Eddu Gray Rock blend, which, in addition to buckwheat whisky, also contains Dalmore malt whisky and Invergordon

grain whisky. There are two explanations for the name Eddu in circulation. Some claim that Eddu is the Old Breton term for buckwheat, while others say that "ed" stands for grain and "du" for black. It is likely that there is some truth in both explanations.

WHISKY
Eddu Silver, 40% ABV, official bottling
Color: Pale amber

TASTING NOTES
This single malt made from malted buckwheat has a wonderfully fruity aroma that includes elements of honey and heather. It is very elegant on the palate, where it produces sweet and fruity notes complemented by strong signs of vanilla. The finish is nicely long and adds elements of apples and oak wood.

WARENGHEM

OWNER	Warenghem
ESTABLISHED	1900
STATUS	In production

LÉON WARENGHEM FOUNDED this distillery in 1900. It is located in Lannion, Brittany, a region where the strong influence of the Celts is visible to this day.

Warenghem produces primarily liqueurs as well as an apple schnapps. In 1987, the first blended whisky was released, named W.B. ("Whisky Breton"). W.B. was followed by Milin Guer, and eventually the first single malt, Armorik, was introduced in 1999. This distillery employs highly traditional methods: the facility includes two lovely pot stills and equipment for

continuous distillation of the grain whisky. Warenghem's whisky matures in stacks of oak casks.

WHISKY
Armorik, 40% ABV, official bottling
Color: Pale amber

TASTING NOTES
Honey and baked apples are dominant in the nose of this traditionally produced single malt, complemented by elements of wood, which, however, vanish on the palate. The flavor brings out a distinct note of caramel and a hint of oranges and chocolate. Armorik has a touch of oiliness and is pleasantly spicy. The spiciness is also noticeable in the medium-long finish.

England and Wales

TOWARD THE END of the nineteenth century, a great many distilleries still existed in England, but they all disappeared in the course of the twentieth century. It was not until 2006 that England could claim a whisky distillery of its own again.

ST. GEORGE'S DISTILLERY

OWNER	James and Andrew Nelstrop
ESTABLISHED	2006
STATUS	In production

ST. GEORGE'S DISTILLERY, owned by James Nelstrop and his son Andrew, is the first distillery licensed in recent times in England. It is located on the A11 between East Harling and Roudham, not far from London.

Construction of the distillery started in April 2006, and by November 27, their first spirit was already being filled into Jim Beam Bourbon casks. It follows that the first single malt can be expected to be released around December 2009, after the

GWALIA AT PENDERYN

OWNER	Welsh Whisky Company Ltd.
ESTABLISHED	1974
STATUS	In production

IN 1974, DAFYDD GITTINS, a colorful figure, founded a whisky production facility in Brecon together with his wife. Their first products were Swn Y Mor and Prince of Wales; they did not bring great sales success. They did bring notoriety when it was discovered that they were both blends of various Scotch whiskies, filtered and bottled in Wales. Gittins had intended to distill his own spirit, but due to a series of technical and legal problems, the nearly-completed facility was never used. In 1997, a few local companies banded together as the Welsh Whisky Company, bought the makeshift outfit and established the Gwalia Distillery at Penderyn. In order to finance the distillery, Tafski vodka, Galn Usk gin, and a whisky liqueur labeled

Legend has it that St. David himself distilled whisky in Wales. What is certain is that ancestors of Evan Williams were producing whisky in the eighteenth century. Williams established the first distillery in the USA in 1783 in what is now Kentucky.

minimum maturation time of three years. Currently, St. George's produces approximately three casks a day. The business has also invested around £1 million to create a visitors center that includes a café, a store, and conference rooms. These all opened to the public in 2007, and given their convenient location near the busy A11 highway, the Nelstrops anticipate up to 100,000 visitors a year. They were also able to hire whisky expert Iain Henderson as manager. It seems that Henderson found retirement a little too quiet: Andrew Symington had successfully convinced him to work for his Edradour Distillery after he had retired from his position at Laphroaig, and in November 2006, the busy retiree joined St. George's, where he was in charge of creating new, interesting whiskies. He has just recently passed the helm to David Fitt.

Merlin were released in the three years in which Penderyn, the distillery's first single malt, aged. Penderyn is distilled in a unique still developed by David Faraday, great-great-grandson of the inventor of the Faraday cage. This special still makes it possible to produce strong spirits in a single-step distillation technique. Penderyn whisky matures in Bourbon casks and is finished in Madeira casks.

WHISKY
Penderyn, 46% ABV, official bottling
Color: Golden yellow

TASTING NOTES
This Welsh single malt has a very sweet aroma with a pronounced oak note. The oak remains on the palate, complemented by an element of spices. The finish, medium-long, again subtly highlights the oak aroma.

Sweden

The Mackmyra Distillery is part of an old industrial complex a few hours north of Stockholm by car. So far, it can claim to be the northernmost distillery in the world.

IN SWEDEN AND FINLAND, whisky production has only started in recent years; Norway will probably follow suit in the foreseeable future. Their late entry into the world of whisky certainly has something to do with the strict regulation of alcohol and high prices paid for it in these countries. At the moment of writing, just one single malt, Mackmyra Preludium, produced by the Swedish Mackmyra Distillery, is on the market. A second Swedish distillery, Gotland Whisky, located on the island of Gotland, has great plans in the works: a strongly peaty and smoky whisky, modeled on Islay whiskies, as well as a milder version, are being developed. The target annual production at Gotland is 200,000 bottles a year. Several other distilleries are in the works.

In Finland, Mika Heikkinen runs a restaurant and a tiny distillery. In 2004, he released Old Buck, a 70 percent ABV whisky, though it was sold mainly to friends and acquaintances. The first bottle was sold at the considerable price of 1,100 euros (more than $1,500). Allegedly, a few casks

of this whisky are still in stock. The Teerenpeli Distillery, which is located in Lathi, has been producing a single malt since 2002; its official release has been announced for 2007 or 2008 (depending on maturation). It is made from slightly smoked malt and matures in Bourbon and sherry casks.

In Norway, a proper whisky distillery has announced it will soon start production. The Lofotr Maltwhisky AS company, which was founded for this purpose, has already registered the distillery with the authorities. It would replace Mackmyra as the world's northernmost distillery.

MACKMYRA SVENSK WHISKY

OWNER	Mackmyra Svensk Whisky AB
ESTABLISHED	1999
STATUS	In production

A GROUP OF EIGHT single malt enthusiasts founded the Mackmyra Distillery in 1999. It is located 125 miles (200 km) from Stockholm in Valbo, a town on the eastern coast of Sweden near Gävle. The Mackmyra Svensk Whisky AB company, which owns the distillery, is owned primarily by the Klingberg family, on whose property the distillery stands. Mackmyra started out experimenting with a small, self-built still that had a capacity of no more than 27 gallons (100 l). The ultimate stills and facilities were installed in 2002, and the first Mackmyra Preludium single malt was presented to the public in 2006. Mackmyra also sells individual casks and offers both a fruity and a smoky whisky. The smoky version derives its aroma and flavor from smoked juniper and Swedish peat. Furthermore, customers are offered

choices as to the type and size of the casks, and even where the whisky is matured.

WHISKY
Mackmyra Preludium 03, 52.2% ABV, official bottling
Color: Golden yellow

 TASTING NOTES
This smoky single malt is matured in Bourbon casks and finished in sherry casks. Its aroma is slightly smoky, fruity, and has a lingering element of butter. On the palate, the butter is complemented by chocolate and notes of raisins and dried figs against a background of oak tones. The finish is slightly bitter at first and brings out the mild notes of smoke toward the end.

Poland and Czech Republic

THERE ARE ONLY A FEW whisky distilleries in Poland. One reason is that the Poles still prefer vodka when it comes to spirits. The few Polish whisky lovers, on the other hand, prefer Scotch and other popular foreign products. In general, the definition of what constitutes a whisky has been a little looser in Eastern European countries compared to other parts of the world. Frequently, brandy with chemical additives was sold as whisky. Since Poland has joined the European Union, however, Polish producers are required to meet European standards and laws.

LUBUSKA WYTWÓRNOA WÓDEK

OWNER	V & S Group
ESTABLISHED	1946
STATUS	In production

A VERY MILD BLEND, ironically called Dark Whisky, is produced by the V & S Group at the distillery in Zielona Góra, which is known by the name of the town. The same group also markets the Scotch whiskies The Famous Grouse and Macallan in Poland.

WHISKY
Dark Whisky, 40% ABV, official bottling
Color: Amber

 **TASTING NOTES**
This rather smooth blend has an aroma with strong notes of fruits, which are continued on the palate and complemented by smooth, slightly velvety elements. There are joined by hints of toffee, which are found again in the smooth finish.

ALLEGEDLY, WHISKY WAS BEING MADE at the Czech Dynybyl Distillery even before World War II. The Halberd Distillery started production in the early 1970s. The Stock Distillery is still producing malt whisky, though it is used exclusively used in blends. The Seliko group, which used to own two distilleries near Olomouc, was quite influential, but went bankrupt. Their distilleries survive, however, as two separate businesses and are still in production.

R. JELÍNEK

OWNER	R. Jelínek
ESTABLISHED	1894
STATUS	In production

After decades of state ownership under the socialist government of Czechoslovakia, the business was privatized in 1989. The distillery uses a Holstein still.

WHISKY
Gold Cock Green Feathers, 12 years old, 43% ABV
Color: Gold

THE JELÍNEK DISTILLERY produces a six-year-old Gold Cock Black and a twelve-year-old labeled Gold Cock Green (malt whisky), as well as a three-year blend, Gold Cock Red, and an entire series called King Barley; the grain whisky used is provided by the Kojetin Distillery. The production facilities are located in the town of Vizovice near Brno. The history of schnapps distillery in this region stretches back into the seventeenth century.

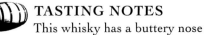 **TASTING NOTES**
This whisky has a buttery nose and notes of toffee with a hint of fruits on the palate. The finish is dry with a touch of leather.

UNITED STATES
OF
AMERICA

UNITED STATES OF AMERICA

The USA is one of the great whiskey-producing nations. Irish and Scottish immigrants brought their techniques for making "firewater" with them from their homelands, and over time the USA developed its own unique styles of whiskey, with Bourbon and Tennessee sour mash leading the way. Today, Jack Daniel's and Jim Beam are among the top ten whiskies in the world.

JACK DANIEL

TO THIS DAY, KENTUCKY and (to a somewhat lesser extent) Tennessee are bastions of the American whiskey industry. Many of the distilleries lie nestled in idyllic natural settings, often deep in the countryside, where life seems to move at a more leisurely pace and follow more traditional ways. There are also enormous whiskey factory complexes clustered in industrial parks, many of them unattractive, surrounded by multistory warehouses. Each distillery, in its own way, is essentially American. Nearly all are all open to the public—and very much worth a visit.

In the land of unlimited possibilities, the ongoing whiskey boom has brought renewed energy to the industry. In recent years many new microdistilleries have opened, producing a wide variety of fine whiskies. Scattered across the country, each seeks its own small niche market, or has already found it. Like their models, the small Scottish distilleries, the microdistilleries are open to the public and prize quality over quantity. Their inventiveness and innovation are most appreciated in the more liberal, progressive states on the east and west coasts, where most of the microdistilleries are located.

For many people, when they think of American whiskey, Jack Daniel's is the first that comes to mind. There are many other notable whiskies in the USA, however, in addition to the famous representative from Tennessee.

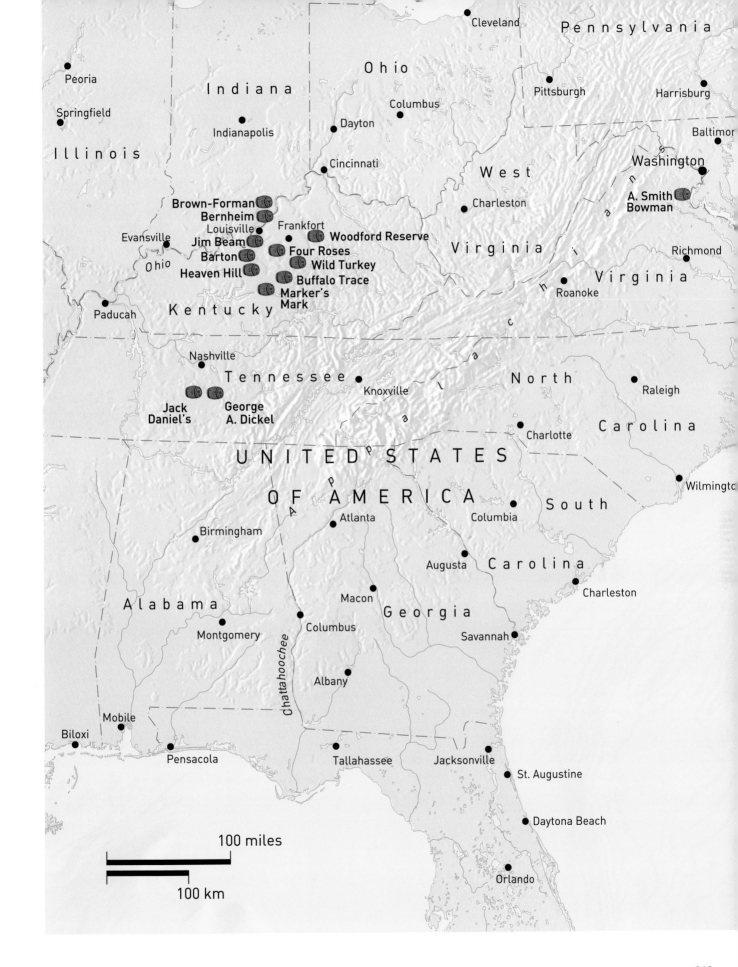

Peoria

Springfield

Illinois

Indiana

Indianapolis

Ohio

Dayton

Columbus

Cincinnati

Evansville

Ohio

Brown-Forman
Bernheim
Louisville   Frankfort
Jim Beam
Barton
Heaven Hill

Woodford Reserve
Four Roses
Wild Turkey
Buffalo Trace
Marker's
Mark

Kentucky

Paducah

Nashville

Tennessee

Knoxville

Jack
Daniel's   **George**
A. Dickel

Pittsburgh

Pennsylvania

Harrisburg

Baltimor

Washington

A. Smith
Bowman

West

Charleston

Virginia

Richmond

Virginia

Roanoke

North

Raleigh

Carolina

Charlotte

Wilmingto

UNITED STATES

OF AMERICA

South

Birmingham

Atlanta

Columbia

Augusta   Carolina

Charleston

Alabama

Macon   Georgia

Montgomery

Columbus

Chattahoochee

Albany

Savannah

Mobile

Biloxi

Pensacola

Tallahassee   Jacksonville

St. Augustine

Daytona Beach

Orlando

100 miles

100 km

History

The first whiskey pioneers

In the second half of the eighteenth century, a veritable flood of settlers from Virginia entered the new states of Kentucky and Tennessee. Still others traveled southwest from Pennsylvania into Kentucky. Scouts, among them the famous Daniel Boone, guided thousands of bold pioneers, many of them from Europe and only recently arrived in the New World. In 1776 alone, more than a quarter million Scots-Irish, most from the Northern Irish province of Ulster, made their way to this area, bringing their whiskey-distilling skills from their old homeland to the new. Often driven from their old homes, their newly-gained freedom gave them the chance to finally put their knowledge to work, adapting it in the process to new crops. The cultivation of rye led to the production of rye whiskey, which was especially popular in Maryland and Pennsylvania, where what was left over from the harvest would be brought to the distilleries for processing. Today, rye whiskey is no longer an important part of American whiskey industry. It was the settlement of the great river valleys in the regions surrounding the Appalachian Mountains, which included both Virginia and what is today Kentucky, that spurred the production of the first corn whiskies.

Many immigrants made whiskey in order to trade it for other goods. Whiskey was actually easier to transport and could be stored for longer periods of time than the grain from which it was made. The settlers carried on a brisk trade with Native Americans, who fell victim to the firewater in ever-increasing numbers. Whiskey was both a medicine and a valuable form of currency, and soldiers would occasionally be recruited with the promise of a daily ration of whiskey.

The government jumped at the opportunity to place a high tax on spirits, whether produced for commercial or household use. This reminded too many Americans of their past quarrels with England, which had taxed whiskey in America from the very beginning of colonial rule. Many recent immigrants began to grumble, seeing the tax as a means of robbing them of their newfound freedoms. Riots broke out in the heart of the whiskey production regions, eventually coming to a head in what is called the Whiskey Rebellion

The Shadow of Danger

If you believe that the traffic in Alcohol does more harm than good— *help stop it!*

Strengthen America Campaign

Strengthen America Campaign - 105 East Twenty Second Street, New York City, N.Y.

This poster from the days of Prohibition was meant to warn of the dangers of alcohol, and whiskey in particular.

of 1797. George Washington, the first president of the United States and himself a whiskey distiller, had to call in over 12,000 soldiers to put down the rebellion. Many of the rebels fled deeper into Kentucky (not yet under federal control at that time), where, in small towns like Harrodsburg, influential settlers like Colonel James Harrod were busy making whiskey from rye and wheat. Many say that Kentucky whiskey was born during this eventful period between 1775 and 1800, when several of the most influential families—including the Böhms (Jim Beam), Browns (Brown-Forman) and Samuels (Maker's Mark)—founded their distilleries.

The birth of Bourbon

Two books were published around that time that would have a lasting influence on the further development of American whiskey. In 1818, the master distiller Harrison Halls published the book *Distiller* in Philadelphia. In it he described how it was more efficient to make whiskey from a variety of grains than from just one. He went on to provide specific information, recommending a blend of corn and rye in which the proportion of rye was no more than 25 percent. For storage he recommended hogshead casks made of soft oak and charred on the inside so as to remove impurities. Was this the birth of Bourbon? No one knows for sure. At the time, rye whiskey from Pennsylvania, especially from the Monogahela Valley, was considered the first true American whiskey; yet today there are no operational distilleries in Pennsylvania. The last one, Mitcher's Distillery, closed in 1989.

Another book, *The Art of Making Whiskey* by Anthony Boucherine, followed in 1819. It also set down standards for the production of whiskey.

Bourbon derives its name from a county in Kentucky, where, in 1821, the first advertisement for Bourbon whiskey appeared in the *Western Citizen* newspaper. The Ohio River, which flows through the county, was the first important shipping route for whiskey; its significance only decreased after 1860, once the railroad crossing the country was built. It often took the whiskey barrels months to reach their destination, leading to the discovery that the quality of whiskey stored for a longer time improved.

happened, in fact. The black market in whiskey flourished, both within and outside the country, making many gangsters, smugglers and moonshiners rich. Foreign whiskey producers who were not averse to smuggling profited, as well. There were also a great many losers, however: the Irish distilleries, for example, that had scruples about smuggling and, above all, the Americans themselves. The ban on alcohol robbed many distilleries of their very means of existence. After the repeal of Prohibition in 1933, there was very little change in the dire situation at first, but over time, the whiskey market recovered. Two American brands in particular, Jack Daniel's and Jim Beam, have developed a worldwide following over the past few decades. Despite this, the number of American distilleries still remains relatively small.

Within the past few years, small microdistilleries have started making a comeback. Seeing an opportunity within the market, they have begun producing not only brandies and fruit-flavored liqueurs, but also first-class whiskies.

Prohibition

Over time, greater and greater quantities of whiskey made their way to the marketplace. It was abundant and inexpensive — anyone could afford it. The temperance movement reacted by devising a plan to ban alcohol, damning whiskey as the very tool of the Devil. They quickly achieved their goal. In some states, such as Tennessee, alcohol was banned as early as 1910. As of January 17, 1920, Prohibition reigned across the entire USA. All the distilleries were shut down except for six, which were allowed to produce alcohol for medicinal purposes.

Of course, the USA was not magically "dried out," as some had expected — quite the opposite

Harry's New York Bar in the late 1940s. It is hard to imagine that the sale of alcohol was once banned in American bars and pubs.

VIRGINIA

"I like whiskey. I always did, and that is why I never drink it."

ROBERT E. LEE

THE COMMONWEALTH OF VIRGINIA was named after Queen Elizabeth I, the "Virgin Queen." When Sir Walter Raleigh founded a settlement on Roanoke Island in 1584 (in what is now North Carolina), he named the territory Virginia in honor of the English queen. Colonial Virginia included an area much larger than that the current state boundaries. Virginia became the tenth state in the Union in 1788, but in 1861 lost its northwestern area to the newly formed state of West Virginia.

These days, corn and wheat both play a major role in agriculture in Virginia, which makes it seem predestined that fine whiskies should be produced here. It is therefore rather astonishing to learn that there is exactly one distillery currently active in the state; all the others fell victim to Prohibition. But this may soon change: the historic distillery

owned by America's first president, George Washington, is being reconstructed at his estate, Mount Vernon, with the help of old drawings and descriptions. Many of the country's most famous whiskey companies are sponsoring the project by releasing special editions earmarked for the project, and using the proceeds to help finance the reconstruction.

Virginia was not always the blank spot on the whiskey map that it is today. In the period before the Civil War, Virginia produced even more whiskey than the neighboring state of Kentucky. The War Between the States brought an end to Virginia's dominance. With the end of the war and emancipation of the slaves, many whiskey operations ceased to exist altogether, while others moved their businesses to other states. By the time

of Prohibition, there were only five distilleries still operating in Virginia. When Prohibition was repealed in 1933, just one came forward: Abraham Smith Bowman Distillery in what is now Reston, near the Potomac River. Founded in 1935, Bowman's Virginia Gentleman brand whiskey was a great success. Bowman was and remains the only active distillery in Virginia, although it is no longer located in Reston.

Unfortunately, there are few historical records of the many and varied distilleries of Virginia's earlier period. Research and archaeological excavation being done at Mount Vernon are the source of nearly all the information we have about George Washington's distillery. The first president inherited the Mount Vernon estate from his brother's widow in 1761 and set himself up as a gentleman farmer. In 1797, upon completing his final term as president, he had a distillery built on the property. It was said to have fifty mash tubs for fermenting the grain and five large copper stills. The whiskey produced there was a blend consisting of 60 percent rye, 35 percent corn and 5 percent barley. In just three years, some 13,000 gallons (50,000 l) had already been produced. The whiskey was shipped, without maturation, to dealers and various prominent persons throughout the state of Virginia.

Top: Mount Vernon, George Washington's estate on the Potomac River in Virginia.
Bottom: Federal officials dismantle an illegal distillery at Mount Vernon in the 1920s, during the Prohibition years.

Opposite: The Shenandoah National Park draws over a million nature lovers to Virginia every year.

A. Smith Bowman

A. SMITH BOWMAN

OWNER	Sazerac Company
ESTABLISHED	1935
STATUS	In production
ANNUAL PRODUCTION	Not specified

TODAY, THE BOWMAN DISTILLERY is located in an industrial park in the charming small town of Fredericksburg, Virginia.

Abraham Smith Bowman founded his distillery in 1935 on his family estate, Sunset Hills Farm. Much of the land was sold in 1961 and became the town of Reston, a planned community that is now a suburb of Washington D.C. Bowman had inherited the property on which he established the farm, and could afford these ventures because he had already earned his fortune manufacturing buses and streetcars. The first whiskey produced in the new distillery was a blend called Virginia Gentleman. Its fame spread quickly among the congressmen in the nearby nation's capital. It was so popular among journalists that a special label, called "Gentlemen of the Press," was produced specifically for sale in the National Press Club.

In the 1960s, the Bowman family sold off the land around the distillery piece by piece until it was completely surrounded by what was becoming the city of Reston. The Bowmans finally shut down their original facility in 1987, moving the entire operation 60 miles (100 km) further south to the small town of Fredericksburg, on the Rappahannock River. They purchased and completely renovated a former cellophane factory there, and one year later, in 1988, the distillery opened its doors again. The new facility produces relatively little whiskey compared to the original one, focusing its production instead on vodka and gin, and occasionally rum. In 2003, the Bowman family sold the distillery, at the time one of the oldest family-owned businesses in the country, to Sazerac. Based in New Orleans, Sazerac is an international beverage company that also owns the Buffalo Trace whiskey distillery in Frankfort, Kentucky. Bowman is now the last surviving distillery in the Commonwealth of Virginia.

Visiting the beautiful city of Fredericksburg today, it is hard to imagine that one of the bloodiest battles of the Civil War was fought here in 1862.

Virginia Gentleman has a wide following far beyond the inviting taverns of Fredericksburg, VA.

Already in production in 1935, the distillery's founding year and just shortly after Prohibition, Virginia Gentleman whiskey remains the firm's workhorse brand. The label on the bottles described it as "Virginia whiskey" until 1996; this has since been changed to "Bourbon whiskey." What is unusual about its production today is that it is only partially produced in the Fredericksburg distillery. Since Bowman's relocation and sale, fermentation and the initial distillation take place in a different state, at the Buffalo Trace Distillery in Kentucky, which serves as a supplier for the Virginia end of the operation. Earlier, a distillery called Heaven Hill filled that role for many years. In both cases, the supplier keeps a close eye on the early phases of the whiskey production process and ensures that the spirit continues to be made exactly according to the original recipe. After the first distillation, the distillate is transported to Fredericksburg by railway, where it is distilled again in a copper doubler, a kind of still that almost looks like a cylinder-shaped pot still. The legendary master distiller Joe Dangler has overseen this second distillation process at Bowman for the past thirty years.

The six-year-old, 90 proof variety (in the USA, 2 proof equals 1 percent alcohol by volume, or ABV) is said to be a blend of 85 percent corn, 8 percent rye and 7 percent malted barley. The high percentage of corn makes this a very sweet whiskey, while the rye lends it a bit of spice. In addition to this bottling, there is also an 80-proof variety, aged for approximately four years. The somewhat older whiskey is definitely to be preferred.

WHISKEY
Virginia Gentleman, 90 proof, 45% ABV, official bottling
Color: Copper red

 **TASTING NOTES**
This approximately six-year-old whiskey has a very sweet nose with a trace of vanilla, a strong honey note and light spice. The scent of oak is also dominant. On the palate, these same scents are very much in evidence, with the vanilla becoming even more prominent still. The finish is very soft.

TENNESSEE

> "... tell me what brand of whiskey that
> Grant drinks. I would like to send a barrel
> of it to my other generals."
>
> ABRAHAM LINCOLN

MENTION THE STATE OF TENNESSEE, and chances are that Jack Daniel's and Lynchburg come to mind right alongside the country music capital of Nashville and Memphis, hometown of rock and roll legend Elvis Presley. Memphis is the largest city in the state, located on the eastern shore of the Mississippi River, and has a climate that is nearly subtropical.

Tennessee, with a population 5.6 million, lies adjacent to Virginia to the southwest, and shares most of its northern border with the whiskey bastion of Kentucky. Nashville, home of the Grand Ole Opry, is its capital city.

Tennessee entered the Union as the sixteenth state in 1796, but with the onset of the Civil War it joined the southern states in seceding on May 7, 1861. Following the war and the emanci-

pation of the slaves, Tennessee was the first rebel state to rejoin the Union on July 24, 1866.

Today, Tennessee still comes across as a very conservative state, particularly in the more rural areas. In fact, it is only legal to produce whiskey in three counties: Coffee, Lincoln and Moore. Throughout the state, the sale of alcohol is subject to stringent regulations. Yet even in Tennessee, time marches on, and the laws are gradually becoming less severe, particularly in the larger urban areas.

Tennessee is an integral part of the region known as the "Bible belt," where Prohibition went into effect as early as 1910. Prohibition was taken seriously here, and distillers were forced to move on to places with greater tolerance for alcohol production. In 1913, the last seven distilleries—of

what had been perhaps 700 distilleries a century earlier—were shut down. While Prohibition was officially repealed throughout the USA in 1933, it remained in place in Tennessee. It was only in 1938 that whiskey production was again permitted—but with the proviso that it could neither be sold nor consumed in Tennessee. It is only since 1995 that distilleries have been allowed to sell whiskey in their gift shops. Drinking whiskey on-site is still forbidden.

Tennessee whiskies are a bit different from the whiskies produced by neighboring Kentucky to the north and, indeed, from all other American whiskies. As Tennessee whiskies are filled into casks for maturing, they are passed through an extra charcoal filter, a procedure sometimes known as the "Lincoln County Process." The more general term is "charcoal mellowing" or "leaching." The charcoal, made from sugar maple wood, is meant to ensure that the whiskey maturing in its casks is even purer, with a more balanced character. Over the years this technique has been further refined, and the term "Tennessee Sour Mash" is now registered as an independent, distinct variety of whiskey. It is not, however, the "sour mash" itself that makes Tennessee whiskey so unique, but the charcoal mellowing. The distilleries throughout the state are naturally proud of their product's special qualities.

Top: The grave of Elvis Presley at Graceland is a pilgrimage site for millions of fans of the King of Rock and Roll.
Bottom: Silent witnesses to the American Civil War at the Chickamauga and Chattanooga National Military Park.

Opposite: Paddle-wheel steamboats on the Mississippi River belong to the era when there were still hundreds of distilleries in Tennessee.

George A. Dickel

GEORGE A. DICKEL

OWNER	Diageo
ESTABLISHED	1870
STATUS	In production
ANNUAL PRODUCTION	4.75 million liters/1.25 million gallons

One of the most popular of George A. Dickel's whiskies is the Sour Mash No. 8.

THE GEORGE A. DICKEL BREWERY can be found near Tullahoma (population 17,000), a small town that first became important because of its railway connection. The distillery itself is located just outside Tullahoma in Cascade Hollow, which was also its name for a long time.

George Dickel was born in Germany in 1818, but immigrated to the USA with his wife in 1844. At the end of the 1860s, he took up the whiskey trade. He would buy bulk whiskey in barrels and then sell it again under his own name. Early on, he developed a strong partnership with the Cascade Distillery (as it was still called at that time), which soon became his exclusive source of whiskey. In 1888, George A. Dickel, together with his brother-in-law Victor Schwab, was able to buy the Cascade Distillery outright. On a side note, the distillery wrote the word "whiskey" the Scottish way—without the "e"—as it still does today.

Unfortunately, Dickel had little opportunity to get involved with his newly purchased distillery. He was injured in a riding accident and died just six years later. Schwab continued to run the facility with his son. When Prohibition got an early start in Tennessee in 1910, they were forced to shut down the distillery and move to Louisville, Kentucky in order to continue production at the Stitzel-Weller Distillery. All too soon, passage of the Eighteenth Amendment halted alcohol production altogether. After Prohibition was repealed, Schenley Distillation purchased the marketing rights for the George Dickel brands, which were then produced at the Ancient Age Distillery near Leestown, Kentucky.

The old, traditional methods were nonetheless preserved, which made it possible, in 1958, to

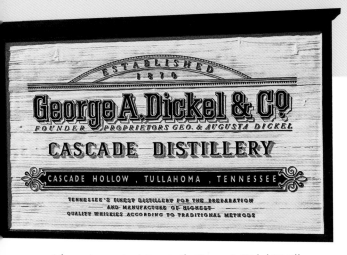

A large sign greets visitors to the George A. Dickel Distillery, founded on this site in 1870.

construct a new distillery barely half a mile away from the original Cascade Hollow location near Tullahoma. Compared to its neighbor, Jack Daniel's, the Dickel operation is downright tiny in scale. There are just twenty-nine workers here, compared to the 400 or so employed by the Lynchburg distillery.

In 1964, the original name of the whiskey was restored. Once again, the label carried the name of George A. Dickel, founder of the company. United Distillers (UD) bought the distillery from Schenley in 1987, and in 1997 it was sold again, this time to international giant Diageo. In 2001, supply greatly exceeded demand, and the new owners shut down production. Many feared that the distillery would be shut down for good. There were also rumors circulating that Diageo wanted to pull out of the American market entirely. When production resumed in 2004, all those involved breathed a deep sigh of relief.

Dickel uses the charcoal mellowing method characteristic of Tennessee whiskies, though the process differs slightly from that of Jack Daniel's. The smaller distillery covers the charcoal with a blanket of wool to ensure that the whiskey drips through evenly, never pooling at any one spot; the whiskey is evenly distributed from the beginning to the end of the filtering process. In addition, the doubler at the Dickel Distillery looks a little odd. Whereas most stills resemble large copper kettles, the Dickel plant uses a doubler made of stainless steel, which is, however, still heated by copper pipes.

George Dickel Old No. 8 is the standard-bearer of the firm. The somewhat older George Dickel Superior No. 12, however, has been named one of the ten best whiskies in the world by no less an expert than Jim Murray, well known author and critic. Murray gives the Superior No.12 Whiskey his highest rating: world class. In addition to these two classic labels, there is also a ten-year-old variety. Dickel whiskies are slightly lighter and more aromatic than the ones produced by neighboring Jack Daniel's.

WHISKY

George Dickel No. 12, 90 proof, 45% ABV, official bottling
Color: Reddish amber

TASTING NOTES

The nose of this whiskey is spicy, but still notably mild. One can discern apple pie, lemon slices, clover honey and a light note of rye. The medium-heavy mouth is spicy and complex, again with apple along with cinnamon and ginger. The finish is very clean, with a final hint of apple pie.

The lovely gift shop on the premises of the Dickel Distillery, whiskey fans can find all kinds of souvenirs and memorabilia.

Jack Daniel's

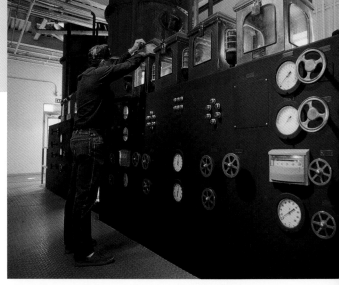

The impressive stills at Jack Daniel's, which date back to the pre-Prohibition era, stand in a seven-story stone building.

JACK DANIEL'S

OWNER	Brown-Forman
ESTABLISHED	1866
STATUS	In production
ANNUAL PRODUCTION	Not specified

LYNCHBURG, TENNESSEE, home to the legendary Jack Daniel's Distillery, is about as picture-perfect a small southern town as one could hope to find. Now as then, the population of Lynchburg is given as 361, just as it was in the very first of the company's famous television ads, regardless of who might have moved in or passed on in the meantime. The pace of life in Lynchburg is slow and leisurely, and people take great care to keep it that way. Completely surrounded by high hills, the town is always decked out in its finest. Most of the shops and businesses date from the golden years of the 1920s. In addition to the distillery, there is also a dry goods store and even a saloon—but as already mentioned, no alcohol can be served there. You can't drink alcohol at the gift shop adjacent to the distillery either, but visitors can enjoy the famous lemonade, also made by Jack Daniel's and sold across the country, that has always been poured instead of the whiskey.

Jack Daniel's grandfather, Joseph Daniel, ran off with the fifteen-year-old daughter of a family of well-off Scots for whom Joseph had worked. They ended up immigrating to America, the land of unlimited opportunities. His grandson, Jack Daniel, whose given name was actually Jasper Newton Daniel ("Jack" was his

The slightly milder Single Barrel is increasingly popular with Jack Daniel's fans.

nickname), also left his family early in life after quarreling with his stepmother, his natural mother having died when Jack was just one year old. Already as a child, Jack worked for the farmer and local distiller Dan Call, who taught him everything he knew about the trade and craft of distilling. But Dan Call was also a fundamentalist lay preacher, and eventually he could no longer reconcile his beliefs with his alcohol business. The solution was to sell the entire production to Jack Daniel, which he did, just around the time Jack turned fourteen years old.

Jack continued to work as a whiskey dealer for the next six years, and in 1866, at the age of twenty, he founded his own distillery in the nearby town of Lynchburg, in the very place where it remains to this day. He chose the location carefully, because he had located Cave Spring, a source of water of unparalleled quality. Jack Daniel had the cave inspected as thoroughly as possible, but the space was too narrow for the distillery to be built directly over the spring.

Daniel drove his whiskey to market in a horse-drawn wagon, promoting the whiskey himself in every way possible. Though he stood not quite 5 feet 3 inches tall, Jack Daniel's unshakable confidence in himself and his product was the whiskey's best advertisement, and his whiskey soon became widely known. Beginning in 1890, he began making what is today the best-selling whiskey in the USA: the famous "No. 7," with its black label and four-cornered bottle. His big breakthrough came at the 1904 St. Louis World's Fair, where Jack Daniel's No. 7 won the gold medal for the best whiskey in the world. Since

Jack never married, in spite of being the most eligible bachelor in the region, he took his nephew, Lem Mortlow, into the firm and groomed him to be his successor. One day, Jack became enraged at a safe that could not be opened and kicked it hard enough to break a toe. That injury never did heal, and he eventually died of blood poisoning in 1911.

Two years earlier, when Prohibition was imposed in Moore County already at the end of 1909, Daniel's nephew Lem had moved the operation to St. Louis, where for a time it was still possible to make whiskey. After Prohibition was repealed in 1933, Motlow wanted to move back to Lynchburg, something the state of Tennessee would only permit him to do five years later, in 1938, when the production of alcohol finally became legal again in Moore County. Upon his return, he expanded the distillery and left it to his four sons upon his death in 1947. Unfortunately, the sons were not able to determine who would be an adequate successor to their father, and sold the operation to the Brown-Forman Corporation in 1956. The sale ensured the continuation of techniques and traditions that led to Jack Daniel's current number one status among all American whiskies.

Jack Daniel's Old No. 7, the most successful whiskey, is a blend of five- to six-year-old whiskies. "Gentleman Jack," as it is affectionately called, is filtered a second time after maturation, making it smoother and slightly sweeter. Another label, Jack Daniel's Single Barrel, is becoming more and more popular. It is not as heavy as others, and because it is a single cask whiskey, its taste can vary from barrel to barrel. This is exactly what makes it so exciting.

WHISKEY
Jack Daniel's Old No. 7,
86 proof, 40% ABV,
official bottling
Color: Copper red

 TASTING NOTES
This five- to six-year-old whiskey is the embodiment of Jack Daniel's. This is not a whiskey for the faint-hearted and should be avoided by those who are newcomers to whiskey. From the start, the nose is full of energy and fiery, phenolic and smelling of oak and liquorices with a somewhat sweet note. It is very heavy on the palate at first, then milder, very oily, with the liquorices continuing along with a dollop of toffee. The finish is improbably long. The oak and the oily flavor are notable, complemented by notes of corn and malt detectable in the aftertaste.

At the Jack Daniel's Distillery, as elsewhere in Lynchburg, people take pride in taking it very easy.

KENTUCKY

"Whiskey is by far the most popular of all remedies
that won't cure a cold"

JERRY VALE

THE STATE OF KENTUCKY, right on the cusp
between the northern and southern states, became
the fifteenth state in the Union on June 1, 1792. It
had previously been part of Virginia. Kentucky's
inhabitants have never been exactly sure where
they belong. Even their two most famous fellow-
citizens stood on opposite sides during the Civil
War: Abraham Lincoln, president of the Union,
and Jefferson Davis, president of the Confederacy.

The name "Kentucky" comes from the Iroquois
word "ken-tah-ten," which means something like
"land of the future." Today, Kentucky is better
known as the "Bluegrass State" after the blue-
green color of the grass that fills its meadows in
the springtime.

Ironically, Bourbon whiskey got its start in
Bourbon County, Kentucky, where no whiskey
has been produced in a very long time. Today,
Bourbon can be made anywhere in the USA provided that certain conditions for its manufacture
and content are met.

Although Kentucky whiskey is a multi-billion
dollar business these days, a wide variety of liquor
laws regulate the sale of alcoholic beverages.
Sixty-one of the 120 counties in the state are "dry,"
despite high profits from whiskey production. The
liquor laws vary widely, making it advisable to get
informed about a particular place well ahead of a
visit. Be forewarned that in most distilleries, not
a drop of whiskey can be drunk: they hand out
candies instead.

The distilleries in Kentucky are divided among
the cities of Bardstown, Clermont, Frankfort,
Lawrenceburg, Loretto, Louisville and Versailles.

Louisville, with a population of 700,000, is by
far the largest city in Kentucky. It is therefore no
surprise that so many distilleries are based in this
metropolis. Its transportation connections—earlier
the Ohio River, and later the railroad—have also
contributed to its appeal. Twelve distilleries once
lined Louisville's famous "Distillery Row." Over
time they grew into extensive industrial complexes

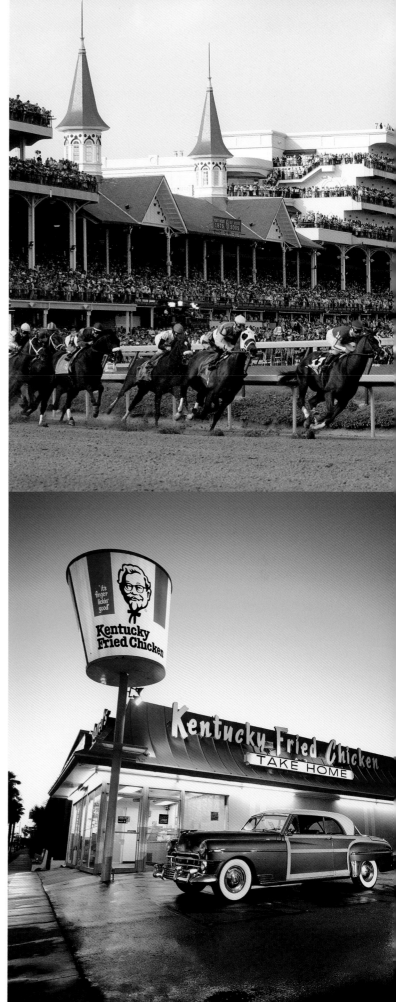

with multistoried brick buildings. Two of these distillery companies are still in production today: Brown-Forman, home of the famous Old Forester brand, and the Bernheim Distillery, which produces whiskey for the Heaven Hill brand in addition to its own labels. Louisville is also the headquarters of the UPS package delivery service, and home of the Kentucky Fried Chicken fast food chain. The latter was founded in 1930 and now includes more than 12,000 restaurants in over eighty countries.

Something else that is strongly associated with Kentucky, right alongside its whiskies, is horses. The state is famous for its thoroughbred breeding as well as the Kentucky Derby, which has taken place here every May since 1875. For two weeks each year, all of Louisville goes wild with excitement. The city is not only a center of the sporting world and economic activity, but also a great cultural center, with many world-class museums and other attractions.

In addition to agriculture, which is the dominating factor by far in Kentucky's economy (horses, cattle, swine, dairy products, grain and tobacco), revenue is also generated through a flourishing manufacturing industry producing automobile parts and machine tools. Coal mining is also profitable, as is, of course, the whiskey.

Top: Every year, Churchill Downs hosts the Kentucky Derby, a Triple Crown horse race that attracts more than 200,000 fans.
Bottom: Another world-famous export from Kentucky, in addition to whiskies such as Jim Beam, Wild Turkey and more.

Opposite: The ease of transportation along the Ohio River made Louisville the center of the Kentucky whiskey industry.

Barton

BARTON	
OWNER	Constellation Brands
ESTABLISHED	1890
STATUS	In production
ANNUAL PRODUCTION	Not specified

THE BARTON DISTILLERY is located in Bardstown, a lovely small town southwest of Louisville with a population of just 7,000. At one time, Barton was the center of whiskey production in the USA, with twenty-two distilleries in operation. These days, only one other, Heaven Hill Distillery, remains in operation in Bardstown.

The brick factory building housing the Barton Distillery sits on 445 acres of prime industrial land. Until recently, Oscar Getz's Whiskey Museum shared this premises, but a few years ago it moved to a new location in an old university building (Spalding Hall) next door to Bardstown's courthouse. Tom Moore built the distillery, which he named after himself, at its current location in 1889. He also owned a second distillery with his partner, Ben Mattingly. Today, the Barton Distillery still calls one of its brands Tom Moore, while Heaven Hill has a brand called Mattingly and Moore. Unfortunately, like so many others, the Tom Moore Distillery fell victim to Prohibition. Businessman Henry Teur tried to reopen the distillery, undertaking a renovation and modernization program in 1934. It was Oscar Getz, however, who, in 1946, turned it into the most technically advanced distillery of its day, rebuilding it from the ground up according to purely functional specifications. Regrettably, this means that the Barton Distillery is not , by any standards, a thing of beauty. The fermentation tanks are located outside the factory, with no roof above them. Only the cap of the stills is made of copper, with the rest of stainless steel. The isolation still, also standing outside the building, is the only piece of equipment made entirely of

Whiskey is matured in barrels stored in giant warehouses on the grounds of the Barton Distillery.

copper. Storage buildings thirty-seven stories high are spread throughout the industrial park. There is really nothing at all left of the original Moore Distillery.

The company and its products reached their present level of quality and popularity under Getz's leadership. Adding to his fame, Getz built the magnificent Oscar Getz Museum of Whiskey History on the grounds and wrote the book *Whiskey, an American Pictorial History*, an endlessly fascinating work of cultural history.

In 1971, Getz expanded his operation to Scotland, taking over the Littlemill Distillery and building a new one on Loch Lomond. After setting up a Scottish subsidiary, the sale and purchase of additional companies and subsidiaries went on for some time, with many rather confusing name changes and shifts of ownership. Today, the Scottish subsidiary belongs to Glen Catrine, and the original American firm is now the property of Barton Brands, itself a subsidiary of the beverage giant Constellation Brands. Barton Brands made its mark primarily with inexpensive supermarket wines. The company's management has frequently been subject to hefty criticism for withholding any information about the production process from the public and generally keeping too much secret. The recipe for the mash, for example, has never been revealed. Despite its critics, Barton has been remarkably successful, recently moving up to become the fourth largest spirits company in the USA, after holding the number eight spot for a very long time. In addition to its for the most part perfectly acceptable and very affordable whiskies, Barton also produces rum, gin, vodka, tequila and a number of other alcoholic beverages in two additional distilleries.

The majority of Barton's whiskies are brands like Barklay's and Colonel Lee, which have received whiskey guru Jim Murray's lowest possible rating. There are many more, including the previously mentioned Tom Moore, the house brand Old Barton, Fleischmann's, Glenmore, Ten High, Kentucky Gentleman and several others.

WHISKEY
Kentucky Gentleman BIB, 100 proof, 50% ABV, official bottling
Color: Amber

TASTING NOTES
This whiskey, long recognized for its character, is difficult to obtain outside of the USA. It is exceptionally powerful, and only a light aroma of malt comes through in the nose. The body is explosively sweet, with strong rye notes and a hint of caramel. The finish is long and dry, with touches of oak and vanilla.

The distillery itself seems very small compared to the expansive property dotted with giant storage warehouses.

Bernheim

Whether it is rye, wheat or malted barley whiskey, the foundation for the fermentation of the grain is laid in the yeast tub.

BERNHEIM

OWNER	Heaven Hill Distilleries, Inc.
ESTABLISHED	1992
STATUS	In production
ANNUAL PRODUCTION	8.5 million liters/2.3 million gallons

THE CURRENT, MODERN BERNHEIM
Distillery is located right in the middle of Louisville's tenth district. It was completely rebuilt in 1992, and only the brickwork of the surrounding massive storage buildings provide any evidence that there was once a much older distillery on the site, the Astor Distillery.

Isaac Wolfe Bernheim (1848–1945), known as Ike, was an immigrant from Germany who started out in Pennsylvania and later moved on to Kentucky. He was the proud holder of the patent for the hip flask, though his invention had not exactly made him rich. Toward that end he joined his brother in the whiskey trade, where he would eventually make his name. Around the turn of the century he built his own distillery in Louisville, right next to the railroad tracks. Since 1888, he had been co-owner of another distillery, which burnt to the ground. The two brothers became best known for their I. W. Harper brand, which brought them great wealth. Bernheim had trademarked the brand as early as 1879. The initials "I" and "W" came from the initials of his first and middle name. He was reluctant to use "Bernheim"; a Jewish name was unlikely to sell the product. "Harper" was the surname of a horse breeder he knew, and he used that instead.

Many whiskey experts around the world consider Rittenhouse rye whiskey to be a hot insider's tip.

Bernheim was a pioneer in the marketing of whiskey, not least because he made sure his was always sold not by the barrel, but in I. W. Harper bottles. During Prohibition, the Bernheim Distillery was one of just six in the USA that were awarded a license to produce alcoholic spirits for medicinal purposes. This allowed the firm to survive financially—just barely—during those difficult times.

After Prohibition, the firm took over the Old Charter brand, along with the rest of the stock of the Stitzel-Weller Distillery. I.W. Harper, the original Berheim brand, went to two whiskey brokers from Chicago, who sold it to Schenley. After Schenley was sold to UD in 1987, the brand was taken over by its current owner, Diageo. At one time, the Bernheim Distillery itself controlled around ninety different brands, of which only a few remain today. In the early 1990s, IDV, the predecessor of Diageo, owned the Stiztel-Weller Distillery just a few miles away from the Bernheim complex, as well as the previously acquired Glenmore Distillery. The new Bernheim Distillery built in 1992 was part of an effort to construct a centralized distilling operation for the production of all of Diageo's Kentucky brands, as well as that of the George A. Dickel Distillery in Tennessee, which is also owned by the giant beverage group. The new plant was designed so that all varieties of Bernheim whiskey, including I. W. Harper and Old Charter, could be produced from a single still.

The Stitzel-Weller brands, which include Weller, Rebel Yell and Old Fitzgerald, were distilled separately, in stainless steel stills—only the beer stills still have copper caps. Almost as soon as the ultra-modern distillery was completed, it had a new owner. As Diageo began to move out of the American market, Heaven Hill took advantage of the situation and purchased the new complex, having lost its own distillery to a catastrophic fire in 1996. In the end, only the Old Fitzgerald brand was transferred to Heaven Hill; the remainder stayed with Diageo. Heaven Hill Distilleries, Inc. continues to produce many whiskey brands for other companies; in fact, this is what Heaven Hill is best known for.

Today, a great number of brands are produced at Bernheim, such as Evan Williams, Elijah Craig, Henry McKenna and Heaven Hill's own house brand, along with the traditional whiskey Old Fitzgerald. Joining these are smaller brands with

limited production. One of these is Rittenhouse, a popular rye whiskey. It is a best-kept secret and hot tip of experts all over the world.

WHISKEY

Bernheim Wheat Whiskey,
45% ABV, official bottling
Color: Gold

TASTING NOTES

This whiskey is a blend that includes 51 percent wheat, giving it a powerful aroma of grain complemented by fruity notes of plums and apricots. The flavor remains fruity on the palate, expanded by woody influences. The entirety has a spicy note that is maintained throughout the medium-length finish.

Parker and Craig Beam, descendants of Jim Beam himself, are the master distillers at Bernheim/Heaven Hill, where they create a wide range of distinctive whiskies.

Brown-Forman

BROWN-FORMAN

OWNER	Brown-Forman
ESTABLISHED	1891
STATUS	In production
ANNUAL PRODUCTION	Not specified

THE BROWN-FORMAN DISTILLERY is located in Shively, a neighborhood on the southwestern outskirts of the port city of Louisville. Louisville was an important mercantile city from very early on due to its prime location on the Ohio River. Trade in hemp rope, tobacco and the region's famous ham flourished. Brown-Forman's simple brick complex is part of the area of Louisville fondly known as "Distillery Row." The storehouses of this otherwise typical industrial building complex are even heated during the winter to maintain optimal conditions for the ageing whisky—note again the spelling without an "e."

What is today the Brown-Forman enterprise began in the year 1860 as the Early Times Distillery, which produced a whiskey of the same name. The name came from the small town near Bardstown where it was originally located, also called Early Times. Its founder was John H. Beam, uncle of the better-known James "Jim" Beam. Today, only the place name itself remains. Brown-Forman bought the distillery in 1923 from owner S. L. Guthrie, relocating the operation to its present address in Louisville shortly after local legislation prohibited the production and storage of alcoholic beverages. The new distillery in Louisville was first called the Old Kentucky Distillery, but in recent years has been known simply as Brown-Forman. Early Times whisky is far from the only brand produced here. It is also the home of Old Forester, considered by experts to be the better of the two. The whisky itself has moved around a bit in the past. Old Forester was

The Brown-Forman Distillery is located on Louisville's Distillery Row. In the golden years of the 1950s, the coopers here made barrels for six different distillers.

first produced in the St. Mary Distillery near the town of Loretto. After that distillery closed, production moved to the Old Forester Distillery in downtown Louisville, not far from the Early Times Distillery. In 1979, Brown-Forman finally closed the Old Forester Distillery for good, consolidating its operations by moving its production to the Early Times complex.

The distillery was put to another use in 1996 after a fire destroyed most of the production facilities of the Heaven Hill Distillery. On short notice, Heaven Hill moved its entire operation to Louisville, renting facilities from Brown-Forman for four days a week until its purchase of the Bernheim Distillery was complete.

How did the distillery come to be owned by Brown-Forman, in control now for well over a generation, in the first place? We first have to take into account that Brown-Forman is a unique company, one of the very few in which family members are still a stockholding majority and take an active role in running the business. In 1750, ancestors of the firm's founder, George Garvin Brown, immigrated to America from Scotland. Together with his half-brother, J. T. S. Brown, George founded a distillery producing Old Forester whisky. Their Scottish background explains why the word whiskey appears on the label without the "e." Brown was one of the first to bottle his whiskey, which he stamped with a quality seal. It was much more common at the time to trade whiskey in full barrels, which often led to the product being illegally watered down or otherwise corrupted while en route. Brown's half brother chose a different path, producing cheap whiskey exclusively. George Brown stuck to his principles and, perhaps as a result, received one of the six licenses issued by the federal government to produce medicinal alcoholic spirits during the Prohibition years.

Today, Old Forester is the standard bearer of the distillery, a fruity whisky aged in charred oak casks. The tendentially nutty Early Times brand is cut with straight Bourbon that has also been matured in charred casks. Today, it is exported all over the world.

The proximity of the Ohio River has provided an important transportation route ever since Louisville was founded. Goods manufactured here were shipped to different states and cities around the country.

WHISKY
Old Forester, 86 proof, 43% ABV,
official bottling
Color: Dark copper

TASTING NOTES
The standard blend is produced according to traditional methods from a mash that consists of 72 percent corn, 18 percent rye and 10 percent barley. The aroma of Old Forester is wonderfully flowery, as is typical for rye blends. This is a whiskey that lingers on the palate, constantly changing. At first it is somewhat dry, then sweet toffee notes with hints of orange emerge, and in the next instant corn and rye are in the forefront. The finish is medium-long and dry, with a spicy oak aftertaste.

Buffalo Trace

BUFFALO TRACE	
OWNER	Sazerac Company
ESTABLISHED	1857
STATUS	In production
ANNUAL PRODUCTION	Not specified

THE BUFFALO TRACE DISTILLERY stands east of Lousville and south of Frankfort. Its water tower is visible from many miles away, as are its multistoried warehouses. Once called Leesville, German immigrants founded the small town now known as Buffalo Trace in 1795 at the place where herds of wild buffalo once regularly forded the river. There are no surviving maps that are detailed enough to show the location of the original settlement.

A man named Benjamin Blanton, a successful gold prospector, returned to Leestown a wealthy man. He bought the nearby Rock Hill Farm and began to distill whiskey. He decided early on to expand his whiskey business further, building the distillery now known as Buffalo Trace in 1865. Four years later he sold the complex to Richard Tobin, who renamed it the OFC (Old Fire Cooper) Distillery. It was under this name that its brands first gained widespread fame in

Buffalo Trace whiskey has been distilled and carefully matured in the small town near Frankfort for nearly 200 years.

Kentucky and neighboring areas. The distillery has had more changes of name than of owners. In 1870, it became part of the spirits empire of Edmund Taylor, who at the time also owned Labrot & Graham. Taylor invested a great deal of money in the distillery, financing regular improvements. Later, as was the case with Labrot & Graham, he sold to George T. Stagg, who renamed it the Old Stagg Distillery. When Stagg sold the complex to Schenley during the Second

An enormous herd of buffalo used to graze near the place where Buffalo Trace Whiskey is made today.

World War, it was renamed first Schenley, and then the Ancient Age Distillery, after its most popular brand. The name Buffalo Trace was bestowed in the year 2000, a reference to both its geographic location and its historical past.

Driven out of Tennessee by the difficult years of the early Prohibition, the George A. Dickel brands were also produced and stored at the Buffalo Trace Distillery, which was outfitted with a building containing the charcoal mellowing filtering apparatus characteristic of Tennessee whiskies. At the time, Schenley owned Dickel as well. Today, there are still two distilleries on the site, although the George A. Dickel brand has since returned to Tennessee. As of 1992, Buffalo Trace belongs to the beverage giant Sazerac.

The warehouses, some of them twelve stories high, are heated in the winter. The total area, including distilleries and storage, includes some 110 buildings on 667 acres. Visitors to the complex cannot possibly overlook the statue of Colonel Albert Bacon Blanton, the son of the founder, who started working at the distillery as an office clerk in 1897 at the age of sixteen. Fifteen years later, he became its manager. In 1952, he finally retired after fifty-five years of service. One of the distillery's most successful whiskies, the first commercially available single cask bottling, is named after him. "Blanton's Single Barrel Bourbon," available since 1984, is one of the most exported in the world. In addition, the Buffalo Trace Distillery has generated increased interest in single cask whiskies with a special bottling

The symbol of the Buffalo Trace Distillery, the water tower with the black Buffalo, is visible from many miles away.

known as the Antique Whiskey Collection, a series of W. L. Weller and Elmer T. Lee single cask bottlings as well as a rye whiskey named after the distillery itself. Its first bottling was an absolute sensation in the whiskey world. The standard brand remains, as before, Ancient Age.

WHISKEY
Blanton's Gold Edition, 51.5% ABV
Color: Amber

TASTING NOTES
The whiskey has a fruity-flowery aroma with a light touch of wood and chocolate. Its flavors are complex and powerful, with the chocolate coming out again in the body along with a hint of cloves. The finish is long, with a vanilla aftertaste and once again the influence of wood.

Four Roses

FOUR ROSES

OWNER	Kirin Brewery Co.
ESTABLISHED	ca. 1860
STATUS	In production
ANNUAL PRODUCTION	11 million liters/2.9 million gallons

THE WONDERFUL BUILDING resembling a Spanish Mission with its little bell tower is located some 12 miles (20 km) south of Frankfort, Kentucky, making the Four Roses Distillery in Lawerenceburg a close neighbor of the Wild Turkey Distillery. The Four Roses Distillery LLC, which has carried that name since 2002, is without a doubt one of the loveliest distilleries in America.

The founder of the distillery was Ire "Old Joe" Peyton. The story goes that he arrived in Kentucky via canoe in 1818 and immediately settled down, starting his whiskey business soon afterward. His whiskey, which he named "Old Joe" after himself, was a great success. Peyton later sold his company to a certain Gratz Hawkins, who renamed the distillery Old Prentice. Its ownership would change frequently over the years, belonging to the Ripley brothers for a time, who had other distilleries in the area as well, and later to Paul Jones, a whiskey dealer. It was he who registered the name Four Roses in 1888, moving the distillery along the road to its current fame.

No one is quite sure why Jones named the whiskey after four roses. Even within the distillery, there are two competing stories. One says that a colonel by the name of Rose had four daughters. The problem is that Colonel Rose actually had five daughters. The other story says that the brand was named after Jones's fiancé, supposedly named Rose. Why, then, four roses?

The Four Roses Distillery with its Spanish colonial style buildings is certainly one of the most beautiful distilleries in America.

The production of whiskey has not been entirely mechanized. The work here in the bottling plant still requires well-trained hands.

Shame on anyone who thinks Mr. Jones might have been up to no good…

The present distillery was constructed in Spanish colonial style from 1910 to 1912. Why this particular architectural style was chosen is something else that remains a little mysterious. In any case, the old Four Roses was produced here in the years before Prohibition. In 1943, it was bought by Seagram's, who moved production to Shively, a suburb of Louisville. It moved back to the site of the Old Prentice Distillery, and thus returned to its roots, in 1986. After Vivendi bought Seagram's in 2001, the distillery was passed on to Kirin, a Japanese partner firm and Japan's largest beer brewer.

Four Roses whiskey is the result of a unique production process. There are two different mash recipes: one uses 75 percent corn, 21 percent rye and 4 percent malted barley; while the other includes 60 percent corn, 36 percent rye and 25 percent sour mash blend. These are fermented with five different yeasts, producing a total of ten different washes (also known as "distiller's beers"). These are fermented for varying periods of time in different kinds of casks, to be blended together for the first time only after the distillation process is complete. In addition, the barrels are not stored in the warehouses next door to the distillery; that is where the Wild Turkey whiskey is aged. Four Roses is kept in

storehouses some fifty miles away on the road that leads to the Jim Beam Distillery. The beauty lies in the details! That is why Jim Rutledge, distillery manager, brought cypress wood from Florida all the way to Kentucky to be able to replace the ageing barrels one by one, as they wore out, rather than ordering the wood new each time and having to wait a year for it to season.

Today there are three different varieties of Four Roses and Bulleit Bourbon produced in Lawrenceburg. Until 2002, the Bourbon was made for export only. It has since found many fans in the USA as well.

WHISKEY
Four Roses Single Barrel, 43% ABV, official bottling
Color: Pale amber with red tones

TASTING NOTES
This single barrel whiskey has a well-defined aroma of malt and vanilla. On the palate, the flavor of rye comes through the spicy and complex flavors. The finish is sweetish, with a strong note of oak.

Heaven Hill

HEAVEN HILL	
OWNER	Heaven Hill Distilleries, Inc.
ESTABLISHED	1890
STATUS	Distillery destroyed by fire in 1996; production continues in Louisville

The 80-proof Bourbon Heaven Hill — the distillery's name brand — is only one of the many whiskies produced under a variety of brand names at the facility.

THE ORIGINAL PRODUCTION FACILITY, which was almost entirely destroyed by a devastating fire in November 1996, was in a river valley just outside Bardstown along the road to Loretto, where Heaven Hill Farm once stood. Some of the storage buildings and the bottling plant are still there, but the company's offices and a beautiful new visitors' center can be found in the center of Bardstown.

The history of Heaven Hill is relatively recent. In the years immediately following Prohibition, the brothers David, Ed, Gary, George and Mose Shapira had saved some money and were looking for an opportunity to get into the whiskey business. They started the company in 1935. It remains a family-owned firm today, run now by children and grandchildren of the founders. The entire enterprise was designed to permit the production of whiskey on a grand scale, and that it does: the

distillery can produce 400 to 500 barrels of spirits per day. It has over thirty washbacks, numerous wash stills and twenty-five of its own storehouses, as well as partial ownership of nineteen more in partnership with the former T. W. Samuels Distillery. Yet this is not all. Heaven Hill not only produces a vast number and variety of its own brands, but also supervises part or all of the production for other bottlers and supermarket chains. The exact number of labels can no longer be calculated, even from within the firm itself. Every time you read the name Bardstown on a whiskey label, with or without the invented name of some fantasy distillery, it is fairly certain that the whiskey comes either from Heaven Hill or Bernheim. Thanks to the dedication and efforts of Max Shapira, the firm has succeeded in introducing its own product lines over the past decades, including whiskies that reach a very high standard indeed. These have made the Heaven Hill name famous all over the world.

On November 7, 1996, the firm suffered a horrible setback when a lightning bolt started a fire in a warehouse. The fire spread rapidly to the stillhouse, destroying all the whiskey production equipment and claiming a total of nine warehouses. In the end, 90,000 barrels were lost in the flaming inferno, seriously depleting the company's

The great whiskey pioneers Elijah Craig and Evan Williams are honored with more than just a museum exhibit; the distillers at Heaven Hill have also named whiskies after them.

stored assets. The loss turned out not to be as great as was originally feared, however. Production could be maintained by renting facilities from the other great family distillery, Brown-Forman, four days a week. Next to Glenfiddich, Heaven Hill still has one of the largest whiskey inventories in the world, more than 600,000 barrels. In March 1999, the company was able to purchase the Bernheim Distillery from Diageo, giving Heaven Hill its own manufacturing base once again. Plans to resurrect the old Heaven Hill site and rebuild the destroyed distillery have been put off indefinitely. Today, Heaven Hill's high-quality brands, such as Elijah Craig or

Though very little of the original Heaven Hill Distillery remained after the 1996 fire, whiskey tastings are still held at the Heaven Hill visitors center in Bardstown.

Evan Williams, both named for pioneers in the Bourbon industry, are greatly appreciated around the world.

WHISKEY

Elijah Craig, 12 years old, 47% ABV,
official bottling
Color: Amber

TASTING NOTES

This whiskey is Heaven Hill Distillery's undisputed star. The twelve years of ageing have served it well. Its aroma is fruity, with notes of peach, apple and cherry. There is also a hint of vanilla and echoes of oak and mint. On the palate, the oak comes to the fore, with a body that is first dry and then somewhat sweet. The finish is very long and complex, with a touch of malt making an appearance.

At the Heaven Hill Bourbon Heritage Center, visitors can learn all about the history and production of Bourbon in interactive exhibits.

Jim Beam

The Jim Beam Distillery is actually two different distilling operations located just about 9 miles (14 km) apart from each other in Kentucky.

JIM BEAM

OWNER	Jim Beam Brands (Fortune Brands)
ESTABLISHED	1795
STATUS	In production
ANNUAL PRODUCTION	40 million liters/10.6 million gallons

JIM BEAM ACTUALLY OWNS TWO distilleries that produce its standard brands. One, known as the original, is located in Clermont, about half an hour south of Louisville by car. The other is in Boston, in Nelson County, about 9 miles (14 km) away. The distillery in Clermont is the favorite with tourists, where visitors can learn a tremendous amoung about the production of whiskey, as well as everything there is to know about the Beam family. You can even visit the Beam family home on the premises.

Jakob Böhm is the one who started it all, a German immigrant who arrived in the land of unlimited opportunity probably around 1788. Settling in Kentucky, he began to distill surplus grain into whiskey. At some point he Americanized his name, becoming Jacob Beam. In 1795, he founded his own company and was soon selling whiskey on a large scale. His son David continued the family business, which was called Old Tub Distillery under his management. David's brother John went on to found the Early Times Distillery. In 1890, Jacob's great-grandson, James "Jim" Beam, took over the helm of the family business, leading it with great skill until Prohibition forced him to shut down all his operations in 1920. Jim Beam stubbornly held on. In 1933, just as the dry years of Prohibition came to an end and at the age of 70, he founded the Clermont Distillery together with his son, Jeremiah.

Black Label is one of the classics from the house of Jim Beam. Its unmistakable label is recognized worldwide.

Since money was tight, he took on Harry Blum, a spirits trader from Chicago, as business partner. In the beginning, he was still producing Old Tub, as the Jim Beam brand was first established in 1942. Sometime during the Second World War, the distillery came completely under the control of Harry Blum, who became its full owner.

Blum was best at the marketing aspects of the whiskey business, setting the Jim Beam brand on its road to success. Demand for it was so high that a second distillery had to be built in nearby Boston in 1953. In 1967, the firm was sold to American Brands, a company primarily involved in the tobacco business. The new owners brought aboard other brands including Old Crow, Old Grand-Dad and Old Taylor, whose distilleries had been closed. Today, these brands are produced in one of the Jim Beam distilleries, still using, it is said, their original yeast cultures.

The entire distilling empire has been renamed a number of times. Its official name today is Jim Beam Brands, and is a subsidiary of Fortune Brands. Although the founding family has not owned the company in decades, many descendants remain intimately involved with the whiskey business. One of Jim Beam's grandchildren, Booker Noe, was a renowned master distiller. His skills as a whiskey ambassador led to a very particular honor: a new whiskey named after him. And the father-son team of Parker and Craig Beam are the master distillers for the Heaven Hill empire.

Exactly how Jim Beam whiskey is produced remains a secret, as the mash formula has never been made public, but it is thought that there are three different mash recipes. Although the two distilleries use exactly the same methods, their water comes from different sources, resulting in very subtle differences in the whiskies. The whiskey from the Boston distillery is considered fuller, with more spice. To ensure consistency, it is likely that the two whiskies are blended with each other before bottling. Production is quite high, more than 600 barrels per day. The "normal" Jim Beam with the white label is the best-selling Bourbon in the world, bested within the USA only by Jack Daniel's Old No. 7. Worldwide, this Jim Beam is one of the top twenty spirit beverages. There is also a Jim Beam Black Label, and a rye whiskey with a yellow label, in addition to the already-mentioned Old Crow, Old Grand-Dad and Old Taylor on offer. Finally, Jim Beam produces the small batch brands Knob Creek and Basil Hayden's, both premium whiskies.

WHISKEY

Basil Hayden's, 8 years old, 40% ABV, official bottling
Color: Amber

TASTING NOTES

This whiskey is one of Jim Beam's high-quality small batch Bourbons, all of which are single cask bottlings. The nose exudes mint and herbs, with a note of tea. On the palate, the flavor of rye comes through, with a bit of peppery spice completed by a hint of sweet honey. The finish is long and dry, with the sweetness of honey emerging once more.

The legendary Jim Beam produces over 600 barrels of its famous whiskey each day, making the company the world's largest Bourbon distiller.

Maker's Mark

MAKER'S MARK

OWNER	Beam Global Spirits & Wine (Fortune Brands)
ESTABLISHED	1805
STATUS	In production
ANNUAL PRODUCTION	8.2 million liters/2.2 million gallons

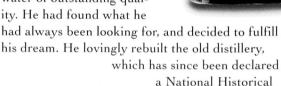

LOCATED ABOUT 4 MILES (6 km) outside the town of Loretto, this distillery's beautiful black- and red-toned wooden buildings stand surrounded by trees and lovely meadows. A narrow brook flows in its masonry red right through the middle of the complex. The idyllic setting makes it easy to believe that nearly everything here is still done by hand, with modern technology barely in evidence.

The distillery is currently supervised by the seventh consecutive generation of the Samuels family, although the firm is no longer family-owned. The Samuels family came to America as immigrants from Scotland. Robert Samuels, a former army officer, moved on from Pennsylvania to Kentucky, setting himself up as a farmer and whiskey distiller. His grandson, Tylor William, began commercial production in 1844. Store-houses from those early days can still be seen—and some are even still in use. After the end of Prohibition, William Isaac and Leslie Samuels made every effort to reopen their old distillery, which they rebuilt and upgraded. Soon afterward, Leslie's son T. William ("Bill") Samuels took over the business, only to sell it in 1943. Ten years later, however, he was drawn back into the whiskey business. He found an old, decrepit distillery outside the town of Loretto. On its grounds he discovered a deep, clear pond with a spring that would provide water of outstanding quality. He had found what he had always been looking for, and decided to fulfill his dream. He lovingly rebuilt the old distillery, which has since been declared a National Historical

Its idyllic location and lovely old wooden buildings make Maker's Mark Distillery one of the most picturesque in the USA.

The souvenir shop at the Maker's Mark Distillery lets visitors select and seal their very own bottle with the famous red wax.

Landmark. Bill also decided to discard the old Samuel's family mash recipes, replacing the rye with milder, more pleasant-tasting winter wheat, and to produce the whiskey itself with minimum recourse to industrial methods.

The distillery was called Star Hill at first, but is today widely known as the Maker's Mark Distillery. The star in the company's logo is a reminder of its original name, and the "S" right next to it refers less to the star than to the role of the Samuels family.

Bill Samuels has remained the driving force behind the company, even following the sale of the company in 1981 to Hiram Walker, a subsidiary of the international firm Allied Domecq. After the breakup of Allied, Maker's Mark became part of Beam Global Spirits and Wine. Despite everything, tradition still rules at Maker's Mark. The work is done exclusively by manual labor, leading to the relatively modest output of just fifty-four barrels per day. Also atypical is that each barrel is left to season, drying in the open air, for an entire year before being filled. Within the warehouses, the barrels are regularly rotated so that the barrels all pass through the higher, warmer levels as well as the lower, cooler ones. The entire

company places a great emphasis on the quality of their product, even when it costs more money to ensure that it is attained. The Glenmorangie Distillery, also known for its wood management, buys its used casks from Maker's Mark. Like everything else, each cask is individual and unique, and each bottle receives its own trademark sealing of red wax.

In addition to the standard Red Seal brand (43–45 percent ABV), there are also white and blue seal versions. In addition, a limited edition 101-proof Gold Seal whisky is produced at regular intervals, and further vintages are planned.

WHISKY
Maker's Mark Red Seal, 45% ABV,
official bottling
Color: Dark gold

TASTING NOTES
This whisky (written without the "e") is without a doubt one of the best artisanal premium brands in the USA. It has a full nose with strong notes of vanilla, wood and a hint of cloves. It is soft on the palate, with vanilla and caramel predominating. The finish is smooth, clean and long.

These are the stills in which Maker's Mark is distilled. The motto of the distillery remains "quality, not quantity."

Wild Turkey

WILD TURKEY	
OWNER	Austin, Nichols and Company (Pernod Ricard)
ESTABLISHED	1869
STATUS	In production
ANNUAL PRODUCTION	10.8 million liters (2.8 million gallons)

LOCATED ALONGSIDE THE KENTUCKY RIVER, the Wild Turkey Distillery reigns over the small town of Lawrenceburg, some 12 miles (20 km) south of Frankfort. The Four Roses Distillery is also nearby.

The Wild Turkey brand is still relatively new. Thomas McCarthy, who was president of the Austin, Nichols and Company beverage firm, a leader in the wine and spirits market, first introduced it in 1942. Although Austin, Nichols and Co. had been around since 1855, McCarthy was the first director to buy Bourbon and gin from other distilleries and resell them under his own label. The name Wild Turkey came to McCarthy one day while he was turkey hunting with some members of his bridge club. His bridge partners, who greatly appreciated his whiskey, asked him to bring some along to the next turkey shoot. He packed a few bottles, which he decorated with labels bearing a wild turkey. They were a great hit, and the Bourbon has carried that name ever since. Nonetheless, it was 1970 before the firm decided to purchase its own distillery, the one in Lawrenceburg. The facility had been founded by D. L. Moore, and then sold to the Irish Ripy brothers in

The Kentucky River valley is the setting for the traditional Wild Turkey Distillery in Lawrenceburg.

The Wild Turkey brand has always symbolized the great tradition of Bourbon.

1907, who also owned a neighboring distillery for a time. It was known as the Boulevard Distillery for a period, but today Wild Turkey proudly bears the name of its primary brand. The Austin Nichols Company was taken over by Pernod Ricard in the 1980s, and it was this change of ownership that led to the worldwide marketing and current popularity of Wild Turkey.

Although production has increased over the past few years, at 60,000 barrels per year its output is still relatively modest compared to that of some of its larger neighbors. Wild Turkey is produced according to slower, more traditional methods. The stills and doubler are still made entirely of copper. High value is placed on loyal employees like Jimmy Russell, their esteemed master blender, who learned his trade under the Ripy brothers and has almost half a century of service to the distillery behind him. Eventually he will turn his job over to his son, Eddie, who himself has been making Wild Turkey for twenty years.

Though the exact mash recipe is a closely guarded secret, it is known that a relatively high proportion of sour mash is used—33 percent, as opposed to a more typical 25 percent. It is also made from less corn and more rye (or malted barley), and all of it only the very best quality. Rumors about the precise proportions abound. The Bourbon is said to be as much as 75 percent corn, 13 percent rye and 12 percent malted barley.

The distillery also produces a rye whiskey. Jimmy Russell is of the opinion that the optimal strength for this whiskey is 100 proof, or "bottled in bond." That is why a variety of bottlings—including Wild Turkey 101, Russell's Reserve and a 12-year-old special bottling—are sold at 101 proof (50 percent ABV). There are also other whiskies, of course, that have a more typical drinking strength. Whiskey expert Jim Murray considers the Wild Turkey Rare Breed to be one of the finest whiskies in the world.

WHISKEY
Wild Turkey Rare Breed, 54.1% ABV, official bottling
Color: Dark amber

TASTING NOTES
The nose begins with a breath of spring flowers, with a light echo of honey. It is nonetheless slightly spicy. It is at first rather strong on the palate, then becomes softer and drier with light notes of honey and orange. A hint of tobacco comes through, as well. The finish is long and nutty, with a lovely aftertaste.

Woodford Reserve

WOODFORD RESERVE

OWNER	Brown-Forman
ESTABLISHED	1812
STATUS	In production
ANNUAL PRODUCTION	Not specified

THE WOODFORD RESERVE DISTILLERY is about 5 miles south of Frankfort in the small town of Versailles. The name it currently bears is that of its best-known whiskey brand. The lovely sandstone buildings are located in an area mainly known for its horse breeding farms amidst a landscape distinguished by splendid farmhouses and bluegrass meadows. The distillery, situated directly on Glenn's Creek, is the only one still in existence of what were once many in this valley.

Elijah Pepper, a whiskey maker from Virginia, came to Versailles in the year 1797 with the intention of taking up his craft anew here. He built a log cabin on the hill overlooking the present distillery, and began farming. He soon added a small distillery where he could make his whiskey. As he produced more and more, the lack of space for storage facilities became a problem, so he moved his operation to Glenn's Creek, where the distillery is still located today. There, he discovered a limestone spring providing water of

outstanding quality. To the south of Versailles, he founded a second distillery in partnership with his brother-in-law.

After Elijah Pepper's death, his son Oscar carried on the family business, bringing in the Scottish gentleman physician Dr. James Crow as a partner. Crow's calling card described him as a doctor, chemist and "distiller with heart and soul." It was Crow who was responsible for perfecting the sour mash method that led to the first production of true Bourbon. He was not, as many have claimed, the inventor of the method—instead, he used his knowledge and scientific background to improve the process and diminish the irregularities in quality and flavor that had plagued the industry. Woodford Reserve therefore has every right to be considered one of the most significant sites in the distilling world.

The sign hanging above the entrance to the distillery still reads: Oscar Pepper Distillery, Est. 1838, Labrot & Graham, Est. 1878. Its inscription testifies to the successful past of the Pepper family. The arrival of Labrot & Graham inaugurated a new era. James E. Pepper, who took over the

An extensive renovation of the entire distillery included building a beautiful visitors center with exhibits and information about the history of the distillery on Glenn's Creek.

Following distillation, the full casks are rolled to the massive sandstone storehouses to mature.

be shut down in 1970 as a result of a steep decline in the Bourbon market, and the property was sold off. In the 1990s, there was a resurgence of interest in distinctive, high quality Bourbons, known as small batch Bourbons. This led to renewed interest in reopening the distillery, but the sales price was by now considerably higher than what had been paid for it in the 1940s. An additional $10 million were invested in the renovations alone. Completed in 1996, the distillery once again shines in its former glory. It is the only distillery in the USA that uses exclusively pot stills imported from Scotland. Of course, what is produced here is not malt whiskey, but Bourbon, composed of 72 percent corn, 18 percent rye and 10 percent malt. To the consternation of many, the distillery was abruptly renamed Woodford Reserve in 2003, after having been traditionally known as Labrot & Graham.

Woodford Reserve and President's Choice are the brands produced here, both of which began as Brown-Forman/ Early Times productions.

WHISKEY
Woodford Reserve, 45.2% ABV, official bottling
Color: Amber-gold

 TASTING NOTES

This whiskey is a blend of triple distilled Bourbon from the Woodford Reserve Distillery and straight Bourbon from the Brown-Forman Distillery. The nose carries an intense aroma of vanilla, with just a hint of fruit. On the palate it is very full, slightly spicy, and not very sweet. The finish is long and warming.

distillery at the age of sixteen after the death of his father, sold the operation to try his luck in New York. A few years later, he returned, but he was by then a poor man. The distillery passed through many hands in this period until it was eventually sold to James Graham and a Frenchman, Leopold Labrot, in 1878. Woodford Reserve whiskey bottles still carry the L&G logo today, a reference to its one-time owner. The initials can also still be found on the distillery's chimney. In 1940, the Brown-Forman Company purchased the distillery for the paltry sum of $75,000. This was an incredible deal, especially when one takes into consideration that more than 25,000 casks of top quality whiskey in the warehouses were included in the sale. This happy circumstance was a great boon for Brown-Forman, since demand for its products had increased so much that it could no longer produce enough whiskey on its own. The newly purchased distillery's inventory of spirits ensured that Brown-Forman could carry on as usual. Unfortunately, the distillery itself had to

Anchor Distilling Co.

IN RECENT YEARS, a number of small-scale distilleries have been established, most of which focus their efforts on the production of vodka, rum or fruit spirits. A good number of them also distill whiskey on the side. In most cases, though, the microdistilleries produce such small quantities that they cannot reasonably distribute it outside their local area. The good news is that most small distilleries are happy to arrange visits to their facilities, by appointment, where one has the opportunity to buy whiskey directly at its source. The trip is nearly always worthwhile.

ANCHOR DISTILLING CO.

OWNER	Fritz Maytag
ESTABLISHED	1993
STATUS	In production

THE ANCHOR DISTILLERY is located right next door to the Anchor Steam Brewing Company in San Francisco's Portrero District.

Fritz Maytag, a descendant of the famous appliance family (Hoover vacuums and Maytag washing machines), purchased the Anchor Steam Brewery in 1965. Many years later, in 1993, he built a small distillery right next door to it. Like many of the whiskey pioneers, Maytag began with the production of rye whiskey. In 1994, after a maturation of just one year in casks that had not been charred, Old Potrero whiskey was introduced to the marketplace. Old Portrero Single Malt Rye Whiskey followed soon thereafter, also aged only one year. What "old" or "malt" has to do with these spirits is hard to say. Maytag followed these successes with Old Portrero Single Malt Straight Rye Whiskey, which was aged three years in charred casks. All of his whiskies are made from a 100 percent rye mash.

WHISKEY
Old Portrero Single Malt Rye Whiskey, 62.1% ABV, official bottling
Color: Pale brown

TASTING NOTES
This whiskey, made from 100 percent rye, ages in new wood casks that are not charred. Its nose is very floral and grassy, with notes of vanilla, nut and cinnamon. The flavors are dominated by the honey-sweetness of the rye. The finish is peppery, with a reappearance of the rye and honey notes.

The Anchor Steam Brewery and its small distillery are located in San Francisco's Portrero District on the east side of the city.

Clear Creek · Domaine Charbay Distillery

CLEAR CREEK

OWNER	Steve McCarthy
ESTABLISHED	1987
STATUS	In production

THE SMALL CLEAR CREEK DISTILLERY is located in downtown Portland, Oregon.

At the end of the 1980s, Steve McCarthy began distilling fruit spirits, grappa, brandy and *Eau de Vie*. He soon added a whiskey made with genuine Scottish peated barley malt. It was named after its creator: McCarthy's Oregon Single Malt Whiskey. It is produced entirely in a still, like a fruit brandy, and probably a pot still, as used in Scotland. When it was first produced, in 1997, McCarthy's was the only genuine American single malt whiskey on the market. Since then, Old Portrero has made the same claim on its label, although it is really a rye whiskey product. McCarthy whiskey is aged in old sherry casks, but also in new wood oak. Given the low production capacity of the distillery, the availability of the whiskey is very much limited. It is estimated that its annual production capacity is approximately 1,200 bottles per year.

WHISKEY
McCarthy's Single Malt Whiskey,
40% ABV
Color: Gold

TASTING NOTES
The nose of this whiskey is dry and smoky, with an earthiness reminiscent of grappa. On the palate it is quite sweet, with some dried fruit. The finish is sweet and syrupy.

DOMAINE CHARBAY DISTILLERY

OWNER	Miles and Marko Karakasevic
ESTABLISHED	1983
STATUS	In production

THIS FAMILY BUSINESS IS LOCATED on Spring Mountain in St. Helena, California, which is part of the famous Napa Valley wine-growing region.

The Karakasevic family immigrated to America from Yugoslavia in 1962. Arriving in California, they started a vineyard. Later, they installed a pot still and began to produce grappa at first, then vodka, apple brandy, and finally walnut liqueur. They first made whiskey in 1999, aged for two years in American soft oak casks. Their malted barley mash is made more aromatic by the addition of hops. The whiskey is bottled in hand-painted bottles and is sold for the bold price of $300 per flask.

WHISKEY
Charbay Whiskey, 2 years old,
40% ABV, official bottling
Color: Pale amber

TASTING NOTES
The nose of this whiskey brings to mind crab apples and fruit cakes. On the palate, the flavor of hops predominates, along with a trace of honey and a light, smoky note. The crab apple note returns during its long finish.

Edgefield · St. George Spirits

EDGEFIELD

OWNER	Mike and Brian McMenamin
ESTABLISHED	1998
STATUS	In production

EDGEFIELD IS A LEISURE CENTER located on the edge of the city of Portland, Oregon. The attractions include hotels, restaurants and bars, movie theaters, a golf course, a winery and, nearby, a small distillery.

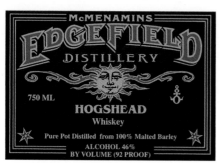

Edgefield got its start when the brothers Brian and Mike McMenamin opened their bar in 1983. They have run the small distillery since 1998, experimenting with brandy and grappa. Later, they produced a well-received gin and a whiskey they named Hogshead, made with genuine barley malt and a pot still that they imported from Germany. This particular model of still, made by the Holstein family from the Lake of Constance region, is particularly appreciated by small distillers because of its flexibility. Hogshead whiskey ages for three years in charred casks made of American oak.

WHISKEY
McMenamin's Edgefield Hogshead Whiskey, 46% ABV, official bottling
Color: Pale golden yellow

 TASTING NOTES
This 100 percent malt whiskey has a strong vanilla aroma with a trace of apricot and grassy, floral notes. On the palate the flavors return anew, along with a sweet maltiness and caramel. Clear honey notes define the finish.

ST. GEORGE SPIRITS

OWNER	Jörg Rupf/Lance Winters
ESTABLISHED	1982
STATUS	In production

ST. GEORGE SPIRITS DISTILLERY is a small facility located in Almeda, California.

Company founder Jörg Rupf grew up in the Black Forest region of Germany before coming to California in 1978 to study law at Berkeley. In 1982, he founded a small distillery, starting with fruit brandies, which he continually refined and improved. Over time he became more and more interested in making whiskey. The malt he uses comes from Wisconsin. He ages his whiskey in Bourbon casks as well as in new wood French oak barrels, and occasionally wine barrels are also used. Like many other microdistillers, Rupf uses a Holstein still.

WHISKEY
St. George Single Malt Whiskey, 43% ABV, official bottling
Color: Golden yellow

 TASTING NOTES
This single malt made from double-rowed malted barley has strong floral and nutty notes, with hints of orange, vanilla and even a little smoke. On the palate, hazelnut flavors come through very clearly. The fruity impression lingers, as does the smoke. The finish is a little chocolatey, with a final wisp of smoke.

Opposite: 0216-259_Whiskeyne of the small stills frequently used by American microdistilleries, shown here at the Edgefield facility

St. James Spirits · Stranahan's

ST. JAMES SPIRITS	
OWNER	Jim Busutill
ESTABLISHED	1995
STATUS	In production

THIS SMALL DISTILLERY is located in Irwindale, California.

Jim Busutill founded his distillery in 1995. Three years later, he began to make a whiskey alongside his usual production of cherry brandy, banana liquor, rum, vodka and raspberry wine. The whiskey ages for three years in old Bourbon casks. Busutill studied chemistry in college and works full time as a biology teacher. His passion, however, is distilling, the techniques of which he learned Germany and Switzerland. His other hobby is falconry, which explains the avian names of his whiskies. In the Scottish style, he writes the word "whiskey" without the "e."

WHISKY

Peregrine Rock — California Pure Malt Whisky, 40% ABV
Color: Golden-yellow with a greenish undertone

 TASTING NOTES
        This single malt made from Scottish malted barley ages for three years in old Bourbon casks. The aroma is fruity with notes of peach and apricot and a light smoky background. The flavors are even smokier, but still discrete. The fruity notes fall away, leaving behind hints of grass and malt. The malt returns in the mild, smoky finish.

STRANAHAN'S	
OWNER	Jess Graber / George Stranahan
ESTABLISHED	2004
STATUS	In production

THE STRANAHAN DISTILLERY is located in Denver, Colorado, right next door to the Flying Dog Brewery.

The distillery and brewery are run very much together. Since 2004, Stranahan's has produced a double distilled whiskey called Stranahan's Colorado. It ages for two years, as it must according to the State of Colorado's regulations. The whiskey is stored in American soft oak casks for two years before it is sold, as it was for the first time in March 2006. The first year's production came to around 6000 bottles. The distillery has big plans for 2007, hoping for a production run of 33,000.

WHISKEY

Stranahan's Colorado Whiskey, 47% ABV
Color: Red brown

 TASTING NOTES
        This whiskey, produced Bourbon-style, has a nose that is exceedingly honey-sweet. On the palate these honey notes reappear, along with spice and light oily notes. The finish is oaky.

Triple Eight Distillery · West Virginia Distilling Co.

TRIPLE EIGHT DISTILLERY

OWNER	Cisco Brewers
ESTABLISHED	1997
STATUS	In production

THE ENTIRE OPERATION, consisting of a winery, brewery and distillery, is on Nantucket Island off the coast of Massachusetts.

The winery was founded in 1981 and expanded to include the Cisco Brewery in 1995. A small pot still was added in 1997 to produce a single malt whiskey under the name Notch. Local personnel were schooled in the art of whiskey-making by none other than Scottish master distiller George McClements of the Bowmore Distillery. After all, the goal was to produce whiskey in the Scottish tradition as authentically as possible. The distillery's location near the sea and water that flows from sandy soil also contribute to conditions that closely resemble those on the Scottish islands.

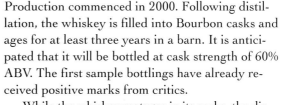

Production commenced in 2000. Following distillation, the whiskey is filled into Bourbon casks and ages for at least three years in a barn. It is anticipated that it will be bottled at cask strength of 60% ABV. The first sample bottlings have already received positive marks from critics.

While the whiskey matures in its casks, the distillery is also producing gin, rum and vodka. Triple Eight's vodka, in particular, is doing a brisk business.

WHISKEY
Notch Single Malt, 60% ABV
Color: Gold

TASTING NOTES
This single malt is made from Scottish malted barley aged in Bourbon casks. The aroma is fruity with notes of peach and apricot and a light smoky background. The flavors are even smokier, but still discrete. The fruity notes fade away, leaving hints of grass and malt. The sweet malt returns in the mild, smoky finish.

WEST VIRGINIA DISTILLING CO.

OWNER	Payton Fireman
ESTABLISHED	1997
STATUS	In production

THIS SMALL BUT MODERN DISTILLERY is located in the mountains surrounding Morgantown, West Virginia.

Payton Fireman, actually a lawyer by profession, distills corn whiskey in his own facility. Instead of filling it into barrels to be aged, however, the corn distillate is blended with neutral grain spirits and bottled as Mountain Moonshine West Virginia Spirit Whiskey. Because it is not aged, it cannot legally be labeled simply "whiskey." Entirely in keeping with the tradition of what used to be illegally distilled moonshine, Fireman produces another product by leaving the distillate

in the still for several weeks, adding chips of oak wood to infuse the spirit with a certain softness. This product is called Mountain Moonshine Old Oak Recipe Spirit Whiskey.

WHISKEY
Mountain Moonshine Old Oak Spirit Whiskey, 40% ABV
Color: Gold

TASTING NOTES
The aroma is very light, with a hint of plums and grapes. The corn flavor comes out on the palate, which is fruity and sugar-sweet, as does the plum and a trace of green apple. Plum is also characteristic of the finish.

CANADA

CANADA

Canada has an abundance of everything that is needed to produce fine whiskies. Distilleries find pure water and enormous areas devoted to agriculture for growing grain. Yet Canadian whisky differs greatly from Scotch or Bourbon. It has a very light flavor, and unique rye lends it spicy and tangy notes. This may be precisely what has led to its popularity.

IT ALL BEGAN at the end of the eighteenth century in Ontario and Quebec, in the areas surrounding the Great Lakes. That is when the first distilleries that produced whiskey on a regular basis came into being. The trade grew rapidly, and by the middle of the nineteenth century there were probably about 200 distilleries in existence. At the beginning of the twentieth century, when US competitors suffered greatly under Prohibition, it was the Scots and their Canadian counterparts who profited from the situation. They delivered the forbidden goods, which were brought to the whiskey-loving American population by smugglers. This "humanitarian aid" paid off. By the time whiskey became legal again in the USA, Canadian distilleries had already positioned themselves in the US market and could always deliver at any time of the day or night. Even today, in the land of Bourbon and Tennessee whiskey, Americans drink more Canadian whisky than their own brands. So it is no wonder that Canada is the world's third largest producer, with around 200 million bottles annually. On the other hand, there are just ten distilleries that continue to make typical Canadian whisky, in which rye whiskey is cut with relatively neutral whiskey.

Rye: the grain that made Canadian whisky famous.

500 miles

500 km

GREENLAND

Beaufort Sea

Baffin Bay

Inuvik

son

on

itory

Labrador Sea

Northern Territories

Hudson Bay

Newfoundland

ritish

Alberta

C

Québec

D

A

A

lumbia

Edmonton

N

Manitoba

Prince Edward Island

Glenora Distillery

Alberta

A

Calgary

Saskatchewan

Gimli

Ontario

Québec

New Brunswick

Nova

ancouver

Potter/ Cascadia

Highwood

Winnipeg

Schenley

Montreal

Scotia

Halifax

Seattle

Lethbridge / Black Velvet

Regina

Maple Leaf

Boston

Boise

St. Paul

Canadian Mist

Toronto

New York

UNITED STATES

Walkerville/ Hiram Walker & Sons

Kittling Ridge

Carson City

Salt Lake City

Chicago

Washington

ncisco

Denver

Indianapolis

Charleston

Las Vegas

O F

Topeka

St. Louis

Raleigh

A M E R I C A

Los Angeles

Nashville

Columbia

Santa Fe

Oklahoma City

Atlanta

Phoenix

El Paso

Dallas

New Orleans

Hermosillo

Houston

ATLANTIC OCEAN

History

Whisky in the New World

The history of Canadian whisky is very similar to that of its big neighbor, the USA. Take note that the Canadians, like the Scots, prefer to spell whisky without the letter "e." Immigrants from Scotland and Ireland brought their whisky know-how with them from the Old World and soon began to distill their own spirits from surplus grain. They sold alcohol to other settlers, hunters and trappers, who needed a warm, soothing drink in the Canadian wilderness. The quality of these spirits continued to improve over time.

John Molson was the pioneer among commercial whisky distillers. He built the first official distillery in 1821, and was already required to pay taxes on it back then. In addition, Molson founded one of the largest breweries in the country. Success on a grand scale, however, only came a half century later. Most whisky pioneers grew their own grains, thus gaining free access to the most important raw material for whisky pro-

Whisky pioneer Hiram Walker had a Renaissance-style palace built on the grounds of the Walkerville Distillery. Today the Distillery Museum is housed in the rooms of the palace.

A Canadian customs official demonstrates the sophistication of whisky smugglers during Prohibition. No wonder so many Americans bought their "bread" on the other side of the border.

duction. Among these were John Philip Wiser, Henry Corby, James Worts, William Gooderham, Hiram Walker and Joseph E. Seagram. The latter two made their companies world famous, thereby making significant contributions to the success of Canadian whisky.

Hiram Walker's ascent

The starting point of this development was very straightforward. Hiram Walker simply was not satisfied with the very sharp, rather low-grade whisky that was then available among his circle of friends, so he started to manufacture an aromatic and relatively pure spirit made from rye and barley malt. But he also produced a refined spirit with a rather neutral taste, made from corn, which was much less expensive. Walker mixed the two and allowed the blended distillate to age in barrels for six years. In addition to these innovations with regard to both production and aging, he also spearheaded marketing improvements. He sold whisky in bottles, rather than in barrels or jars, and the label read "Club Whisky." By doing so, Hiram Walker had not only created the light

Canadian style still prized today, but also the first brand-name whisky in the country.

Next to Hiram Walker, it was Joseph E. Seagram who would make whisky history in Canada. The son of an English immigrant, in 1883 he began to make whisky at a distillery he had bought shortly beforehand in Waterloo, Ontario. The success story of Seagram's V.O. began in 1916, and it soon made him the largest producer of rye whisky in the land. However, the company's ascent began in earnest during the period of Prohibition in the neighboring United States.

Neighborly aid for the USA

There was also a temperance movement in Canada that aimed to forbid the use of all alcohol. In the lead was Father Chiniquy, who called himself an "apostle of abstinence," although he did not entirely refrain from alcohol consumption himself. Chiniquy was finally excommunicated after he was found guilty of arson, embezzlement and—as if that weren't enough—amorous missteps. Nellie Mooney McClung was able to exert a much greater influence. This teacher and author got a kind of women's movement started and motivated numerous, long-suffering women whose husbands were alcoholics to get strongly behind the prohibition of alcohol. And it worked! As early as 1914, alcohol was strictly forbidden. In fact, the ban was in effect nationwide for a brief period in 1918; but the Canadian government quickly realized that the ban was senseless and lifted it that same year. Lawmakers may have been motivated by more

than the realization that such a law was futile: it also may have been a calculated business decision. Prohibition was just around the corner in the USA, and it was probably a smart move on the part of the Canadian government not to hamstring the Canadian producers. As soon as the alcohol ban went into effect in the neighboring country, no one had any qualms about smuggling in a supply of high-quality whisky. Naturally, black market distillers in the USA were placed at an unfair disadvantage, due to possible domestic surveillance. Their own products were mainly of inferior quality, whereas Canadian whisky enjoyed an outstanding reputation following the fourteen years of Prohibition. While US production had to get up and running again, the Canadians could jump right into the breach. Canadian whisky has been the undisputed Number One in the USA ever since. Thus, it is no wonder that numerous American companies now own Canadian brands and distilleries. And European corporations have numerous shareholdings in the country's approximately ten operating distilleries. The whisky market is in constant flux, also in Canada.

Toronto's Distillery District was once home to the largest distillery complex in Canada. The forty-five Victorian-era brick buildings have been converted into a residential and cultural district.

NOVA SCOTIA

"The tools I need for my work are paper,
tobacco, food and a little whiskey."

WILLIAM FAULKNER

*Cabot Trail on Cape Breton Island is among the most
spectacular coastal roads anywhere.*

THE NAME OF THE PROVINCE of Nova Scotia
is Latin and means "New Scotland." It is Canada's
second smallest province in terms of area and
consists of a peninsula and Cape Breton Island,
a large island off the mainland. This is where the
province's only distillery is situated. The hilly
landscape, rugged cliffs and sleepy little seaports
are immediately reminiscent of the terrain in
Scotland, which made it an ideal environment in
which to revive the Scottish whisky tradition.

Nova Scotia's largest and most important city is
Halifax, which has a population of about 360,000.
It is also the capital of the province. Halifax was
established in 1749 by approximately 2,500 settlers
to serve as a British military outpost to guard
against the French. Later on, Halifax was a strategic hub for logistics during World War I and
World War II. Today, the city's harbor is an important trading center with two large container
terminals, numerous loading docks for automobiles
and other machinery, and a direct connection to
the railroad.

Approximately 80 percent of Nova Scotia's
inhabitants have ancestors who once came from
Great Britain, and a large portion of these were
Scots. That is why Scottish Gaelic, as well as
English, was spoken for a very long while in this
province. Many of the Scottish immigrants had
been banished from their homeland in the course
of the Highland Clearances, and they were able
to carry on many of their traditions in Nova
Scotia. They brought along that very special
cultural asset, whisky, and soon started to produce
it in their new home.

Since many Scots had taken up residence on
Cape Breton Island, in particular, they really still
needed a distillery there. The dream of having
their own Glenora Distillery was finally realized,
even though it required numerous attempts.
Glenora produces malt whisky, which is rather
atypical for Canada, but entirely in the tradition
of the immigrants' Scottish forefathers.

Glenora

THE DISTILLERY IN GLENVILLE, on Cape Breton Island, is located in surroundings that could hardly be more Scottish, an area with a valley, mountains, meadows, forests and clear, fresh water.

Canadian businessman Bruce Jardine dreamed of building a distillery here, based on the Scottish model. He found the perfect water source in MacLellan's Brook. The distillery has a pagoda roof and owns a Forsyth of Rothes mash tun and pot still. Naturally, the architect for the facility was from Scotland. Morrison Bowmore trained the staff. When the first whisky flowed in September 1990, everything seemed perfect; but in December, the distillery had to close it doors again for lack of funds. The owners secured new capital in 1991 and production continued until 1993,

GLENORA	
OWNER	Lauchie MacLean
ESTABLISHED	1989
STATUS	In production
ANNUAL PRODUCTION	50,000 liters/13,200 gallons

when they unfortunately had to close their gates once more. Lauchie MacLean has owned the distillery since 1995, and it has been producing again since that time. It was not until 2000 that Glen Breton, Glenora's ten-year-old single malt whisky, was first released. In addition to this malt whisky, two kinds of rum are also produced in-house. Moreover, they are trying to attract tourists with their own shop, inn and chalet. The concept seems to be catching on.

WHISKY

Glen Breton Rare, 10 years old, 43% ABV, official bottling
Color: Gold

TASTING NOTES

A genuine Canadian single malt whisky, produced in Scottish pot stills. The nose evinces hints of heather, honey, a bit of butterscotch and a little ginger in the background. On the palate it is creamy and has a toasted oak note, as well as almond and caramel. The medium-long finish is sweet, ending with a smoky note.

Exactly in keeping with Scottish tradition — right down to the little pagoda roof — the distillery is nestled in a valley in Nova Scotia.

QUEBEC

"Whiskey has killed more men than bullets,
but most men would rather be
full of whiskey than bullets."

LOGAN PEARSALL SMITH

QUEBEC, CANADA'S LARGEST PROVINCE (approximately three times the size of France), has a majority French-speaking population. The capital is Quebec City, with a population of roughly 500,000. In 1985, UNESCO declared Quebec City a World Heritage Site. Apart from the cities, the rest of the province itself is rather sparsely populated.

Quebec once played an important role in the whisky industry. Two of the most important distilleries that "supplied the need" for whisky in the USA during Prohibition, LaSalle and Beaupre, were located here. Today there is only one distillery still active, Valleyfield Schenley, and it has meanwhile fallen into American hands. While the Beaupre Distillery, which used to belong to Seagram, was situated near Quebec City, the owners of LaSalle produced their whisky in a suburb of Montreal.

Montreal, with a population of 1.8 million, is a major commercial center and Canada's second

With its pretty shoreline promenade and excursion steamers on the river, the Canadian capital, Quebec City, seems very French.

largest city. A total of 3.6 million people live in the greater Montreal metro area. This city on the St. Lawrence River achieved prominence in the eighteenth century through the fur trade. When the railroad connection between Montreal and New York was established in 1853, the city became the second largest commercial center in all of North America for a period of time. Today, though, even within Canadian borders, she lags behind Toronto. Because the French-speaking population here has always seen itself as disadvantaged, and this has often led to great conflicts with the federal government, many large corporations have preferred to avoid the turbulence and settle in other provinces. The consequences are reflected in what is, by Canadian standards, high unemployment and the city's declining population figures.

Valleyfield/Schenley

THE VALLEYFIELD DISTILLERY, also known as the Schenley Distillery, lies about an hour's drive west of Montreal. It is located in the province of Quebec, which has a French-speaking majority. This also makes it the only remaining distillery in the francophone areas of Canada.

Schenley founded the distillery in 1945 and sold it to a group of Canadian businessmen in 1981. The company was then bought by UD in the 1980s. In 1999, it was sold for the last time to the present owner, Barton Brands, and its parent company, Constellation Brands.

The Valleyfield Distillery produces Schenley's Golden Wedding and Canadian O.F.C. brands, both of which are available only in Canada. Furthermore, the distillery manufactures the Gibson's, MacNaughton, Order of Merit and Royal Command brands. Gibson's now belongs to William Grant & Sons (Glenfiddich). All UD brands used to be produced here, as well as rum and vodka.

VALLEYFIELD/SCHENLEY	
OWNER	Barton Brands Inc.
ESTABLISHED/STATUS	1945/In production
ANNUAL PRODUCTION	24 million liters/ 6.34 million gallons

WHISKY
Schenley OFC, 8 years old, 40% ABV, official bottling
Color: Pale gold

TASTING NOTES
This Canadian whisky, designated Original Fine Canadian (OFC), has a nose with plenty of sweet caramel, toffee notes and traces of citrus fruits. On the palate the toffee influence is again present, complemented by vanilla and a light rye zest. The finish is soft, with the familiar caramel and toffee character.

The Schenley Distillery was founded in 1945 near the large metropolis of Montreal on the St. Lawrence River.

ONTARIO

"Whenever someone asks me if I want water
with my Scotch, I say I'm thirsty, not dirty."

JOE E. LEWIS

ONTARIO IS CANADA'S most populous province, and around 39 percent of all Canadians
live here. Toronto, with a population of about
2.5 million, is the capital of the province and the
largest, most important city in the country. The
most densely populated area, which includes
nearby Mississauga, the province's third largest
city, continues to grow steadily. Thus, in 2005,
there were about 5.3 million residents in Toronto's
commuter belt. From a political viewpoint, the
most important city in the province is Ottawa, the
capital of Canada, with its 775,000 residents.

Ontario is a province of lakes. With about
250,000 lakes and rivers, there are more than
62,000 miles (100,000 km) of waterways to be
found here. The name Ontario can mean either
"beautiful water" or "beautiful lake" in the
Iroquois language, which makes perfect sense in
light of the geographical reality.

Toronto was called York until 1850. Great
water and natural gas accessibility, as well as the

*The famous Niagara Falls are located near London, Ontario,
straddling the border between Canada and the USA.*

railway lines that were built later, ensured that the
city would boom.

The Distillery District, today a residential and
entertainment quarter, used to be home to a giant
distillery complex. William Gooderham and James
Worts founded the Gooderham and Worts Distillery here in 1832, and it grew into the largest in
the entire British Empire. The company then
merged with Hiram Walker in 1926, but was
forced to close its doors permanently in 1990.

In those days, proximity to the USA and to
high-quality water supplies attracted many whisky
entrepreneurs, including Hiram Walker. It is
therefore no surprise that there are still three
distilleries operating in this province: Walkerville,
Canadian Mist and Kittling Ridge. Canadian Club,
a typical Canadian whisky, is one of the brands
that is among today's export hits.

Canadian Mist

CANADIAN MIST	
OWNER	Brown-Forman
ESTABLISHED	1967
STATUS	In production
ANNUAL PRODUCTION	15 million liters/4 million gallons

Canadian Mist's blends were the most popular brands in the United States until 1998. That spot has been taken over by Diageo's Crown Royal.

THE CANADIAN MIST DISTILLERY, which produces whisky by the same name, is located approximately 60 miles (100 km) from Toronto in the tiny village of Collingwood.

The Barton Company created the Canadian Mist brand in 1965, and Melcher produced it. The blended whisky met with such overwhelming success that they decided to build their own distillery. The Canadian Mist Distillery was built in the record time of only four months and finally went into operation in 1967.

Brown-Forman has owned the brand since 1971. They took great pains in marketing and succeeded in making their whisky the top seller in the USA. It was at the top of Canadian whisky sales worldwide for a long time, but finally had to cede the field to Crown Royal in 1998.

The manufacturing process for this whisky is rather special. The Canadian Mist Distillery uses a mixture of corn and malted barley, which is highly unusual for Canadian whisky. The portion of rye whisky that is also required is produced at the Brown-Forman Distillery (sometimes also called Early Times) in Kentucky.

In order to cut the Canadian whisky with a little bit of Bourbon, it is driven in tank trucks from Canada to Kentucky.

WHISKY
Canadian Mist, 3 years old, 40% ABV,
official bottling
Color: Golden

TASTING NOTES
This Canadian blended whisky, very popular in the USA, is cut with just a small amount of Bourbon and is rather light. It has a sweet berry and caramel aroma with light sherry and honey notes. Creamy caramel emerges strongly on the palate and is prominent again in the finish.

The distillery plays an important economic role in its hometown of Collingwood.

Hiram Walker & Sons

HIRAM WALKER & SONS	
OWNER	Pernod Ricard
ESTABLISHED	1858
STATUS	In production
ANNUAL PRODUCTION	45 million liters/11.9 million gallons

The Hiram Walker Distillery in Walkerville surely has the richest tradition of all Canadian distilleries. The distillery museum provides a lovely glimpse into the company's history.

THE CITY OF WALKERVILLE on Lake Erie was named after the founder and builder of this distillery, Hiram Walker. In the course of the last century, Walkerville has merged with the city of Windsor.

Hiram Walker settled here in 1858 and built the Walker Windsor Distillery. Since the whisky business went well from the start, Mr. Walker gradually had homes, a school, a church and, in 1869, even a post office built around the distillery for the benefit of his employees. The locality was named Walkerville in honor of Hiram Walker, the very name the distillery still goes by today. Some sources prefer to call it by the original company name of Hiram Walker & Sons. Currently, the company belongs to Pernod Ricard, which had purchased the previous owner, Allied Domecq, in 2005.

Canadian Club whisky, which first established the typical Canadian style and is still considered a classic among Canadian whiskies today, originally came out of this distillery. The Canadian Club brand now belongs to Fortune Brands, however, and it would seem to be only a matter of time before this whisky is no longer produced in Walkerville, but rather in Alberta, where Fortune Brands is based. The

Walkerville Distillery facility has column stills for the continuous distillation process as well as a pot still.

In addition to Canadian Club, the distillery makes other brands, including the Wiser's series, Imperial (not to be confused with the distillery of the same name in Scotland, although they both have the same owner), Meagher's 1878 and Gooderham & Worts, among others.

WHISKY
Canadian Club Classic, 12 years old, 40% ABV, official bottling
Color: Pale amber

TASTING NOTES
This twelve-year-old Canadian blend is still a classic, even if it is somewhat older than most Canadian whiskies. The aroma is pleasantly fruity and mild with a hint of cream caramel. Rye shows up clearly on the palate, with just a hint of vanilla. It is dry, mild and thoroughly soft. The finish exhibits the same dryness, along with a smoky touch.

Kittling Ridge

THE KITTLING RIDGE DISTILLERY, which uses pot stills for whisky production, is located only about 15.5 miles from Niagara Falls in Grimsby. It operates on a much smaller scale than others in Canada.

It was built in the early 1970s by Otto Rieder, a brandy distiller of Swiss descent. Rieder distilled only fruit spirits and brandies to begin with, yet he was able to make a name for himself with two blended whiskies, in spite of the fact that their component whiskies came from other distilleries. John K. Hall, a wine merchant, bought the company in 1992 and began to distill his own whisky, Forty Creek, something that Rieder was never able to do. Rieder had experimented with a variety of whiskies in his day, but was never able to develop them into a presentable product. Hall brought the Forty Creek Barrel Select on to the market in 2003. This whisky was distilled from a

KITTLING RIDGE	
OWNER	John K. Hall
ESTABLISHED	1992
STATUS	In production
ANNUAL PRODUCTION	Not specified

combination of corn, barley and rye, stored in charred oak casks for early ageing, and further matured in sherry barrels. The whisky derived its name from the little stream, Forty Mile Creek, on which the distillery was built. Although Hall has been very successful with his whisky, as well as a vodka, the wine business remains his principal occupation.

WHISKY
Forty Creek Barrel Select, 40% ABV, official bottling
Color: Amber

 **TASTING NOTES** This Canadian blended whisky has always gotten high marks from whisky critics. The nose already yields aromas of vanilla, toasted oak and fruity influences. Vanilla appears anew on the palate, further complemented by walnut, honey and spices. Vanilla surfaces once more in the finish, which is rather smooth.

Unlike most other Canadian distilleries, the Kittling Ridge Distillery in Grimby does not use column stills; instead, whisky is distilled in two traditional copper pot stills.

MANITOBA

"My God, so much I like to drink Scotch that
sometimes I think my name is Igor Stra-whiskey."

IGOR STRAVINSKY

*Grain fields as far as the eye can see: Manitoba's fruitful soil
has always attracted lots of whisky distillers.*

Manitoba, Canada's easternmost prairie province, is also known as the Land of 100,000 Lakes, a reference to the immense Lake Agassiz, which came into being when a giant glacier retreated at the end of the last ice age.

About 10 percent of Canada's original inhabitants (Indians and Métis) live in Manitoba today. The greatest number of immigrants came from Great Britain, followed by Germans, French, Poles, Ukrainians, Philippinos and many others. Since this 211,600 square mile (548 km²) province has fewer than 1.2 million inhabitants, there are just 5.6 residents per square mile.

Winnipeg is the capital of the province, as well as its largest municipality. More than half of Manitoba's inhabitants, or about 620,000 people, live in the capital city. Winnipeg lies on the flood plain of two rivers, the Red River and the Assiniboine; an overflow canal has been constructed to protect the city from major flooding. The region has a continental climate. While pleasant tem-

peratures prevail during the summer months, Winnipeg is one of the coldest cities on earth in the wintertime: the average temperature in January is −4°F (−20°C).

Agriculture remains one of the most important sectors of the economy here. In addition to vast areas devoted to growing grains (especially wheat and barley), peas, sunflowers and canola are also cultivated.

Thanks to the bountiful yield in the grain-growing areas, a good number of whisky distillers have settled in Manitoba over the years. It is thus not surprising to find that the Gimli Distillery, the largest in the country and a legacy of Seagram, is located here. There is another distillery in Winnipeg, the Maple Leaf Distillery. In spite of new ownership there, the future of Maple Leaf remains somewhat uncertain.

Gimli

THE GIMLI DISTILLERY is located on the western shore of Lake Winnipeg, and lies just short of 100 miles (160 km) north of the provincial capital, Winnipeg.

The distillery complex with its many warehouses was constructed in 1968, and holds the distinction of being the last distillery build by Seagram that is still in operation today. Other Seagram distilleries, such as Waterloo, Beaupre or LaSalle in Quebec, were either shut down or torn down entirely.

Prior to that, however, the firm made sure that Gimli was in a position to produce each of the whiskies that had formerly been produced elsewhere. Gimli is also the home of Seagram's Crown Royal, the most successful Canadian whisky in the world. Crown Royal was still produced in Waterloo, Ontario until 1992, but like additional Seagram brands—such as Seagram's V.O., Seagram's 5 Star, Seagram's 83 and more—Crown Royal is now made at Gimli. The distillery, including all of its brands, was acquired by Diageo in 2001. Seagram's whisky trade names are the only traces left of what was once the largest spirit enterprise. In any event, the brands that were formerly owned by an industry giant became the property of what is currently the largest corporate group.

Distillation takes place in three beer stills and a four-stage column still, as well as in another facility with two additional column stills. The blend is a combination of up to fifty different whiskies. Most of the whisky is aged in charred American oak barrels. There are no fewer than forty-six warehouses on the grounds, containing 1.25 million barrels. A thousand barrels of whisky are distilled here every day.

The prairie provinces are Canada's breadbasket. Every day, trucks laden with grain from Manitoba's fields arrive at the Gimli Distillery.

GIMLI	
OWNER	Diageo
ESTABLISHED	1968
STATUS	In production
ANNUAL PRODUCTION	3.65 million liters/9.6 million gallons

WHISKY

Seagram's Crown Royal, 40% ABV, official bottling
Color: Pale amber

 TASTING NOTES

This Canadian blended whisky is Canada's best-selling brand, which means that it is readily available worldwide. The aroma is sweet, with noticeable traces of malt. A bit of oak and rye emerge on the palate, but it is smooth and sweet. The mild finish is very well-balanced.

Maple Leaf

MAPLE LEAF	
OWNER	Angostura Canada/Burn Stewart (CL Financial)
ESTABLISHED	1997
STATUS	Currently closed

THE MAPLE LEAF DISTILLERY was founded in 1997, right in the middle of Manitoba's vibrant metropolis, Winnipeg. Even these few years later, it can already look back on an eventful past.

The distillery was established for the purpose of producing a whole range of spirits. Among the approximately 135 brands, there was but one whisky, Canadian Cellars. Despite steady financing, the firm's accounts exhibited numerous financial irregularities, and the two CEOs, C. Alatiotis and D. Wolinsky, had to declare bankruptcy in January 2006. The future of the distillery remains very uncertain. The Canadian division of Angostura bought the distillery in the summer of 2006 for $3.6 million (Canadian dollars), most likely because of the brands rather than the distillery itself. The assumption is that Burn Stewart Distillers will attend to Maple Leaf's concerns in the near future. However, it was announced that all personnel would be retained. It remains to be seen whether, in addition to its many other brands and products, the company will continue to produce whisky.

WHISKY

Canadian Cellars, 40% ABV, official bottling
Color: Pale gold

TASTING NOTES

This Canadian blended whisky is in scarce supply right now. The aroma has light caramel notes and is somewhat reminiscent of toasted white bread. Toffee influences characterize the palate, which has a bit of oak and nuttiness. The finish is peppery.

The Maple Leaf Distillery is based in the heart of Winnipeg, at the confluence of the Red and Assiniboine Rivers. Fifty-five percent of Manitoba's population lives here.

THE RISE AND FALL OF SEAGRAM

After studying economics for a year in the USA, Joseph E. Seagram returned to Canada in the 1860s to become head of the Waterloo Mill in Ontario, which was already manufacturing alcoholic beverages from surplus grain in those days. He took on the leadership of the entire business in 1883 and founded the Joseph E. Seagram Flour Mill & Distillery Company. This explains the origin of the name for his first whisky: Seagram's 83. The firm changed its name to Joseph E. Seagram & Sons in 1911 and rang in an era of great success with the release of Seagram's V.O. (meaning "very own") in 1916.

Impressed by the company's success, the largest spirit producer at the time, Distillers Corporation Limited (DCL), entered into a partnership with Seagram in the 1920s. DCL also had a 50 percent holding in Samuel Bronfman's business. Bronfman was a Soviet émigré, a mover and shaker, whose smuggling operation delivered copious amounts of alcohol to the USA during Prohibition. But founder Joseph Seagram did not live to see any of this, since he died in 1919. What DCL was aiming at in its liaison with Bronfman is unclear today. In any case, things got too hot, DCL withdrew from the business, and

The success story of the Canadian firm began with Seagram's V. O.

Bronfman was then able to purchase Seagram as sole proprietor.

Samuel Bronfman knew for certain that sooner or later, Prohibition would end. In anticipation, he had built up enormous reserves of whisky and, when the alcohol ban in the USA was repealed in 1933, he was perfectly positioned to flood the market on a grand scale. The Americans couldn't fall back on old whiskey inventories of their own at that point in time, and first had to build up their production again. So the success of Canadian whisky was surely due to Bronfman and Seagram, as well as to Walker. When Bronfman expanded extensively after the Second World War, the Seagram Company Ltd. became the largest spirit distiller in the world. Seagram soon bought Chivas Brothers, among others, consequently acquiring distilleries like Strathisla in Scotland; Kirin in Japan; as well as

other firms in India, Thailand, South Korea and elsewhere.

The Bronfmans also enjoyed Hollywood glamour and bought MGM Studios in the 1960s for an exorbitant sum. They later purchased MCA, including Universal Studios and its associated music and book publishers, which unfortunately brought them nothing but multi-billion-dollar losses.

But the big surprise came in 2001. The French conglomerate, Vivendi, purchased Seagram in a stock swap. Since Vivendi was only interested in the media business, however, the spirit firms were thrown to the proverbial lions. Diageo snapped up the largest portion, and Pernod Ricard definitely got the highlights with the Chivas & Glenlivet Group, making it the second-largest spirit company after Diageo. And thus what was once largest spirit enterprise on earth was divided.

ALBERTA

"There is no such thing as a bad whiskey.
Some whiskies just happen to be
better than others."

WILLIAM FAULKNER

ALBERTA IS CANADA'S WESTERNMOST
prairie province and borders British Columbia
in the west. Like Manitoba, the province is
characterized by seemingly endless expanses of
prairie, and the foothills of the Rocky Mountains
determine the landscape in the west. The city of
Edmonton, with a population of around 666,000,
is the capital of the province. Calgary is the largest
city, however, as well as the province's economic
and cultural center. After black gold was discovered in Alberta in the 1970s, numerous oil
companies settled here. The city went into a major
economic slump when oil prices fell, but was able
to recover somewhat, especially thanks to the
1988 Winter Olympic Games. Tourism, first and
foremost, has helped to improve the economy.

Alberta's agricultural and oil industries are
both very successful. Cattle farming and grain
cultivation, the latter of which also served as an
incentive for a number of whisky distillers to set

*The Valley of Ten Peaks in Banff National Park is one
of Alberta's tourist attractions. The peaks of the Rocky
Mountains border the endless western prairie expanses.*

up operations here, are other important economic
sectors. The export of these goods to the USA is
an especially important factor.

The region offers many advantages for whisky
distilling: in addition to gigantic areas devoted
to grain cultivation, whisky pioneers found the
water quality at the foot of the Rocky Mountains
to be perfect. So it is not any wonder that at least
three distilleries are still in operation today:
Alberta, which still produces some of its whisky
from pure rye; Highwood, a large liqueur and
brandy manufacturer; as well as the Black Velvet
Distilling Company in Lethbridge, which sells
about 2 million bottles of its house brand, Black
Velvet, annually.

Alberta Distillers

ALBERTA DISTILLERS IS LOCATED in an area near Calgary that is particularly well suited to whisky production. After all, this is Canada's largest grain-growing region. In addition, plenty of high-quality water is available.

The distillery was built in 1946 and has been owned by Fortune Brands since 1987. Luckily, production methods did not change at all with the change of ownership. This is the only distillery in Canada to make its whisky exclusively from rye. Additionally, it is unusual for the base whisky, which is highly distilled to approximately 95 percent alcohol, to be made from rye and to be made in-house. Rye gives this whisky the requisite piquancy. Alongside the standard house brands, Alberta Carrington (three years old), Windsor (four years old) and Tangle Ridge (ten years old), there are two others on the market, Alberta Premium (five years old) and Alberta Springs (ten years old). Some labels contain the designation, "charcoal mellowing." This has nothing whatsoever to do with the filtering method used to make Tennessee whiskey. Instead, they filter conventionally here with activated charcoal, as with Bourbon. The distillery also delivers in bulk by tank truck to their parent company, which sells the whisky in the USA under the Autumn Gold, Canadian Gold and Canada House labels.

ALBERTA DISTILLERS	
OWNER	Beam Global Spirits & Wine (Fortune Brands)
ESTABLISHED	1946
STATUS	In production
ANNUAL PRODUCTION	20 million liters/5.3 million gallons

WHISKY

Alberta Tangle Ridge Double Casked, 10 years old, 40% ABV, official bottling
Color: Amber

TASTING NOTES

This Canadian rye whisky has aged for ten years in a new oak cask, then transferred to a second cask and matured further. These oak notes are present in the nose, complemented with sherry and vanilla. Oak is again noticeable on the palate, along with a sweet, fruity influence, and this sweet note reappears in the medium-long finish.

Albert Distillers is located in an area that ranks as Canada's largest grain-cultivating region.

Black Velvet · Highwood

BLACK VELVET

OWNER	Barton Brands Inc.
ESTABLISHED	1973
STATUS	In production
ANNUAL PRODUCTION	18.5 million liters/4.9 million gallons

THE BLACK VELVET DISTILLERY, which also goes by the name of Lethbridge, as well as by the name of Palliser Distillery, stands on the eastern edge of the Rocky Mountains in the little town of Lethbridge, beautifully nestled amid fields of corn and rye.

W. A. Gilbey, Ltd., an English firm, built the "old" Palliser Distillery in the 1930s near Toronto. With the dramatic success of its main brand, Black Velvet, which is among the top five Canadian whiskies on the world market, a new and larger distilling facility was eventually needed. It was established in Lethbridge in 1973 for the production of the leading whisky, as well as McMasters blended whisky, but the decisive factor was their best-selling vodka, Smirnoff. With the restruc-

turing of Gilbey's parent company, Diageo, the distillery and both whisky brands were sold to Barton (part of Constellation Brands) in 1999. Needless to say, Diageo did not let go of its powerhouse, Smirnoff.

WHISKY
Black Velvet, 40% ABV, official bottling
Color: Pale gold

 TASTING NOTES
This Canadian whisky is among the best-selling blends in Canada, and is also readily available in Europe. A distinctly peppery note emerges in the nose, as do corn and rye. On the palate it is slightly sweet with caramel and chocolate notes. The finish is very short and just a little spicy.

HIGHWOOD

OWNER	Highwood Distillers Ltd.
ESTABLISHED	1974
STATUS	In production
ANNUAL PRODUCTION	Not specified

ONE OF THE NEWEST DISTILLERIES in Canada has settled in the little town of High River near Calgary.

The distillery was founded in 1974 under the name Sunnyvale Distillery. In 1987, it was re-named Highwood Distillers in honor of its parent company, a private firm with headquarters in neighboring Calgary. Highwood is one of the fastest-growing operations in the country. It purchased the Potter Distillery, which is located in British Columbia, in 2005. The distillery is proud of the fact that it uses nothing but wheat for its basic whisky, as well as for its house vodka. The company also manufactures gin, rum, tequila and

various mixed drinks. With the purchase of Potter, the company's product portfolio expanded considerably. Its own whisky brands are Centennial and Highwood.

WHISKY
Centennial Limited Edition, 10 years old, 40% ABV, official bottling
Color: Pale golden yellow

 TASTING NOTES
This Canadian rye whisky is surely one of the purest and most restrained whiskies in the country. Caramel and cherry are the dominant aromas in the nose. The palate again consists of caramel and honey-dipped grains. The finish is extremely gentle.

Opposite: Men and machines work in tandem during the wheat harvest in Alberta.

BRITISH COLUMBIA

"Happiness is having a rare steak, a bottle of whiskey,
and a dog to eat the rare steak."

JOHNNY CARSON

BRITISH COLUMBIA IS CANADA'S western-most province, and its west coast directly borders the Pacific Ocean. The province was named after the Columbia River, whose source lies within its borders.

The capital of the province is Victoria on Vancouver Island, not Vancouver itself, as is often assumed. With a population of approximately 590,000, however, Vancouver is certainly the largest city in the province (Victoria has just under 80,000 residents). In fact, 2.14 million people reside in the greater Vancouver metro area. This multi-cultural city is composed of a mishmash of immigrants from every imaginable background. These days, the excellent quality of life it offers makes Vancouver one of the most popular cities on earth. Vancouver has Canada's largest harbor and is one of North America's largest transshipment centers for commercial goods. The city is also home

In many parts of British Columbia, totem poles bear witness to the traditions of Canada's original inhabitants.

to several good universities, which help supply local businesses with new intellectual talent. Thus, in recent years, many software and biotech companies have established themselves here.

With its spectacular scenery, it is only natural that the region thrives on tourism. Winter sports venues, such as the Whistler ski resort, attract a large number of tourists from all over the world. The 2010 Winter Olympics will take place in Vancouver and Whistler.

So it is all the more mysterious that this region has never especially attracted whisky distillers. Despite mountain water of the highest quality, the accessibility of good connections for commerce and further amenities, only the Potter Distillery remains more or less active in this area.

Potter / Cascadia

IN THE BEAUTIFUL
OKANAGAN VALLEY,
known more for its wine
cellars than for whisky, lies
the Potter Distillery in the
little town of Kelowna. It
is also known as the
Cascadia Distillery. The
Granville Island Brewery
shares the same site.

The Potter Distillery
opened in Langley in 1958,
but since 1990 has been
producing in Kelowna. It
primarily manufactures
basic whisky and blends it
with whiskies from other
distilleries. Hence, the
distillery currently pro-
duces just enough to be
able to maintain its license.
Apart from that, the site
is used by the neighbor-
ing brewery. In 2005, the
distillery was finally bought by Highwood
Distillers. This independent company wanted
to expand its portfolio and, having experienced
substantial growth in recent years, it sought an
alternative distillery since its own production
capacity would eventually be reached.

POTTER / CASCADIA	
OWNER	Highwood Distillers Ltd.
ESTABLISHED	1958
STATUS	In production part of each year
ANNUAL PRODUCTION	Not specified

WHISKY
Potter's Special Old, 14 years old, 40% ABV,
official bottling
Color: Pale gold

TASTING NOTES
This Canadian rye whisky is quite
difficult to obtain at present, because very little
of it is currently being produced. The aroma
presents a clear rye note, but this is typical of a
fine Canadian whisky. Light caramel is evident
on the palate, while walnut, toffee and rye are
also clearly present. In addition, it turns out to be
somewhat oily. A bit of vanilla and oak appear in
the medium-long finish.

*The pretty Okanagan Valley, home of the Potter Distillery,
is best known for its extensive vineyards.*

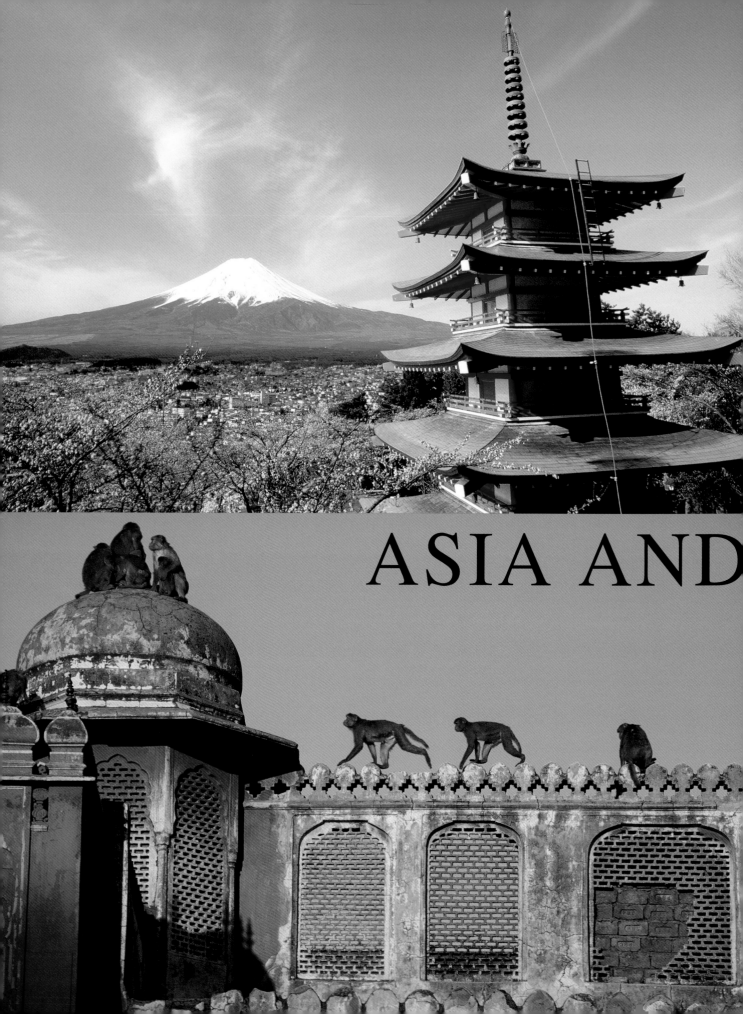

ASIA AND

OCEANIA

ASIA AND OCEANIA

The history of whisky in Japan is still relatively young, originating only around 1923. Strong alcoholic drinks played a much less important role here than in Europe and the USA. In the former British colonies of India, Australia and New Zealand, it was an entirely different story. There, the strong influence of the Motherland led to establishment of a whisky tradition early on.

CURRENTLY, THERE ARE about a dozen distilleries in Japan. They produce whisky with a characteristically soft style and have made Japan into one of the world's largest whisky producers. Despite its unique characteristics, it is very similar to Scotch whisky, and is manufactured along the same lines.

Indian whisky is also gaining ground. A ban on alcohol that is still in effect in three states does not change this one iota. Whisky has been distilled here for over 120 years. Since 1992, smaller distilleries in Australia have been permitted to produce whisky again, and a new distillery was founded in New Zealand several years ago.

NEPAL

New Delhi

Katmandu

BHUTAN

Sikkim

BANGLA-
DESH

Ahmadabad

I N D I A

Calcutta

Nagpur

Mumbai

B a y   o f

B e n g a l

McDowell's/
Ponda

A
r
a
b
i
a
n

S
e
a

Amrut

Bangalore

Madras

400 miles

400 km

SRI
LANKA

Hokkaido

Yoichi

Sapporo

H
O
N
S
H
U

Akita

*J
a
p
a
n*

Sendai/
Miyagikyo

Karuizawa

Hakushu

*S
e
a

o
f*

Fukui

Tokyo

Matsue

Fuji-
Gotemba

Kyoto

Fujiyama

Yamazaki

H
O
N
S
H
U

Kochi

K y u s h u

P A C I F I C   O C E A N

200 miles

200 km

JAPAN

THE HISTORY OF WHISKY IN JAPAN first began around 1923. In the Land of the Rising Sun, strong alcoholic beverages have traditionally played a much less important role than in Europe and North America. This makes it all the more surprising that within a very short period of time, Japan has developed into one of the greatest whisky producers in the world. Furthermore, the largest distillery on earth is located here, although it has not been producing at full capacity for the past several years.

There are around twelve distilleries in Japan at present. About half manufacture malt whisky, and the rest specialize in grain whisky, since here as elsewhere, the majority of whiskies flow into blends. All Japanese whiskies share a smooth palate and high-quality production.

Distilled alcoholic beverages were first produced in Japan in the mid-seventeenth century, or possibly somewhat earlier. A rice liquor by the name of awamori was the forerunner. It was followed by shochu, which was made from rice, buckwheat, millet, potatoes and similar ingredients. A kind of Japanese vodka, this beverage was admittedly looked down on as the "poor people's schnapps," but it was able to establish itself alongside beer and sake nonetheless.

In the course of the economic reforms of the 1868 Meiji Restoration, as well as the westernization and modernization associated with them, Japanese society started to take an increased interest in Europe, and in cultural matters, a special interest in Scotland. People in the upper class began to import Scotch and played golf or

The Japanese always build their whisky distilleries according to the Scottish model. These pot stills in the Hakushu Distillery could just as well be found in the Scottish Highlands.

rugby. Thus, it was only natural that they would inaugurate a whisky of their own.

Two Japanese men are primarily credited with the move to domestic production and can confidently be called the fathers of today's successful business. Although he was actually a wine merchant, Shinjiro Torii, the founder of Suntory, established Yamazaki, the country's first whisky distillery, in 1923. He hired Masataka Taketsuru as head of production, and it was Taketsuru who later founded the Yoichi Distillery and paved the way for Nikka, which is now the country's second largest whisky producer. Taketsuru had studied in Scotland and could put his whisky know-how to use during his employment at the two distilleries. His style had a profound influence on Japanese whisky and was a model for many of his successors.

But the first Suntory whisky, which was introduced on the market in 1929, did not quite prevail. Not until 1950 did the Suntory Old single malt bring the desired results. Meanwhile, Suntory has established itself as one of the world's five largest beverage groups, even though the company plays only an ancillary role in the whisky market. Even when asserting itself internationally with the Morrison Bowmore Group—which owns the Scottish distilleries Bowmore, Auchentoshan and Glen Garioch, among others—Suntory achieves the highest volume of sales in Japan. Suntory whisky has a domestic market share of about 70 percent. Nikka has another 10 percent, and the rest is divided among the remaining companies and foreign imports.

Since the Japanese prefer to drink lighter alcoholic beverages such as sake with meals, typical single malts from Scotland are often considered to be overly strong. The perspicacious founder of Suntory, Shinjiro Torii, had a bright idea: he opened a number of "Torii whisky bars" throughout the country, which were set up entirely in the style of American bars, but offered exclusively Suntory's own whiskies and brands. This marketing strategy soon proved extremely successful, and the firm's sales vastly increased.

As a rule, Torii's whiskies are diluted with water (the resulting beverage is called "mizuwari"), and thus have a very light taste, making them quite enjoyable with food. In fact, they have been advertised as an alternative to sake. Many Japanese whisky lovers even have their own personal bottle reserved just for them at their favorite bars. After each visit, the bottles are neatly stored on the bar shelf until their next visit.

In addition to wine and whisky, the Suntory firm—which is continually expanding and acquiring additional products—produces beer, mineral water and a variety of foods. The firm also owns subsidiaries in other business sectors, including publishing, pharmaceuticals and biotechnology.

Despite the unique drinking culture in Japan, Japanese producers of whisky are utterly committed to having their products come as close as possible to their Scottish ideals. When the first distilleries were established, they initially imported great quantities of what is known as bulk whisky for use in blends and pure malt whiskies. Today they have large and flexible distilleries at their disposal that are capable of producing malt and grain whiskies of their own. In the meantime, imports of malt whiskies have sharply decreased—and this is by no means due only to the country's long-lasting recession.

It is sad but true that despite the major international success they have achieved, Japanese single malts are to a large extent underrated.

Fuji Gotemba · Hakushu

FUJI GOTEMBA

OWNER	Kirin Brewery
ESTABLISHED	1973
STATUS	In production
ANNUAL PRODUCTION	12 million liters/ 3.2 million gallons (incl. grain)

AT THE FOOT OF MOUNT FUJI in the city of Gotemba lies a distillery of the same name. It is the most important departure point for ascending the sacred mountain.

The Kirin Brewery Company founded the Gotemba facility in collaboration with Seagram in 1973. Kirin took care of sales and marketing, as well as the distribution of Chivas's Glenlivet whiskies, which belonged to Seagram at that time. In return, the Japanese profited from the years of experience and know-how of the Canadians and Scots. Single malt whisky has only been bottled regularly here since 2002, following the breakup of Seagram. The distillery has both pot stills and column stills, so that both malt and grain whisky can be produced. Imported malt whiskies from Scotland and Ireland are also used.

WHISKY
Gotemba, 15 years old, 43% ABV, official bottling
Color: Dark straw

TASTING NOTES
This single grain is sweet in the nose, almost like a liqueur, and displays notes of honey, sesame, orange peel and coconut. It has a soft feel around the edges and an oaky flavor, both very luscious and delicate at the same time. The sweet finish of this Japanese whisky is once again reminiscent of oak.

HAKUSHU

OWNER	Suntory
ESTABLISHED	1973
STATUS	In production
ANNUAL PRODUCTION	26 million liters/ 6.9 million gallons

THE HAKUSHU DISTILLERY is about 75 miles (120 km) west of Tokyo in the mountains of Yamanashi Prefecture, which is among the country's most important wine regions. It comes as no surprise that there is a winery right next door to the distillery.

This distillery holds the distinction of being the largest whisky-producing facility in the world. With twenty-four column stills, close to 6.9 million gallons (26 million l) of spirits can be produced here annually. Hakushu was founded in 1973 and added another building with twelve pot stills in 1981, further increasing annual production by about 1.6 million gallons (6 million l). Only this "smaller" facility is in operation at the moment. Naturally, most of the whisky is used for blends. There is a very interesting whisky museum on the grounds, which contains information about whisk(e)y all over the world. Approximately 800,000 barrels, on average, are stored in the numerous warehouses.

WHISKY
The Hakushu Single Malt Whisky, 18 years old, 43% ABV, official bottling
Color: Amber

TASTING NOTES
A lemony-fruity note with a bit of barley emerges in the nose. The barley is developed on the palate, along with a malty sweetness. The finish reveals light traces of chocolate and vanilla.

Karuizawa · Sendai/Miyagikyo

KARUIZAWA

OWNER	Mercian
ESTABLISHED	1955
STATUS	In production
ANNUAL PRODUCTION	135,000 liters/
	35,000 gallons

THE KARUIZAWA DISTILLERY is located west of Tokyo in the health resort of the same name at the foot of Mount Asama.

This small business was founded in 1955. Here, the entire production process (mashing, fermentation and distillation) takes place within a single building, which has led to fond comparisons to the Scottish mini-distillery, Edradour. Karuizawa owns four pot stills and was the first distillery in Japan to bottle its whisky as a single malt. Thus far, however, it has only been produced in

relatively small quantities. The viticultural concern, Mercian, has owned the distillery for several decades.

WHISKY
Karuizawa 1991, twelve years old, 40% ABV, official bottling
Color: Gold

 TASTING NOTES
This is a very fresh malt whisky. This freshness as well as a touch of malt are already perceptible in the aroma. On the palate it is lovely and clear, with the sweetness of brown sugar and light vanilla notes making a very pleasant impression. These sweet notes also reappear in the finish.

SENDAI/MIYAGIKYO

OWNER	Nikka
ESTABLISHED	1969
STATUS	In production
ANNUAL PRODUCTION	5 million liters/
	1.3 million gallons (incl. grain)

THE SENDAI DISTILLERY LIES in the lovely Hirose Valley on the outskirts of Sendai, a city of more than a million residents in Miyagi Prefecture. The complex is located about half an hour west of downtown.

The founders searched for nearly three years to find a suitable location, and finally chose this valley due to the excellent water quality of the Nikkawa River. The red brick building was constructed in 1969 along Scottish lines, right down to a characteristic pagoda roof. From the

very beginning, there were two distillery buildings. One was equipped with pot stills for malt whisky production, and the other was designed primarily for producing grain whisky.

WHISKY
Nikka Sendai, 12 years old, 45% ABV, official bottling
Color: Intense gold

 TASTING NOTES
This is a pleasant-drinking single malt from the House of Nikka. The nose is rather gentle, with a leafy aroma and an autumnal note. The palate is characterized by a fruity, oily note. It has a distinctly sweet, light and pleasantly dry finish.

Yamazaki

YAMAZAKI

OWNER	Suntory
ESTABLISHED	1923
STATUS	In production
ANNUAL PRODUCTION	3.5 million liters/ 925,000 gallons

Suntory's Yamazaki Distillery, with its unique facade, is beautifully situated in a valley surrounded by thickly forested hills.

JAPAN'S OLDEST DISTILLERY is located north of Osaka on the outskirts of Kyoto, the former capital. Although the most densely populated areas of Japan are not far from away, everything seems rather pastoral here. The brick buildings with their rather distinctive towers fit right into the forested valley. The pride of Japanese cutting-edge technology passes right in front of the large buildings: the Shinkansen, or Japanese Bullet Train, one of the most modern high-speed trains, connects the major metropolitan areas of Tokyo and Yokohama with the area around the cities of Kyoto, Osaka and Kobe.

Although Yamazaki was only founded in 1923, it is nevertheless the oldest whisky distillery in the land. Shinjiro Torii founded this distillery with money he earned in the wine business. In order to realize his dream, one of the first things he did was to hire Masataka Taketsuru, who had learned the trade in Scotland. Taketsuru was able to achieve great things at the firm and, after ten years of service, he decided to strike out on his own.

The first Yamazaki whisky was released on the market six years after the distillery was built. In 1971, the company decided to discontinue malting on its own and dismantled its kiln. Since that time, they have tended to import Australian malt especially, but Scotland and North America also count among their suppliers. They also used to import a larger proportion of Scottish malt in order to give the blends greater complexity. After all, Japanese whiskies have a somewhat milder character. In order to make up for this potential deficiency, the fourteen pot stills, which were previously set up like sets of identical twins, were replaced in the 1990s with a multiplicity of stills in various shapes and sizes. This move has enable the firm to produce a larger and more varied selection of whiskies.

The managers also realized early on that it was important to offer visitors tours of the facility, in order to drum up potential clientele for their outstanding whiskies. Twelve- and fifteen-year-old Yamazaki whiskies are available today around the world. The fifteen-year-old whisky is bottled at cask strength, or 57 percent ABV.

WHISKY

Suntory Yamazaki, 12 years old, 43% ABV, official bottling
Color: Pale amber

TASTING NOTES

This is a noble, full-bodied pure malt. The nose is very pleasing with aromas of honey and dried fruits. On the palate it is slightly spicy, but with a very pleasant feel in the mouth and a nicely dry, lingering woody note.

Yoichi

THE SECOND OLDEST DIS-
TILLERY in Japan is based
in Yoichi, a harbor city with
about 20,000 residents, approximately one hour from
Sapporo. It is the sole distillery on the northern island of
Hokkaido. With its attractive
pagoda roofs, Yoichi must
certainly be among the loveliest distilleries in the country.
With the exception of the
roofs, which are painted
entirely in bright red, everything here is based on the
Scottish paradigm.

Masataka Taketsuru
founded the distillery in 1934.
He had attended university
in Scotland, and then appren-
ticed at Hazelburn Distillery
in Campbeltown and Lagavulin
on the Isle of Islay. While there, he lived with a
widow and fell in love with her daughter, Rita.
The two married in 1920, but without the approval
of either family—a bride had already been arranged for Masataka in Japan. For Rita, this was
the start of a difficult life in Japan, because she
initially spoke very little Japanese, the war made
Japan and her homeland enemies, and provisions
were scarce. Many items were rationed, including
the all-important barley. Prior to introducing his
first whisky in 1940, and in order to make ends
meet, Taketsuru financed the whisky distillery by
producing fruit juices. After surviving hard times,
Rita became ill and died in the early 1960s. Her
husband outlived her by nearly twenty years and
died at the end of the 1970s. Their adopted son,
Takeshi, kept the operation going for a few more
years before it all became the property of the
present owner, the Nikka Whisky Distilling Co.

Taketsuru paid careful attention to Scottish
production methods, relying on peated malts of
various strengths and using different yeast strains

*The red pagoda roofs are something of a Yoichi
trademark. Scottish influences are ever-present
at this handsome facility.*

YOICHI	
OWNER	Nikka Whisky Distilling Company
ESTABLISHED	1934
STATUS	In production
ANNUAL PRODUCTION	2 million liters/ 528,000 gallons

in order to be able to produce varying whiskies.
The distillery now owns six pot stills and is still
heated with coal.

WHISKY
Nikka Yoichi, 15 years old, 45% ABV,
official bottling
Color: Deep gold

TASTING NOTES
This single malt has received numerous
awards and gets excellent marks from whisky
guru Jim Murray. A light smokiness, a touch
of salt and sweet fruitiness arise in the nose. A
smoky spiciness is prominent on the palate, along
with a fruity note and malt. The finish is wonderfully long and well balanced.

INDIA

ALTHOUGH INDIA IS ONE OF the largest whisky producers in the world, with production growing at an annual rate of up to 50 percent, people in western countries unfortunately know very little about it. That is certainly in part because Indian whisky is very difficult for us to come by. In addition, liberal laws permit a distillate made from molasses to be sold as whisky, which is not particularly compatible with western quality standards. Indian malt whisky frequently contains only malt extracts, and spirits made from molasses would be classified as rum here. In addition to single malts, blends are prevalent in India and are often enhanced with Scotch malt whisky. However, blends need only contain 4 percent malt whisky.

The British brought Scotch whisky to India during colonial rule, but only the affluent segments of society were able to afford it. Even today, more than 265,000 gallons (1 million l) of it are still imported each year. When compared to the total population, this amount quickly becomes relative. The first efforts at domestic distillation were also made during the period of British rule. The firm of Shaw Wallace & Co. was founded in 1886, and was supposed to supply the colonial regiments with whisky. The country's largest spirit company, UB Group, now owns that firm. The first distillery founded by Indians was built in Daurala in 1943, which was still during the colonial era.

Currently there are fifteen malt distilleries in India, as well as numerous distilleries that produce rum, gin, brandy and other alcoholic beverages. Certain provincial governments, however, are not exactly positively inclined toward whisky and other spirits. Even today, alcohol is completely banned in three federal states.

The following pages introduce some of the whiskies that are available internationally.

Amrut

INDIA'S LARGEST DISTILLERY, Amrut, is based in Bangalore, which is known these days as the Indian Silicon Valley, thanks to its many high-tech and software firms. The state of Karnataka, where the distillery is located, is known for a number of things, including its liberal attitude regarding the pleasures of alcohol.

Radhakrishna Jagdale founded the company in the year 1948. He began by producing liqueurs at first, which he bottled at his own plant. The Jagdale Group gradually developed into a large and highly diversified concern, which now includes pharmaceuticals, foods, pet food, IT services and much more.

Amrut, which means "water of life" in Sanskrit, was the first Indian whisky that managed to gain an international foothold, and it is now available worldwide. The company's primary goal intially was to make sure its whisky was available in a great number of Indian restaurants while Britannia still ruled the waves. The idea was that this would eventually lead to a greater market penetration of the brand, one step at a time.

Amrut whisky is made from barley grown in the Punjab and Rajasthan provinces, as well as from Himalayan water. The malting generally takes places in Jaipur and Delhi. In tropical atmospheric conditions, the whisky is aged for three years in Bourbon and oak casks. In addition to its single malt whisky, Amrut sells blends such as MaQintosh, Prestige, Gold Star and several others. These blends, however, are based largely on inexpensive molasses. Only with single malts can you be sure that they contain exclusively pure whisky.

AMRUT	
OWNER	Jagdale Group
ESTABLISHED	1948
MEANING	Water of life
STATUS	In production
ANNUAL PRODUCTION	2 million liters/ 528,000 gallons

WHISKY
Amrut Single Malt, 40% ABV, official bottling
Color: Flaxen

TASTING NOTES
This single malt whisky, made from unpeated malt, is now available worldwide. The nose reveals a rather fruity and sweet malt note. Robust on the palate, the flavor conveys this fruity sweetness as well as a hint of black coffee. A clear oak note is discernable in the finish.

Jagdale's Amrut Distillery is based in the newly booming city of Bangalore.

Opposite: At present, Indian whisky is still something of a "sleeping giant." Considering the immense growth of the industry, however, that may soon change.

McDowell's/Ponda · Sikkim

MCDOWELL'S/PONDA

OWNER	United Spirits Ltd (UB Group)
ESTABLISHED	1988
STATUS	In production
ANNUAL PRODUCTION	Not specified

THE MCDOWELL'S DISTILLERY is also called Ponda Distillery because it is located in the locale of the same name in the state of Goa. All business matters, however, are conducted through the head office in Bangalore.

In 1988, a malt distillery with a stainless steel mash tub, six small fermentation tanks and two pot stills was built next to an already existent brewery and distillery, which was equipped for continuous distillation. The peat to be used for malting is imported specially from Scotland. The whisky is aged in Bourbon casks, and furthermore, no caramel color is added. One really gets the impression that McDowell's takes the single malt designation seriously, and that Scotland serves as their main model. The firm, founded as

McDowells & Company, is now a part of United Spirits Ltd. and as such belongs to the world's third largest spirit concern, UB Group (United Breweries).

WHISKY
McDowell's Single Malt, 42.8% ABV, official bottling
Color: Golden

🛢 TASTING NOTES
The nose of this truly successful single malt is virtually indiscernible from that of a Scotch whisky. It displays a very malty, grassy note, as well as a touch of citrus fruits and light peat smoke. A clear element of oak emerges in the fresh, slightly smoky flavor. At the same time, it is also malty-sweet, with a mildly bitter streak. The sweet finish is astonishingly short and gently warming.

SIKKIM

OWNER	SDL
ESTABLISHED	1954
STATUS	In production
ANNUAL PRODUCTION	Not specified

SIKKIM DISTILLERIES LIMITED (SDL), a corporation founded in 1954, produces whisky, rum, brandy, gin and various liqueurs in this Himalayan distillery at the foot of Kanchenjunga, the third-highest mountain in the world. It is equipped with both pot stills and column stills. The state of Sikkim is the largest shareholder, owning about 50 percent.

WHISKY
Sikkim Old Gold Premium Single Malt Whisky, 42.8% ABV, official bottling
Color: Golden

🛢 TASTING NOTES
This whisky, designated as single malt, consists of both malt whisky and industrial alcohol, as is familiar from the Canadian example. It is also available in a rather unusual, dagger-shaped bottle. The scent of alcohol is shown off to perfection in the nose, along with caramelized sugar and some vanilla. A bit of coffee appears on the palate. The finish is somewhat bitter. All in all, this whisky takes some getting used to.

Opposite: The Sikkim Distillery is in Sai Baba Nagar, Rangpo, in the foothills of the Himalayas.

Australia

THANKS TO THE INFLUENCE of British colonial rule, Australia looks back on a great whisky tradition. But the distilleries in operation today were only able to begin producing in the mid-1980s. The Commonwealth Distillation Act of 1901 only allowed for large-scale operations that included a wash still with a minimum volume of 715 gallons (2700 l).

Bill and Lyn Lark, who dreamed of opening a distillery in Hobart on the island of Tasmania, introduced a plea for a legal change, and it was successful. In 1992, they were granted the first license to distill since 1839. Their first single malt, introduced in 1998, sold out faster than they could have imagined in their wildest dreams.

There is another distillery on the island, the Tasmania Distillery, which experienced two changes of ownership within a very short time and was closed for a short time starting in 2002. It is in production again and offers Sullivan's Cove Single Malt. Hellyers Road Distillery, a very ambitious project of Whisky Tasmania Pty Ltd., has been distilling since 1999 and already has thousands of barrels ageing. A fourth distillery, Bakery Hill, has received numerous awards, and connoisseurs consider it the best whisky in Australia.

BAKERY HILL

OWNER	David Baker
ESTABLISHED	1998
STATUS	In production
ANNUAL PRODUCTION	Not specified

DAVID BAKER OWNS A SMALL DISTILLERY in the vicinity of Melbourne called Bakery Hill. This skilled food chemist manufactures Australian single malt here in a small pot still, using the Scottish method. He first started distilling in 2000, two years after he founded the business. His malts come from both domestic and Scottish sources. Meanwhile, the business has expanded with the addition of a small brewery.

David Baker offers five different varieties of single malt whisky, all of which are single-cask bottled. These include Bakery Hill Classic Single Malt and Bakery Hill Peated Malt, which are bottled both at cask strength (60 percent ABV) and with the customary alcohol content of 46 percent. Bakery Hill Double Wood Malt, finished in port wine casks, is offered along with them.

WHISKY
Bakery Hill Cask Strength Classic Single Malt, 60% ABV, official bottling
Color: Rich gold

TASTING NOTES
This smoky, cask strength single malt whisky has a lingering, very smoky, slightly salty aroma with notes of lemon and cherry. In addition to smokiness, the palate contains a bit of caramel, honey, a strong malty note, and the same salty influence. The finish is long, warming and well-rounded. Once again, smoky effects are shown to advantage here.

New Zealand

TRUE WHISKY ENTHUSIASTS will probably still know the name Milford and the former Lammerlaw brand from New Zealand. But the Wilson Distillery, New Zealand's first and the producer of this whisky, was forced to close its doors in 1997. After the buildings were torn down in 2002, a spirit distributor snapped up the remaining inventories and currently still offers them under the name of Milford. In the meantime, a new commercial distillery has been established in New Zealand, the Southern Distilling Company, also known as Timaru, where it is located.

THE DISTILLERY COMPLEX IN TIMARU, New Zealand is a conglomeration of previously existing operations in Canterbury and Otago.

Both of the owners, Peter Wheeler and Malcom Willmott, have been in the business for more than twenty-five years and have installed two small pot stills, as well as a facility for continuous distillation of grain whiskey, in this new location. The distillery produces according to Scotch tradition (except for the name, which is spelled "whiskey") and uses exclusively peated barley malt for its single malt, called "The Coaster." Along with The Coaster, they also manufacture a blend, The MacKenzie. Old Hokonui is yet another of their products. This whisky is made from a recipe that dates back to 1892, which was once used to make illegal moonshine.

WHISKEY
The Coaster Single Malt, 40% ABV, official bottling
Color: Amber

SOUTHERN DISTILLERIES	
OWNER	Peter Wheeler and Malcom Willmott
ESTABLISHED	2000
STATUS	In production
ANNUAL PRODUCTION	15,000 liters/3,900 gallons

TASTING NOTES
This New Zealand single malt whiskey is currently only available via the distiller's own museum and Internet shop. The smokiness of the rather full-bodied palate is accented by caramel. These smoky effects reappear in the incredibly fine finish.

The Canterbury region on New Zealand's South Island is dominated by the stunning backdrop of Mount Cook.

WHISKEY TASTING

Whiskey Tasting

A WHISKEY TASTING BEGINS with a visual inspection of the glass and its contents. Then, the smell of a whiskey is explored before taking a sip. This is repeated several times; sometimes, a little water is added. The following criteria come into play when forming a judgment:

APPEARANCE

The color of a whiskey can range from almost transparent to a beautiful, dark, syrupy brown. The spirit proper is completely colorless at the time of casking; a whiskey's unique color develops during maturation. It is hardly possible to make general statements about color, since the end result depends on the length of maturation, on the type of casks used for maturation and, of course, on whether any additives have been used to enhance the color.

The alcohol content of a whiskey can be assessed by watching the bubbles that result from swirling it. If it is lower than 50 percent—i.e., in whiskies of typical drinking strength, there are few bubbles that vanish quickly. Another thing that becomes apparent when swirling is whether the whiskey is clear or more cloudy, that is, whether it contains any fine particles. Many whiskies are chill filtered and therefore appear to be clear. Chill filtration, however, by extracting fine particles, robs a whiskey of certain aromas. For that reason, some distilleries do without this procedure, which is stated by the term "unchillfiltered" on the label.

A whiskey's color can range from pale straw yellow to an intense, syrupy brown. In most cases, the final color is a result of the type of cask in which it matures.

The traces it leaves on the glass are an indication of a whiskey's oiliness: the longer they take to flow down, the more body the whiskey has.

SMELL

Even the first impression of smell characterizes a whiskey as pungent, aromatic, warming or brisk, to name only a few typical characteristics. The

SETTING AND AMBIENCE ARE IMPORTANT

- The room where the tasting takes place should be free of any odor; cigarette smoke or food smells strongly interfere with our highly sensitive sense of taste.
- It is best to use proper whiskey snifters. Professional connoisseurs own measured and standardized glasses with ounce or centiliter marks. Sherry copitas will work, as well, and even Cognac snifters will do if nothing else is at hand.
- The water served should be still and contain as few minerals as possible in order to prevent interference with the whiskey's aroma. It may be advisable

to serve table water. A pipette can be used to add drops of water to a whiskey. The bouquet of a cask strength whiskey, in particular, will open up when a little water is added because it is more difficult to differentiate the various aromas when the alcohol concentration is very high.

- Traditionalists will say that the room's temperature should be approximately 59°F/15°C, which used to be the average room temperature of an old Scottish house. More typical present-day room temperature is acceptable as well. The whiskey itself should have the same temperature.

impression the whiskey leaves is referred to as "nose feel." After the first sniff, the glass is nosed thoroughly while swirling the whiskey in order to let the aroma unfold. If the aroma does not develop, warming the glass in one's hands is usually quite helpful. In most cases, the first impression is the most reliable one, and it does not help to continue nosing for several minutes.

TASTE

After nosing, it's time for a sip. Again, the first impression is the one that matters most. The entire tongue and mouth should be coated with whiskey, allowing the flavors to first unfold on the tongue and the aromas to then travel along the upper respiratory tract. The whiskey's bouquet is essential to its overall flavor.

FINISH

After swallowing, there is a certain time during which the whiskey lingers on the palate. A very short finish is usually associated with freshness, while a very long one is common with a particularly rich whiskey. Medium to long finishes are most common, and are preferred by most connoisseurs. There are whiskies that linger on the palate for hours after drinking.

WATER

If a little water is added to a whiskey, the ester chains start to break down, releasing further aromas. In the case of cask strength bottlings,

adding water is frequently a necessity. Usually, no water is added to drinking strength whiskies, though it doesn't hurt if one does in most cases.

FURTHER TIPS

Professional tasters attend to other things, as well. They cover the glasses with lids or glass covers in order to prevent unnecessary contact with the air, which may lead to slight changes in flavor and smell. It is quite common to taste the same whiskey a second time after leaving the glasses uncovered for half an hour or an hour.

Master blenders prefer to arrange tastings during the morning hours, because our senses are more acute during that time of day. In the evening, especially after a big meal, this may not be the case any longer.

Whiskies tend to taste different depending on the time of day. A light whiskey often tastes better around lunchtime than in the evening. A heavy, full whiskey, on the other hand, is perfect after a fine dinner. Taking notes on your own tasting experiences helps keep track of what kind of whiskey was tasty at what time of day. This is a good method for learning about your personal sense of taste.

By swirling and warming a glass in one's hand, the whiskey's aromas are set free. The impression on the nose plays a major role in forming an opinion about a whiskey.

Tasting Terminology

WHEN READING TASTING NOTES, one encounters across a wide range of terms. In a great many cases they are rather self-explanatory, but almost as often they are not. Some tasters presumptuously use fantastic, flowery imagery that can be too much for the readers' powers of imagination at times. Terms and phrases such as "Bruyère wood," "old-fashioned oilskins" or "smells like a spice rack hung in an old tack room" will probably be incomprehensible to most people. This is why the author of this book recommends using descriptions that will be easily understood by the majority of whiskey lovers. Many terms have become widely known, and they are frequently encountered in specialized publications. While the mouth-feel may be difficult to describe, the characterization of flavor perceptions is easier; comparisons with impressions familiar from food or common drinks help.

The following list of common terms may be helpful with the difficult task of describing sensory experiences.

COMMON TERMS

Soft	no alcoholic edge
Light	good balance between aromas and flavors, subtle
Young	has not yet fully matured
Smoke	rather acrimonious taste, of average quality
Pungent	too intense, interfering aromas, unpleasant
Hard	astringent on the nose, metallic elements
Clean	no interfering aromas; mostly refers to young whiskies
Spicy	tingling on the nose and/or on the palate
Peppery	spicy pepper note, provoking a sneeze
Oily	rather high viscosity, but may still be pleasant
Rich	very powerful impression, intense
Metallic	rather cold and unpleasant
Round	well-balanced flavors and aromas
Flat	rather boring, average, without flavor
Watery/thin	rather fluid, with little flavor
Mild	perfect maturation, subtle alcohol, unobtrusive

Pepper is among the terms most frequently used by whiskey tasters to characterize the taste of a whiskey on the palate.

Dry	astringent effect, rather short-lived taste
Heavy	intense aromas and flavors, laid back, not always desirable
Fresh	pleasant, invigorating, rather light
Neutral	alcohol is dominating, few aromas
Robust	very intense aromas and flavors

Tasting Wheel

A TASTING WHEEL CAN HELP with assigning tasting terms to various flavors. Whether one uses these expressions or not, of course, is a matter of personal preference. However, anyone with a genuine interest in whiskey will come across such terms and phrases again and again, whether in magazines or on the Internet, and the illustration below can be used to help provide orientation. A tasting wheel is also a good illustration of the fact that all the tasting descriptors are not made up out of thin air, but can actually be broken down to a few basic categories. Even if someone is not capable of distinguishing quite as many different notes, it is still obvious that most experts are not arbitrary about their descriptions and that tasting notes have a solid basis in fact.

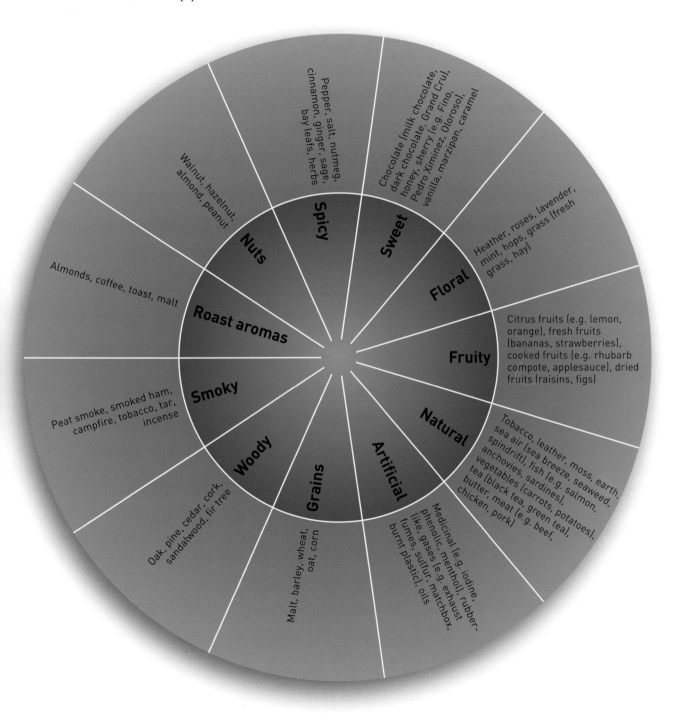

Whiskey and Food

THE QUESTION OF WHICH DRINK should be chosen to go with a nice meal is most commonly answered by "good wine!" However, the answer might just as well be "good whiskey." The range of whiskies available today is so wide that it is relatively easy to find an appropriate whiskey for each course of a meal. Of course, not just any whiskey is guaranteed to go well with a given course.

Considerable knowledge and experience is required to choose just the right whiskey for a meal. One needs to be familiar with the selection of whiskies; ideally they should have been tasted personally, so the whiskey's aromas are known well enough to narrow down the choice. On a side note: only one dram of whiskey (maximally 1 oz/ 30 ml) is served with each course. Most people drink a generous quantity of water alongside it, just as with wine.

With the growing popularity of whiskey in recent years, many quality restaurants have started holding events with names like "Whiskey & Dine"—and with great success, for that matter. Several-course menus are served with a complementing whiskey to accompany each course, plus aperitif and digestive whiskies.

Which whiskey goes with what type of food? That is another question that cannot be answered in general terms; however, there are a few rules of thumb that can be followed when narrowing down the available choices. Lighter whiskies go well with salads and light summer dishes, but also with fish, seafood and vegetables (such as spinach, for instance).

Rich whiskies complement more opulent or hearty dishes that are often served in winter: duck, goose, beef, but also sweet Christmas specialties such as baked apples with cinnamon. A nice whiskey with a strong sherry note goes nicely with beef tartar. That kind of whiskey is best served at cask strength for it to develop its full potential.

Some people think that smoked fish, such as salmon, does not harmonize with a smoky Islay whiskey; the concern is that the whiskey could cancel out the taste of the smoked fish. At the same time, many whiskey aficionados, including the author of this book, appreciate this combination of flavors. Bourbon-cask whiskey, with its characteristic vanilla note, is a great match for clams, soft cheeses and various desserts.

On a cool day in late fall, a nice pumpkin soup with a bit of malt whiskey is a wonderfully warming yet light meal.

A LITTLE SUGGESTION

Rich cream soups go well with whiskies, and this is one of the author's favorites. Since autumn is pumpkin season (Halloween), why not try serving a homemade pumpkin cream soup and two different whiskies to go with it? One good choice is a ten-year-old Laphroaig, cask strength (57.3% ABV) for those who enjoy a smoky malt, or a Marker's Mark Red Seal, 45% ABV. These combinations are guaranteed to meet with your guests' approval.

Whiskey and Chocolate

WHAT DO WHISKEY AND CHOCOLATE have in common? Both of them are luxury articles that, in most cases, are carefully produced according to high standards of expertise and quality. Both can be tasted. For high-quality Grand Cru chocolate, there are tastings and tasting wheels very similar to those for whiskey. What could be more obvious than combining the luxury food with the luxury drink? In recent years, more and more parallel tastings have begun to take place.

But how is a luxury chocolate different from regular, mass-produced chocolate? Many factors come into play. The widespread belief that a high percentage of cocoa is equal to high-quality chocolate is entirely misguided; luxury chocolates often do not contain more than 65 percent cocoa. The same mistake is also responsible for the misconception that high-end chocolate will inevitably taste very bitter, which is equally untrue. One important prerequisite for the production of high-quality chocolate is the choice and cultivation of the different cocoa crops. The largest share of cocoa is grown in Venezuela, Ecuador, Bolivia, Madagascar and Java. Cocoa beans grow on Theobroma trees and have to be harvested, fermented and dried before further processing. Top-quality crops are stored in large quantities in order to bridge years that yield cocoa of inferior quality. Next, the beans are roasted. They are given a lot of time—a practice generally familiar from whiskey production, although the actual time spans cannot be compared. During the next stage, the cocoa nibs are stoneground; particular care is taken during this phase to preserve the cocoa's aroma. Conching, a sophisticated finishing process that made Swiss chocolate world-famous, is the stage during which the actual chocolate is created. This stirring and airing technique may take up to seventy-two hours.

Chocolate should be experienced and enjoyed with the senses of sight, small, taste and touch. In order to smell the chocolate, you may even rub it between your fingers. When biting into chocolate, pay attention to softness and crispness; in general, high-quality chocolate will tend to be harder than milk chocolate. Chocolate reveals its aromas when it melts on the tongue. Ideally, chocolate is tasted shortly before lunchtime (around 11 a.m.) or early in the evening (around 6 p.m.), because those are

A truly elegant combination: gourmet chocolate served with an outstanding malt whiskey. Enjoyed simultaneously, chocolate and whiskey cause virtual explosions of flavors on the palate.

times of day when the senses are most acute for experiencing its flavors and aromas.

Regarding the combination of whiskey and chocolate, there are no general rules that state which whiskey complements which chocolate; here, too, the choices will depend on individual preferences. Chocolate aromas and flavors are almost as varied and unique as whiskey, which is why there are so many possibilities for combining the two. Once again, the proof of the pudding is in the eating (and drinking)!

Whiskey Cocktails

LITERALLY HUNDREDS OF COCKTAILS can be mixed with whiskey as an ingredient. Here we present just a few of the most delicious examples that include whiskies of all kinds.

MANHATTAN

According to legend, this cocktail was first invented by Winston Churchill's mother, Jennie, who was originally a citizen of the USA.

---

1 DASH ANGOSTURA BITTERS
2 OZ (60 ML) RYE WHISKEY
¾ OZ (20 ML) SWEET VERMOUTH
CRUSHED ICE
1 MARASCHINO CHERRY

---

1 Combine the liquid ingredients and the crushed ice in a mixing glass and stir everything well.
2 Strain the drink into a chilled cocktail glass and top with the cherry.

IRISH COFFEE

This decadent beverage was probably invented in the 1940s by Joe Sheridan, who was the head chef of the Shannon Airport in Ireland at that time.

1½ OZ (40 ML) IRISH WHISKEY
SUGAR
STRONG, FRESHLY BREWED COFFEE
1½ OZ (40 ML) CREAM

---

1 Pour the whiskey into a preheated glass that can withstand head, and add sugar to taste.
2 Add the coffee to the glass and stir well.
3 Then pour the cream very slowly over the back of a spoon so that it runs into the coffee. The spoon should just come into contact with both the coffee and the glass itself.
4 Slowly continue until all of the cream forms a layer on the surface of the coffee.
5 Do not stir, but instead drink the coffee through the cream.

HIGHLAND FLING

Blended whiskey is the best suited for mixing in cocktails. Noble single malts should always be enjoyed pure, or with a little water. As for the cheapest bottles, which are more closely related to mouthwash than genuine whiskey, you can mix them with as many drinks as you like – the result will still more closely resemble rocket fuel than a cocktail.

CRUSHED ICE
1 DASH ANGOSTURA BITTERS
1½ OZ (40 ML) SCOTCH WHISKEY (CHIVAS REGAL)
¾ OZ (20 ML) SWEET VERMOUTH
1 COCKTAIL OLIVE

1 Fill a mixing glass with crushed ice.
2 Pour a dash of Angostura over the ice.
3 Add the whiskey and vermouth.
4 Stir well and strain into a chilled cocktail glass.
5 Decorate with the olive.

WHISKEY SOUR

This classic drink has a long tradition in the American South and is prepared with the best American whiskey. There are innumerable variations, as well, made with vodka, gin or other spirits.

¾ OZ (20 ML) LEMON OR LIME JUICE
1½ OZ (40 ML) BLENDED WHISKEY
1 TSP SUGAR OR SUGAR SYRUP
ICE
1 SLICE LEMON OR LIME
1 MARASCHINO CHERRY

1 Combine the first three ingredients with ice in a cocktail shaker, shake vigorously, then strain into a cocktail glass.
2 Top off the drink with a slice of lemon or lime and a maraschino cherry.

Glossary

THERE ARE A NUMBER OF TERMS specific to the world of whiskey that come up in conversations and in the literature about whiskey, some of which did not find a place in this book. The following pages provide explanations for some of these terms.

Analyser
In patent still distillation, the first column is also referred to as the analyser.

As we get it
This expression is used to refer to whiskey that has been bottled directly from the cask, meaning it was bottled at cask strength. Ian Macleod, an independent bottler from Edinburgh, has been producing an entire series under this label.

Ball of malt
What the "dram" is in Scotland, the "ball of malt" is in Ireland: another name for a glass of whiskey.

Barley loft
The barley loft is the place where barley is stored before it is malted.

Barrel proof
An American equivalent for "cask strength."

Burnt ale
Refers to the liquor left in the first still (wash still) after the first distillation, which is often turned into animal fodder.

Cask strength
Refers to whiskey that has been bottled at the strength it has when it is poured out of the cask, without any dilution (i.e., at 57–63% ABV). Cask strength whiskey may be consumed at full strength, but is usually watered down in the glass. Some people find cask strength whiskey with a drop of water superior in taste to regular whiskey.

Dephlegmator xxx
A bubble-shaped condenser at the neck of some stills.

Double matured
Refers to whiskey that has been aged in two different casks.

Draff
The spent grains after mashing.

Dram
In common language, this often refers to a "sip" of whiskey, and a dram of whiskey is often offered in Scotland. In spite of their reputation of being penny pinchers, however, the author would like to state that he has never seen such well-filled glasses as in Scotland. Originally a unit of measurement used by British pharmacists, equivalent to one-eighth of an ounce.

Feints
An alternative term for tails or aftershots, this is the final spirit cut from the low wines. This portion has a low alcohol content and contains impurities and undesirable flavor elements. It is returned to the low wines for re-distillation.

Finishing
A second, optional maturation stage after the primary ageing in barrels. To add further notes and flavors, whiskey is sometimes refilled into different casks that have been used previously for the maturation of wine. Popular finishes include sherry, Madeira and port.

Grist
Term referring to barley after it has been shredded and ground.

Head
Another term sometimes used to refer to the foreshots of the distillation.

Heart
Term used to refer to the middle cut of the distillation. The middle cut is the "prime" cut that is eventually filled into casks.

High proof
Term used in connection with cask strength. If a whiskey is flammable, it is stronger than 57% ABV. This value is referred to as "100 proof" in Scotland; in the USA, however, "100 proof" means 50% ABV. Thus, a 100 proof European spirit corresponds to a 114 proof US spirit.

Independent bottlers
A term that refers to companies that buy individual, select casks of whiskey for bottling, marketing and selling. While independent bottlers sometimes rebrand their products, they are usually allowed to use the name of the distillery on their labels. Also, the labels of such "independent" or "private" bottlings frequently provide information regarding the cask's number, the number of the individual bottle, the vintage year and the length of maturation.

Keepers of the Quaich

An exclusive Scottish society founded with the aim of furthering the prestige and popularity of whiskey all over the world. Membership is restricted to persons who have a strong record of association with whiskey for at least five years and who are recommended by at least two existing members. This is why the society counts many important figures from the whiskey industry and politics among its ranks, in addition to connoisseurs, writers and collectors. The Keepers were established in 1988 by four large whiskey manufacturers; today, almost all the renowned companies are members. As of early 2007, there were more than 1,400 members from all over the world, all of whom share a passion for fine Scotch whiskies.

Low wines

The distillate obtained from the first still, which is why that still is sometimes also referred to as "low wines still."

Lyne arm

Term referring to the neck of a pot still.

Maltman

In distilleries that do their own malting, the maltman was traditionally the person in charge of the entire malting process, including drying the malt in the kiln and inspection of it. Today, members of this profession are primarily found in industrial malthouses, where they also oversee the entire malting procedure. Present-day distilleries without their own malthouse employ maltmen to inspect malt as it is received, and to clean and grind the malt prior to distillation.

Master blender/malt master

After the spirit has matured, the master blender (also referred to as the malt master, or the "nose") selects those casks that will be bottled into single malts, Bourbons and/or blends. In many distilleries, the master blender is also responsible for cask quality and wood finishing.

Maturation

Refers to the period of time, usually between three and twenty-five years, during which a whiskey is aged in a wooden cask, maturing from raw spirit to a fully developed whiskey. The type of cask used for maturation is sometimes specified on the bottle label, e.g.: "Matured in a sherry cask."

New make

Refers to the newly distilled spirit, which is still colorless at that stage.

O. F. C.

Often found on Canadian whiskey labels, this stands for "Old Fine Canadian."

Official bottling

Statement that indicates that a whiskey has been bottled directly by the producer (the distillery), or at least by its owner, as opposed to by an independent bottler.

On the rocks

Not recommended for Scotch single malts: the ice strongly compromises our sense of taste and prevents certain flavors from developing.

Pure malt whiskey

Also known as vatted malt whiskey, this is a blend of different whiskies, all of which must be single malts.

Quaich

Variation of the Gaelic word *cuach*, meaning a cup. This is a drinking vessel used for ceremonial whiskey drinking. Originally, they were made of wood, but today a quaich is likely to be made of silver.

Saladin box

A mechanized means of turning the barley with rakes during germination, rarely used nowadays.

Sample safe

Alternative term for spirit safe.

Shiel

A wooden shovel used for turning over the barley malt in malthouses.

Slainthe (*mhath*)

Gaelic expression that means "good health," something like "cheers!" It is pronounced *slanj avah*. There are long and short forms of the first word, and today's spelling varies widely: *Slante, Slainthé, Slàinte, Slainthé mhat*, etc.

Stillman

The stillman oversees the entire process of distilling. He is the only one who knows the details and secrets about how and when to proceed from foreshots to middle cut to feints.

Tail

Frequently used alternative word for feints.

Ullage

Gaelic expression equivalent in meaning to "angels' share."

Vintage

Vintage whiskey was produced in a clearly specified year.

Books and Websites

Books

Banks, Iain. *Raw Spirit: In Search of the Perfect Dram*. London: Arrow, 2004.

Buxrud, Ulf. *Rare Malts: Facts, Figures and Taste*. Shrewsbury: Quiller, 2006.

Elder, Andrew (ed.). *Whisky Map of Scotland*. London: Collins, 2005.

Hills, Philip (ed.). *Scots on Scotch: The Book of Whisky*. Edinburgh: Mainstream Publishing, 2002.

Jackson, Michael. *Michael Jackson's Malt Whisky Companion*. London: Dorling Kindersley, 2004.

Jackson, Michael. *The World Guide to Whisky*. London: Dorling Kindersley, 1993.

Jefford, Andrew. *Peat Smoke and Spirit: A Portrait of Islay and Its Whiskies*. London: Headline, 2005.

MacLean, Charles and Jason Lowe. *Malt Whisky*. London: Mitchell Beazley, 2006.

Murray, Jim. *Classic Blended Scotch*. London: Prion, 1999.

Murray, Jim. *Jim Murray's Whisky Bible*. London: Carlton, 2007.

Ronde, Ingvar. *Malt Whisky Yearbook*. Shrewsbury: MagDig Media Ltd, 2007.

Russell, Inge, Charles Bamforth and Graham Stewart. *Whisky: Technology, Production and Marketing*. London: Academic, 2003.

Smith, Gavin D. *Scotch Whisky*. Stroud: Sutton, 1999.

Smith, Gavin D. *Whisky, Wit & Wisdom*. Glasgow: Neil Wilson, 2003.

Smith, Gavin D. *Whisky: A Brief History*. Hewitt, NJ: AAPPL Facts, Figures & Fun, 2007.

Udo, Misako. *The Scottish Whisky Distilleries: the Ultimate Companion for the Whisky Enthusiast*. Edinburgh: Black & White, 2006.

Wilson, Neil. *Island Whisky Trail: Scotland's Hebridean and West Coast Malt Whisky Distilleries*. Northampton, MA: Interlink Publishing Group, 2003.

Internet Links:

www.anquaich.ca
Website of the Canadian An Quaich society of whiskey enthusiasts, with many links.

www.bestofwhisky.com
A weblog reporting whisky industry news.

www.dcs.ed.ac.uk/home/jhb/whisky/
The Edinburgh Malt Whisky Tour, a site with much practical and historical information about Scotch whiskies and distilleries.

www.malts.com
A website with extensive information on classic malts.

www.olddutchman.nl
Very extensive website with up-to-date news, a forum, events, etc.

www.scotch-whisky.org.uk
This is the website of the Scotch Whisky Assocation.

www.scotchwhisky.com
Scotland-based website with clear information about whiskey itself, as well as Scottish single malts and blends.

www.scotchwhisky.net
Large website with a wealth of information about Scotch (partly in different languages, as well).

www.singlemalt.tv
Internet TV channel with streaming videos on the history and production of whisky (news, special features, interviews, etc.).

www.smws.com
The official website of the Scotch Malt Whisky Society, with links to their regional branches around the world.

www.straightbourbon.com
Extensive website with information about Bourbon whisky.

www.whisky-distilleries.info
A wealth of information on all Scottish distilleries.

www.whiskymag.com
Big website of Whisky Magazine, with news, a database of whiskies and tasting notes, forums, a newsletter and more.

www.whisky-pages.co.uk
Frequently updated website with a wealth of news and information, edited by Tom Cannavan and well-known whisky writer Gavin D. Smith.

Distillery Addresses

THE FOLLOWING is a list of distilleries with their addresses and contact information, in the order in which they appear in the book. A few additional firms that could only be mentioned briefly in the text have been included, as well.

🛈 = Visitors center

SCOTLAND

LOWLANDS/CAMPBELTOWN
Auchentoshan
Dalmuir, Clydebank,
Dumbartonshire, G81 4SJ
Tel. +44-1415-58 90 11
www.auchentoshan.co.uk
🛈 yes

Bladnoch
Bladnoch, Wigtownshire, DG8 9AB
Tel. +44-1988-40 26 05
www.bladnoch.co.uk
🛈 yes, also offer a whisky school

Glen Scotia
12 High Street, Campbeltown, Argyll,
PA28 6DS, Tel. +44-1586-55 22 88
🛈 no, but visits can be arranged in the summer months

Glenkinchie
Penkaitland, Tranent, East Lothian,
EH34 5ET, Tel. +44-1875-34 20 04
🛈 yes

Girvan
Girvan, Ayrshire, KA26 9PT
🛈 no

Strathclyde
40 Moffat Street, Glasgow, G5 0QB
🛈 no

Springbank/Killkeran
85 Longrow, Campbeltown, Argyll,
PA28 6ET, Tel. +44-1586-55 20 85
www.springbankdistillers.com
🛈 yes, in the summer and by appointment only

ISLAY AND THE ISLANDS
Ardbeg
Port Ellen, Islay, Argyll, PA42 7DU
Tel. +44-1496-30 22 44
www.ardbeg.com
🛈 yes, incl. a shop and café

Arran
Lochranza, Isle of Arran, Argyll,
KA27 8JH, Tel. +44-1770-83 02 64
www.arranwhisky.com
🛈 yes, incl. a shop and restaurant

Bowmore
Bowmore, Islay, Argyll, PA34 7JS
Tel. +44-1496-81 06 71
www.morrisonbowmore.co.uk
🛈 yes, incl. a shop

Bruichladdich
Bruichladdich, Islay, Argyll,
PA49 7UN
Tel. +44-1496-85 02 21
www.bruichladdich.com
🛈 yes, incl. a shop

Bunnahabhain
Port Askaig, Islay, Argyll, PA46 7RP
Tel. +44-1496-84 06 46
www.bunnahabhain.com
🛈 yes

Caol Ila
Port Askaig, Islay, Argyll, PA46 7RL
Tel. +44-1496-84 02 07
🛈 yes, by appointment only

Highland Park
Kirkwall, Orkney, KW15 15U
Tel. +44-1856-87 46 19
www.highlandpark.co.uk
🛈 yes

Jura
Craighouse, Jura, Argyll, PA60 7XT
Tel. +44-1496-82 02 40
www.isleofjura.com
🛈 yes, incl. a shop

Kilchoman
Rockside Farm, Bruichladdich, Islay,
Argyll, PA49 7UT
Tel. +44-1496-85 00 11
www.kilchomandistillery.com
🛈 yes, incl. a shop

Lagavulin
Port Ellen, Islay, Argyll, PA42 7DZ
Tel. +44-1496-30 27 30
🛈 yes

Laphroaig
Port Ellen, Islay, Argyll, PA42 7DU
Tel. +44-1496-30 24 18

www.laphroaig.com
🛈 yes, incl. a shop

Scapa
St. Ola, Kirkwall, Orkney,
KW15 1SE, Tel. +44-1856-87 20 71
www.scapamalt.com
🛈 yes, by appointment only

Talisker
Carbost, Isle of Skye, IV47 8SR
Tel. +44-1478-64 03 14
🛈 yes

Tobermory
Tobermory, Isle of Mull, PA75 6NR
Tel. +44-1688-30 26 45
www.burnstewartdistillers.com/
tobermorydistillery.htm
🛈 yes

Port Ellen
Port Ellen, Islay, Argyll, PA42 7AH
🛈 no

WESTERN AND NORTHERN HIGHLANDS
Balblair
Edderton, Tain, Ross-shire, IV19 1LB
www.inverhouse.com
🛈 no

Ben Nevis
Lochy Bridge, Fort William,
Inverness-shire, PH33 6TJ
Tel. +44-1397-70 02 00
www.bennevisdistillery.com
🛈 yes, incl. a shop

Brora/Clynelish
Brora, Sutherland, KW9 6LR
Tel. +44-1408-62 30 00
🛈 yes

Dalmore
Alness, Morayshire, IV17 0UT
Tel. +44-1349-88 23 62
www.thedalmore.com
🛈 yes

Glen Ord
Muir of Ord, Ross-shire, IV6 7UJ
Tel. +44-1463-87 20 08
🛈 yes, incl. a shop

Glengoyne
Dumgoyne, Near Killearn, Glasgow,
G63 9LB, Tel. +44-1360-55 02 54

www.glengoyne.com
ℹ yes

Glenmorangie
Tain, Ross-shire, IV19 1PZ
Tel. +44-1862-89 24 77
www.glenmorangie.com
ℹ yes

Loch Lomond
Lomond Estate, Alexandria,
Dumbartonshire, G83 0TL
Tel. +44-1389-75 27 81
www.lochlomonddistillery.com
ℹ no; visits possible by appointment

Oban
Stafford Street, Oban, Argyll,
PA34 5NH, Tel. +44-1631-57 20 04
ℹ yes

Old Pulteney
Huddart Street, Wick, Caithness,
KW1 5BD, Tel. +44-1955-60 23 71
www.oldpulteney.com
ℹ no; visits possible by appointment

Teaninich
Alness, Ross-shire, IV17 0BX
Tel. +44-1349-88 50 01
ℹ no; visits possible by appointment

SPEYSIDE
Aberlour
Aberlour, Banffshire, AB3 9PJ
Tel. +44-1340-88 12 49
www.aberlour.co.uk
ℹ yes, incl. a shop and a café

Allt-à-Bhainne
Glenrinnes, Dufftown,
Banffshire, AB55 4DB
Tel. +44-1340-78 33 31
ℹ no

An Cnoc/Knockdhu
Knock, near Keith, Banffshire,
AB54 7LJ, Tel. +44-1466-77 12 23
www.inverhouse.com
ℹ no

Ardmore
Kennethmont, Aberdeenshire,
AB54 4NH, Tel. +44-1446-83 12 13
ℹ no; visits possible by appointment

Auchroisk
Mulben, Banffshire, AB55 3XS
Tel +44-1542-86 03 33
ℹ no

Aultmore
Keith, Banffshire, AB45 3JT

Tel. +44-1542-82 27 62
ℹ no; visits possible by appointment

Balmenach
Cromdale, Grantown-on-Spey,
Morayshire, PH26 3PF
Tel. +44-1479-87 25 69
www.inverhouse.com
ℹ no; visits possible by appointment

Balvenie
Dufftown, Banffshire, AB55 4BB
Tel. +44-1340-82 00 00
www.balvenie.com
ℹ yes, but by appointment only

Benriach
Longmorn, Morayshire, IV30 8SJ
Tel. +44-1343-86 28 88
www.benriachdistillery.co.uk
ℹ no

Benrinnes
Aberlour, Banffshire, AB3 9WN
Tel. +44-1340-87 25 00
ℹ no; contact through Dailuaine

Benromach
Invererne Road, Forres, Moray,
IV36 3EB, Tel. +44-1309-67 59 68
www.benromach.com
ℹ yes

Cardhu/Cardow
Aberlour, Banffshire, AB38 7RY
Tel. +44-1340-87 25 55
ℹ yes, incl. a shop

Cragganmore
Ballindalloch, Banffshire, AB37 9AB
Tel. +44-1807-50 02 02
ℹ yes

Craigellachie
Craigellachie, Banffshire, AB38 9ST
Tel. +44-1340-88 12 12
ℹ no; visits possible by appointment

Dailuaine
Carron, near Aberlour, Moray,
AB38 7RE, Tel. +44-1340-81 03 61
ℹ no

Dallas Dhu
Forres, Morayshire, IV36 2RR
www.historic-scotland.gov.uk
ℹ yes, incl. a museum

Dufftown
Dufftown, Keith, Banffshire,
AB55 4BR
Tel. +44-1340-82 02 24
ℹ no

Glen Elgin
Longmorn, Morayshire, IV30 8SS
Tel. +44-1343-96 02 12
ℹ no

Glen Grant
Rothes, Morayshire, AB38 7BS
Tel. +44-1542-78 33 18
www.glen-grant.com
ℹ yes, incl. a shop

Glen Moray
Bruceland Road, Elgin, Morayshire,
IV30 1YE, Tel. +44-1343-54 25 77
www.glenmoray.com
ℹ yes

Glen Spey
Rothes, Morayshire, AB38 7AU
Tel. +44-1340-83 20 00
ℹ no; visits possible by appointment

Glenallachie
Aberlour, Banffshire, AB38 9LR
Tel. +44-1340-87 13 15
ℹ no; visits possible by appointment

Glenburgie
Mains of Burgie, Moray, IV36 2QY
Tel. +44-1343-85 02 58
ℹ no; visits possible by appointment

Glendronach
Forgue, Aberdeenshire, AB5 6DB
Tel. +44-1466-73 02 02
www.theglendronach.com
ℹ yes

Glenfarclas
Ballindalloch, Banffshire, AB37 9BD
Tel. +44-1807-50 02 57
www.glenfarclas.co.uk
ℹ yes

Glenfiddich
Dufftown, Banffshire, AB55 4DH
Tel. +44-1340-82 00 00
www.glenfiddich.com
ℹ yes, incl. a shop and a café

Glenlossie
Elgin, Morayshire, IV30 8FF
Tel. +44-1343-54 78 91
ℹ no; visits possible by appointment

Glenrothes
Burnside Street, Rothes, Moray,
AB38 7AA, Tel. +44-1340-87 23 00
www.glenrotheswhisky.com
ℹ no

Glentauchers
Mulben, Keith, Banffshire,

AB5 2YL, Tel. +44-1542-86 02 72
❶ no

Inchgower
Buckie, Moray (Banffshire),
AB56 5AB, Tel. +44-1542-83 11 61
❶ no

Kininvie
Dufftown, Banffshire, AB55 4DH
Tel. +44-1340-82 03 73
www.glenfiddich.com
❶ no

Knockando
Knockando, Moray, AB38 7RT
Tel. +44-1340-81 02 05
❶ no

Linkwood
Elgin, Morayshire, IV30 3RD
Tel. +44-1343-55 38 00
❶ no; visits possible by appointment

Longmorn
Elgin Morayshire, IV30 3SJ
Tel. +44-1542-78 30 42
www.pernod-ricard-swiss.com/DE/
marken/longmorn.html (German)
❶ no; visits possible by appointment

Macallan
Craigellachie, Banffshire, AB38 9RX
Tel. +44-1340-87 22 80
www.themacallan.com
❶ yes, incl. a shop

Macduff
Macduff, Banff, Aberdeenshire,
AB45 3JT
Tel. +44-1261-81 26 12
❶ no; visits possible by appointment

Mannochmore
Elgin, Morayshire, IV30 8FF
Tel. +44-1343-54 78 91
❶ no

Miltonduff
Miltonduff, Elgin, Morayshire,
IV30 3TQ, Tel. +44-1343-54 74 33
❶ no; visits possible by appointment

Mortlach
Dufftown, Banffshire, AB55 4AQ
Tel. +44-1313-37 73 73
❶ no; visits possible by appointment

Royal Brackla
Cawdor, Nairn, Nairnshire,
IV12 5QY
Tel. +44-1667-40 20 02
❶ no

Speyburn
Rothes, Aberdeenshire, AB38 7AG
Tel. +44-1340-83 12 13
www.inverhouse.com
❶ no; visits possible by appointment

Speyside
Glen Tromie, Kingussie,
Inverness-shire, PH21 1NS
Tel. +44-1540-66 10 60
www.speyside.com
❶ yes

Strathisla
Seafiled Avenue, Keith, Banffshire,
AB55 3BS, Tel. +44-1542-78 30 44
www.pernod-ricard-swiss.com/DE/
marken/strathisla.html (German)
❶ yes, incl. a shop

Strathmill
Keith, Banffshire, AB55 5DQ
Tel. +44-1542-88 50 00
❶ no; visits possible by appointment

Tamdhu
Knockando, Morayshire, AB38 7RP
Tel. +44-1340-87 22 00
❶ no

Tamnavulin
Tomnavoulin, Ballindalloch, Moray,
AB37 9JA, Tel. +44-1807-59 02 85
www.whyteandmackay.co.uk
❶ yes, together with the mill

The Glenlivet
Ballindalloch, Banffshire,
AB37 9DB, Tel. +44-1542-78 32 20
www.theglenlivet.com
❶ yes, incl. a shop

Tomatin
Tomatin, Inverness-shire, IV13 7YT
Tel. +44-1808-51 14 44
www.tomatin.co.uk
❶ yes

Tomintoul
Ballindalloch, Banffshire, AB3 9AG
Tel. +44-1807-59 02 74
www.angusdundee.co.uk
❶ no

Tormore
Advie, Morayshire, PH26 3LR
Tel. +44-1807-51 02 44
www.tormore.com
❶ no; visits possible by appointment

EASTERN HIGHLANDS
Fettercairn
Distillery Road, Laurencekirk,

Kincardineshire, AB30 1YE
Tel. +44-1561-34 02 44
www.whyteandmackay.co.uk
❶ no

Glen Garioch
Distillery Road, Oldmeldrum,
Aberdeenshire, AB51 0ES
Tel. +44-1651-87 34 50
www.morrisonbowmore.co.uk
❶ yes

Glencadam
Brechin, Angus, DD9 7PA
Tel. +44-1356-62 22 17
www.glencadam.com
❶ no; visits possible by appointment

Royal Lochnagar
Craithie, Ballater, Aberdeenshire,
AB35 5TB, Tel. +44-1339-74 27 16
❶ yes, incl. a shop

MIDLANDS
Aberfeldy
Aberfeldy, Perthshire, PH15 2EB
Tel. +44-1887-82 20 11
www.dewarswow.com
❶ yes

Blair Athol
Pitlochry, Perthshire, PH16 5LY
Tel. +44-1796-48 20 03
❶ yes

Dalwhinnie
Dalwhinnie, Inverness-shire,
PH19 1AB, Tel. +44-1540-67 22 19
❶ yes

Deanston
Deanston, near Doune, Perthshire,
FK16 6AG
Tel. +44-1786-84 14 22
www.burnstewartdistillers.com/
deanstondistillery.htm
❶ no; visits possible by appointment

Edradour
Pitlochry, Perthshire, PH16 5JP
Tel. +44-1796-47 20 95
www.edradour.com
❶ yes, incl. a shop

Glenturret
Crieff, Perthshire, PH7 4HA
Tel. +44-1764-65 65 65
www.glenturret.com
❶ yes, incl. a shop and restaurants

Tullibardine
Blackford, Perthshire, PH4 1DG
Tel. +44-1764-68 22 52

www.tullibardine.com
✪ yes, incl. a shop and a café

IRELAND
Cooley
Riverstown, Cooley, County Louth
Tel. +353-42-937 61 02
www.cooleywhiskey.com
✪ yes, at the Kilbeggan Distillery

Midleton
Midleton, County Cork
Tel. +353-21-463 18 21
www.jameson.ie
✪ yes

Old Bushmills
Bushmills, County Antrim,
BT57 8XH, Tel. +44-2820-73 15 21
www.bushmills.com
✪ yes

Jameson
Old Jameson Distillery,
Bow Street, Dublin
www.jameson.ie
✪ yes

Kilbeggan
Locke's Distillery Museum,
Kilbeggan, County Westmeath
Tel. +353-506-321 34
www.cooleywhiskey.com
✪ yes

Powers
John's Lane, Dublin
✪ no

Tullamore
Bury Quay, Tullamore, County Offaly
Tel. +353-57-932 50 15
www.tullamoredew.com
✪ yes, incl. a shop, pub and
restaurant

EUROPE

GERMANY
Blaue Maus
Bamberger Straße 2,
91330 Eggolsheim-Neuses
Tel. +49-9545-74 61
www.fleischmann-whisky.de
✪ no

Slyrs/Lantenhammer
Obere Tiefenbachstr. 8,
83734 Hausham/Schliersee
Tel. +49-8026-92 48-0
www.slyrs.de

✪ no
ADDITIONAL DISTILLERIES
Gruel
Neue Straße 26, 73277 Owen
Tel. +49-7021-5 99 85
✪ no

Rabel
Berghof, 73277 Owen-Teck
Tel. +49-7021-86 19 61
www.berghof-rabel.hoffrisch.de
✪ no; visits possible by appointment

Höhler Brewery
Kirchgasse 3, 65326 Aarbergen
Tel. +49-6120-13 21
www.brennerei-hoehler.de
✪ no

Mösslein Vineyard
Untere Dorfstraße 8,
97509 Zeilitzheim
Tel. +49-9381-15 06
www.weingeister.de
✪ yes, incl. a shop

Sonnenschein (private brewery)
Alter Fährweg 7–9, 58456 Witten-
Heven, Tel. +49-2302-56 00 6
www.sonnenschein-brennerei.de
✪ no, but there is a shop

Volker Theurer Brewery
Gasthof Hotel Lamm, Jesinger
Hauptstraße, 72070 Tübingen
Tel. +49-7073-91 82-0
www.lamm-tuebingen.de
✪ no, but restaurant and hotel

Obst Korn Brennerei Zaiser
Hussengasse 1, 73257 Köngen,
Tel. +49-7024-8 22 24
www.obstbrennerei.de
✪ no

AUSTRIA
Reisetbauer
4062 Axberg, Tel. +43-7221-63 69 0
www.reisetbauer.at
✪ no

Waldviertler Roggenhof
3664 Roggenreith
Tel. +43-2874-74 96
www.roggenhof.at
✪ no

ADDITIONAL DISTILLERIES
Wolfram Ortner Destillerie
Untertscherner Weg 3,
9546 Bad Kleinkirchheim
Tel. +43-4240-76 0
www.wob.at

✪ no
Destillerie Weidenauer
Leopolds 6, 3623 Kottes
Tel. +43-2873-72 76
www.weidenauer.at
✪ no

SWITZERLAND
Brennerei-Zentrum Bauernhof
Talacher, 6340 Baar
Tel. +41-41-711 80 70
www.swissky.ch
✪ no; visits possible by appointment

Whisky-Brennerei Holle
Hollen 52, 4426 Lauwil
Tel. +41-61-941 15 41
www.swiss-whisky.ch
✪ no; visits possible by appointment

ADDITIONAL DISTILLERIES
Whisky Castle
Käsers Schloss AG, Schlossstr. 17,
5077 Elfingen, Tel. +41-62-876 17 83
www.whisky-castle.com
✪ no; visits possible by appointment

Maison les Vignettes
Les Vignettes, 1957 Ardon
Tel. +41-27-306 44 79
www.swhisky.ch
✪ no; visits possible by appointment

Destillerie Zürcher
Nägeligässli 7, 2562 Port
Tel. +41-32-331 85 83
✪ no

Brauerei Locher AG
9050 Appenzell
Tel. +41-71-788 01 50
www.locherbier.ch
✪ no; visits possible by appointment

FRANCE
Distillerie des Menhirs
Pont Menhir, 29700 Plomelin
Tel. +33-298-94 23 68
www.distillerie.fr
✪ no; visits possible by appointment

Warenghem
Route de Guingamp, 22300 Lannion
Tel. +33-296-37 00 08
www.distillerie-warenghem.com
✪ yes

ADDITIONAL DISTILLERIES
Claeyssens
1 rue de la Distillerie,
59118 Wambrechies
Tel. +33-320-14 91 91
www.wambrechies.com

ℹ yes, incl. a restaurant
Distillerie Artisanale Glann ar Mor
Celtice Whisky Compagnie,
Crec'h ar Fur, 22610 Pleubian
www.glannarmor.com
ℹ no; visits possible by appointment

Guillon
Hameau de Vertuelle, 51150 Louvois
Tel. +33-326-51 87 50
www.whisky-guillon.com
ℹ yes

ENGLAND
St. George's Distillery
Harling Road, Roudham, Norfolk
NR16 2QW, Tel. +44-1953-71 79 39
www.norfolkwhisky.co.uk
ℹ yes

WALES
Penderyn/Gwalia
Penderyn, CF44 0SX
Tel. +44-1685-81 33 00
www.welsh-whisky.co.uk
ℹ no

SWEDEN
Mackmyra Svensk Whisky
Bruksgatan 4, 81832 Valbo
Tel. +46-26-54 18 80
www.mackmyra.com
ℹ no; visits possible by appointment

POLAND
Lubuska Wytwórnoa Wódek
Ul. Jednosci 59, 65018 Zielona Góra
Tel. +48-68-325 48 41
www.vsluksusowa.pl
ℹ no

CZECH REPUBLIC
R. Jelínek
Razov 472, 763 12 Vizovice
Tel. +420-577-686 120
www.rjelinek.cz
ℹ no

UNITED STATES

VIRGINIA
A. Smith Bowman
1 Bowman Drive,
Fredericksburg, VA 22408
Tel. 1-540-373-4555
www.asmithbowman.com
ℹ yes

TENNESSEE
George A. Dickel
Cascade Hollow,

Tullahoma, TN 37388
Tel. 1-931-857-3124
www.georgedickel.com
ℹ yes, incl. a shop

Jack Daniel's
Lynchburg, TN 37352
Tel. 1-931-759-6183
www.jackdaniels.com
ℹ yes, incl. a shop

KENTUCKY
Barton
Bartstown, KY 40004
Tel. 1-502-348-3991
www.bartonbrands.com
ℹ yes, as well as the
Oscar Getz Museum in town

Bernheim
West Breckenridge,
Louisville, KY 40210
Tel. 1-502-585-9186
www.heaven-hill.com
ℹ yes, incl. a shop

Brown-Forman
Louisville, KY 40201-1105
Tel. 1-502-774-2960
www.brown-forman.com
ℹ no

Buffalo Trace
1001 Wilkinson Boulevard,
Franklin County, KY 40601
Tel. 1-502-696-5926
www.buffalotrace.com
ℹ yes, incl. a shop

Four Roses
1224 Bondsmill Road,
Lawrenceburg, KY 40342-9734
Tel. 1-502-839-3436
www.fourroses.us
ℹ yes, incl. a shop; tours given
by appointment

Heaven Hill
1311 Gilkey Run Road,
Bardstown, KY 40004
Tel. 1-502-337-1000
www.heaven-hill.com
ℹ yes, incl. a shop

Jim Beam
Clermont, KY 40110
Tel. 1-502-543-2221
www.jimbeam.com
ℹ yes, incl. a shop

Maker's Mark
3350 Burks Spring Road,
Loretto, KY 40037

Tel. 1-270-865-2881
www.makersmark.com
ℹ yes, incl. a shop

Wild Turkey
Lawrenceburg, KY 40342
Tel. +1-502-839-4544
www.wildturkey.com
ℹ yes, incl. a shop

Woodford Reserve
7855 McCracken Pike,
Versailles, KY 40383
Tel. 1-859-879-1812
www.woodfordreserve.com
ℹ yes, incl. a shop

MICRODISTILLERIES
Anchor Distilling Co.
1705 Mariposa Street,
San Francisco, CA 94107
Tel. 1-415-863 83 50
www.anchorbrewing.com
ℹ yes, but only by appointment

Clear Creek
2389 NW Wilson,
Portland, OR 97210
Tel. 1-503-248-9470
www.clearcreekdistillery.com
ℹ yes, but only by appointment

Domaine Charbay Distillery
St. Helena,
Napa Valley, CA 94574
Tel. 1-800-634-7845
www.charbay.com
ℹ yes, but only by appointment

Edgefield
2126 Southwest Halsey Street,
Troutdale, OR 97060
Tel. 1-503-669-8610
www.mcmenamins.com
ℹ yes, incl. a pub and a hotel

St. George Spirits
2601 Monarch Street,
Alameda, CA 94501
Tel. 1-510-769-1601
www.stgeorgespirits.com
ℹ yes, tours given without prior
appointment every Saturday

St. James Spirits
Irwindale, CA 91706
Tel. 1-626-856-6930
www.saintjamesspirits.com
ℹ no; visits by appointment only

Stranahan's
2405 Blake Street,
Denver, CO 80205

Tel. 1-303-296-7440
www.stranahans.com
❶ no; visits possible by appointment

Triple Eight Distillery
5 & 7 Bartlett Farm Road,
Nuntucket, MA 02584
Tel. 1-508-325-5929
www.ciscobrewers.com
❶ yes

West Virginia Distilling Co.
1425 Saratoga Ave, Suite C,
Morgantown, WV 26505
Tel. 1-304-599-0960
www.mountainmoonshine.com
❶ no

CANADA

NOVA SCOTIA
Glenora
Route 19/Ceilidh Trail, Glenville,
Cape Breton, Nova Scotia
Tel. 1-902-258 26 62
www.glenoradistillery.com
❶ yes, incl. a shop, restaurant, pub
and chalets (overnight accomodations)

QUEBEC
Valleyfield/Schenley
Salaberry-De-Valleyfield, Quebec,
J6T 2G9
Tel. 1-450-373 32 30
www.bartonbrands.com
❶ no

ONTARIO
Canadian Mist
Collingwood, Ontario, L9Y 4J2
Tel. 1-705-445 46 90
www.canadianmist.com
❶ no; visits possible by appointment

Hiram Walker & Sons
Walkerville, Windsor, Ontario
N8Y 4S5, Tel. 1-519-254 51 71
www.canadianclubwhisky.com
❶ yes

Kittling Ridge
Grimsby, Ontario, L3M 1Y6
Tel. 1-905-945 92 25
www.kittlingridge.com
❶ yes, from April to September

MANITOBA
Gimli
Gimli, Manitoba, R0C 1B0
Tel. 1-204-642 51 23
www.crownroyal.com
❶ no

Maple Leaf
251 Saulteaux Crescent, Winnipeg,
Manitoba, R3J 3C7
Tel. 1-204-940 70 00
❶ no

ALBERTA
Alberta Distillers
Calgary, Alberta, T2G 1V9
Tel. 1-403-265 25 41
www.albertadistillers.com
❶ no

Black Velvet
Lethbridge, Alberta, T1H 5E3
Tel. 1-403-317 21 00
www.bartonbrands.com
❶ no

Highwood
High River, Alberta, T1V 1M7
Tel. 1-403-652 32 02
www.highwood-distillers.com
❶ yes

BRITISH COLUMBIA
Potter/Cascadia
Kelowna, British Columbia,
V1Y 2K6
Tel. 1-250-762 33 32
www.highwood-distillers.com
❶ yes

ASIA AND AUSTRALIA

JAPAN
Fuji-Gotemba
Shizuokaken Gotemba,
Shibanuta 970
Tel. +81-135-23 31 31
www.kirin.co.jp/english
❶ yes

Hakushu
Kita-Koma-gun, Yamanashi
408-0316, Tel. +81-551-35 22 11
www.suntory.com
❶ yes

Karuizawa
Naganoken, Kitasakogun,
Miyotamachi, Oaza Maseguchi
1795-2, Tel. +81-267-32 20 06
www.mercian.co.jp/karuizawa
❶ yes

Sendai/Miyagikyo
Miyagiken, Sendaishi, Aoba,
Nikka 1, Tel. +81-22-395 28 65
www.nikka.com
❶ yes

Yamazaki
Shimamoto-cho, Mishima-gun,
Osaka, Tel. +81-75-962 14 23
www.suntory.com
❶ yes

Yoichi
Yoichigun, Yoichimachi,
Kurokawacho 7–6
Tel. +81-135-23 31 31
www.nikka.com
❶ yes

INDIA
Amrut
36, Sampangi Tank Road,
Bangalore, 560 027
Tel. +91-80-222 19 87
www.amrutdistilleries.com
❶ no

McDowell's/Ponda
51, Le Parc Richmond,
Richmond Road, Bangalore, 560 025
Tel. +91-80-222 10 705
www.clubmcdowell.com
❶ no

Sikkim
Sai Baba Nagar, Rangpo, 737 132
Tel. +91-3592-24 08 22
www.sikkimdistilleries.com
❶ no

AUSTRALIA
Bakery Hill
28 Ventnor Street,
North Balwyn Victoria 3104
Tel. +61-3-9857 70 70
www.bakeryhilldistillery.com.au
❶ no; visits possible by appointment

NEW ZEALAND
Southern Distilleries
Stafford Street, Timaru
Tel. +64-686-65 15
www.hokonuiwhiskey.com
❶ yes, incl. a museum

Index

Picture Credits

Amrut 295

Arran 71

Benriach 114

Bernheim 236, 237

Bruichladdich 75 (middle and bottom)

Buffalo Trace 240 (top and bottom)

Canadian Mist 271 (top)

Chivas Brothers/Pernod Ricard 6, 30 (bottom), 83, 106, 126, 127, 128 (bottom), 138, 147, 150 (bottom), 160

Cooley Distillers 190, 191, 199

CORBIS 170, 177, 195, 220, 223 (bottom), 225, 230, 235, 249 (bottom), 264 (bottom), 274, 299; P. Adams 288; Atlantide Phototravel 182/183; R. Antrobus 153, 163 (bottom); J. Arnold 285 (bottom); S. Austin 95; R. Benali 284 (bottom); N. Benvie 20 (top); W. Bibikow 276; S. Boyle 233 (top); J. Butchofsky-Houser 283; Car Culture 233 (bottom); N. Clark 55 (top); A. Clopet 104; T. Craddock 260/261; M. Cristofori 2; R. Cummins 186, 188; M. Fife 54, 57, 62; K. Fleming 216/217; J. Fuste Raga 284 (top); R. Gehman 34 (top), 222, 248; T. Gipstein 227 (top); Goodshoot 270; P. Gould 41 (bottom), 218, 231; M. Grandmaison 275, F. Grehan 277, 302 (top); C. Gryniewicz 208; D. and J. Heaton 285 (top); R. Holmes 254; D. G. Houser 227 (bottom); W. Kaehler 223 (top), 262; C. Karnow 42 (top), 43, 125, 171 (bottom); V. Kessler 204/205; R. Klune 192; B. Krist 268; M. Listri 202; Macduff Everton 8/9, 14, 30 (middle), 40, 55 (bottom), 58, 73, 110, 120, 136, 149, 152, 158, 184, 187, 196; W. Manning 278; B. Mays 226, 239; W. McNamee 294; K. R. Morris 232, 250; S. Pitamitz 189; J. Richardson 107; Riou/photocuisine 306; D. S. Robbins 297; C. Rotkin 238; Ryman/photocuisine 303; Skyscan 69, 99; P. A. Souders 279, 281, 282; L. Snider 224; J. Sparks 76, 87; M. St. Maur Sheil 19 (right), 197; Stapleton Collection 50 (top); J. Sugar 27 (top); S. Vannini 44, 53, 105 (bottom), 121, 148, 166, 198; P. Ward 128 (top); R. W. Weir 163 (top); A. Woolfitt 171 (top); M. S. Yamashita 269

John Dewar & Sons/Bacardi/ G. Wylie 111, 119, 140, 144

Dettling & Marmot 300/301, 307

Diageo 19 (left), 31 (top), 32 (left), 32 (right), 34 (bottom), 35, 52, 59, 60, 65, 67 (top), 77, 84/85, 94, 96 (top), 96 (bottom), 102, 103, 115, 118 (bottom), 122, 132, 135, 137, 143, 156, 168, 169, 228, 229

Edgefield Mcmenamins 257

Edrington Group 12/13, 178 (bottom)

D. Flury 15, 18, 20 (bottom), 46/47, 51, 66, 88, 90, 100, 117, 123, 134, 139, 145, 162

Four Roses/M. Manning 42 (bottom)

Fortune Brands 246, 247, 249 (top), 264 (top), 272

GETTY IMAGES 29 (top), 151, 175, 293, 302, 303; First Light 265; J. J. Mitchell 74, 75 (top); Y. Joel 221

Glenfarclas 17, 30 (top), 33, 38 (bottom), 129

Glenmorangie 98, 124

Glenrothes 133

Gordon & Macphail 116

William Grant & Sons 27 (bottom), 28 (left), 37 (left), 37 (right), 113, 130, 131

Heaven Hill 244, 245 (top and bottom)

M. A. Hoffmann 11, 21 (middle), 26, 28 (right), 36, 38 (top), 39, 41 (top), 67 (bottom), 70, 72, 80, 81, 86, 89 (top), 89 (bottom), 91, 93, 101, 105 (top), 118 (top), 142, 150 (top), 154, 164, 165, 167, 172, 173, 174, 178 (middle), 179

Inver House 92, 109, 112

Irish Distillers/Pernod Ricard 193

Jelínek 206

Jura 79 (top and bottom)

R. Kalberer 97

M. Kellstrand 234, 241, 251

Kittling Ridge 273

Mackmyra 214

M. Manning 242, 243

M. Merkle 82

Morrison Bowmore 56

National College of Art & Design, Dublin 200

Parragon 306 (top), 306 (bottom), 307 (left), 307 (right)

Printbig 209

G. Schlaich 24/25

Scoma 267

Speyside 146

Springbank 16, 22/23

Suntory 289, 292

Tullamore Dew Heritage Centre 201

Tullibardine 180, 181

I. Vollmeier 29 (bottom), 61, 78

Holle 211

D. Wollers 266

Woodford Reserve 10, 21 (bottom), 252, 253

For the use and reproduction of the labels and bottles pictured we thank the producers as well as:

M. A. Hoffmann

Héron Marc © la Maison du Whisky

www.whiskyworld.de

www.scoma.de

www.whisky-fox.de

www.royalmilewhisky.com

www.hotel-forellenhof.de

www.mister-bourbon.de

Basis for the maps: Mountain High Maps, © Copyright © 1995 Digital Wisdom, Inc.

GLENBURGIE

Glenfiddich

SINGLE MALT
SCOTCH WHISKY

GLEN GRANT

GLEN SPEY

ST. GEORGE

SINGLE MALT
WHISKEY

KILBEGGAN
Finest
IRISH WHISKEY

Glenkinchie
THE EDINBURGH MALT

10
YEARS OLD

TOMATIN
SCOTCH WHISKY

GREENORE
Single Grain
IRISH WHISKEY

GLEN ELGIN
SPEYSIDE SINGLE
POT STILL MALT WHISKY

HAND CRAFTED

AGED **12** YEARS

ABERLOUR
TRADE   MARK
DISTILLERY

GLENTURRET

KNOCKANDO
PURE SINGLE MALT
SCOTCH WHISKY

HIGHLAND
GLEN DEVERON
SINGLE MALT
SCOTCH WHISKY

AULTMORE

SCOTCH WHISKY